The
Family *of* Abraham

JEWISH, CHRISTIAN, AND MUSLIM INTERPRETATIONS

Carol Bakhos

 Harvard University Press

Cambridge, Massachusetts
London, England   2014

Library of Congress Cataloging-in-Publication Data

Bakhos, Carol.
  The family of Abraham: Jewish, Christian, and Muslim
interpretations / Carol Bakhos.
    pages cm
  Includes bibliographical references and index.
  ISBN 978-0-674-05083-9
  1. Abraham (Biblical patriarch) 2. Abrahamic religions.
3. Religions—Relations. I. Title.
  BS580.A3B335 2014
  222'.11092—dc23   2013040577

To Vivienne, for planting and watering the seeds

Contents

Note on Transliteration   ix

Introduction   1

1.   Scriptures and Interpreters   15

2.   The Biblical and Qur'anic Abraham   51

3.   The First Monotheist   80

4.   The Wives of Abraham   106

5.   Sibling Rivals   137

6.   Firstborn Son   154

7.   The Sacrifice of Isaac and Ishmael   190

Conclusion   214

Notes   221

Acknowledgments   275

Index   277

Note on Transliteration

THIS BOOK is written for both general and scholarly readers. Some will be familiar with Arabic and Hebrew, and others with neither language. One of my objectives is to make both languages as accessible as possible to all readers. I have therefore adopted a simplified system of rendering Hebrew and Arabic into English. With the exception of the Arabic *hamza* and *'ayn*, I have not used any diacritical marks or special characters in personal names, unless of course the names appear in a quotation or are included in a term such as *dīn Ibrāhīm*. For Arabic terms and book titles, I have followed the system of transliteration used by the *International Journal of Middle Eastern Studies* (IJMES). Anglicized derivatives of Arabic words have not been transliterated. For Hebrew words, I have employed the general-purpose system of transliteration used by the Society of Biblical Literature (SBL), with one exception: the *khet* is rendered *ḥ* (proper names notwithstanding). I trust that my colleagues in the fields of Jewish and Islamic studies understand my need to adopt a more basic system of transliteration and forgive any inconsistencies.

Introduction

OVER THE PAST SEVERAL YEARS, the term "Abrahamic religions" has gained purchase in scholarly and ecumenical circles to refer to Judaism, Christianity, and Islam. Its purchase in these arenas has seeped into common parlance and secured its widespread usage, especially by those who seek to foster peaceful interactions among believers in the three religions. But an emphasis on the common spiritual threads, the shared scriptural heritage and ethical teachings, can lead to major differences being swept under the rug and, ironically, breed misunderstanding. It is crucial to ask, then, exactly what *is* Abrahamic about Judaism, Christianity, and Islam?

In the person of Abraham, we are introduced to a new conception of the divine—the one and only God who has called his people to worship him. According to all three traditions, he is the father of monotheism, the true *Urmonotheismus*. But *in* each faith he plays a major role as well. To Jews, Avraham (the Hebrew name) is the father of the Jewish people; to Christians, Abraham is the father of the Christian family of faith; and to Muslims, Ibrahim (Arabic) is the father of prophets in Islam. Thus he is at once a unifying and divisive figure with respect to how we conceive of these religions.

Central to all three is the belief in the one true God, but articulation of God's attributes is manifestly distinct in each religion. Even the common scriptural heritage—the bedrock of each religion— and similar beliefs and practices are given unique expression. What is common is at once different; the very familial feature that permits comparison is that which demands contrast. While one can appreciate the impulse to accentuate what is common to all three, that endeavor should not come at the expense of a more refined understanding of the particular role Abraham plays in each of the religions, or at the devaluation of the complexity of the ways in which religious systems evolve and the role that historical exigencies play in that process.

And what better illustration of what is involved in comparing these three traditions than the ever-pervasive "Abrahamic" taxonomy, which draws attention to a common narrative of origins yet at the same time distorts each tradition and propagates assumptions about Abraham? The term is highly problematic and requires critical consideration. To what extent is "Abrahamic" a useful analytical tool for interrogating the complex relationship of Judaism, Christianity, and Islam as a family of religions?

Two more or less concomitant trends have contributed to the use of "Abrahamic." One is the well-intentioned attempt to underscore nodes of commonality; the other is the reevaluation of descriptive categories such as "Western monotheisms." Islam, Christianity, and Judaism were commonly referred to as the monotheistic, or Western monotheistic, traditions, as opposed to Eastern religious traditions such as Buddhism, Hinduism, Taoism, and Shinto. In an effort to avoid misguided assumptions that Islam, Christianity, and Judaism are the only three monotheisms and that they are practiced only in the West, scholars have suggested alternative nomenclature. Martin Jaffee's term "elective monotheisms" is an attempt to illuminate the ways these religions are "equally rich, historical embodiments of a single structure of discourse that underlies the historically developed symbol systems specific to each community,"[1] while recognizing that that single structure is one form of monotheism. Thus, Jaffee discusses "metaphysical" monotheism as distinct from "elective" monotheism. Whereas the first gives voice to the relationship between the eternal and the ephemeral world of beings, the second makes specific claims about a specific creator, God, who desires a relationship with a specific community that is commanded to love and serve him. Throughout history the latter form of monotheism has benefited from the former, Jaffee notes, but they are nonetheless *"phenomenologically* distinct."[2]

There are many advantages to using Jaffee's "elective monotheisms" to associate Judaism, Christianity, and Islam and set them off typologically from other forms of monotheism. It is not just that these faiths all acknowledge the belief in one God; it is that they all espouse the belief in and worship of the one God who created ex nihilo, who revealed God's being to a distinct community, and who requires that community to live according to God's will. The descriptor "elective" emphasizes the selective nature of God's revelation and at the same time draws attention to unsettling aspects of this form of monotheism. "On the plane of history," Jaffee writes, "the capacity of God to love intensely and exclusively is translated, as often as not, into the human capacity to hate intensely."[3] For even though each of these monotheisms gives voice, whether stridently or sotto voce, to universalism and inclusivity, there is an inherent exclusivity that runs through them. We would not refer to them as the exclusive monotheisms, yet election is also essentially a form of exclusion. Moreover, while the notion of election or chosenness resonates throughout different iterations of Judaism and Christianity, the notion does not play much of a role in Islam, which is supracovenantal, such that neither "elective" nor "exclusive" sufficiently categorizes it. Given the lack of fit with Islam and the way "elective" has implied "exclusive," Jaffee's term does not provide an entirely satisfying way to refer to the three religions.

Judaism, Islam, and Christianity are also referred to as the Semitic monotheisms. "Semitic" relates to or denotes a family of languages that includes Hebrew, Arabic, and Aramaic, as well as ancient languages such as Phoenician and Akkadian. "Semitic" can also refer to peoples of the Near East and northern Africa. An argument can be made that the term is appropriate because it was in the region where Semitic languages were spoken that these monotheisms originated and because their Scriptures, the New Testament notwithstanding, were originally disseminated in a Semitic language—Hebrew, Aramaic, or Arabic. But this argument, too, is problematic, for it disregards the wider Greco-Roman cultural context in which Judaism developed and from which Christianity emerged.

The shift in nomenclature from "monotheistic" to "Abrahamic" is also a byproduct of interfaith dialogue and a desire for greater cooperation among faith communities. Like the similarly distorting descriptor "Judeo-Christian," "Abrahamic" is employed for the purpose of emphasizing common roots. Especially after 9/11, ecumenists recognized the need to include Islam, and thus "Judeo-Christian" was replaced with the more inclusive "Abrahamic." The French scholar Louis Massignon (1883–1962), a devout Roman Catholic equally drawn to Islam and Arabic culture, was one of the initial proponents—and perhaps the most influential proponent—of the notion, in the mid-twentieth century.[4] His spiritual gravitation to Abraham was so great that when he became a lay member of the Franciscan community he adopted the religious name Ibrahim. Invoked as an expression of Massignon's deep commitment to interfaith dialogue and to the belief in Jewish, Christian, and Muslim peaceful coexistence in the Middle East, Abraham (or Avraham or Ibrahim) also played a vital role in his writings. Massignon's legacy is still felt today.

Examples abound of the multifarious uses of the patriarch Abraham as an emblem of confraternity of religious and political communities. One instance is Abraham's Vision, "a conflict transformation organization that explores group and individual identities through experiential and political education." According to its website, its purpose is to examine "social relations in and between the Jewish, Muslim, Israeli, and Palestinian communities."[5] The organization aims to empower participants to practice just alternatives to the status quo. Another is the Abraham Path Initiative, which organizes walking tours that "follow the footsteps of Abraham or Ibrahim through the Middle East." By retracing his path, the organizers hope to provide journeyers with an opportunity to connect with "people of all faiths and cultures, inviting us to remember our common origins, to respect our cultural differences, and to recognize our shared humanity."[6] Moving from the religious to the political, consider the Abraham Fund, a nonprofit organization aspiring to advance "a cohesive, secure and just Israeli society by promoting policies based on innovative social models, and by conducting large-scale social change initiatives, advocacy and public education."[7]

These organizations take as their starting point the notion that Abraham is the progenitor of Jews and Palestinians, Jews and Arabs, or Jews, Christians, and Muslims, and in the case of the Abraham Path Initiative, he is the forebear of all peoples and cultures. The beloved ancestor, the monotheist who rails against idolatry and obeys the will of the one true God, the father of a multitude of nations, is pressed into the service of promoting goodwill among divergent political and religious groups. (Here I use the term "divergent" intentionally, because the assumption is that Abraham or that which is Abrahamic is the common point of origin from which the groups diverged.)

A popular work by Bruce Feiler, *Abraham: A Journey to the Heart of Three Faiths*, is a good example of the contemporary contortions Abraham undergoes to satisfy people's need to make him not only the father of Judaism, Christianity, and Islam but "the father of all"[8]—that is, to claim him for all humanity. "The great patriarch of the Hebrew Bible is also the spiritual forefather of the New Testament and the grand holy architect of the Koran,"[9] Feiler writes. "He is the linchpin of the Arab-Israeli conflict. He is the centerpiece of the battle between the West and Islamic extremists." The grand holy architect, the linchpin, the centerpiece—the Abraham in Feiler's portrayal is pulled in so many directions that he is almost unrecognizable.

The qur'anic notion *millat Ibrāhīm*, the faith of Abraham, which precedes the three religions of the People of the Book, is taken in modern times as a foundation on which to build interreligious solidarity.[10] Indeed, Judaism, Christianity, and Islam present Abraham as a believer in the one true, creator God and as obedient to God, yet at the same time each tradition casts Abraham in another light: a Torah-observant Jew, father of the Jewish nation; the believer in Christ; a precursor to Muhammad. His role is fashioned by and fosters particular beliefs and teachings of each monotheistic tradition—beliefs and teachings that rub against one another.

The shape Abraham's role takes in each tradition is significant, and significantly different. The difference is obfuscated when we reduce the three traditions to misconceived notions of shared origination, and in this way we undermine the main purpose of interfaith dialogue—that is, to arrive at a deeper understanding of traditions other than our own. The insistence on a common story, in other words, is a superficial approach to Scripture, an approach that distorts minor and major differences.[11] In the biblical story, Abram, whose name is changed to Abraham, "father of nations," is commonly understood to be the father of Jews and of Christians. Both Jews and Christians trace their theological lineage—and in the case of the Jews, their ancestral lineage as well—to Abraham through his son Isaac, born of Sarah; and Muslims locate their ancestry back to Abraham via Ishmael, the son of Abraham and Hagar the Egyptian maidservant.[12] In the Islamic tradition, Ishmael plays a greater role than Isaac, who is also considered a prophet. Ishmael plays no positive role in Christian and Jewish interpretive traditions, however.

The often-evoked "Father Abraham" gives one the impression that Abraham established one religion with three denominational variants, an impression that does not withstand historical scrutiny.[13] As members of the Abrahamic family of religions, Judaism, Christianity, and Islam are considered siblings, but nothing could be more foreign to Judaism and Islam than the notion of a triune Godhead. For that matter, the belief that Muhammad is the Seal of Prophecy could not be more alien to Judaism and Christianity. The theologies, liturgical calendars, scriptural traditions, and ritual practices of the three religions are different, and in some instances radically so. In fact, we can easily make the case that the three religions have very little in common and that the notion of familial affinities must be abandoned altogether.

And yet, if we use a wider lens and consider the spectrum of world religions, we come to see that despite their enormous differences these three religions do share many ritual rhythms and theological beliefs. While their sacred canons are vastly different, common narratives permeate the Jewish and Christian Bibles, as well as the Qur'an. In a group of religions that includes those of Indian origin (Hinduism, Buddhism, and Jainism) as well as those of Chinese origin (Confucianism, Taoism, and Chinese Buddhism), one cannot help but notice the striking resemblance of Christianity, Judaism, and Islam.[14] Theirs is a monotheistic, omnipotent, omniscient, creator God, who reveals godself in history and who in the future will judge the righteous and the wicked accordingly; they share a scriptural heritage (mutatis mutandis), engage in similar practices, and espouse a two-pronged ethical system based on one's relationship to God and fellow creatures. At the same time, the term "Abrahamic" artificially cordons off Judaism, Christianity, and Islam, thus potentially blinding us to other connections and exigencies with respect to religious traditions relegated beyond the Abrahamic pale.

With the rise of university chairs in "Abrahamic religions" and the extensive use of the term among academics, scholars have begun to question the very category.[15] In Jon Levenson's view, Judaism, Christianity, and Islam are "a confraternity of three communities devoted to the one God whose character was discovered and taught by their common revered antecedent. And to that extent, too, the appeal to Abraham as a source of commonality and kinship among these three groups makes eminent sense and can help defeat the widespread notion that strong religious commitments can be a source only of division and discord."[16] What Levenson objects to is the stronger use of the term that "in effect creates a new religion that both encompasses and supersedes them."[17] Although the notion attempts to attenuate communal boundaries, Abraham is conceived in specific notions of what it means to be Jewish, Christian, and Muslim. "One of the most salient historical characteristics of all three Abrahamic traditions," Levenson notes, is "their disbelief in the very proposition that *each* is as Abrahamic as the other two."[18]

Aaron Hughes, in his reflections on the term "Abrahamic religions," points out, as others have, its vague nature, "its worrisome nebulousness."[19] He unpacks the category's use and abuse in academic circles and discusses the threat it poses to critical analysis. Among his concerns is that the sweeping reach and monolithic presence of "Abrahamic" dull the polychromatic character of each religious tradition. Yet, Hughes acknowledges, there are similarities and patterns that "justify the creation of common categories or terms with which to group or label them."[20]

I share many of the concerns of Hughes and others who question the validity and usefulness of "Abrahamic," but I have reluctantly come to accept its inclusion in everyday parlance. I acknowledge its limited usefulness and encourage a circumscribed application. As fraught and imperfect as the term may be, on a practical level it serves

as shorthand for referring to Judaism, Christianity, and Islam. This
purpose is especially useful when highlighting commonalities.

Like all categories, even those such as "Jewish," "Christian," and
"Muslim," it has its share of deficiencies. In its attempt to locate the
resemblances among the traditions vis-à-vis the polyvalent figure of
Abraham, it presents him as one-dimensional, as a father of these
three traditions. Moreover, this understanding of Abraham is rooted
neither in Scripture nor in early interpretive traditions but rather in
the rhetoric of twentieth-century ecumenical advocacy of religious
tolerance and understanding.

This work attempts to reclaim the variety of portrayals of Abraham and his family in ancient and early medieval Jewish, Christian,
and Islamic literary sources. Whenever possible, I will underscore
the commonalities that entice us to create flawed but at times useful
categories. After all, what makes it possible for us even to consider
Judaism, Christianity, and Islam as belonging to a category? Ignoring the elements that allow comparison is as egregious as emphasizing them at the cost of recognizing distinctions. As we consider the
threads that run through all three traditions, we must always bear
in mind that the thread is woven in each tradition uniquely, mixing
and mingling with other threads in order to fashion a new fabric—
one that, while made of some of the same raw materials as the other
fabrics, is not the same. This is the challenge of situating the three
traditions together: to find what we can compare and what we must
contrast. It is not enough—in fact it is problematic—merely to refer to
common stories, yet at the same time we cannot overlook their commonality as they take on different forms and meanings in TaNaKh,
the Old and New Testaments, and the Qur'an, or as they are retold
and refashioned in exegetical traditions.

One drawback to the term "Abrahamic" is the homogenizing
effects it has on the three traditions. In the Hebrew Bible Abraham's
name is Avram, prior to Genesis 17:5, and then it is Avraham; in
the Qur'an his name is Ibrahim. I have chosen to use the English
"Abraham"—but is Abraham the same as Ibrahim? Are Ishmael and
Isma'il one and the same? Yitzhaq and Ishaq? By adopting English
usage, have I created a new figure unlike the biblical Avraham and

qur'anic Ibrahim? If I were to adopt their Hebrew and Arabic names, would I run the risk of obfuscating the shared narrative elements that make aspects of the story recognizable across traditions? And what aspects of Avraham would be familiar to Christians who know him as Abraham?

Moreover, using the term "Abrahamic" gives Abraham a privileged position in each of the three religious traditions. Nancy Calvert-Koyzis writes: "Descent from Abraham in either physical or spiritual terms is often seen as central to what identifies each of these different groups as God's people in contrast to those who are not privileged with this lineage."[21] Many share Calvert-Koyzis's impression of Abraham's role in Islam, but the notion of descent from him is not unequivocally central. In fact, one must qualify his centrality with respect to all three religions. The more central figure in the case of Judaism is Moses; in Christianity Jesus; and in Islam Muhammad.

The family of Abraham is conceptualized differently in each tradition. In Judaism, Abraham is the father of a people to whom God makes an everlasting, exclusive covenant, the Jews. He is the first of three patriarchs—Abraham, Isaac, and Jacob—invoked throughout Jewish history. In Christianity he is the father of all who believe. In this case, his descendants are not biological but spiritual: his family is that of believers.

In the Qur'an, Abraham is the first monotheist, a model of faith and piety, and the father of two prophets, Ishmael and Isaac. Through Ishmael he is the father of the Arab people; through Isaac the father of the Jewish people. Neither a Christian nor a Jew himself, Abraham is an upright man who surrenders to the will of God—a *ḥanīf* (true monotheist)—and an important prophet in a long line of prophets leading up to and culminating in Muhammad. With his son Ishmael, Abraham builds the sacred sanctuary (the Ka'bah) in Mecca.

There are many compelling reasons to locate Judaism, Christianity, and Islam together in a scriptural arena. Both bonds and divisions exist at the very heart of what we deem "Abrahamic." Any exploration of the ways in which the three traditions converge and diverge—either scholarly or ecumenical—must be critical, sensitive, responsible, and meaningful; it must maintain the integrity of each religious tradition and must respect religious, theological, and hermeneutical assonance. As Patrick Ryan aptly remarks, "irenical trialogue between Jews and Christians and Muslims would be better served by our frank recognition of the different ways, based on our historical experiences of faith, we think of Abraham."[22]

Overview

This work sets out to introduce readers to the Scriptures and interpretive traditions of Judaism, Christianity, and Islam and to explore the relationship between these traditions in order to shed light on the extent to which we can refer to them as Abrahamic religions. I examine ancient and early medieval narratives and scriptural interpretations of Abraham and his immediate family (Sarah, Hagar, Ishmael, and Isaac). Often Scripture is received through commentary literature generated by the canonical texts. More often than not, we read verses with preconceived notions informed by that extrascriptural tradition, and in many instances the afterlife of a canonical text, its *Nachleben*, even serves as a substitute for it.[23] Contemporary interpretations focus on aspects of scriptural stories that earlier readers, occupied by other concerns, overlooked. The afterlife of the scriptural figures under discussion is colored by living readers, who mold and deploy these characters according to their own needs, displaying their underlying exegetical, theological, social, and political assumptions in the process. In fact, the very notion of "Abrahamic" is informed by contemporary concerns and interests—that is, by the need to understand Scripture in light of three separate but related traditions.

How each religion conceives of its scriptural heritage—how it receives, transmutes, and transmits it—must be understood as a process susceptible to political, social, and historical exigencies. The nature and character of scriptural interpretation in any given tradition is complex and multifaceted. An effective way of appreciating the transmission of scriptural narratives through interpretation and storytelling is in connection with the methods and forms of other traditions. Comparative studies of early Christianity and late antique Judaism have yielded such significant works that the study of the common cultural ground from which they emerged has become de rigueur.

What was once the novel thesis of books and articles published decades ago—that each generation interprets Scripture from the perspective of its own historical circumstance, that an examination of the exegesis of an individual must take into account the writer's theological, sociocultural, and historical embeddedness—is now widely assumed. What is of concern is no longer to prove that interpretation is a product of various theological, sociocultural, and historical forces and factors but to detect those factors and forces at work, as well as to elucidate how interpretations have in turn shaped religious traditions.

The past several decades have given rise to cultural and inter- and cross-disciplinary studies. As a result, scholars' interest in comparative studies, as well as in broadening the horizons of their own subfields, has increased. They have embraced the need to comprehend religious systems from a perspective that respects the uniqueness of each tradition while at the same time detecting and highlighting the specific elements shared by different religious traditions. Several scholars of rabbinic exegesis have, for example, turned their attention not only to early Greek and Latin Christian texts but also to Syriac sources. Scholars of the Talmud are now actively excavating the sociocultural setting of Sasanian Babylonia in their examination of rabbinic law and literature.

Furthermore, in order to understand rabbinic biblical interpretation (midrash), scholars of ancient and early medieval Judaism not only have looked to the texts themselves—the Hebrew Scriptures—but also have explored the ways in which they are situated in the context of Greco-Roman literature and history. These scholars have also noted the similar aspects of rabbinic and patristic biblical interpretation, despite the sui generis character each interpretive tradition often claims for itself. Those working in the arena of Jewish exegesis, however, have yet to engage in the study of early Islamic hermeneutic practices and principles in order to appreciate the peculiarities of the implicit laws of interpretation that different communities of exegetes espouse. Be that as it may, recent scholars have come to recognize that they must attend to the various internal and external stimuli that give rise to particular interpretations and must look at how those stimuli, though shared among traditions in the same cultural setting, yield different interpretations.

I hope to shed light on variations with respect to portrayals of biblical and qur'anic figures, as well as narrative expansions, and to highlight working theological and hermeneutical assumptions on which interpretations are based. Noting similarities and differences among and in the three monotheisms provides a portal into the theological teachings of each tradition. The documentation of the variations and similarities in the literature under examination will in turn serve as a locus for addressing the extent to which one can talk about Judaism, Christianity, and Islam as Abrahamic.

Because one of the aims of this work is to introduce specialists in related fields, as well as general readers, to the literary sources of each religion, I will for the most part use texts that are easily available in English. Although mine is not an exhaustive treatment of the family of Abraham—far from it!—it nonetheless examines major themes and exegetical concerns that limn the basic characteristics of Jewish, Christian, and Muslim interpretive traditions. Modern conceptions of Abraham are shaped by these long-standing traditions, but for the most part even believers are unfamiliar with the underlying historical and exegetical issues. Introducing readers to them is the aspiration that animates this book.

There is an overabundance of ancient and medieval sources that deal with Abraham and his family in all three traditions. My objective is not to survey all or even many of them but to spotlight those portrayals that in one form or another continue to accompany these scriptural figures, as well as those that tease out aspects of how Jews, Christians, and Muslims addressed thorny scriptural issues or dealt with the burning issues of the day, that is, how they employed Scripture for political and social purposes. I examine interpretive traditions from a variety of sources roughly spanning the first century BCE to the twelfth century CE.

I begin in Chapter 1 with a brief introduction to the Bible and the Qur'an and some of their interpreters. Then I turn to the story of Abraham in the Bible and the Qur'an, before examining specific portrayals and interpretations. Given the nature of this topic, there are few academics, let alone general readers, who are conversant with all three scriptural traditions beyond the rudiments. This book necessarily covers territory that is partly unfamiliar even to the professional academic, and the general reader may not know much beyond general plotlines or names. Thus, I retell the scriptural stories—the stories in the Bible and the Qur'an—in Chapter 2. Highlighting the biblical and qur'anic ambiguities and uncertainties is helpful if we are to appreciate how the exegetical traditions function in fleshing out and making sense of those ambiguities and uncertainties.

Chapter 3, the first in a series of thematic chapters, discusses the depiction of Abraham as the first monotheist and the various exegetical reasons that contribute to that portrayal. Why is the image of Abraham as the monotheistic iconoclast prominent especially in Jewish and Muslim traditions? Chapter 4 explores how Sarah and Hagar are depicted in ancient and early medieval sources as well as the factors that bring about a variety of interpretations of these women's stories in Judaism, Christianity, and Islam. This chapter also includes contemporary readings of the wives of Abraham, including Keturah, to illustrate how interpretation functions.

Chapter 5 is devoted to the relationship between Ishmael and Isaac and the extent to which they are sibling rivals. The chapter also explores notions of family in Judaism, Christianity, and Islam. Chapter 6 focuses on Ishmael in order to illustrate the ways scriptural figures are used as political tools. The figure of Ishmael, though employed for different purposes in Christian and Muslim internecine debates of the medieval period, functions in a similar way, namely to cast aspersions on coreligionists.

Chapter 7 takes up the sacrifice of Abraham's son in all three traditions and draws attention to how each tradition celebrates Abraham's willingness to sacrifice his son and at the same time presents a critical perspective. By allowing the cries of Sarah and angels to be heard, for example, Jewish, Christian, and Muslim interpreters subvert this parade example of Abraham's faithfulness. The near-sacrifice of the son is heralded as the supreme act of obedience to God, but the interpretive traditions also subtly, yet even at times stridently, call it into question.

This work takes partially familiar stories about Abraham and his family—stories that we all, Jews, Muslims, Christians, Hindus, Sikhs,

Buddhists, atheists, think we know but do not really know—and produces a new understanding. The new understanding arises in part from simply juxtaposing the three traditions (it becomes clear, for instance, that Ishmael and Isma'il are not mere facsimiles of each other) and in part from a close reading of the texts themselves, which are often surprisingly different from the popular versions that have been passed from generation to generation.

Over the course of my close examination of the scriptural and extrascriptural texts, I will draw attention to how exegetes recast Abraham and his family in order to accommodate philological, theological, and political concerns.

1

Scriptures and Interpreters

At the core of Judaism, Christianity, and Islam is the belief that God revealed himself[1] to humans through a series of revelations. For Jews and Christians, this revelation is known as the Bible, from the Greek *ta biblia*, "the books." Each religion, however, understands "Bible" and its content differently. Often we speak of canon and Scripture as if they were synonyms, but the term "canon"—meaning the collection of writings deemed holy—would have been foreign to ancient Jews and Christians. Canon assumes Scripture, in that it is a cataloguing, a listing, but Scripture does not require canon. Furthermore, the process of canonizing a set of writings is just that—a process, one that spans a lengthy period of time. Although "canon" has different meanings, I use it here to refer to a set of immutable, authoritative texts.[2] It is a closed, static list of books, yet the dynamic act of interpretation keeps it unfastened. In other words, while we do not add to the list of works that make up the Bible or any canon, through interpretation we continue to make the collection of texts relevant and meaningful, open to new insights and understanding. In this way, the canon is at once fixed and fluid.[3]

TaNaKh/Old Testament

The Jewish and Christian traditions both claim the Bible to be the authoritative word of God, but what constitutes the Bible is different for these two communities. The Jewish Bible, known by the acronym TaNaKh, is divided into three sections: the Torah (also known as the Pentateuch or the First Five Books of Moses), the Prophets (Nevi'im), and the Writings (Ketuvim). The Jewish Bible is also known as the Hebrew Bible. Although by and large the Jewish Bible is written in Hebrew, parts of it, such as portions of Daniel and Ezra, are in Aramaic. The books contained in the Jewish Bible (Hebrew Bible)[4] also make up what Christians refer to as the Old Testament; however, the Catholic and Eastern Orthodox canons include additional writings known as the Apocrypha or Deuterocanonical Books.

Many assume that the Jewish Bible is the Old Testament; in fact, it is not uncommon to hear Jews refer to their Bible in that way. But calling it the Old Testament undermines a theological cornerstone of Judaism—the covenantal relationship between God and the Jewish people. According to Judaism, there is nothing "old" about the Jewish Bible. For Jews, it is the only Testament, the only covenant, and it is everlasting. Christians, in contrast, believe that God made another covenant through Jesus, hence the New Testament.[5]

How the books are organized hints at how the communities of believers understand their Scriptures. The first section of the Jewish Bible, the Torah or Pentateuch, ends with a series of five speeches Moses gives to the Israelites as they prepare to enter the Promised Land. Following a similar pattern, the very last book of the Jewish Bible as a whole, 2 Chronicles, recapitulates the history of the Israelites after the destruction of the First Temple and closes with the new Persian king (Cyrus) giving permission to the Jews living in exile in Babylonia to go back and rebuild their Temple. The order is not chronological: Ezra and Nehemiah, the two books that precede 2 Chronicles, recount what occurs *after* the exiles return. As the books are arranged, however, TaNaKh ends with an image of those in exile returning to the Promised Land to live "happily ever after," and the reader is left with an echo of the "happily ever after" ending

of the Torah and the sense that what is expected will take place—
that is, that the covenant between God and the people of Abraham,
Isaac, and Jacob will be fulfilled. The *expectation* of fulfillment, not
its playing out, is the important part. In this way, the canon, which
one might see as closed, locked in the eternal past, is open to the
future, to the expectation of Jews living in the land and keeping the
commandments in fulfillment of the covenant. Prayers, liturgy, and
engagement with the biblical accounts through narrative expansions as well as other exegetical activities transform this eternal past
into the eternal present. The ordering of the Jewish Bible is thus
also an interpretation of its contents.

The Christian canon of sacred Scripture consists of all the books
of the Hebrew Bible, ordered differently, and adds the New Testament afterward. What for Jews is the abiding covenant in and of
itself for Christians finds fulfillment in the "new and everlasting
covenant" in the person of Jesus of Nazareth, whose life, death, and
resurrection are proclaimed in the New Testament. The Christian
ordering of the books of the Old Testament signals the shift in the
understanding of the covenant. Like the Jewish Bible, the Christian
Old Testament begins with the Pentateuch, but the Christian version ends with Malachi, a prophetic work that announces the coming of a messenger whom God will send. The messenger will reunite
and purify all of Israel prior to the "great and terrible day of the
Lord" (4:5).[6] The central theme of Malachi is fidelity to the Lord's
covenant, faithfulness to his teachings. The prophet Malachi condemns the priests for their corruption and exhorts obedience to God,
the father of all (2:10), in anticipation of the day of the Lord.[7] The
Old Testament therefore ends with an expectation, an anticipation
of a future event that will begin with the birth of Jesus in Matthew,
the first book of the New Testament. The end of the Old Testament
leads into the beginning of the New Testament: "Behold, I will send
you Elijah the prophet before the great and terrible day of the Lord
comes. And he will turn the hearts of fathers to their children and
the hearts of children to their fathers, lest I come and smite the land
with a curse" (Mal. 4:5). The verse anticipates the arrival of the coming of Jesus.[8] The very ordering of the Christian canon testifies to
the belief that Jesus is the fulfillment of Scripture.

The end of the New Testament reflects the Christological understanding of the Hebrew Bible, thus rendering it a First, or Old, Testament. The New Testament, which includes four Gospels, letters
of the apostle Paul, and others, as well as a chronicle of the apostolic
age (Acts of the Apostles), concludes with the Book of Revelation,
an apocalypse[9]—a magnificently imaginative, powerful vision of the
final days when Jesus will come to make a final judgment on the living and the dead and usher in a new heaven and earth. The book
ends with the expectation of the coming of the Lord: "He who testifies to these things says, 'Surely I am coming soon.' Amen. Come,
Lord Jesus!" (22:20).

Like the Old Testament, the New Testament—and thus the entire
Christian Bible—culminates in the image of a future event that
some Christians believe is already in the process of being fulfilled.
The Christian Bible, like the Jewish Bible, ends with an image of
the future. There is a marked difference between the two, however,
since the end of the Jewish Bible, the book of 2 Chronicles, looks
forward to a future that already took place historically. We are asked
to envisage the inhabitants of Judea returning from exile to rebuild
the Temple, but we know from the books of Ezra and Nehemiah
that the rebuilding already took place. The future suggested at the
end of the Jewish Bible is oriented to the present; its fulfillment is
not in the future but has already come to pass. Moreover, it does not
anticipate a cataclysmic end to the world as we know it, an end that
affects all the inhabitants of the earth, but is centered on the covenantal relationship between God and his people.

The overall shape of the Jewish and Christian Bibles in many
ways represents how these two religions overlap and diverge, how
they share books and at the same time differ significantly. Considering the Old Testament and the Jewish Bible to be exactly the same
work would betray theological claims central to each religion. Yet it
would be a mistake to draw sweeping conclusions about Judaism
and Christianity from the arcs of their biblical narratives, such as
that Judaism is marked by a presentist orientation while Christianity's gaze is toward the future. Jews tailored the Bible to address
political, social, and theological exigencies. They extended the biblical telos into the future by employing the narrative of apocalypse

and visions common to other Near Eastern cultures and religions. At the same time they drew on classical midrashic (rabbinic interpretive) motifs that were also adapted to accommodate the realities of the day, and in doing so they gave voice to future expectations. Christian interpreters and homilists, for their part, regarded biblical personages as role models of rectitude, as exemplars for living a Christian life in the here and now.

The Qur'an

Consisting of 114 suras ("chapters"), ordered for the most part from the longest to the shortest, the Qur'an is the sacred text of Islam.[10] It is considered the word of God revealed through the angel Gabriel to the prophet Muhammad over a period of twenty-two years. According to the Islamic tradition, God made known his laws and teachings also to Jews and Christians, but over time these laws and teachings were corrupted, falsified by Jews and Christians who distorted *(taḥrīf)* and altered *(tabdīl)* the divine message.[11] Unlike the New Testament, for example, the Qur'an is not conceived or understood as a continuation of the Jewish Bible/Old Testament but is a continuation and perfection of revelation.

Taḥrīf is the notion that the Jews and Christians who received divine revelation corrupted God's word, that they tampered with their own Scriptures.[12] According to Islam, the Old Testament/ Jewish Bible and New Testament as they are preserved today are not the authentically revealed word of God, for what was revealed to Jews and Christians is not preserved. Rather, the Qur'an is the true word of God, sent from above to the prophet Muhammad, who is considered the Seal of Prophecy.

In the medieval period there were two prevalent notions of *taḥrīf,* which modern scholars term *taḥrīf al-naṣṣ* (or *taḥrīf al-lafẓ*), having to do with the corruption of the text, and *taḥrīf al-maʿna,* having to do with the distortion of meaning. The concept was adapted and developed over time. Moreover, Muslims were well aware of the Bible and in many instances used it polemically against Jews and Christians.[13] It was also utilized for apologetic purposes to argue that it predicted the coming of the prophet Muhammad and—by exegetes—to demonstrate the authority of the Qur'an. "Many Muslim intellectuals acquired an extensive knowledge of the Bible," the scholar Walid Saleh notes. "Converts, some eager to put their previous knowledge in the service of their new faith, wrote scathing works that became part of the Islamic polemical repertoire."[14]

Geographically set in the Arabian peninsula, the Qur'an is regarded as the recapitulation of previous revelations and at the same time the final revelation. It emerged predominantly out of a larger, multicommunal scriptural tradition that also included nonbiblical Jewish and Christian traditions. It recounts many of the same stories as those in Genesis and Exodus, for example, and on numerous occasions refers to other stories of the Bible elliptically, so much so that it generally assumes "scriptural literacy."[15] Many of the biblical dramatis personae make an appearance in the Qur'an.

According to the Islamic tradition, several of the major characters of the Old Testament/Jewish Bible and the New Testament are referred to as prophets and messengers. The most common term, *rasūl*, which is used over three hundred times in the Qur'an, usually means "messenger," "apostle," or "someone who was sent." It also has a more specific meaning: one who has been appointed by God to communicate a particular message. Among those explicitly referred to as messengers are the biblical prophets Noah, Ishmael, Moses, Lot, and Jesus and the nonbiblical prophets Hud, Salih, and Shu'ayb.[16] The term *nabī* ("prophet") occurs less often in the Qur'an than *rasūl*, but it is used in connection with many more biblical characters: Lot, Abraham, Isaac, Jacob, Joseph, Aaron, David, Solomon, Job, Idris (Enoch), Jonah, Zechariah, John the Baptist, Elisha, and Elijah. And there are qur'anic passages that refer to prophets but do not name specific ones.

These messengers and prophets were sent to their people to spread the same belief that Muhammad would preach in the seventh century BCE. As the Qur'an states in 6:84–90, it is to these men (Idris is not listed) that the Book, wisdom, and prophethood are given, so that they may guide the people and exhort them to follow the straight path. Other passages likewise express the notion that these biblical figures were recipients of revelation. Thus we read in Qur'an 3:84,

"Say: We believe in God and that which is revealed to us and that which was revealed to Abraham, Ishmael, Jacob and the tribes, and that which was given to Moses and Jesus, and the prophets from their Lord. We make no distinction between any of them, and to Him have we surrendered."[17] The prophets preached monotheism and the need to accept and live by God's revelation. Thus the message of the Qur'an is not radically different from that of the Old Testament/Jewish Bible and New Testament. In fact, it purports to be a continuation of the message of the revelation sent to Jews and Christians. Furthermore, God's revelation in the Qur'an is explicitly for all humankind: all are exhorted to follow the path set out by God through the prophets. Those who follow it will be rewarded; those who reject or stray from it will be held accountable for their actions on the Day of Judgment.

The Qur'an randomly refers to episodes in no sequential manner. Unlike the Jewish Bible, which begins with Creation and has a specific trajectory, the Qur'an is a series of revelations that recount the attempts by generations of prophets to call people to the worship of the one true God. The Qur'an often mentions prophetic figures in passing, but exegetes *(mufassirūn)* and storytellers *(quṣṣāṣ)* recount events from the prophets' lives in greater detail.

Stories about Adam and Eve, Noah, Abraham, Joseph, and other scriptural figures, as well as legends about the biblical patriarchs, rabbis, monks, and martyrs, were circulated widely in Arabia well before the seventh century CE by Jews and Christians.[18] Although we possess no extant Arabic translation of parts of the Bible from pre-Islamic Arabia, in all likelihood such translations circulated among the Christians of pre-Islamic Arabia for liturgical and missionary purposes.[19] Moreover, as with the Aramaic-speaking Jews who read the Bible in Hebrew and explained it to listeners in Aramaic, it is reasonable to assume that the Arabian Jews read the Bible in Hebrew and explained it in Arabic.[20] Apart from Jewish and Christian stories, however, different types of narratives were also widespread and popular among the inhabitants of Arabia,[21] and are no less part of the qur'anic literary contexts.

The Relationship between the Bible and the Qur'an

One of the many challenges that scholars of Near Eastern literature of late antiquity confront is how to describe the relationship of
the Qur'an to its intertexts, without at the same time subsuming the
Qur'an under all that is "biblical" or creating a sense that it is derivative. That is, how can one appreciate the ways in which the Qur'an
is part and parcel of the broader scriptural landscape of the late antique Near East and not merely a product of that landscape?

Past efforts to detect exegetical motifs, narrative plots, and similar
stories found in Muslim and Jewish (as well as Muslim and Christian) sources resulted in the use of the term "borrowing," which implies that elements found in a later tradition belong to the earlier
source. Attempts at "source-hunting"[22] contribute to the sense that
the later tradition, in this case Islam, is derivative and owes a huge
debt to the earlier source or tradition. The idea that all roads lead to
the Bible is, perhaps needless to say, exceedingly wrongheaded; it
creates the reductionist impression that one tradition owns a host of
ideas, stories, or motifs and that the iteration of those ideas, stories,
or motifs within a different literary or religious matrix must inevita-
bly involve an attenuated form. But the Qur'an is not simply another
interpretation of the Bible. (Nor, for that matter, is the New Testament derived from the Old.) Philological investigations inform understanding of a word or verse in the Qur'an and explain how literary
texts migrated from one locus to another, but descriptive language
that assumes that the Qur'an is derivative or that it resides within the
biblical penumbra compromises such inquiries.[23]

Literary traditions do not move in only one direction, of course.
The sources attest to means by which Islamic literary material
made its way back into Jewish interpretation, and Islamic theology,
too, left its imprint on Jewish and Christian theology. The phenomenon of literary, cultural, and philosophical diffusion and
crosscultural dissemination must be understood in terms of the
power and vitality of that which is transmitted and of that which is
transformed.[24] Traditions taking shape in new contexts should be
understood not as "borrowing," then, but as a facet of how a religious system develops in multiple arenas of discourse, how it shapes

and is shaped by its milieu, whether literary, theological, social, or cultural.[25]

Eschewing the language of "borrowing" and the implications of a genealogical approach to the Qur'an and the larger Islamic tradition, recent scholars have begun to offer alternative explanations for parallels between Jewish and Muslim exegetical literature. Rather than searching for the qur'anic "Urtext," some have turned to orality and intertextuality[26] as explanations for the transmission of Jewish and Christian interpretations known to Muslims, and have attributed intentionality to the transmission and absorption of Jewish cultural artifacts by Muslim exegetes.[27] Along with rejecting the notion of "borrowing," accepting a more complex notion of intertextuality, and attributing intentionality to the absorption of late antique Jewish, Christian, and Greco-Roman sources, recent scholarship also recognizes the symbiotic relationship of self-definition between Jews and Christians, Christians and Muslims, and Muslims and Jews.[28]

Understanding biblical allusions in the Qur'an is not only a matter of identifying what the references are and to whom they were addressed; it is also a matter of discovering how Muslims considered these allusions to function within their religious horizon. In this regard, the work of Angelica Neuwirth has forged groundbreaking paths in Qur'anic studies and reinvigorated the field, advancing it well beyond reductive approaches.[29] She offers insight into why themes in the Qur'an emerge and recur in light of historical exigencies.

The move away from mining the Islamic textual tradition for Jewish and Christian sources is an important and necessary shift in understanding the role Muslim exegesis plays in its own tradition, for to regard the Qur'an and Islamic exegesis as derivative or as a reaction to what preceded it is to ignore the role that Scripture and scriptural interpretation played and continue to play in creating, and fostering, a group's self-definition and self-understanding. At the same time, to deny that Islam absorbed Near Eastern motifs and literary narratives, to ignore the existence of literary traditions found in other cultures and religions, is to strip it of its historical embeddedness, to deny it its rightful relationship to Judaism and

Christianity and its place within the late antique Near Eastern realm.

Over the course of centuries, all three religions developed exegetical traditions that gave new meaning to the Holy Word. Political, social, and religious exigencies gave rise to different readings of Scripture. Particular contexts gave shape to the ways in which exegetes revitalized the word of God. Readers of the Bible and Qur'an continue to unpack and tease out new meaning, new understanding of a biblical narrative or qur'anic verse that has resonance for the reader personally or throws light on a current social or political matter. The interpretive endeavor can take one so far afield that the Abraham of Genesis is no longer the father of Isaac and Ishmael but rather the father of all peoples.

Jewish, Christian, and Islamic scriptural interpretations, whether ancient or modern, share many fundamental assumptions inherent to the hermeneutical process. They approach Scripture as a seamless whole, perfect in its message to humanity. The Word of God is neither self-contradicting nor subject to mutability. Its interpretation, however, is far from monolithic, and subject to differing perspectives. Interpretation is a context-dependent activity. The questions addressed, the manner in which they are addressed and answered, the matter of who is addressing and answering and to what audience—all these factor into understanding scriptural interpretation. In other words, awareness of the historical situation of the interpreter and of that which is interpreted provides a portal into exegetical texts and the practices that give rise to specific readings of Scripture.

What follows is a very brief overview of Jewish, Christian, and Muslim interpretive traditions of the late antique and early medieval periods, traditions that played a role in later exegetical developments in each religious tradition. Far from exhaustive, this general discussion seeks to familiarize the reader with underlying exegetical concepts—some of them common to all three Abrahamic religions, some of them unique to one religion—as well as with several important works and interpreters whose impact remains palpable today.

Often our knowledge of scriptural stories comes less from our direct engagement with the Bible and the Qur'an than from our exposure to extrascriptural legends and tales told about them. Accreted traditions and confessional assumptions shape our images of scriptural personages. Many are surprised to discover that in the Bible Adam and Eve do not eat an apple, Abraham does not smash his father's idols, and Ishmael does not diddle his younger brother, and that in the Qur'an Ishmael is not explicitly named as the sacrificial son—in short, that what we think we know about scriptural personages and events is not quite what we read in the Bible and the Qur'an. Clothed in layer upon layer of tradition, scriptural characters take on a life of their own. Events are imbued with meaning exceeding the literal limits of verses and chapters.

The stories in the Jewish Bible and the Qur'an, characteristically terse, leave readers with many unanswered questions about the details of any given narrative. Exegetes both creatively expand stories and bridge gaps in them, and troubling passages are explained away in order to whitewash the patriarchs and matriarchs who are believed to embody religious teachings and to behave in exemplary ways.

Ancient and Early Medieval Jewish Exegesis

The Bible, the source for exegesis for Christians and Jews, itself includes numerous examples of interpretation. That is, many biblical passages tailor earlier material to construct new meaning. The inner-biblical exegetical phenomenon takes on many forms and functions and is consonant with later interpretive literature.[30]

Works that are especially interesting to consider include *Jubilees*, an elaborate second-century BCE[31] narrative covering events that take place from Genesis to Exodus 12; one of the Dead Sea Scrolls that is extant in fragmentary form, composed between the early and middle second century BCE, *Genesis Apocryphon;* and the second-century CE *Biblical Antiquities (Liber Antiquitatum Biblicarum)* of Pseudo-Philo, which ends with the death of Saul.[32] These works embellish and amplify the biblical narrative, but they may not regard the Bible as canonical. That is, the Bible is not necessarily their starting point; its centrality during the Second Temple period is questionable. By contrast, midrash—rabbinic biblical interpretation—takes the Bible as its starting point.

Though by most accounts the ancient Jewish historian Josephus (37–ca. 100 CE) was not an exegete, his history of the Jewish people from the biblical period in his *Jewish Antiquities* is part of the long trajectory of Jewish scriptural interpretation. Josephus promises to cover the entire biblical history systematically, and for the most part he delivers on that promise. His retelling of events and embellishment of characters, while not a verse-by-verse exposition of the Bible, contributed to the reception of biblical stories in antiquity.

Another important figure is Philo (ca. 20 BCE–ca. 50 CE), a Jewish Hellenistic philosopher and interpreter of Scriptures. His approach to the Bible made less of an impact on Palestinian rabbinic interpretation than it did on the writings of the church fathers (patristics). His interest in the etymologies of Hebrew names, a form of allegorical interpretation, was for example adopted and popularized by early church biblical exegetes. In contrast to Josephus, who set out to give an account of biblical history, Philo was concerned mostly with philosophical matters and with understanding biblical personages in light of Hellenistic philosophical values.

The *pesher* ("interpretation") of prophetic works of the Bible found at Qumran exhibits traits similar to those of rabbinic midrash—an atomistic approach to scriptural verses and the use of double entendre, anagram, and paronomasia (wordplay).[33] It is a distinct form of interpretation, however, and should not be conflated with rabbinic forms of interpretation.[34] The Qumran *pesher* engages the past to address the present but does so with respect to the future. Although there are no traces of the *pesher* per se in the New Testament, the *pesher* has affinities with the New Testament's use of prophetic literature as a key to unlocking the meaning of past events.

Rabbinic literature, primarily midrash, is an important source for my examination of depictions of the members of Abraham's immediate family. In common parlance, midrash (Hebrew root *drsh*, "to investigate, seek, search out, examine") refers to interpretation of any text, sacred or secular, ancient or contemporary. In its strictest sense, however, it is a process of scriptural exegesis that characterizes classical rabbinic interpretation. It also refers to the vast and varied rabbinic compilations of the late antique and medieval periods that preserve oral traditions prior to their redaction (roughly the third to the thirteenth century).[35]

The decline of Palestine as the center of intellectual activity in the mid-fourth century may have given rise to the need and interest in compiling such works. Christian claims to the biblical heritage also may have factored into the need to preserve rabbinic discourse in writing. Given that the rabbis made no effort to state explicitly their priorities, concerns, and desiderata, we can only speculate as to the reasons why they collected their musings, opinions, and teachings on legal and nonlegal matters into massive volumes.

Midrash, both the process and the very fruit of that process, grew out of an attempt to understand laconic or obscure biblical verses in order to make meaning out of Scripture. It is the means by which the rabbis made biblical ordinances relevant, taught moral lessons, told stories, and maintained the Jewish metanarrative that shaped and continues to sustain the Jewish people. The rabbis probed Holy Writ for responses to the burning theological issues of the day, as well as for answers to a changing cultural and political reality. The Bible was a vehicle for looking both backward and forward.

Not all rabbinic interpretation, however, should be understood as a response to contemporary religious or social concerns. Gaps in the biblical text, superfluous wording, and seeming contradictions occupied the rabbis' attention. Hence the philological aspects of midrash are essential to understanding the rabbinic enterprise itself. Midrash's versocentric, intertextual orientation is its fundamental feature. But not all midrashim can be understood in these hermeneutic terms. Social, theological, and political issues precipitated by historical events such as the rise of Christianity and Islam played a role, significant or otherwise, in the rabbinic reading of some biblical verses. The point is that midrash, like any form of interpretation, did not develop in a vacuum, void of interaction with ambient peoples, religions, and cultures. On the contrary, both the content and the exegetical methods employed in midrashic literature betray features of Greco-Roman, Christian, Persian, or later Islamic sources, depending on whether the rabbinic work is of the late antique or medieval period.

Many of the rabbinic sources to be examined come from *Genesis Rabbah* (ca. fifth century, of Palestinian provenance), the premier example of an aggadic (nonlegal, also known as nonhalakhic), exegetical compilation. It contains commentaries on almost the entire book of Genesis. Here we find both simple and elaborate explanations of words and phrases of the verse at hand, often in Aramaic. Most of the *parashiyot*, or chapters,[36] contain one or more *petihtot*, or proems. The *petihta*—usually from the Writings, especially from Psalms or the Wisdom literature, sometimes from the Prophets, and only rarely from the Torah—at first may seem extraneous but is connected through a chain of interpretations to the verse at the beginning of the section.

An important feature of rabbinic compilations is the inclusion of competing opinions on how to interpret a verse. Consider, for instance, this midrash from *Genesis Rabbah:*

So it came about that the Lord scattered them [*wayyafets*] from there over the face of the entire world and they stopped building the city (Gen. 11:8). R. Yudan said: "The people of Tyre went to Sidon and the Sidonites to Tyre, while Mizraim [Egypt] retains his land." R. Nehemiah said: "Everyone held onto their own land for their original settlement was there, and to that they returned." So what is meant by ". . . the Lord scattered them . . ."? All the peoples entered the mountain peaks and absorbed their own inhabitants. The Rabbis said: "scattered [*wayyafets*] is to be read swept away [*wayyatsef*]: the sea came up and swept away thirty families." R. Pinchas said in R. Levi's name: "No misfortune comes to a man which does not profit somebody. How were those thirty families replaced? From Abraham, sixteen from the sons of Keturah and twelve from Ishmael, and as for the remaining two—And the Lord said unto her, 'Two nations are in your womb.'" (*Gen. Rab.* 38:10)[37]

The midrash concerns God's response to humanity's building of a tower after the Great Flood (Gen. 11:8): "The Lord came down to look at the city and tower [called Babel in verse 9] that man had built, and the Lord said, 'If, as one people with one language for all, this is how they have begun to act, then nothing they propose to do will be out of their reach. Let us, then, go down and confound their speech there, so that they shall not understand one another's speech.' Thus the Lord scattered them from there over the face of the whole earth." What does it mean that God scattered the people from there over the whole earth? Did not the people already "branch out over the earth" after the Flood? Rabbi Yudan understands the scattering to mean that people exchanged places, but Rabbi Nehemiah interprets it as meaning that people went back to where they belonged before the Flood. In the third explanation, the rabbis, true to form, transpose letters, turning *vayyafets,* "scattered," into *vayyatsef,* "swept away," and explain that the verse means that thirty families were swept away and replaced by the progeny of Abraham. Where did the rabbis come up with thirty? From the nations or families of Abraham: twelve from Ishmael, two from Isaac, and sixteen from the children Abraham has with Keturah. The image is that of sweeping away and scattering—sweeping away nations that engage in building a tower to reach the heavens, and scattering Abraham's family throughout the world.

The example illustrates recurring aspects of rabbinic interpretation. First, it asks what is meant by the scattering of people from over the face of the whole earth, in light of Genesis 10:32: "the nations branched out over the earth after the Flood." It tackles the question by offering different explanations, including one based on wordplay. But it does more: it also asserts who constitutes the family. Abraham's family includes the children he had with Hagar and Keturah.

Through philological associations and intertextual wordplay, the rabbis unpack the meaning of biblical verses. Moreover, by drawing on verses from the Prophets and Writings to explicate a verse in Torah, the rabbis demonstrate the underlying notion that TaNaKh is a seamless whole whose parts shed light throughout from beginning to end. For example, on Genesis 1:1, we read in *Genesis Rabbah:* R. Oshaya opened his explication of the verse: "I was with Him as a nursling [*amon*], a source of delight every day; rejoicing before him at all times" (Prov. 8:30). By drawing on a variety of verses (Num. 11:12, Lam. 4:5, Esther 2:7), the midrash offers different explanations for the meaning of *amon*—"tutor," "covered," "hidden," and "great." The connection is philological, based on assonance between *amon* in Proverbs 8:30 and a word in each prooftext. In this manner, the midrash unpacks Proverbs 8:30, which in turn explicates Genesis 1:1, "In the beginning God created." In the final interpretation, "*Amon* is a workman [*uman*]." Torah (Wisdom) speaks: "I was the working tool of the Holy One, blessed be He." The midrash continues:

> In human practice, when a mortal king builds a palace, he builds it not with his own skill but with the skill of an architect. The architect moreover does not build it out of his head, but employs plans and diagrams to know how to arrange the chambers and the wickets. Thus God consulted the Torah and created the world, while the Torah declares, "In the beginning God created," beginning referring to the Torah, as in the verse, "The Lord made me as the beginning of His way." (Prov. 8:22)

In addition to wordplay, we find scores of stories, maxims, and parables, *meshalim* (singular *mashal*). The Hebrew parables about kings are the signal form of narrative in rabbinic exegetical literature. Nearly all rabbinic *meshalim* consist of a bipartite structure—the fictional narrative, which is the *mashal* proper, and its application, the *nimshal*, which usually concludes with a biblical verse serving as the *mashal*'s prooftext. Formulaic phrases mark the two parts: *mashal le*, "it is like" (also, *mashal lema hadavar dome le*, or simply *le*), and *kakh*, "so, too, similarly."[38]

Rabbinic exegetical methods employed in halakhic and aggadic midrashim vary. The *qal wahomer* (literally "light and heavy") establishes an argument based on the inference that if something applies in a minor case, it will also apply in the major. This form of reasoning is found in both halakhic and aggadic midrashim, and was common in Greco-Roman argumentation (*a minore ad maius*). The *gezera shavah*, however, is more common to halakhic midrashim. By means of verbal analogy, a particular detail of a biblical law in one verse is derived from the meaning of the word or phrase in the other. Other rules that characterize halakhic midrashim include the *binyan av* (a specific law in one verse may be applied to all other similar cases), *kelal uperat, perat ukelal* (rules of inference between general and specific statements and vice versa), and *hekkesh* (inference by analogy, whether explicit or implicit between two subjects—not words—within the same or similar context).

These aforementioned rules are employed in halakhic exegesis, but biblical nonlegal passages are often explained by paronomasia (wordplay). Philology provides a lynchpin for rabbis to draw analogies between verses. It also can take the form of gematria, whereby the arithmetical value of Hebrew letters is used to interpret a word or verse, and *notarikon*, shorthand writing whereby individual letters are used to signify words. In other words, Hebrew words are understood as acronyms so that each letter stands for another word, which in turn forms a phrase or sentence.

In the medieval period we find anthologies (*Midrash ha-Gadol* and *Yalkut Shim'oni*, known simply as the *Yalkut*), for example, of midrashic material. The *Yalkut*, compiled from more than fifty works and covering the entire span of the Jewish Bible, is one of the most well-known and comprehensive anthologies. There are several other collections of midrashic works from this period, collections that blend collation and commentary. A noteworthy work of the eighth/early ninth century that falls into the category of neither midrash nor anthology is *Pirke de Rabbi Eliezer (PRE)*.[39] It transmits both classical rabbinic and nonrabbinic material and utilizes earlier motifs and narratives from the Second Temple Period.[40] The status of *PRE* in the rabbinic corpus is problematic. Its narrative structure as biblical expansion is similar to that of the book of *Jubilees* (second century BCE), and its style is significantly different from that of earlier midrashim. Even though several sources were used, its structure indicates that it is ostensibly the work of one author, probably a Palestinian. It seems to represent a transition between the mythical perspective of rabbinic literature and that of kabbalah.[41] Given its dating and the inclusion of material that betrays familiarity with Islam, the composition sits at literary as well as cultural crossroads.

This later period saw a rise in commentaries on the Bible, but the interest in midrash continued nevertheless. Midrashim of the ancient and early medieval periods were often mentioned or alluded to in Bible commentaries. Rashi (1040–1105), the greatest Jewish medieval Bible and Talmud commentator, transmitted rabbinic exegetical traditions. Even today midrashim find their way into contemporary sermons, for they are part of the very bedrock of the Jewish tradition that exhorts readers of the Bible to "turn it over again and again, for everything is in it" (Pirke Avot 5:22).

The later rabbinic compilations include stories found in Islamic sources. While previous scholarship generally assumed that the Islamic texts adapted Jewish material, recent scholars have compellingly argued for a more fluid circulation of stories and motifs that may indeed have originated in Islamic circles.

Christian Exegesis

Many literary genres shaped early Christian biblical interpretation. In homilies, letters, and commentary, the church fathers engaged with the meaning of individual verses as well as longer passages and entire books of the Bible. The role played by scriptural interpretation in the formation of doctrine, and indeed in all areas of the life of the church, contributed to the vitality and development of Christianity over the centuries. The interaction flowed in two directions: scriptural interpretation both influenced and was influenced by doctrinal discussions. How the early Christian exegetes understood biblical passages throws light on the way Christian communities conceived of themselves.

Like their Jewish counterparts, Christian interpreters made sacred texts relevant and accessible to Christian audiences, finding lessons in the lives of biblical characters. Since most Christians could not read the Bible, their understanding of God's word was mediated by the early church writers, who in a sense rewrote the narrative as a teaching tool. The church fathers also waged internecine debates on theological matters, drawing on Scripture to bolster their positions, and engaged in polemics against Jews and Muslims as well.

The fathers of the church unequivocally and universally accepted the inspired nature of Christian Scriptures. They differed with respect to determining the meaning of the divine word, when to take it figuratively, and when to read it literally—that is, in the sense intended by the writer. Christian exegetes acknowledged that the explicit literal meaning might also include an implicit or metaphorical sense. Early Christian scriptural interpretation took into account the need for a variety of approaches; otherwise, how could one understand Exodus 21:24, "eye for eye, tooth for tooth," when, for example, a toothless baby was murdered? Or how does one read anthropomorphic statements about God in Genesis: "They heard the sound of the Lord God moving about in the garden" (Gen. 3:8)? As Chrysostom (347–407) would explain (in Ps. 9:4), "We interpret some passages by the letter, others with a meaning different from the literal and figurative."[42] In his analysis of early Christian exegesis the scholar Charles Kannengiesser notes that even the most literal-minded exegetes who rigorously "applied the rules and principles of a philological analysis to the sacred text" instinctively approached "the literality of the biblical text as gifted in itself with supernatural power. 'The meaning deserves to be explored because divine scripture says nothing that would be useless or out of consideration' . . . (*Quaestiones* 10,1)."[43] The literal sense was not always apparent, and often proved problematic. Cultural chasms resulted in unfamiliar phrases and foreign geography. The "ordinary" sense of a word or phrase was not always readily available, so Christian writers consulted lists,[44] among them those of Philo, whose interpretation of proper names often opened up the meaning of obscure terms.

Interpreters were primarily concerned with maintaining the continuity between the Old Testament and the New. The notion that Christians are the spiritual inheritors of the Old Testament with respect to its sacred teachings and divine revelation is paramount to understanding early church interpretation. Through allegory and typology, Christian exegetes fostered the unity of the testaments. "The New is in the Old concealed, the Old is in the New revealed," ran a popular medieval Latin saying.[45] The notion that the Old and New Testaments are intrinsically connected, not as two separate parts of a whole but as one in which each testament is part and parcel of the other, is fundamental to unlocking Christian approaches to Scripture.

One sign of that intrinsic connection is the Christological reading of prophetic literature. Beginning with Paul, the events of the

Old Testament prefigured Jesus and the church. They in turn reveal the deeper meaning of events recorded in the Old Testament. Examples of prefiguration include Adam as a type of Jesus in Paul's writing. The fulfillment statements in Matthew exemplify how the New Testament reads the prophetic writings of the Old. Other examples include Matthew 21:42–43 and Acts 8:32–35, in which Isaiah 53:7–8 is explicitly read as a reference to Jesus:

> Now the passage of the scripture that he [Ethiopian eunuch] was reading was this: "Like a sheep he was led to the slaughter, and like a lamb silent before its shearer, so he does not open his mouth. In his humiliation justice was denied him. Who can describe his generation? For his life is taken away from the earth" [Isa. 53:7–8]. The eunuch asked Philip, "About whom, may I ask you, does the prophet say this, about himself or about someone else?" Then Philip began to speak, and starting with this scripture, he proclaimed to him the good news about Jesus. (Acts 8:32–35)[46]

The second-century CE Marcion controversy and the ongoing debates with gnostic thinkers contributed to the linkage between the Old and New Testaments, as many writers went to great lengths to respond to theological challenges that compromised the relationship between the testaments. Gnostic dualism and disregard for the material world led some to reject the Old Testament entirely, for it was deemed the product of a foolish demiurge, in contrast to the supreme, good God of the New Testament.[47] Marcion, too, dismissed the Old Testament in toto. The testaments, even his New Testament, which differed from what eventually became canonized, to his mind, were irreconcilable. Marcion believed that the God of the Old Testament was vengeful yet righteous, but for many gnostics the creator God of the Old Testament was inherently evil, proof of which could be found in the world he created. Early church exegetes employed a variety of strategies in order to secure the relationship between the Old and New Testaments, throwing light on the meaning of individual words, phrases and verses, and entire stories. Here a brief review of terms commonly used in discussions of patristic methods of interpretation—such as "literal sense" and "plain sense," allegory, typology, and *theoria*—may be helpful.[48]

The literal sense was often referred to in terms of "lower" and "closer," whereas the spiritual sense was "higher" and "deeper." The relationship between the literal and spiritual "senses" of Scripture informs the use of allegory in Christian exegesis. *Allegory* is a Hellenistic term derived from the Greek, meaning roughly "to say something else in public speech." It is a form of interpretation, as Irmgard Christiansen explains, "thanks to which a core idea ('Ideeneinheit') implicitly included in the letter is explicated, a notion equivalent to the written expression but of a broader significance being joined to it."[49] In Greek antiquity, commentators produced allegorical interpretations of Homer and Hesiod. The Latin tradition, too, utilized allegory for exegetical purposes; there is no shortage of it in Philo.[50] In every instance, allegory was a means by which interpreters situated themselves vis-à-vis society and culture.[51]

Typology is a form of allegorical interpretation. According to the writings of the church fathers, a biblical place, person, event, or institution can function as a type, or *typos*, insofar as the place, person, event, or institution signifies someone or something that will be fulfilled or manifested in the future through God. What sets typology apart from allegory is connection to historical reality: typology attaches itself to history, whereas allegory need not have any connection to an original event in order to derive meaning. Isaac, Joseph, Joshua, and David are regarded as *typoi* of Jesus. Typological readings are widespread among the church fathers.[52]

Events such as the crossing of the sea are also read typologically. Thus, in *Pseudo-Barnabas* (12:2–3), the prayer of Moses as he extends his hands during the battle between the Israelites and the Amalekites is understood as a *typos* of the cross and crucifixion. In the *Dialogue with Trypho*, the law as discussed in the Old Testament is a *typos* of Christ and the Church. Gregory of Nyssa explains the Red Sea as a *typos* of baptism. Theodore of Mopsuestia provides numerous examples of events in the Old Testament that can be understood as *typoi* of events in the New Testament. The liberation of the Israelites from Egypt, for instance, is read as a prefiguration of the death of Jesus and freedom from sin.

Not all early Christian interpretation is nonliteral. Clement, for example, employs exempla throughout his writings, drawing on Old Testament characters to exhort believers to behave morally. Cain, Esau, and Aaron serve as illustrations of the effects of jealousy, and Abraham, Job, and David display the virtue of humility. And while early Christian exegetes interpreted the lovers in the Song of Songs as Christ and the church, Theodore read it as a love song, and hence did not accept its canonicity.

When discussing early Christian interpretation, scholars of patristics[53] often refer to two general schools of interpretation, the Alexandrian and the Antiochene, even though the latter was not a formal school (didaskaleion). In Alexandria, an actual school was established under the aegis of a local bishop. In Antioch, by contrast, no formal school existed; there was simply a group of exegetes and theologians who came together for a common purpose, although some, such as the founder of the school, Diodorus (late fourth century), took on private teaching roles.[54] Earlier scholarship in the field adhered rigidly to the "Alexandria versus Antioch" dichotomy, but the customary distinctions have recently been modified in order to underscore the importance of figural representation to all forms of early Christianity.[55] For one thing, the expected patterns might be reversed—an Antiochene scholar might allegorize a verse that the Alexandrian takes literally, rather than the other way around. For another, rigid categorization tends to homogenize the exegetical process in such a way that differences among interpreters in a school are obscured.[56] Antiochene exegetes, for example, may use the same method but come to different interpretations.[57]

The characteristics that mark the work of Origen (ca. 185–ca. 253 CE), among them allegory, etymology, and the symbolism of numbers, may be found in the work of his predecessors, such as Clement, but under Origen the school of Alexandria reached its apex.[58] Known for his encyclopedic learning and productivity, and for his staggering facility with the biblical text, Origen stands out as one of the greatest scholars of the early church. His interpretation took the form of commentaries on entire books, homilies preached in Caesarea, and scholia—that is, collections of explanations for select passages in Exodus, Leviticus, Isaiah, and Psalms 1–15. Other exegetes tended to concentrate on a few books of the Old Testament; the more expansive Origen included Ecclesiastes and Job. In fact, he wrote on all the books of the Old and New Testaments. What he received from his predecessors he widened and deepened, and at the same time he produced what was perhaps the first attempt at a critical edition of the Old Testament, his sixfold Bible, commonly known as the *Hexapla*. Although he knew little Hebrew and thus relied on rabbis for the significance of Hebrew names, he set himself the task of producing the most reliable biblical text by placing six translations side by side.

Origen's approach to Scripture was philological and marked by the recognition of the inexhaustibility of the Word of God. His *De Principiis* outlines a theory of exegesis that informed his interpretive work and espouses notions generally accepted by Christian exegetes—that Scriptures convey knowledge about God and Jesus, the world, and evil, and demonstrate divine salvific actions. In *De Principiis* (4.3.5), Origen notes that while all of Scripture has a spiritual significance, that is not the case with respect to the literal, since one can identify several instances where the literal sense is impossible.

The Antiochene school, which flourished in the fourth and fifth centuries, is often described as antiallegorical, but such a portrayal is inaccurate. Theodore of Mopsuestia (ca. 350–428), one of the leading figures of the school of Antioch, would in 553 be renounced as a heretic at the Second Council of Constantinople for his Christological views, but at the time of his death he was regarded as one of the outstanding biblical exegetes and theologians of his time. Known today as the father of Nestorianism, Theodore was a towering critic of Origen's allegorical interpretation. He maintained a literalist orientation as well as one directed toward eschatological readings of Scripture.

John Chrysostom (ca. 347–407), "the golden-mouthed," was a close friend and classmate of Theodore and a fellow monk. Renowned for the oratory excellence that earned him his name, Chrysostom was an interpreter of Scriptures whose literary legacy was unsurpassed among the Greek church fathers. In addition to the exegetical homilies that make up the largest part of his writings, he wrote sermons, treatises, and letters. He adhered to the Antiochene exegetical precepts, yet, he explained, "we interpret some passages by the letter, others with a meaning different from the literal, others again as literal and figurative."[59]

For Origen, every word of the Bible had a possible spiritual message; Theodore, in contrast, renounced Origen's allegorical readings and emphasized the historical dimension of Scripture, which in his view was undermined by allegory. But even Theodore, whose position was extreme, understood the nonliteral dimensions of Scripture, and those who took their cue from Philo and Origen did not diminish the intrinsic value accorded the letter.

The Alexandrian exegete Didymus (also referred to as Didymus the Blind) (ca. 313–398) was heavily influenced by Origen and was admired by Jerome. Like his Alexandrian predecessors, Didymus read Scripture in order to unveil the supernatural mysteries therein. Thus, etymologies of Jewish names are pregnant with meaning, as are animals and numbers. While he read beyond the literal, he was far less concerned with textual criticism than Origen.

We see Origen's influence in Didymus's *Commentary on Genesis*, putatively the oldest commentary by a Greek Christian author on the first book of the Bible. Didymus makes the same distinction that Origen did between the lighter, spiritual bodies of the prelapsarian period and the weighty body after the Fall, for example. Furthermore, he draws on Philo's interpretation of Sarah and Hagar. Whereas Sarah is emblematic of perfect virtue, Hagar symbolizes a preliminary stage leading up to virtue.

Ephrem (ca. 306–373) is considered one of the best-known writers of the golden age of Syriac literature, which spanned the fourth to eighth centuries. He is best remembered for his teaching and scriptural interpretation. His extensive oeuvre may be divided between prose, including expository as well as rhetorical works, and poetry. He was most famous for his poems: dialogue poems and metrical homilies *(memre)* and "teaching songs" *(madrashe)*, often referred to as hymns.[60] According to Jerome, these compositions were recited publicly after the reading of Scriptures.[61] As many have noted, their closest analogues might be "the Hebrew *Piyyutim*, synagogue songs which enjoyed great popularity in Palestine from the eighth century

on, and which feature biblical themes and literary devices very similar
to those regularly used by Ephraem."[62] The purpose of *madrasha*
(singular), however, is akin to that of its Hebrew cognate, midrash:
to instruct.

The Syriac and Greek traditions refer to him as having commented on all the books of the Bible; however, his *Commentary on
Genesis* is the only extant work in Syriac. Many of his commentaries
are preserved in Armenian and some in Syriac fragments. Rather
than giving a verse-by-verse exposition, Ephrem focused on passages he considered significant, such as the first three chapters of
Genesis on Creation and the Adam and Eve narrative.

Ephrem's exegetical works point to a familiarity with Jewish interpretation and reflect the influence of his Mesopotamian milieu.
They are also shot through with Christian faith. But one can say
the same of all his work, not just the exegetical—for example:

> The scriptures are set up
>   like a mirror;
> one whose eye is clear
>   sees there
> the image of the truth.
> Set up there
>   is the image of the Father;
> depicted there
>   is the image of the Son,
> and of the Holy Spirit.[63]

Whether in his refutations against those who hold opposing theological views, in his commentaries, or in his *memre* and *madrashe*,
his concern was to draw the reader or listener closer to truth, which
for him is the life, death, and resurrection of Christ:

> See, the Law carries
>   all the likenesses of him.
> See, the Prophets, like deacons,
>   carry
> the icons of the Messiah.

Nature and the scriptures
  together carry
The symbols of his humanity
  and of his divinity.[64]

Indeed, as highly regarded as his prose was, it was his poetical works that brought him wide acclaim, for it was through them that he conveyed his theological teachings, displayed his mastery of Semitic poetic devices, and exhibited his artistic genius.

Jerome (ca. 347–419/420) may be charged with lacking originality or methodological coherence, but there is no shortage of philological rigor to his commentaries. Even during his lifetime he gained authority in the realm of sacred Scripture.[65] His translation of the Old Testament, the Vulgate, directly from the Hebrew contributed to his renown as one knowledgeable in scriptural matters and, more important, became the basis "on which would rest from now on any edifice of the explication of the Scriptures in the Christian West."[66]

Origen's profound influence on him is clear in Jerome's *Hebrew Questions on Genesis*, but his approach, unlike Origen's, is twofold, taking into account the literal and spiritual senses of Scripture.[67] Moreover, he engaged with rabbinic sources to an unprecedented degree. Jerome's personal trajectory equipped him with the proper exposure to the cultural and philological tools necessary to produce commentaries that enriched Christian exegesis.

Literal and allegorical readings are more intertwined in the writings of the church fathers than scholarly designations lead us to consider. Cyril of Alexandria (ca. 375–444) was one of the most prolific Christian Bible commentators of late antiquity.[68] Like his Alexandrian counterparts, he engaged in allegorical readings of Scripture. At the same time, he recognized the importance of the literal meaning:

The discourse of the holy prophets is always obscure. It is [full of] hidden ideas, and, with labor, it speaks to us in advance about the divine mysteries. For Christ is the end of the law and prophets, just as it is written. However, I say that those who wish to make clear the subtle and hidden breath of spiritual insights must hasten to consider thoroughly, with the eye of the mind, on the one hand, the exact historical meaning . . . and, on the other hand, the interpretation resulting from spiritual contemplation. They should do this so that, in every way, benefit might come to the readers, and the explanation of the underlying ideas be lacking in nothing.[69]

Yet, while he attempts to explain historical contexts and to shed light on obscure names and foreign vocabulary, it is in order to uncover the mystery hidden in types.

For Cyril the resurrection of Christ unlocks the Bible. His reading of Scripture is through and through Christological. As Robert Wilken explains, "Christ is Cyril's true subject matter. Yet without the Bible there is no talk of Christ. Cyril knew no way to speak of Christ than in the words of the Bible, and no way to interpret the words of the Bible than through Christ. His biblical writings are commentaries on Christ and only if one reads them in that spirit can one appreciate his significance as interpreter of the Bible."[70]

Even the briefest overview of Christian interpreters must include Augustine (345–430), whose interpretive work took many forms—homily, commentary, and quaestio. His *De Doctrina Christiana (On Christian Teaching)* is largely a treatise on biblical interpretation. In it he espouses the notion that there is a multiplicity of interpretations that may be offered for a scriptural passage. "Sometimes not just one meaning but two or more meanings are perceived in the same words of scripture," he writes (*De Doctrina*, Book 3, 38).[71]

In addition to *De Doctrina Christiana*, two other works mark an important phase in Augustine's career as biblical commentator: *De Genesi ad Litteram (The Literal Meaning of Genesis)*, a unique attempt to produce a proper commentary of Scripture, and the *Confessions*. Especially in the *Confessions* we encounter the inextricable links between the human condition and scriptural interpretation and are exposed to the ways in which theology, philosophy, and an individual's personal spiritual journey commingle with exegetical endeavors. In these works Augustine affirms both the diversity and oneness of Scripture and acknowledges that the multiplicity of opinions is acceptable, as long as an interpretation draws us toward love of God and of neighbor.[72]

Early Christian interpreters exhibited two tendencies. On the one hand, their wish to read the Old Testament Christocentrically, against Jews and gnostics, pushed them toward allegory; on the other, the dangers of the gnostics' exaggerated allegorism fostered a more literal interpretation of scriptural sources. Despite the prominence of symbolic interpretation among Christian exegetes, then, the early church writers cannot be characterized as mere allegorists. Loosely speaking, the Alexandrian and Antiochene schools represented these two trends—the Alexandrians on the allegorical side, the Antiochenes on the literal side—but recent scholarship has benefited from moving beyond the oversimplification of earlier decades. The shift in scholarly discussions in turn reveals a more vibrant picture of Christian exegetical approaches to Scripture.

Qur'anic Exegesis

Tafsīr is derived from the Arabic root *fassara*, to explain, expound, or reveal. Like its Jewish analogue, midrash, *tafsīr* refers both to the act of exegesis and explanation and to actual corpora of interpretation.[73] The chronological span of *tafsīr* literature is expansive; its scope is vast and its physical size voluminous. It exhibits the cumulative and innovative nature of the exegetical enterprise par excellence. Extant commentaries on the Qur'an represent a sustained engagement that continues to the present.

Traditional *tafsīr* commentaries hew to a fairly standard format. As their starting point they take the qur'anic chapters from first to last, and they include a range of interpretations attributed to earlier authorities. While the individual commentator *(muffasir)* preserves the exegetical tradition, he also transforms the tradition through his selection process, as Jane Dammen McAuliffe observes: "the authorities that he cites define and demarcate the exegetical lineage within which he writes. Further, it is in the very process of selection, organization, presentation, and assessment of this material from one's exegetical predecessors that the individuality and originality of the particular commentator demonstrates itself."[74]

The *isnād* (chain of transmission) goes all the way back to the Companions and successors of the Prophet. These reports provide the basis of the voluminous *tafsīr* compilations.[75] Traditional commentaries include an *isnād* and the interpretation itself, the *matn*. Given the breadth of the *tafsīr* corpus, generalizations are untenable. We can safely assert, however, that Muslim exegetes repeatedly addressed questions and concerns having to do with when and why a verse was revealed *(asbāb al-nuzūl)*, the meaning of an uncommon word or phrase, syntactic matters, and morphological irregularities. Qur'anic exegesis of the classical period—roughly from al-Tabari (d. 923 CE)[76] to the twelfth century—is intertextual, in that parallel words and phrases occurring in other verses are brought to bear on the meaning of the verse at hand. Furthermore, traditions of *ḥadīth* (sayings attributed to the prophet Muhammad) are also included in the commentaries.

Often, *tafsīr* literature is divided into two broad categories: *al-tafsīr bi'l-ma'thūr* (also known as *al-tafsīr bi'l-riwāya*) and *al-tafsīr bi'l-ra'y*. The first refers to inherited tradition and is more conservative and constrained, whereas the second is based on personal opinion. About *al-tafsīr bi'l-ra'y*, it is reported that Muhammad categorically stated: "Whoever talks about the Qur'ān on the basis of his personal opinion *(ra'y)* or from a position of ignorance will surely occupy his seat in the Fire!"[77] As other ḥadīth indicate, during the classical period exegesis itself was less of a concern than the issue of whether or not someone unqualified would venture into such matters.[78] The prevalence of *al-tafsīr bi'l-ma'thūr* may be attributed to Ibn Taymiyya (1263–1328), whose exegetical paradigm categorically rejected as valid sources other than those inherited.[79] While scholars today continue to use these categories to categorize *tafsīr*, one must question their analytical utility. The very act of selecting and organizing "received tradition" reveals that which is unique to the *muffasir*.[80]

Some of the major collections of *tafsīr* that I will draw on are those of Muqatil ibn Sulayman,[81] al-Tabari, al-Tha'labi (d. 1035 CE), and Ibn Kathir (d. 1373 CE).[82] Muqatil ibn Sulayman was one of the earliest *mufassirūn* to show less interest in grammar and more in narrative expansion.[83] Although he was generally considered a great qur'anic commentator, later generations denigrated his contribution. This sea change, according to Claude Gilliot, "betrays a discernible historical trend of backward projection, whereby ancient scholars come to be judged according to standards which only find wide-spread acceptance long after the scholar in question has died."[84]

Muqatil ibn Sulayman al-Balkhi (d. 150/767) was born in Balkh, in modern-day Afghanistan, and lived in Iraq, but his scholarly pursuits sent him on peregrinations as far as Beirut and Mecca. The scholarly consensus maintains that his *al-tafsīr* is most likely the earliest extant qur'anic commentary. Because Muqatil drew heavily on what was later considered *isrā'īliyyāt* literature, he was accused of having borrowed his narratives from the Jews. He was also reproached for anthropomorphisms and heavily criticized for not providing *isnāds* for his exegesis.[85] Viewing him as unreliable and a liar, later Sunni traditionalists *(aṣḥāb al ḥadīth)* did not mention his corpus of interpretation. It is important to note that Muqatil engaged with the Qur'an at a time when *isnāds* were not considered the fixed pathways of transmission and that his work was composed before the Mu'tazilite (the dominant Muslim theological school of the ninth and tenth centuries CE) attack on anthropomorphism. In any event, there is no question that his work left an indelible mark on later exegetes.

One of the most famous exegetes is the polymath par excellence Abu Ja'far Muhammad ibn Jarir al-Tabari, whose Qur'an commentary, *Jāmi' al-bayān 'an ta'wīl āy al Qur'ān* (popularly known as *Tafsīr al-Tabari*), is considered the beginning, and perhaps the apex, of the classical period of Qur'an commentary.[86] McAuliffe notes that "his biographers never tire of repeating the remark laid to the credit of Abu Hamid al-Isfara'ini: 'If a man were to travel to China so as to acquire the book of *tafsīr* of Muḥammad b. Jarīr, that would not be too far.'"[87] The incorporation of *ḥadīth*, around thirty-eight thousand, and thirteen thousand different *isnāds* in *al-Tafsīr* alone is staggering.[88] In attempting to be as comprehensive as possible, al-Tabari included interpretations he himself did not favor. Sometimes his preferences are made explicit; at other times they are subtly revealed by the way in which the *ḥadīth* are arranged. In either case, he constantly displayed independent judgment *(ijtihād)*,[89] favoring reasoned, commonsensical interpretations over those marked by flights of fancy.

Unlike Muqatil, whose reception by his contemporaries was less than favorable, al-Tabari was regarded by his peers as a foremost authority. A scholar's scholar and consummate compiler, he laboriously gathered and systematically organized the exegetical, linguistic, and historical opinions of previous generations on the verses of the Qur'an, which resulted in his *al-Tafsīr*, the most celebrated example of the approach known as *al-tafsīr bi'l-ma'thūr* (based on reports). His other crowning achievement, which he wrote before his commentary, was his *Ta'rīkh al-rusul wa'l-mulūk* (*The History of the Prophets and Patriarchs*, simply known as *Ta'rīkh* [al-Tabari]), a universal history of the world.[90]

According to al-Tabari, there are several fundamental exegetical principles that must be followed:[91] (1) The moral and legal implications of a verse must be applied generally unless it is restricted in a prophetic *ḥadīth*.[92] While most *ayat* (verses) of the Qur'an deal with a particular situation, the moral or legal implication is valid for all similar occasions. This principle is already witnessed in early exegetical writings. (2) Verses have both exoteric (*ẓāhir*) and esoteric (*bāṭin*) meaning. An interpreter cannot jettison the exoteric meaning in favor of the esoteric unless the esoteric meaning or a prophetic *ḥadīth* furnishes reason to do so.[93] (3) Ambiguity in a verse cannot be resolved by bringing another verse, even if that verse is unambiguous. Such analogies are not acceptable.[94] Each verse must be interpreted on its own, and done so exoterically, that is, according to the literal or apparent meaning. (4) The Qur'an possesses no ambiguities. It is manifestly clear (*bayān*). No word, not even a letter, of the Qur'an can be rendered meaningless or incorrect. (5) Mastery of the Arabic language is a prerequisite. The meaning of an *aya* (verse) is determined by its proper usage. (6) What precedes or follows a specific pericope is important in determining meaning. Passages must be understood in context (*siyāq*). (7) Whenever there is a case of conflict regarding variant readings or questions of pronunciation, the orthography of the Qur'ans in common use (*rasm al-maṣāḥif*) serve as arbiters. (8) The authority of experts in specialized fields of learning such as grammar and history is highly regarded when several variants are acceptable. (9) With respect to generic nouns (*ism li-kull*), all meanings are equally possible. (10) That which is unspecified should not be arbitrarily rendered specific. Arbitrarily specifying details or presuming knowledge (*takalluf*) in order to fill in gaps in a verse such

as providing the answers to "who," "when," or "how much" assumes
a false kind of authority.[95]

Ahmad b. Muhammad al-Tha'labi (d. 427/1035), a native of
Nīshāpūr, was a prominent *mufassir,* considered by some "the most
important Qur'an exegete of the medieval Islamic world."[96] His major exegetical work, *al-Kashf wa'l-bayān 'an tafsīr al-Qur'ān (The Unveil-
ing and Elucidation in Qur'an Exegesis),* commonly known as *al-Kashf,*
is a massive interpretation of the Qur'an. Characteristics that set
al-Tha'labi's work apart from other medieval commentaries include
the self-conscious way he embarked on the task before him. The
introduction evaluates the status of the field, enumerates all utilized
sources, discusses earlier exegetes, and explains why the Mu'tazilite
tafsīr tradition, for example, was not included. Al-Tha'labi drew on
personal notes from well over three hundred scholars and, meticulous in amassing material, availed himself of all recensions.[97] Because
al-Kashf also included most of al-Tabari's material, it became the
treasured resource of later exegetes. Al-Tha'labi is also known for
his *Qiṣaṣ al-Anbiyā' (Tales of the Prophets),* a recounting of the prophets preceding the birth of Muhammad.

Born in Bosra in 1300, Ibn Kathir was a historian and traditional-
ist of Mamlūk, Syria. Most famous for his *al-Bidāya wa-l-nihāya
(The Beginning and the End),* a major historical work that became the
basis of later works, he also produced a Qur'an exegesis, *Tafsīr al-
Qur'ān al-'aẓīm,* and a popular collection of tales of the prophets.

In addition to the *tafsīr* compilations, interpretation of the Qur'an
takes on other forms, among them histories and stories of the prophets. Known as *qiṣaṣ al-anbiyā'* (tales of the prophets), these narratives
share details found in Jewish and Christian sources, fill in the gaps
of the qur'anic narrative, and flesh out characters with homiletic and
historical flourishes.[98] These stories are also known as the *isrā'īliyyāt,*[99]
a term applied to narratives about the "children of Israel" (Banū
Isrā'īl),[100] that is, the ancient children of Israel. A precise definition
of this term has eluded scholars; perhaps it is best defined as Muslim
renditions of narratives also found in the Jewish tradition.

Qiṣaṣ al-anbiyā', unlike the Qur'an itself, are ordered for the most
part chronologically. In fact, linear chronology may be considered
the most significant aspect of this literature. As Roberto Tottoli

notes, "if, in historiography, the succession of prophets constitutes the initial stage of a history based on three periods—prophets, Muhammad, and Islamic history—the *qiṣaṣ al-anbiyā'* represent a type of genre limited to the description of the first among these. Here, in a temporal and literary space that goes from Creation to the advent of Muhammad, medieval Islamic authors gather stories and traditions of different kinds to alternate with and link to Qur'an verses and passages."[101]

During the early Islamic period, those gathering traditions looked favorably on these stories, considered early testimonies of the true religion, Islam. In fact, in the Qur'an God instructs Muhammad to consult those who have read the Book if he doubts what God reveals to him (10:94). Consulting these traditions for legal advice, however, was prohibited, and by the fourteenth century the term *isrā'īliyyāt* had come to designate dubious traditions with objectionable content.[102] Ibn Kathir was in all likelihood the first to use the term systematically to designate unreliable traditions of direct Jewish origin.[103] In any event, the normative attitude toward the *isrā'īliyyāt* did not prevent their wide readership and preservation in various literary corpora throughout the centuries.[104] The terms *qiṣaṣ al-anbiyā'* and *isrā'īliyyāt* should not be conflated, for the latter is a pejorative term that develops much later than the former.[105] After all, Ibn Kathir produced his own collection of *qiṣaṣ al-anbiyā'*. *Isrā'īliyyāt* implies judgment on the reliability of a tradition, in contrast to *qiṣaṣ al-anbiyā'*, which are perfectly acceptable.

Al-Tha'labi, whose collection of tales is one of the most widely known and thus figures prominently in my discussion, enumerates in the introduction to his *Tales of the Prophets ('Arā'is al-Majālis fī Qiṣaṣ al-Anbiyā')* five reasons for transmitting stories about the prophets: (1) to put forth a "manifestation of his [Muhammad's] prophethood and a sign of his mission"; (2) because "God told him about the noble characters of the preceding messengers and prophets, the saints and pious men, and praised them, so that these men would serve him as a model and example, so that his people might avoid the transgression of those commandments for which the nations of the prophets were punished and for which they deserved punishments and chastisements"; (3) in order to confirm him and make his nobility, as well as his people's, known; (4) to serve as instruction and guidance; (5) to keep the memory and legacy of preceding prophets and saints alive.[106] These stories affirm Muhammad's prophethood and offer moral instruction. Through the preceding prophets' exemplary behavior, they guide all who are subject to transgressions. Accounts of the moral depravity of previous generations and the fate they faced as a consequence of their wretchedness assure Muhammad and his followers of the favor God bestows on those who live righteously. These stories also secure the prophetic legacy for posterity. Far from bland, didactic disquisitions, they are fanciful, colorful tales that entertain and edify. They convey Muslim beliefs and mores in the same way that Jewish *aggadah*, nonlegal narrative, not only fills in scriptural and theological lacunae but also transmits rabbinic teachings and religious, social, and cultural values.

In addition to collections of tales of the prophets, there exist copious compilations of extra-qur'anic traditions dealing with qur'anic narratives and personae. The historical works of the late ninth and early tenth centuries synthesize earlier traditions and in turn become foundational for later writings.[107] Al-Tabari's massive classical history *Ta'rīkh al-rusul wa 'l-mulūk (The History of the Prophets and Patriarchs)*, for example, was copied or abridged to suit the purposes of later chroniclers. His monumental account spans the period from the creation of the world to 914–915, the last years before his death. Indeed, the synthetic corpus of this indefatigable collector of traditions, considered an author by some,[108] is hardly a mere collection of random reports.

Observations

This survey of Jewish, Christian, and Muslim interpreters of the ancient and early medieval periods is a very brief introduction to various exegetes and writings that I will draw on throughout the ensuing chapters, and an entrée to some of the ways in which they approached Scripture. The cursory nature of this discussion makes it difficult to draw far-reaching conclusions, but some observations are in order. Some of the rules outlined in al-Tabari correlate to some degree with those that the rabbis also embraced, even though rabbinic

compilations do not enumerate the principles underlying their exegesis. To be sure, the seven rules of Hillel and the thirteen rules
of Rabbi Ishmael articulate fundamental principles operative in halakhic midrashim, but compilations of aggadic midrashim do not
include reference to a system of exegesis. Many of the rules, however,
are antithetical to rabbinic approaches to Scripture. For example,
al-Tabari's rule that a verse must be understood in context, that what
comes before and after the verse is important in determining its meaning, goes against the rabbinic atomistic, verso-centric approach.[109]
For the rabbis, verses are removed from their immediate context and
are recontextualized vis-à-vis other texts ostensibly by means of word
association. Discrete verses serve as the midrash's *tesserae*. The rabbinic orientation toward intertextual reading runs in the opposite
direction of reading verses in situ. They are to be read in isolation
of that context and in light of other verses. Furthermore, one of al-
Tabari's rules cautions against filling in the gaps, that is, providing
answers to "who," "when," or "how much" because it assumes a false
kind of authority. The rabbis, on the other hand, leave no gap unfilled.
Philological play is their implement.

Ancient and early medieval exegetes did not for the most part
expound their musings on hermeneutics, theories of interpretation,
or interpretive rules and principles. They were nonetheless guided
by fundamental principles and held dearly to an understanding of
the Word of God that assumes its unity. Church fathers read the New
Testament through the Old and the Old Testament through the
New. The rabbis' remarkable mastery of every jot and tittle of the
Bible afforded them the opportunity to read across "books" and
"chapters," and make associations such that Proverbs 8:30 illumines
Genesis 1:1. Understanding that the Bible is a seamless whole undergirds their intertextual readings. Seeming contradictions in the Bible or Qur'an were just that—seeming.

Contradictions do not exist. It is the limitation of human understanding that leads to the assumption that there is a contradiction.
The Qur'anic prophets, while human and subject to error, were to
the degree possible portrayed favorably. So, too, biblical figures in
Jewish and Christian writings were generally cast in the most positive light. Interpretation, whether in the form of stories, homilies,

letters, or grammatical analyses, served to make Scripture relevant to its readers, listeners, and adherents.

The multifarious writings of the church fathers, the rabbis, and Muslim exegetes reflect the richness of each tradition's engagement with its sacred texts. They also attest to the diversity of interpretations within each tradition. A quote from the Qur'an captures the unending quest for understanding the meaning of Scripture: "And if all the trees of the earth were pens and the oceans ink, with many more oceans for replenishing them, the word of God would never come to an end" (31.27), as does a saying from *Pirqe Avot* ("The Sayings of the Fathers"), a collection of rabbinic maxims and teachings: "Turn it over again and again, for everything is in it" (5:22).

2

The Biblical and Qur'anic Abraham

Songs, stories, and tales about Father Abraham abound, but we know nothing of the real Abraham, who he was, where and when he lived. No mention of him is made in any of the hundreds of thousands of ancient Mesopotamian, Egyptian, and Syro-Palestinian documents in our possession. It is in the Book of Genesis that we first meet Abraham and his family.

Genesis 1–11 is an account of primordial history from the creation of the world to God's unsuccessful attempts to maintain a relationship with human beings. Beginning with Adam and Eve and leading up to the Tower of Babel, human beings continually disappoint and disobey God. Although the covenant that God makes with all humanity after the Flood is never annulled, he makes a different covenant with Abraham and his offspring.[1] From Genesis 12 onward, the narrative lens focuses on one person, one family, and one nation so unswervingly that TaNaKh/the Old Testament may be summed up as the story of the relationship between God and his chosen people, the Israelites. From Genesis through the last book—2 Chronicles in TaNaKh and Malachi in the Old Testament—the real subject is the ebb and flow of the Israelites' dramatic, turbulent relationship with their God, the God of Abraham, Isaac, and Jacob. In that covenantal relationship lies not only rejection, pain, and suffering but also redemption and renewal.

The Jewish metanarrative begins with the call of Abraham in Genesis 12, where God summons Abraham to leave his family, his home, and his homeland, Ur of the Chaldeans, and journey to an unknown destination that God will show him. In the biblical narrative the call of Abraham marks a significant shift from a story of God's relationship with humanity at large to his relationship with a specific person who will become the father of a nation, a nation that will in turn become the focus of the rest of TaNaKh/the Old Testament.

The covenant God makes with Abraham and his progeny is foregrounded in the first eleven chapters of Genesis. From Adam and Eve in the Garden of Eden to the attempt to build the Tower of Babel, human beings disobey and challenge God, so much so that he regrets making humankind (Gen. 6:6). In this context, the call of Abraham in chapter 12 is understood as God's attempt to be in a covenantal relationship with one person and his descendants. Genesis 1–11 serves as a framing device: the unique call of Abraham and the sui generis promise made to his descendants through his son Isaac enable the audience of these verses to appreciate God's plan for all peoples. It is through the lives of Abraham and his family that all nations will be blessed.

The family intrigues, the moral dilemmas, the complexity of characters such as Abraham, Sarah, Jacob, and Esau, Dinah's tragedy, the episode between Judah and Tamar, to say nothing of the Joseph novella, offer readers insights into the human condition. In other words, beyond their theological and religious import for both Jews and Christians, the stories have a universal appeal. And yet the Book of Genesis with all its implications and attendant theological ramifications is the story of a birth of a people, commencing with its progenitor, Abraham, who commands the attention of scholars and nonscholars, believers and atheists alike.[2]

The Jews trace their theological, national, and genealogical lineage back to Abraham, whom God singled out among all the inhabitants of the world. Whether Jews identify religiously or ethnically,

Abraham is considered the forebear of the Jewish people, of *am Yisrael*. His encounter with God, who makes a covenant with him and his descendants, sets the Jewish people apart from the nations of the world (*umot ha-olam*). Even though God announces to Abraham that he will be a father of many nations, the covenant God makes with him and his seed is through Isaac, not through Ishmael or the sons he has with Keturah (Gen. 25:1–2). The chosen status of Isaac and his descendants as heirs of the covenant is quite explicit:

> And God said, "Sarah your wife shall bear you a son, and you shall call his name Isaac, and I will establish my covenant with him for an everlasting covenant with his offspring to come. And as for Ishmael, I have heard you. Behold, I have blessed him, and I will make him fruitful, and exceedingly numerous; twelve princes he shall beget, and I will make him a great nation. But I will establish my covenant with Isaac." (Gen. 17:19–21)[3]

That the covenant is maintained through Isaac is often clouded by apologetics and interfaith rhetoric that go to great lengths to attenuate the special status bestowed on Isaac. It is, however, a crucial point in apprehending the conceptualization of the family of Abraham in the Jewish and Christian traditions. It is also important for understanding the family rivalry his election poses. Hearing Abraham's concerns about his oldest son, God also blesses Ishmael, but the covenant is made through Isaac and his descendants. Although Ishmael is circumcised along with Abraham and the male members of Abraham's household, he is not part of the covenant. In short, the younger sibling is chosen over the older.

We first encounter the motif of election—who is chosen and who is not—in the story of Cain and Abel. We see it again in the stories about Isaac, Jacob, Levi, Judah, Joseph, Ephraim, Moses, Eleazar, Ithamar, Gideon, David, and Solomon. Ishmael and Isaac, Esau and Jacob, Leah and Rachel, Ephraim and Manasseh—all contribute to the playing out of this motif.[4] In fact, as Robert Alter observes, the entire book of Genesis "is about the reversal of the iron law of primogeniture, about the election through some devious twist of destiny of a younger son to carry on the line," thus "the first born very often seem to be losers in Genesis by the very condition of their birth."[5]

The distinction between Isaac and Abraham's other progeny is reinforced in Genesis 25: "Abraham took another wife, whose name was Keturah. She bore him Zimran, Jokshan, Medan, Midian, Ishbak, and Shuah . . . Abraham gave all that he had to Isaac. But to Abraham's sons by concubines, he gave gifts while he was still living and sent them away from Isaac his son" (Gen. 25:1–6). Once Ishmael and these other sons are sent away, we no longer hear about them in Genesis. The rest of the narrative focuses on Abraham's lineage via Isaac and his son Jacob. At the very end, the Israelites are in Egypt, reunited with Joseph, who assures his brothers that God will take them to the land that he promised Abraham, Isaac, and Jacob.

For a host of reasons, the concept of election may be unsettling to believers and secularists alike.[6] Indeed, the notion of a just and loving God who gives preferential treatment to one individual over another or to one people over others is theologically as well as morally troubling to many. "A truly rational and universal God, it is maintained, could not do anything so arbitrary as to 'choose' one particular group out of mankind as a whole," Will Herberg writes. He continues: "God is the God of all alike, and therefore, cannot make distinctions between nations and peoples. To this is added the moral argument that the doctrine of 'chosenness' is little better than crude ethnocentrism, in which a particular group regards itself as the center of the universe and develops doctrines that will flatter its pride and minister to its glory."[7] However unsettling, however disturbing, Genesis is about God's relationship with Abraham and Sarah's descendants.

For Christians, too, this rich narrative recounts the unique relationship God has with his chosen people. Each religion makes an exclusive, yet radically different, claim to God through Abraham and his seed. Whereas the Jewish claim to Abraham manifests itself in the notion of a particular people set apart from all others, Christianity's claim runs in a countervailing direction: the Christian idea of the covenant, although still exclusive, includes all believers. The family of Abraham is thus transformed from a genealogical to a spiritual family that manifests itself as the church, or community of believers in Jesus.

The interpretive traditions of Judaism and Christianity reinforce this distinction, especially in prevalent portrayals of the patriarch. The Abraham (Avraham) of TaNaKh is not the same as the Abraham of the Christian Old Testament. God makes a covenant with the Abraham (Ibrahim) of the Qur'an also, but here the covenant with Abraham and his offspring is not the focal point, as it is in the Hebrew Bible. In the Qur'an, God also makes a covenant with Adam, Noah, Moses, the children of Israel, the People of the Book; through the prophets he makes a covenant with all humankind. Covenant frames the relationship between God and his chosen people in the Hebrew Bible and undergirds the Christian understanding of the relationship between the Old and New Testaments.

The covenants God makes in the Qur'an, *mīthāq* and *'ahd*, occur about seventy-five times and refer to agreements that God establishes and to which people respond. Thus we read in the Qur'an 3:81–82: "When God made his covenant with the prophets, He said, 'Behold the Scriptures and the wisdom which I have given you. Afterward a messenger will come to you, confirming them. Believe in him and help him.' He said, 'Do you agree to this and accept the burden which I lay upon you in this matter?' They responded, 'We agree.' God said, 'Then bear witness, and I will bear witness with you. One who rebels hereafter is a transgressor.'"[8]

The terms for covenant can also refer to political contracts and civil agreements, but in the Qur'an their predominant use is in connection with agreements God makes with prophets and their followers. The Qur'an mentions the covenant with the Israelites on several occasions. "Oh, children of Israel, remember the favor I bestowed upon you. Fulfill your part of the covenant and I shall fulfill mine" (Q. 2:40) is perhaps the best example of the bilateral nature of covenant found in the Qur'an. Those who enter into the covenant and uphold their part receive God's protection; he is their *walī* (guardian). Those who reject his will, however, incur his wrath: "And when we made a covenant with the prophets, and with you [Muhammad], and with Noah and Abraham and Moses, and Jesus son of Mary, we made a solemn covenant with them, that God might question the truth about their truthfulness. But for the unbelievers, He has prepared a painful punishment" (Q. 33:7–8).[9]

The Abrahamic covenant in Genesis is a turning point in the narrative that, as noted, shifts the focus from humanity at large to the figure of Abraham. But who is Abraham? What does Genesis actually tell us about him? What do we know about him from the New Testament and the Qur'an? In this chapter I narrate and reflect on the story of Abraham as it appears in the scriptural traditions; in Chapters 3 through 7 I will analyze interpretive sources.

The Story of Abraham in the Book of Genesis

The Jewish Bible/Old Testament opens with Creation and narrates the story of humankind's failure to maintain a relationship with God marked by obedience to his laws. Humankind transgresses from the outset and continues to do so even well after God makes a covenant with Abraham. Moving from the macro to the micro, from the span of human existence to a single individual, the narrative shifts its focus in Genesis 12, when Abram, whose name is changed to Abraham in Genesis 17, is summoned from Ur of the Chaldeans[10] to leave his father's house and travel to the land God will show him. God tells Abraham: "I will make you a great nation, and I will bless you; I will make your name great, and you shall be a blessing. I will bless those who bless you and curse him that curses you; and all the families of the earth shall bless themselves before you" (Gen. 12:2–3).[11]

The shift from the universal scope of Genesis 1–11 is rather striking and puzzling, for there is no indication that Abraham has set himself apart from all others, no hint as to why God has summoned him from Mesopotamia. Later interpreters fill in the details of his early life and justify his chosenness by relating the story of his fight against his father's idolatry, and the rabbis portray him as having indeed distinguished himself, becoming worthy of the covenant and the promises that come with it.

Thus, at the age of seventy-five, Abraham (then still called Abram), along with his wife, Sarai, whose name becomes Sarah in chapter 17, and his nephew Lot, leaves all that is familiar and ventures into the unknown.[12] Abraham's response to God's command is the first sign of trust on Abraham's part, or, according to some traditions, the first of ten trials he must endure.[13]

While Abraham is sojourning, God appears to him and informs him that his seed is to inherit the land that he has entered, the land of Canaan: "The Lord appeared to Abram and said, 'I will assign this land to your offspring.' And he built an altar there to the Lord who appeared to him" (Gen. 12:7).[14] Abraham is thus promised land, a nation, and a blessing, a promise that is reiterated in one form or another throughout Genesis, and reinterpreted as God's response to Abraham's willingness to sacrifice his beloved son, Isaac, in Genesis 22: "Because you have done this and have not withheld your son, your favored one, I will bestow My blessing on you and make your descendants as numerous as the stars of heaven and the sands on the seashore; and your descendants shall seize the gates of their foes. All the nations of the earth shall bless themselves by your descendants, because you have obeyed My command" (Gen. 22:15–18).[15]

During his peregrinations toward the Negev in the land that God has just promised him, there is a famine in the land that forces Abraham to go to Egypt. Just before entering Egypt, he tells his wife, "I know what a beautiful woman you are. If the Egyptians see you, and think, 'She is his wife,' they will kill me and let you live. Please say that you are my sister, that it may go well with me because of you, and that I may remain alive thanks to you" (Gen. 12:11–12).[16]

Abraham's concerns are well founded: Sarah's captivating beauty makes her the center of attention. The Pharaoh, thinking she is Abraham's sister, bestows sheep, oxen, servants, she-asses, and camels on him. Abraham profits from the deceit, but the Pharaoh pays a price for his amorous advances: "The Lord afflicted Pharaoh and his house with mighty plagues because of Sarai, Abram's wife" (Gen. 12:18).[17]

With his now ample household and livestock, Abraham continues to travel from the south back to where he first built an altar to God. Lot with his herds accompanies him, but as the land cannot accommodate both men's flocks, herds, and tents, tension develops between them, and Abraham suggests that they separate. Lot chooses the plain of Jordan, and Abraham settles in Canaan. On

Lot's departure, the Lord appears to Abraham and reiterates his earlier promise of land for Abraham and his offspring: "Lift up now your eyes and look from the place where you are northward, and southward, and eastward, and westward; for all the land which you see, I give to you and your offspring [seed] forever. And I will make your offspring as the dust of the earth so that if one can count the dust of the earth, then your offspring shall also be counted" (Gen. 13:15–16). The Lord commands Abraham to walk through the land "in the length and breadth of it." Abraham settles in the plain of Mamre, which is Hebron, and builds another altar to God (Gen. 13:18).

In the next episode of his life, one that is underplayed in postbiblical sources, Abraham is depicted as a warrior waging battle on an international stage in order to rescue Lot, who has been captured by an alliance of kings. Here he encounters King Melchizedek of Salem (probably Jerusalem; see Ps. 76:3), who bestows a blessing on him: "Blessed be Abram of God Most High, Creator of heaven and earth. And blessed be God Most High, who has delivered your foes into your hand" (Gen. 14:20).[18]

In Genesis 15, God appears to Abraham in a vision, saying: "Fear not, Abram. I am a shield to you; your reward shall be very great." For the first time Abraham speaks in response, concerned that he has no progeny and that his steward will be his heir: "What can you give me, seeing that I shall die, and the one in charge of my household is Dammesek Eliezer?"[19] God assures him that he will have a son, and again he reassures Abraham of his multitudinous seed, pointing Abraham skyward to the stars and suggesting that his seed will be vast as the stars in heaven: "and because he put his trust in the Lord, he reckoned it to his merit" (Gen. 15:7).[20] Then, God proclaims his relationship with Abraham and his descendants in salvific terms: "I am the Lord who brought you out of Ur of the Chaldeans, to give you this land to inherit" (Gen. 15:7).[21] When Abraham inquires as to how he will know that he will inherit (a rather strange question, given that in the preceding two verses he has put his trust in the Lord), the Lord enters into a covenant with him.

This type of covenant, known as a grant covenant, is found in Mesopotamia and is mentioned elsewhere in the Bible (2 Sam. 7:8–

16; Ps. 89:20–37). The covenant God makes with Abraham in this passage is explicitly an inheritance of land: "To your offspring I assign this land, from the river of Egypt to the great river, the river Euphrates: the Kenites, and the Kenizzites, and the Kadmonites, and the Hittites, and the Perizzites, and the Rephaims, and the Amorites, and the Canaanites, and the Girgashites, and the Jebusites." The territory delineated here—not the same as that in Numbers 34:1–12—seems to represent the maximal borders of the Promised Land.

Before the covenant is made, while Abraham is in a trance, the Lord forewarns him of the plight of his people: they will be enslaved for four hundred years but the nation they will serve as slaves will be judged by God. It is also made known to Abraham that he will be buried along with his fathers in a good old age, but that "they shall return here in the fourth generation, for the iniquity of the Amorites is not yet complete" (v. 16).[22]

Abraham's wife, Sarah (still called Sarai at this point in the narrative), not trusting God's promise of progeny, approaches her husband with the idea that he should have a son with Hagar, her Egyptian maidservant, so that through Hagar she herself can obtain children. (This practice was not unusual in Near Eastern societies.)[23] Abraham complies with his wife's request; Hagar conceives, and Ishmael is born. The Bible tells us, however, that when Hagar conceived, "her mistress was lowered in her esteem" (Gen. 16:4). Sarah complains to Abraham, who tells her that she should do as she wishes with Hagar. When Sarah deals harshly with Hagar, she flees into the wilderness, where the messenger of God finds her.[24] He informs her that God will multiply her seed exceedingly, that she is with child, and that she shall call him Ishmael, which means "God hears," because the Lord "has paid heed to your suffering and heard your affliction" (Gen. 16:11).[25]

In Genesis 17 God commands Abraham at the age of ninety-nine to walk before him and be perfect, for God will make an everlasting covenant with him and his offspring: "You shall be the father of a multitude of nations. And you shall no longer be called Abram, but your name shall be Abraham [father of a multitude] . . . I will make you exceedingly fertile, and make nations of you; and kings shall come forth from you. I will maintain my covenant between Me and you and your offspring to come, as an everlasting covenant throughout the ages, to be God to you, and to your offspring to come. I assign the land you sojourn in to you and your offspring to come, all the land of Canaan, as an everlasting holding. I will be their God" (Gen. 17:4–8).

As for Abraham and his seed, they shall keep God's commandment: "Every male among you shall be circumcised. You shall circumcise the flesh of your foreskin; and that shall be the sign of the covenant between Me and you . . . Every male child born in the house, or bought with money of any stranger, which is not of your seed, shall be circumcised. As for the homeborn slave and the one bought from an outsider . . . they must be circumcised, homeborn and purchased alike, and my covenant shall be in your flesh for an everlasting covenant" (Gen. 17:10–13).

Sarai's name is changed to Sarah. When God informs Abraham that Sarah will bear a son, Abraham marvels at the thought that he, who is one hundred years old, and Sarah, who is ninety, can produce a child. Abraham says to God, "Oh that Ishmael might live by Your favor!"[26] God responds that Sarah shall bear his son, whom he will name Isaac, and it is with Isaac that God will maintain his covenant, "as an everlasting covenant for his offspring to come." As he promised Hagar, God promises Abraham that Ishmael shall be a great nation: "For Ishmael, I have heeded you; I hereby bless him, I will make him fruitful, and exceedingly numerous. He shall be the father of twelve chieftains, and I will make him a great nation" (Gen. 17:19–20). Like Isaac, through whom twelve tribes are established, Ishmael will father twelve chieftains, but the covenant will be maintained only through Isaac, not Ishmael.

The biblical presentation of Abraham calls into question whether he puts his trust in God, at least before Genesis 22. That is to say, although depictions of Abraham in extrabiblical literature underscore his unwavering faith in the Lord, the biblical story in Genesis 12–21 suggests that Abraham doubted God's promise of progeny, despite God's assurances. By turning various events leading up to Abraham's test in Genesis 22 into trials that he endured and through which he exhibited righteous, faithful behavior, extrabiblical depictions dispel any doubts the reader of Genesis may have about his steadfast faithfulness.

The far-reaching theological implications of the divine promise in Genesis 17 cannot be overemphasized. In effect, the promise concerning Ishmael extends God's blessing beyond the Israelites to other peoples. Although the covenant is carried through Isaac and his line of progeny, God is ever mindful of those outside the covenant whom he increases and blesses and to whom he grants greatness. Abraham's descendants through Isaac are not the sole recipients of God's blessings. At the same time, the Genesis plotline emphasizes the promise destined for Isaac. Divine blessings are bestowed on non-Israelites (Gen. 12:1–3 and 22:18), but the futures of Ishmael and Isaac are distinctly different.

There is an inherent paradox here. Like his father and his brother, Ishmael will be the father of a great nation, yet God will maintain his covenant only with Isaac and his seed—not with Ishmael and his offspring and not with Abraham's other descendants.[27]

Ishmael is included—"Then Abraham took his son Ishmael . . . and he circumcised the flesh of their foreskins on that very day" (v. 23)—but also excluded—"But my covenant I will maintain with Isaac" (v. 21). Ishmael is not only placed under the auspices of the God of Israel, he is also a member of Abraham's family—indeed, his firstborn. But therein lies the rub. In line with the narrative motif of Genesis, as firstborn Ishmael is pushed aside. He and his descendants are relegated to the margin, a very tenuous position that at best generates ambiguous portrayals and at worst engenders hostile depictions in extrabiblical literature. Genesis 17:15–21 no longer refers to the covenant that includes Ishmael and all those circumcised along with Abraham. Now it is a covenant that excludes all but Abraham's descendants through Isaac.[28]

Genesis 17 ends with Abraham circumcising Ishmael and all the male members of his household according to God's instructions. The next chapter in the life of Abraham concerns the destruction of Sodom and Gomorrah. After Abraham and Sarah receive three strangers (angels) with great hospitality, God reveals his plan to destroy Sodom and Gomorrah. Abraham asks God, "Will you also destroy the righteous with the wicked? There might be fifty righteous

within the city. Will you also destroy and not spare the place for the
fifty righteous therein? That be far from you to do after this manner, to slay the righteous with the wicked: and that the righteous
should be as the wicked, that be far from you. Shall not the Judge of
all the earth do right?" (Gen. 18:23–25). God agrees that because of
fifty—or even as few as ten—righteous people in Sodom, he will
not destroy the cities. In the next chapter, the city is destroyed.[29]

In chapter 20, as at the end of chapter 12, Abraham again conceals Sarah's identity. This time it is Abimelech, the king of Gerar,
who is duped. The situation is more complex, and not until verses
11–13 is the reader made aware of why Abraham hands over his wife
to another man—namely, that there is no fear of God among the
inhabitants of Gerar. Again Abraham's life is threatened on account
of Sarah. In this episode, too, Sarah claims that Abraham is her
brother, and when Abimelech confronts Abraham about his deception, he replies, "And besides, she is in truth my sister, my father's
daughter though not my mother's; and she became my wife" (Gen.
20:12). The exchange between Abimelech and Abraham in verses
9–10 presents the Gentile king chastising Abraham, who in verse 7
is referred to as a "prophet," for his immoral error. Despite Abraham's behavior toward him, Abimelech displays generosity toward
Abraham, restoring his wife, permitting him to settle wherever
he pleases, and giving him money.[30]

Genesis 21 ushers in the son of the covenant and ushers out the
son of the maidservant. Sarah gives birth to Isaac, and on the day he
is weaned Abraham makes a banquet. One mother's joy is another's
sorrow: "Sarah saw the son whom Hagar the Egyptian had borne to
Abraham playing [*metsaḥeq*, from the Hebrew root *tsḥq*]. She said to
Abraham, 'Cast out that slave-woman and her son, for the son of
that slave shall not share in the inheritance with my son Isaac'"
(Gen. 21:9–10). The matter greatly distresses Abraham, but God intervenes and tells him to listen to Sarah. God allays his concerns
about Ishmael's fate, and Abraham sends Hagar and her son into the
wilderness of Beersheba.

In Genesis 17 God "hears." In Genesis 16:11, he has "heard"
Hagar's affliction; now (Gen. 21:17), he hears the cries of Ishmael.
As in Genesis 17, God promises to make Ishmael a great nation.

The expulsion of Hagar and Ishmael in Genesis 21, however, is in many respects unprecedented.[31] Ancient and modern commentators alike have grappled with the verse in which Sarah changes her mind about her maidservant's place in the family. Why does Sarah, who provided Abraham with Hagar for the purposes of procreating, now want her and her son "cast out"? What does *metsaḥeq*, "playing," mean? In what horrendous act was Ishmael engaged?[32]

One of the best-known narratives in the life of Abraham, perhaps arguably in the entire Book of Genesis, is Abraham's near sacrifice of Isaac. God tests Abraham by asking him to offer up his only son—that is, the only one he loves—Isaac. Voicing no objections, Abraham rises early in the morning and sets out with Isaac and two other lads to the land of Moriah, as God commands. On the third day, Abraham orders the two other boys to stay put while he and Isaac go up to the mountain to worship God. Abraham has Isaac carry the firewood for the offering and takes the fire and the knife himself, and they walk together. Isaac inquires, "Behold, the fire and the wood, but where is the lamb for the burnt offering?" Abraham replies, "My son, God will provide himself a lamb for a burnt offering." On arriving at the place God shows him, Abraham builds an altar, arranges the wood, binds Isaac, and lays him on the altar. As he is about to slay his son, the angel of the Lord calls out to Abraham, saying, "Abraham, Abraham! Do not lay your hand upon the lad, nor do anything to him, for now I know that you fear God, seeing you have not withheld your son, your only son from me" (Gen. 22:12). Abraham lifts his eyes and sees a ram tangled in a thicket. He takes the ram and offers him up as a burnt offering in lieu of his son. The angel calls out a second time to Abraham, blessing him: "Because you have done this thing, and have not withheld your son, your only son, that in blessing I will bless you and in multiplying I will multiply your seed as the stars of the heaven, and as the sand which is upon the sea shore; and your seed shall possess the gate of his enemies; and in your seed shall all the nations of the earth be blessed because you have obeyed my voice" (Gen. 22:16–18). Abraham returns to the young men, and they go together to Beersheba. Why doesn't Isaac return with his father? Jewish exegetes also ask why the angel of God calls out to Abraham twice. I take up the near sacrifice of Isaac in Chapter 7.

In the next chapter, Sarah dies in Hebron in the land of Canaan at the age of 127. Abraham acquires the field of Machpelah from Ephron the Hittite and buries Sarah in the cave of Machpelah. He orders his oldest servant, Eliezer, to find a suitable wife for Isaac from among Abraham's kin. The servant goes to Mesopotamia, to the land of Nahor, and brings Rebekah back to Isaac, who takes her as his wife. In chapter 25, Abraham takes Keturah to be his wife, and she bears him six sons. He gives gifts to the children of his concubines but bequeaths everything he has to Isaac. Abraham dies at the age of 175 (Gen. 25:7), and both Isaac and Ishmael bury him in the cave where Sarah was buried.

Thus concludes the life of Abraham in the Book of Genesis. Abraham is mentioned relatively infrequently in other works of the Jewish Bible/Old Testament. References to the seed of Abraham are scattered throughout a few books such as Joshua 24:3, Isaiah 41:8, Nehemiah 9:8, and 2 Chronicles 20:7. In prophetic literature, readers are reminded of the covenant God made with Abraham and God's loyalty to that covenant: "Look back to Abraham your father and to Sarah who brought you forth. For he was only one when I called him, but blessed him and made him many" (Isaiah 51:2).[33] In the Jewish Bible/Old Testament Abraham does not figure prominently; it is the history of the Israelites' relationship with God that takes center stage. Abraham is forefather and plays a small, yet significant, role in the sweep of that history.

The apocryphal (that is, not included in the Jewish and Protestant biblical canons) work Wisdom of Jesus ben Sira (Sirach; Ecclesiasticus), composed around 180 BCE in Jerusalem, describes Abraham as the father of a multitude of nations (44:19–22) through whom God maintains his covenant with Isaac and his progeny. In chapters 44–50 Ben Sira praises the Jewish forefathers.[34] Abraham is praised for his faithfulness and recognized as the progenitor of Israel as well as father of a multitude of nations in line with Genesis. In other words, early Jewish literature, in fact even rabbinic literature, acknowledges that Abraham is father of a multitude of nations, but the Jewish metanarrative emphasizes his role as father of the Israelites and by extension the Jewish people. Christianity highlights his role as both father of the Israelites with whom God makes a covenant and father of a multitude of peoples.

This quick review of the focal points in his life provides a background for understanding the issues Jewish and Christian readers take up as they amplify the narrative in order to fill in gaps and to justify the behavior of their matriarch and patriarch.

Abraham in the New Testament

The story of Abraham and his family as narrated in the Book of Genesis provides the basis for his depiction in the New Testament. Here, as in the Qur'an, mention is made of Abraham, and in many instances it is assumed that the reader is aware of aspects of his biography detailed elsewhere. In fact, the Qur'an tells us a great deal more about Abraham than the New Testament. I will highlight a few specific references to Abraham in the New Testament that provide a general understanding of his role in it.[35]

The New Testament opens with the genealogy of "Jesus Christ, the son of David, the son of Abraham," one of seven mentions of Abraham in the Gospel of Matthew.[36] The significance of linking Jesus and Abraham cannot be overstated. Jesus Christ, seen by Christians as the fulfillment of God's promise of salvation for humankind, is understood here as the fulfillment of the covenantal promise, the seed of Abraham through whom all nations will be blessed. That the first pages of the New Testament proclaim this ancestry is noteworthy in light of the relationship between the Old and New Testaments. It is especially in the Gospel of Matthew that Jesus is emphasized as the Jewish Messiah who fulfills the prophets and the hopes of the Jewish people.[37] In several places the Gospel of Matthew uses what scholars have called "fulfillment citations," not found in the other gospels. Fulfillment citations—that is, verses from the prophetic literature of the Hebrew Bible that are cited in the gospel—do not have a specific formula, but the general thrust is that an event occurred to fulfill "what was spoken by the prophet."[38]

The Gospel of Matthew connects Jesus with David as well, portraying Jesus as the fulfillment of not only the Abrahamic covenant but also the Davidic messianic covenant. The fact that David is mentioned more often in the Gospel of Matthew than Abraham need not compromise the important role Abraham plays in the gospel, which depicts Jesus as the Jewish Messiah and savior of all, as the physical and spiritual descendant of Abraham.[39]

Paul's writing, especially the Epistle to the Romans, is central to the history of Christian thought.[40] Abraham is depicted in Paul as a model of faith, most famously in Romans 4. The longest and most complex of Paul's letters, it was instrumental in Augustine's conversion and helped shape his theology and writings, which in turn contributed significantly to the development of medieval Christian theology. Romans took center stage in debates between Protestants and Catholics during the sixteenth century, and even today church leaders and congregants alike continue to investigate and debate its meaning.[41]

Given its understanding of Abraham's merit and its importance in Christian thought, the chapter deserves quotation in full:

What then are we to say was gained by Abraham, our ancestor according to the flesh? For if Abraham was justified by works, he has something to boast about, but not before God. For what does the scripture say? "Abraham believed God, and it was reckoned to him as righteousness."[42] Now to one who works, wages are not reckoned as a gift but as something due. But to one who without works trusts him who justifies the ungodly, such faith is reckoned as righteousness. So also David speaks of the blessedness of those to whom God reckons righteousness apart from works: "Blessed are those whose iniquities are forgiven, and whose sins are covered; blessed is the one against whom the Lord will not reckon his sin" [Ps. 32:1–2]. Is this blessedness, then, pronounced only on the circumcised, or also on the uncircumcised? We say, "Faith was reckoned to Abraham as righteousness." How then was it reckoned to him? Was it before or after he had been circumcised? It was not after, but before he was circumcised. He received the sign of circumcision as a seal of the righteousness that he had by faith while he was still uncircumcised. The purpose was to make him the ancestor of all who believe without being circumcised and who thus have righteousness reckoned to them, and likewise the ancestor of the circumcised who are not only circumcised but also follow the example of faith that our ancestor Abraham had before he was circumcised. For the promise that he would inherit the world did not come to Abraham or to his descendants through the law but through the righteousness of faith. If it is the adherents of the law who are to be the heirs, faith is null and the promise is void. For the law brings wrath; but where there is no law, neither is there violation. For this reason it depends on faith, in order that the promise may rest on grace and be guaranteed to all his descendants, not only to the adherents of the law but also to those who share the faith of Abraham (for he is the father of us all, as it is written, "I have made you the father of many nations" [Gen. 17:5]—in the presence of the God in whom he believed, who gives life to the dead and calls into existence the things that do not exist. Hoping against hope, he believed that he should become "the father of many nations," according to what was said, "So numerous shall your descendants be" [Gen. 15:5]. He did not weaken in faith when he considered his own body, which was already as good as dead (for he was about a hundred years old), or when he considered the barrenness of Sarah's womb. No distrust made him waver concerning the promise of God, but he grew strong in his faith as he gave glory to God, being fully convinced that God was able to do what he had promised. Therefore his faith was "reckoned to him as righteousness." Now the words, "it was reckoned to him," were written not for his sake alone, but for ours also. It will be reckoned to us who believe in him who raised Jesus our Lord from the dead, who was handed over to death for our trespasses and raised for our justification.[43]

Romans 4 is best understood in light of the theme of the letter as a whole, best captured by Paul's two verses: "For I am not ashamed of the gospel; it is the power of God for salvation to everyone who has faith, to the Jew first and also to the Greek. For in it the righteousness of God is revealed through faith for faith; as it is written [in Habakkuk 2:4], 'The one who is righteous will live by faith' "

(Rom. 1:16–17). Salvation, according to Paul, is based on faith, and both Jews and Gentiles through their faith are made right with God. Paul turns to Abraham to illustrate that the gospel message is rooted in Scripture. Abraham is a paragon of faith, for he was justified by trusting in God's promise before he was given the sign of circumcision (4:10). He is the ancestor of those who believe—whether or not they are circumcised, whether or not they are Jews. What is important for salvation is not the works of law but faith. It is not his flesh-and-blood progeny who are the children of Abraham but rather those who continue to trust in God and in his promises, which are now fulfilled in the death and resurrection of Jesus.

And how is Abraham a model of faith, according to Paul? What did Abraham believe in? To begin with, Abraham believed in the God "who gives life to the dead and calls into existence the things that do not exist" (Rom. 4:17). Furthermore, despite the promise of descendants at an advanced age, and despite Sarah's barrenness, Abraham did not falter in his faith (4:19). He was given credit for his faith. So, too, all those who believe in the God "who raised Jesus our Lord from the dead" (4:24) are considered righteous in the eyes of God.

The inclusion of Gentiles and Jews in God's salvific purposes is taken up again in Romans 9–11. In Romans 9:6–8 Paul makes a distinction between descendants of the flesh and those of the promise: "It is not as though the word of God had failed. For not all Israelites truly belong to Israel, and not all of Abraham's children are his true descendants; but 'It is through Isaac that descendants shall be named for you' [Gen. 21:12]. This means that it is not the children of the flesh who are the children of God, but the children of the promise are counted as descendants." The dilemma Paul confronts in Romans 10:18–21 is that the Jews, the children of the flesh, have not all accepted the gospel message, while the Gentiles have. Does this mean, however, that God has abandoned Jews who do not believe? Paul asks and answers in 11:1–2: "By no means! I myself am an Israelite, a descendant of Abraham, a member of the tribe of Benjamin. God has not rejected his people whom he foreknew." As Jeffrey Siker observes, "if in Romans 4 . . . Paul drew attention to the way in which Abraham demonstrates the legitimacy of gentile inclusion within God's people, in Romans 9–11 Paul draws attention to the way in which Abraham points to God's continued election of the Jews."[44]

Although Romans portrays Abraham as the man of faith whose descendants are believers, children of the promise, he is also the father of Jews. According to Paul, God has not abandoned unbelieving Jews: "As regards the gospel they are enemies of God for your sake; but as regards election they are beloved, for the sake of their ancestors; for the gifts and the calling of God are irrevocable" (11:28–30). In other words, even though they oppose the gospel message, the election of the Jews is immutable.

Contrary to the arguments of Gentile Christians in Rome who maintain that Jewish rejection of Christ is tantamount to exclusion from God's promises, Paul asserts their irrevocable election. Even though they do not believe, Jews are assured of God's faithfulness. In Romans, Paul safeguards God's abiding faithfulness to non-Christian Jews. Gentiles are brought into the family of Abraham since they are included among the children of Abraham, the father of nations. Believers are children according to the spirit, and Jews are children according to the flesh.

That Paul speaks of Abraham differently in his letter to the Galatians continues to challenge Pauline scholars attempting to reconcile Galatians and Romans. Although they debate the specific circumstances that occasioned Galatians, scholars all agree that it was in response to a severe crisis. Written to communities in the Roman province of Galatia (present-day Turkey),[45] Paul's impassioned letter is concerned primarily with the issue of whether Gentile followers of Christ had to follow the Mosaic law—that is, whether they had to be circumcised, keep kosher, and observe the laws given to the Israelites at Mount Sinai.[46] In the view of some missionaries or a group of teachers, whose identity remains unresolved, Gentiles could not be true followers of Jesus unless they followed these laws.[47] Their view was an affront to the gospel message Paul preached to the Gentile Galatians: "I am astonished that you are so quickly deserting the one who called you in the grace of Christ and are turning to a different gospel—not that there is another gospel, but there are some who are confusing you and want to pervert the gospel of Christ" (Gal. 1:6–7). Galatians, therefore, is about the law as it relates to Gentile

Christians. Refocusing one's lens on Paul's attitude toward Gentile observance of the law is crucial to reading Galatians in its proper context and for understanding the ways he draws on the Genesis story of Abraham.[48]

Paul's frustration is obvious: "You foolish Galatians! Who has bewitched you? . . ." (Gal. 3:1); "Are you so foolish? Having started with the Spirit, are you now ending with the flesh?" (Gal. 3:3). Because the rival teachers have used Abraham in endorsing observance of the law, and in particular the necessity of circumcision, Paul turns to Abraham to demonstrate how the blessings given to him are extended to all people. Paul thus establishes the identity of the sons of Abraham as the sons of the promise: "Just as Abraham 'believed God, and it was reckoned to him as righteousness,' so, you see, those who believe are the descendants of Abraham. And the scripture, foreseeing that God would justify the Gentiles by faith, declared the gospel beforehand to Abraham saying, 'All the Gentiles shall be blessed in you.' For this reason, those who believe are blessed with Abraham who believed" (Gal. 3:6–9).

In Galatians Christ is the singular offspring, *sperma*, of Abraham through whom all who believe become children of Abraham. They are "children of the promise, like Isaac," whereas in Romans stress is placed on the notion that all who believe as Abraham does are his offspring. Furthermore, Galatians seems to imply that unbelieving Jews have no standing before God, but Romans demonstrates God's enduring concern for the Jews. In both epistles Abraham is typical of all who have faith and Gentiles are included in the promise God makes to Abraham, despite the differences between the two letters in tone, intended audience, and those who are identified as Abraham's heirs.[49]

In the Gospel of John, Abraham is used in polemics between Johannine Christians and their opponents. During a confrontation between Jesus and the Jews, Abraham is presented as subordinate to Jesus. In John 8:56 Abraham rejoices to see Jesus' day, and in verse 54 it is the Father who glorifies Jesus. Moreover, the Gospel of John distinguishes between descendants (*sperma*) of Abraham and children (*tekna*) of Abraham, the former a reference to genetic lineage, the latter to spiritual descent. Jews are depicted as assuming that the two go hand in hand, but the gospel disconnects them; physical paternity is not necessarily relevant to spiritual descent.[50] The Jews, according to John's Gospel, should behave as he does, for descent has to do with how one behaves.

In the Epistle to the Hebrews,[51] the author seeks to exhort a Christian community that has grown weary to persevere and to have patience in the face of persecution: "Therefore lift your drooping hands and strengthen your weak knees, and make straight paths for your feet, so that what is lame may not be put out of joint, but rather be healed" (Heb. 12:12). Abraham is singled out as a model of patience—"And thus Abraham, having patiently endured, obtained the promise" (6:13)—and is paraded as a prime example of patient faithfulness.

The author repeatedly evokes the importance of faith: "Now faith is the assurance of things hoped for, the conviction of things not seen. Indeed by faith, our ancestors received approval. By faith we understand that the worlds were prepared by the word of God, so that what is seen was made from things that are not visible" (Heb. 11:1–3). After listing examples of faith displayed by Abel, Enoch, and Noah, the letter turns to Abraham, who demonstrated obedience to God's command to leave his homeland without knowing where he was going. Moreover, because of Abraham's faithfulness, he received "the power of procreation" (11:11), but according to Hebrews it is God's trustworthiness that makes Abraham's faith possible. As in the Epistle to the Romans, the author invokes Abraham's willingness to offer Isaac (it is as if he did so, "figuratively speaking" [en parabole]) as a demonstration of his faith in the resurrection (11:19).

Those who put their faith in God's promise—Jesus—are counted among the true descendants of Abraham, even those who came before the Christians: Abel, Enoch, Noah, Moses, the Israelites who crossed the Red Sea, Gideon, Barak, Samson, Jephthah, David, Samuel, and all the prophets who displayed faith. These were models of faithfulness, the patriarchs of the family of faith, of which Christians who persevere faithfully are members. About the letter's spiritualizing dimension, James Swetnam writes: "The 'seed' which was promised to Abraham seems to have been realized in the eyes of the author of Hebrews not merely in the numerous offspring which come to

Abraham through Isaac and his physical descendants as a result of a promise, but in the spiritual 'seed' composed of all those who, like Abraham, have faith when they are tested in God's power to raise from the dead."[52]

A mention of Abraham in Hebrews 7 is used to illuminate the superiority of Jesus' priesthood over the Levitical priesthood. Christ's eternal priesthood is rendered through a typological reading of Abraham's encounter in Genesis 14:17–20 with Melchizedek:

> When he returned from defeating Chedorlaomer and the kings with him, the king of Sodom came out to meet him at the Valley of Shaveh, which is the Valley of the King. And King Melchizedek of Salem brought out bread and wine; he was a priest of God Most High. He blessed him saying, "Blessed be Abram of God Most High, Creator of heaven and earth. And blessed be God Most High, Who has delivered your foes into your hand." And [Abram] gave him a tenth of everything.

We read about Melchizedek in Hebrews 7:1–2a: "This King Melchizedek of Salem, priest of the Most High God, met Abraham as he was returning from defeating the kings and blessed him; and to him Abraham apportioned "one-tenth of everything." But who was this Melchizedek? The author tells us: "His name, in the first place, means 'king [*melech*] of righteousness [*tsedek*]'; next he is also king of Salem, that is, 'king of peace.' Without father, without mother, without genealogy, having neither beginning of days nor end of life, but resembling the Son of God, he remains a priest forever" (7:2b–3). He was so great that Abraham the patriarch gave him a tenth of the spoils that he received from having rescued Lot and his family from the army of four eastern kings (Gen. 14).

In Hebrews, Abraham serves as a paragon of persistent faithfulness but is also a type for the Levitical priests. Melchizedek, a type of Christ, is greater than Abraham and hence greater than the priesthood, for it is Abraham who pays the tithe to Melchizedek. And "just as Christ's priesthood is superior to the Levitical priesthood," Siker notes, "so the covenant inaugurated in Christ is superior to the covenant under which the Levitical priests served."[53]

Thus we read: "accordingly Jesus has also become the guarantee of a better covenant" (7:22). In Hebrews, Christ and Abraham meet only indirectly, insofar as Christ in the person of Melchizedek encounters Abraham, but according to the logic of the typology, Christ appears before the Levitical priesthood.

James 2:20–24 also depicts Abraham in terms of modeling what it means to be a person of faith: "Do you want to be shown, you senseless person, that faith apart from works is barren? Was not our ancestor Abraham justified by works when he offered his son Isaac upon the altar? You see that faith was active along with his works, and faith was brought to completion by the works. Thus the scripture was fulfilled that says, 'Abraham believed God, and it was reckoned to him as righteousness,' and he was called the friend of God."[54] Here James argues against the idea that one is justified by faith alone. Works complete faith, or, to put it another way, faith is meaningless without works.

The Christian exegetical tradition takes up this image of Abraham as the man of faith but gradually jettisons his role as forebear of the Jewish people. Some early authors such as Marcion relinquished Abraham to the Jews, whereas others, among them Barnabas, Ignatius, and Philip, Christianized him. The use of Abraham in early Christian polemics against Jews takes on many forms, in genres ranging from letters and commentary to apology and treatise, and is given different expressions, but over time the most persistent image of Abraham in the Christian tradition is that of a man obedient to God and in whose faith in God all believers partake and are blessed.

The Qur'anic Abraham

Abraham (*Ibrahim*)[55] figures prominently—second only to Moses (Musa)—in the Qur'an. The qur'anic portrait of Abraham is a composite of various references strewn throughout. His life is not narrated sequentially, nor is it replete with details. He is depicted primarily as the first true believer, the prototypical Muslim: "Truly, Abraham was a model of virtue, obedient to God, upright, and not one of those who associate" (Q. 16:120).[56] More than 245 *ayas* (verses) of the Qur'an refer to him, although, as is typical of the Qur'an, each of the references appears in several places. Various appellations such as Khalīl Allah, Friend of God,[57] and *ḥanīf*,[58] "upright" or "pure of faith," and *ṣiddīq*, "truthful," are used to describe him. The Qur'an also makes reference to *millat Ibrāhīm*, commonly glossed as *dīn Ibrāhīm*, "religion of Abraham." *Dīn Ibrāhīm* does not itself appear in the Qur'an; *millat Ibrāhīm*, however, occurs in six qur'anic verses: 2:130, 2:135, 3:95, 4:125, 6:161, and 16:123. What *millat Ibrāhīm* consists of is not explained in the Qur'an, although Patricia Crone and Michael Cook suggest that it centered on the practices of circumcision and sacrifice.[59] The term *milla* may have been adapted from Hebrew or Aramaic, or from the Syriac *melltā*, which, as Gerald Hawting notes, "is sometimes used for the Greek *logos*."[60]

According to the Qur'an, Abraham is neither a Jew nor a Christian; he is the paradigmatic monotheist, the quintessential Muslim, who vies against idolatry:

> And when Abraham and Ishmael were raising up the foundations of the House [they prayed]: "Our Lord, Accept [this] from us, for You are the Hearer, the Knower. Our Lord, Make us submitters *muslimīn* to You and our progeny a submissive people to You. Show us the ritual places and turn toward us, for You are the most relenting, the Merciful. Our Lord, send them a messenger from among them who will recite for them Your signs and teach them the Book and wisdom and make them pure and good. For You are the Mighty, the Wise." Who could dislike the religion of Abraham other than those who fool themselves? We have chosen him in [this] world. And in the hereafter, he is among the righteous. When the Lord said to him: Surrender! [*Aslim*], he answered: "I surrender to the Lord of the universe." Abraham charged his sons, as did Jacob: "O my sons! God has chosen the right religion for you. When you die, die as submitters to God." (Q. 2:127–132)

One of the words used to describe Abraham is the problematic term *ḥanīf*, which is often left untranslated. Translations into English include "upright," "firmly and truly," "true believer," "true monotheist." In other Semitic languages—in the Syriac *ḥanpā* and the Hebrew *ḥanef*—the term seems to take on a meaning opposite to the Islamic "true monotheist," instead conveying the sense of "heathen" or "pagan."[61] The term appears in the Qur'an at verses 2:135, 3:67, 3:95, 4:125, 6:79, 6:161, 16:120, 16:123, and 30:30, and in eight instances it refers explicitly to Abraham. Of those verses that mention Abraham, five include the phrase *millat Ibrāhīm*. In addition, *ḥanīf* appears twice in the plural, in verses 22:31 and 98:5. The most plausible explanation is that the word is used in reference to people who reject the polytheism of their fellow Arabs but who accept neither Judaism nor Christianity. (Some, however, are reported to have embraced Christianity.)[62] They are often portrayed as people who adhere to elements of the religion of Abraham, and thus we find, as Gerald Hawting writes, "the equation of the religion of Abraham with the status of a *ḥanīf* (*dīn Ibrāhīm: al-ḥanīfiyya*)."[63]

Abraham's extraordinary birth, his marriage to Sarah, and their journey westward, episodes all absent in the Qur'an, are detailed in the *qiṣaṣ al-anbiyā'*, and *tafsīr* literature.[64] The Qur'an alludes only to Abraham's emigration (Q. 19:48–49, 21:71, 29:26, 37:99) and does not explicitly state that Abraham rejected the beliefs of the Chaldeans, who were widely known for their knowledge of astronomy and astrology, which were considered a single field at that time.[65] Interpreters took his willingness to leave as a sign of his abandoning their ways, and the Qur'an relates his moment of enlightenment.[66] Sura 6, "The Cattle" (al-An'ām), where unbelievers are summoned to submit to the Lord of all the worlds, the most powerful and all-knowing, and to follow his guidance, is the first sustained reference to Abraham's discovery. In fact, the renunciation of other idols is embedded in a sura that on the whole both celebrates God the creator of all, who is omnipotent as well as omnipresent, and draws attention to the waywardness of unbelievers. In this context we read about Abraham's father, Azar, whom Abraham rebukes for taking idols as gods, reprimanding his father and his people for straying. At that point God shows Abraham the kingdom of the heavens and the earth, so that he might be of those who possess certainty:

When the night grew dark over him he saw a star and said, "This is my Lord," but when it set, he said, "I do not like things that set." And when he saw the moon rising he said, "This is

my Lord," but when it too set, he said, "If my Lord does not
guide me, I shall be one of those who go astray." Then he saw
the sun rising and cried, "This is my Lord! This is greater!" But
when the sun set, he said, "My people, I am free from all who
associate with God. I have turned my face as a true believer
towards Him who created the heavens and the earth. I am not
one of the idolaters." (6:74–80)[67]

Abraham's recognition of God comes not only from his contemplation of the celestial realm but also from God's revelation to Abraham: "Thus We showed Abraham the kingdom of the heavens and
the earth, so that he might be of those who possess certainty."[68]

Sura 6 ends with a recapitulation of many of the themes and ex-
hortations expressed throughout. Muhammad is warned to keep
clear of divisive figures and is commanded to announce that he is
guided on the straight path, in the religion of Abraham, who was
not an idolater. The final verses remind the reader of the episode
between Abraham and his father and proclaim the greatness of the
one true, creator God: "Say, 'should I seek a Lord other than God,
when He is the Lord of all things?'" (6:164).

The most prevalent qur'anic image of Abraham is that of the defi-
ant son who ardently battles against his father's idolatry. He is the
believer par excellence in God, and because of his unflinching conviction he incurs the people's wrath. Told often and in great detail
in the Qur'an, the story depicts Abraham as the valiant defender of
God. Here and elsewhere in the Qur'an, Abraham is the precursor
of the prophet Muhammad and, like Moses, serves as a model of
Muhammad, who confronts unbelievers in Mecca as well as Jews
and Christians who do not accept his revelation.[69]

Qur'an 19:43–49 recounts a dialogue between Abraham and his
father. The son implores his father to follow him in the right path
and to cease worshipping Satan lest he be punished. In turn, Azar
threatens to have his son stoned. On leaving his father and rejecting
his father's idols, Abraham is rewarded by God: "Thus, when he left
them and the idols they worshipped, We bestowed on him Isaac and
Jacob, and made each of them a prophet, And bestowed on them
some of Our blessings, and gave them high renown."

In the third account (Q. 21:51–73) Abraham physically smashes the idols and faces life-threatening consequences:

> We had earlier given Abraham true direction, for We knew him well. When he said to his father and his people: "What are these idols to which you cling so passionately?" they replied, "We found our fathers worshipping them." He said, "You and your fathers are in clear error." They replied, "Are you speaking in earnest, or only jesting?" He responded: "In fact it was your Lord, the Lord of the heavens and earth, who created them; and I bear witness to this. I swear by God I will do something to your idols when you have turned your back and gone." So he smashed them up to pieces with the exception of the biggest, so that they may turn to it. [When they returned] They asked, "Who has done this to our gods? He is surely one of the evildoers." They said, "We heard a youth talk about them. He is called Abraham." "Bring him before the people," they said, "that they may bear witness." "Did you do this to our gods, O Abraham?" they enquired. "No," he said. "It was done by that chief of theirs. Ask him in case they can speak." Then they thought and observed: "Surely you are yourselves unjust." Then crestfallen [they confessed]: "Truly, as you know, they cannot speak." Abraham replied, "Then why do you worship something apart from God that cannot profit you or do you harm? Fie on you and those you worship besides God! Will you not understand?" They retorted, "Burn him, and save your gods, if you are men of action." "Turn cold, O fire," We said, "and give safety to Abraham." They wished to entrap him, but We made them greater losers. So We delivered him and Lot, and brought them to the land We had blessed for all people. And we bestowed on him Isaac, and Jacob as an additional gift, and made them righteous. And we made them leaders to guide [the people] by Our command.

Muslim accounts found in the tales of the prophets discuss these events in great detail. Moreover, the story is told with an emphasis on God's saving power toward those who believe and follow him.

Reiterating themes found elsewhere in the Qur'an, verses 26:68–86 depict God's might and mercy. Abraham pronounces his complete reliance on God, God who sustains him with food and drink, who heals him and will, he hopes, forgive him his faults on the Day of Judgment, cause him to die and renew his life. Then Abraham prays that he might be considered among the righteous and be counted among the inheritors of Paradise. He furthermore asks for forgiveness on behalf of himself and his father, who "was surely among those who went astray" (Q. 26:86).

Although Sarah and Hagar are not explicitly named in the Qur'an, in Islam they are included as members of Abraham's family, along with both Ishmael and Isaac. This is not the case in Christianity, which includes Sarah and extends Abraham's spiritual paternity only to Isaac, excluding Ishmael and Hagar. In Judaism, Ishmael is a member of Abraham's family, but he is marginalized, sent away with his mother, and both of them, along with the children Abraham fathers with Keturah, are excluded from the family blessing.

Like his brother, Isaac is considered a prophet in the Qur'an, one who stands before God, one who is a reward to Abraham when he renounces his people's idolatry and who is himself rewarded, as noted earlier: "And when Abraham cast off his people and their idols, We gave him Isaac and Jacob. Each of them We made a prophet and We bestowed on them Our mercy and granted them a high renown" (Q. 19:49). The absence of Ishmael in the text is noteworthy. To be sure, the Qur'an mentions Ishmael as he assists Abraham in building the holy sanctuary in Mecca, but Ishmael's role in the Qur'an is far from prominent. Over time he gained importance in the Islamic metanarrative, and he is now unequivocally considered the son intended for the sacrifice, whereas early exegetes were not in agreement as to whether it was Isaac or Ishmael.

Abraham and his family are the focus of ancient and medieval works that at times gloss over troubling verses or flesh out details of elliptical passages. Extrascriptural sources amplify Abraham's attributes while attenuating or attempting to justify his questionable behavior. Even within a single tradition one will find different, competing portrayals of the forefather and his family. How did readers imagine Abraham's life before God chose him, and why did

God choose him in the first place? Why is there rivalry between Ishmael and Isaac? Why does Sarah demand the expulsion of Abraham's firstborn and his mother? What fanciful tales and traditions were told and sermons given about the first family of Judaism, Christianity, and Islam? It is to those questions that I turn in the chapters that follow.

■ 3

The First Monotheist

THE BIBLE TELLS US very little about Abraham's family prior to his departure from his homeland, and even less about Abraham himself:

> Now this is the line of Terah: Terah begot Abram, Nahor, and Haran; and Haran begot Lot. Haran died before his father Terah,[1] in his native land, Ur of the Chaldeans. Abram and Nahor took to themselves wives, the name of Abram's wife being Sarai and that of Nahor's wife Milcah, the daughter of Haran, the father of Milcah and Iscah. Now Sarai was barren, she had no child. Terah took his son Abram, his grandson Lot the son of Haran, and his daughter-in-law Sarai, the wife of his son Abram, and they set out together from Ur of the Chaldeans for the land of Canaan; but when they had come as far as Haran, they settled there. The days of Terah came to 205 years; and Terah died in Haran. (Gen. 11:27–32)

With this sketchy background, Abraham's story begins in Genesis 12:1–3, where God commands him to leave his country, kindred, and father's house to journey to a land that God will show him. God tells Abraham that he will make him a great nation and bestow blessings on him. Why Abraham merits God's attention is not made clear in the Bible, but extrascriptural sources offer explanations and justifications, filling in this lacuna with examples of Abraham's worthiness.

As terse as the Bible is in rendering details of Abraham's early years, tales of his special birth, precociousness, recognition of the one true God, and fearless revolt against Nimrod gained popularity throughout the centuries and took on a variety of forms in Jewish, Christian, and Islamic sources. The fairly widespread image of Abraham the idol smasher emerges in sources other than the Bible and is the prominent portrayal of the qur'anic Abraham. Many readers of the Bible are surprised to discover that the story is missing from the Genesis narrative.

The Book of Genesis does not mention the idolatrous ways of Abraham's father or how Abraham's monotheistic devotion came about. We read only of his call to leave his homeland and go to the land that God will show him. The Book of Joshua, however, refers explicitly to Terah's idol worship: "Then Joshua said to all the people, 'Thus said the LORD, the God of Israel; In olden times, your forefathers—Terah, father of Abraham and father of Nahor—lived beyond the Euphrates and worshipped other gods. But I took your father Abraham from beyond the Euphrates and led him through the whole land of Canaan and multiplied his offspring'" (Joshua 24:2–3). The verses do not quite dissociate Abraham from his father's behavior. In fact, in an effort to absolve Abraham, as well as Abraham's family, Pseudo-Philo's *Biblical Antiquities* (*Liber Antiquitatum Biblicarum*), a first- to second-century Jewish retelling of the Hebrew Bible from Adam to the death of King Saul,[2] renders the verse as follows: "And when those inhabiting the land were being led astray after their own devices, Abraham believed in me and was not led astray with them."

It is unclear from the biblical text whether God singled him out as a reward for rejecting idolatry or in order to reveal himself to Abraham and thus protect him from idolatry. Interpreters emphasize the point that Abraham was blessed on account of his rejection of idol worship. For ancient interpreters, God singles out Abraham because he alone, in an environment rife with astrologers and astronomers, did not worship other gods.

In the ancient period, the Chaldeans were famous for their astronomical expertise, so much so that the word *Chaldean*, as James Kugel notes, "itself came to be a synonym for 'astronomer' in Greek and Aramaic." Astronomy went hand in hand with astrology; Kugel explains that the Chaldeans' pursuit of astronomy "was not merely out of curiosity about the makeup of the universe: like many ancient peoples, they believed that the stars controlled human destiny . . . indeed, by seeking the favor of this or that god identified with a certain celestial body, one might actually influence things for the good."[3]

Jubilees, a Palestinian work from the beginning of the second century BCE,[4] perhaps conveys the first account of Abraham's separation from his father's ways and his destruction of idols. After learning that Abraham (Abram) was named after his maternal grandfather, we are told that he "began to realize the errors of the earth—that everyone was going astray after the statues and after impurity. His father taught him (the art of) writing. When he was two weeks of years [= 14 years], he separated himself from his father in order not to worship idols with him. He began to pray to the creator of all that he would save him from the errors of mankind and that it might not fall to his share to go astray after impurity and wickedness" (11:16–18).[5] From the outset, *Jubilees* tells us of Abraham's powers of discernment, his rejection of idol worship, and his recognition of God, the Creator of all things, whom he implores for help. Unlike Genesis, *Jubilees* opens with biographical verses that foreshadow Abraham's separation from his idolatrous surroundings and from his father, who not only worships idols but manufactures them.

Abraham confronts his father: "What help and advantage do we get from these idols which you worship and before which you prostrate yourself? For there is no spirit in them because they are dumb. They are an error of the mind. Do not worship them. Worship the God of heaven who makes the rain and dew fall on the earth and makes everything on the earth. He created everything by his word; and all life (comes) from his presence. Why do you worship those things which have no spirit in them?" (12:2–4).[6] He goes on to explain that the idols are fashioned by human hands. Not only are they of no help to him, but they cause great shame to those who make them. Terah's reply to Abraham is noteworthy. While some Jewish sources indict Abraham's father for idol worship, in *Jubilees* he responds, "I, too, know (this), my son," but he fears those who surround him, whose souls cleave to idols, and thus he advises his son to keep silent.[7] One evening Abraham burns down the house of idols. In attempting to save the idols, Abraham's brother Haran dies in the fire, and Terah and his sons leave Ur of the Chaldeans.[8]

Another second-century BCE work, the Book of Judith, an apocryphal novella, explains why Abraham left Chaldea:

> Then Achior, the leader of all the Ammonites, said to him [Holofernes, the general of the Assyrian army] . . . This people is descended from the Chaldeans. At one time they lived in Mesopotamia, because they would not follow the gods of their fathers who were in Chaldea. For they had left the ways of their ancestors, and they worshipped the God of heaven, the God they had come to know; hence they drove them out from the presence of their gods; and they fled to Mesopotamia, and lived there for a long time. Then their God commanded them to leave the place where they were living and go to the land of Canaan. There they settled, and prospered, with much gold and silver and very many cattle. (Jth. 5:5–9)

Interestingly, while the Book of Judith provides a background to the Israelite ancestry and their presence in Canaan, it does not single out Abraham. God does not command that they leave, nor do they leave of their own volition; rather, the Chaldeans drive out Abraham and his family because they no longer worship their ancestral gods.

Contrary to Joshua 24:2–3, which indicts Terah and Nahor in idol worship, Judith tells us that Abraham and his family reject the ways of their people and that this results in their expulsion. After they settle in Mesopotamia, God commands all of them, not just Abraham, to migrate to Canaan.

Like Judith and *Jubilees*, the Jewish historian Josephus, of the first century CE,[9] describes Abraham's departure from Chaldea (*Jewish Antiquities*, 1.7.1 [1.154–157]),[10] but Josephus, unlike Judith, applauds him for his monotheism. Josephus tells the reader of Abraham's exceptional sagacity and virtue. Josephus's Abraham—the father of the Jewish people, who was obedient to the laws before they were even given—was the first to make public monotheistic proclamations and polytheistic renunciations that drew the wrath of the Chaldeans. Fearing for his life, Abraham by God's command and with his assistance immigrated to Canaan.

Josephus's Abraham is a Greek philosopher who combats Chaldean views that maintain the power of heavenly bodies. Abraham's discovery of God comes about through celestial contemplation and recognition of the irregularity of the stars, which effect changes in the land and sea: "For he said that if they had the power they would have provided their own orderliness; but since they lack this, it is evident that as many things as they contribute to our increased usefulness they perform not by their own authority but in accordance with the power of their commander, on whom alone it is proper to confer honor and gratitude."[11] This portrayal of Abraham as one who refutes the divine power of heavenly orbs is also found in Philo of Alexandria (20 BCE–50 CE), who commonly attributes Greek philosophical views to biblical characters.

Philo similarly accords Abraham pride of place as the first to believe in God (*On Virtue*, 216). The son of a Chaldean astrologer, "the most ancient member of the Jewish nation,"[12] Philo's Abraham rejects his inherited Mesopotamian views, which consist of believing that "the stars and the whole heaven and universe are gods, the authors . . . of the events which befall each man for good or for ill, and hold that there is no originating cause outside the things we perceive by our senses."[13] Abraham leaves behind those misconceptions when he comes to understand the one true God:

In this creed [that the world itself was God, thus likening the created with the Creator] Abraham had been reared, and for a long time remained a Chaldean. Then opening the soul's eye as though after profound sleep, and beginning to see the pure

beam instead of the deep darkness, he followed the ray and dis-
cerned what he had not beheld before, a charioteer and pilot
presiding over the world and directing in safety his own work,
assuming the charge and superintendence of that work and of
all such parts of it as are worthy of the divine care. (*On Abraham*, 70)[14]

Philo depicts Abraham's conversion from astrology to faith in
God the creator as a process of moving from darkness to light.
Abraham's departure from his home is understood allegorically
and in similar terms, as a departure from a place of darkness—
Chaldea—to a place of understanding, a place of light. The soul's
sudden awareness of God's presence propels Abraham to abandon
his former way of thinking of God. Whereas in *Jubilees* and Josephus Abraham grasps God through observable phenomena, in Philo
Abraham is awakened to God, and his migration is the soul's journey, set out in several stages, that will ultimately lead him to the
Promised Land, that is, to the one true God. Josephus and Philo
portray Abraham's discovery of God differently, yet both emphasize that Abraham, and Abraham alone, makes that discovery. His
family plays no role in it.

One of the most fanciful accounts of Abraham's departure from
his father's house is found in the *Apocalypse of Abraham*,[15] a second-
century CE pseudepigraphical work, which is told in the first person singular and opens with an amusing tale about his discovery of
the one true God. One day while he is fulfilling his father's sacrificial duties to the gods in the temple, he notices that Marumath,[16] a
god made of stone, has fallen at the feet of the iron god Nahon. He
seeks his father's assistance in bringing Marumath back to his
proper place, but in the process Marumath's head comes off. Terah
quickly fashions a headless Marumath, places on it the head of the
first Marumath, and shatters its remains. Terah makes five more
gods, which he commands Abraham to sell. While performing his
vending duties, Abraham encounters Syrian merchants whose camel
makes a sound that frightens his donkey, and three of the gods
smash to the ground. The merchants purchase the two remaining
gods and pay for the three broken ones, which Abraham casts into

the water of the river Gur. They sink into the depths, and there is nothing left of them.

On his way home, Abraham begins to ruminate, "Behold, Marumath fell and could not stand up in his sanctuary, nor could I myself lift him until my father came and we raised him up. And even so not able (to do it) and his head fell off of him." He continues to consider the fact that his father had to set Marumath's head on another stone god, which his father made without a head, and furthermore the broken fragments never emerged from the river. Thus he concludes: "If it is so, how can my father's god Marumath, which has the head of another stone and which is made from another stone, save a man, or hear a man's prayer, or give him any gift?"

On returning and greeting his father, he gives his father the silver, which gladdens Terah, who exclaims, "You are blessed, Abraham, by the god of my gods, since you have brought the price of the gods, so that my labor was not (in) vain." Abraham replies, "Listen, my father, Terah! The gods are blessed in you because you are a god for them, because you made them, for their blessing is their perdition, and their power is vain. They did not help themselves; how then can they help or bless me?" Needless to say, Terah is incensed. He commands Abraham to gather the splinters of wood out of which he makes gods. While preparing the afternoon meal for his father, Abraham finds a little god, on whose forehead is written "God Barisat."[17] Deciding not to disclose his discovery to his father, he continues to prepare his father's meal. As he is about to leave the kindling fire for a moment, he speaks threateningly to Barisat: "Pay careful attention that the fire does not die down, but if it seems to be dying out, rekindle it by blowing on it." When Abraham returns, he sees that Barisat has fallen backward and is horribly burnt. Abraham bursts into laughter and says to himself, "Barisat, truly you know how to light a fire and cook food!" The fire consumes Barisat.

Abraham sets the meal before Terah, who eats with a happy heart and blesses Marumath, at which point Abraham interjects, "Father Terah, do not bless Marumath your god, do not praise him! Praise rather Barisat, your god, because, as though loving you, he threw himself into the fire in order to cook your food." The sarcasm is lost on Terah, who replies, "Great is the power of Barisat! I will make another today, and tomorrow he will prepare my food." Abraham laughs to himself and with indignation wonders how it is that a god whom his father manufactures is of help to his father. Now directing his thoughts to Terah, he questions him directly about the worth of his gods in comparison to his brothers' gods, such as Zucheus, made of gold. Then Abraham commences a disquisition on the relationship between the natural elements and begins an attack on the rationale for worshipping them:

> Behold, the fire is more worthy of honor than all things formed because even that which is not subjected is subjected to it, and things easily perishable are mocked by its flames. But even more worthy of honor is the water, because it conquers the fire and satisfies the earth. But even it I do not call God, because it is subjected to the earth under which the water inclines. But I call the earth much more worthy of honor, because it overpowers the nature of the water. Even it, however, I do not call god because it too is dried up by the sun, and is apportioned to humans to be tilled.[18]

Abraham continues to discount the heavenly bodies, one after the other, and then turns to his father and proclaims, "I will make known to you the God who has made everything, not these we consider gods. Who then is He? Or what is He? Who has crimsoned the heavens, and made the sun golden, And the moon lustrous, and with it the stars. And has made the earth dry in the midst of many waters and set you in . . . Yet may God reveal Himself to us through Himself!" Instantly, the voice of God comes down from heaven in a fiery cloudburst, saying, "Abraham, Abraham!" To which Abraham replies, "Here I am." The Almighty continues: "You are seeking in understanding of your heart the God of Gods and the Creator; I am He; Go out from your father Terah, and the house, lest you be slain in the sins of your father's house." He heeds the command, and as he leaves, thunder strikes Terah, his house, and all its inhabitants. Abraham is thus saved because of his rejection of idolatry and because of his obedience to God. Had he ignored God's command, he would have died along with the others.

This marvelously humorous tale about the vanity of idol worship explains why Abraham was set apart from his family: God called him forth because he called forth to God.[19] Through his observation of the world, he deduces the existence of the one true God. He attempts to share his discovery with his father, but to no avail. *Jubilees* and Josephus—and the Qur'an and other Islamic sources—also depict him as unsuccessfully preaching monotheism and, because of that, being endangered and needing to flee. In the works examined above, Abraham's surroundings leave much to be desired. In other traditions, his leaving Terah's home is considered the first of ten trials.

The rabbis also portray Abraham as someone who rejects idolatry through consideration of the sensory world. To explicate Genesis 12:1, "Now the LORD said unto Abram, 'Get thee out of your country," the rabbis offer the following parable:

> This may be compared to a man who was travelling from place to place when he saw a building in flames. He wondered, "Is it possible that the building lacks a person to look after it?" The owner of the building looked out and said, "I am the owner of the building." Similarly, because Abraham our father said, "Is it conceivable that the world is without a guide?" the Holy One, blessed be He, looked out and said to him, "I am the Guide, the Sovereign of the Universe." (*Gen. Rab.* 39:1)[20]

In this passage Abraham looks out into the world and concludes that surely someone must master it, but another passage from rabbinic literature depicts God as guiding Abraham and showing him the vanity of astrology (*Gen. Rab.* 39:1).[21]

In *The Making of a Forefather*, Shari Lowin explores the ways Jewish and Islamic sources portray Abraham's turn to the worship of God as either by means of intellection or with God's guidance. She argues that in Sunni and Shi'i Islamic narratives God plays an active role but midrashic sources depict a more independent Abraham who chooses God independently. As she notes, however, in *Genesis Rabbah* 95:3 Abraham's knowledge comes from his kidneys, the body's seat of intellect. Whereas she points to this midrash as an example of Abraham discovering Torah (not knowledge of the Five Books of Moses, but general instruction and spiritual knowledge) through the use of his natural faculties, with no outside help from a pedagogue or angel, I would argue that it suggests he was indeed guided by God.[22]

The prooftext in *Genesis Rabbah* 95:3 is "I bless the Lord who has guided me. At night my innards instruct me." The nightly cogitation is about God—all night with deep inner cogitation (in "my innards"—literally, kidneys).[23] According to Lowin, R. Levi formulates the matter more simply as "Abraham learned Torah for himself." On the contrary, the midrash should be read as offering two different positions: R. Shim'on contends that Abraham was given Torah, and R. Levi maintains that he learned it on his own. The Jewish and Islamic sources portray Abraham as one who has on his own accord discovered God, and as one who relies on God to show him the way.

Cave of Treasures is a Syriac text traditionally attributed to the fourth-century CE Ephrem Syrus (the Syrian), or Ephrem of Nissibus, but scholarly consensus places it, in the form in which it is preserved, no earlier than the sixth century. The work contains similar stories about Abraham's rejection of idolatry and recognition of God, "the maker of the universe." As in other renditions, Abraham abuses and smashes the idols his father has commanded him to sell. While on the road, he sets the images down and says to them, "I wonder if you are able to do what I ask you at this moment, and whether you are able to give me bread to eat or water to drink?" When none answers him, he verbally and physically assaults them, and still they do not respond. He strikes the face of one and kicks another, and the third he breaks into pieces. He asks them, "If you are unable to save yourselves from one who has injured you, or retaliate against someone who has injured you, then how can you be called gods? Those who worship you do so in vain and I utterly deplore you." He then turns his face to the East, stretches out his hands, and says, "Be my God, O Lord, Creator of the heavens and the earth, Creator of the Sun and Moon, Creator of the sea and dry land, Maker of the majesty of the heavens and the earth, and of that which is visible and invisible. O Maker of the universe, be my God. I place my trust in You, and from this day forth I will place my trust in no other save yourself." At that moment a blazing chariot of fire appears. Abraham is frightened and falls on his face, and God says to him, "Fear not, stand upright."[24]

Many Christian writers take up the allegorical interpretation found in Philo, understanding Abraham's journey from Chaldea to the Promised Land as a spiritual journey. Leaving the land is like leaving the body. The most prominent image of Abraham in early Christian writings is that of a man of faith. As the fourth-century Alexandrian theologian Didymus writes:

> It is not by chance that God orders Abraham to leave his land and his relatives but because he saw in him something that made him worthy of divine solicitude, that is, his faith in God. It was inappropriate for one who had faith in God to remain among perverse people—Abraham's father was in fact an idolater— because the company of the wicked often does harm to zealous people, especially to those whose zeal is new. This is why the Savior also proclaims, "If anyone wishes to follow me and does not hate his father, his brothers, his sisters, and even his wife and children, he cannot be my disciple" [Luke 14:26; Matt. 16:24]. The Lord did not say that in order to cause hatred of one's parents, but if one of them becomes an obstacle to virtue, it is necessary to hate him for virtue's sake. That is what the apostle did, who said, "Look, we have left everything in order to follow you" [Mark 10:28]. Such is the order given now to the patriarch, and God announces to him that he will show him a land in which to live, that he will make of him a great nation, that he will bless and magnify his name.[25]

Didymus tells us that it was Abraham's faith in God that merited God's special attention, as it was unfitting for a believer to dwell among idolaters. In addition, Didymus makes a connection between God's command to Abraham to leave his place of origin and Jesus' call to follow him but notes that if one is to follow Jesus, one must renounce one's family lest it draw one astray.

Caesarius of Arles interprets "leave your kinsfolk" as a reference to becoming purified from the vices and sins that humans inherit but rid ourselves of through baptism (Sermon 81.2).[26] Further-more, Abraham's journey is not explicitly one from polytheism to monotheism but one from vice to virtue, from the devil to God. In Caesarius's sermon the devil is the father of humans in the sense that we imitate his wicked ways: "Indeed, they could not have been born of him, but they did want to imitate him. This fact that the devil was our first father the psalmist relates in the person of God speaking to the church: 'Hear, O daughter, and see; turn your ear, forget your people and your father's house'" (Sermon 81.3).[27]

The emphasis in Christian sources is less on discovering the one true God than on believing in him. Knowledge of the creator God, as Ephrem comments, was known to the first generations: "the Creator had been manifest to the mind of the first generations, even up to the [generation of the] Tower. The fact that creatures were created was also publicly taught. And it was general knowledge that the creatures were created things. Moreover from [the generation of] the Tower un-til [the generation of] Moses there was no lack of men among the sons of Shem to preach these things" (*Commentary on Genesis, Prologue 2*).[28] This is not to suggest that Christians did not enjoy fanciful stories of Abraham's discovery of God, such as the one in which he escapes from the clutches of Nimrod, but to note that for the church fathers, Abraham's faith alone made him worthy of the covenant.

Nimrod and the Pyre

Although the Bible tells us little about Nimrod, extrascriptural sources of the first century provide a more fleshed-out picture of him.[29] Perhaps the earliest attestation of Abraham's encounter with Nimrod is found in Pseudo-Philo's *Biblical Antiquities*. Chapter 5 of this work opens with the statement that the sons of Ham made Nimrod their leader.[30] Nimrod and Abraham are mentioned in Pseudo-Philo's account of the building of the Tower of Babel. In Genesis 11:3, when the people decide to build a tower, they say, "Come, let us make bricks and burn them hard," evoking fire imagery on which Pseudo-Philo expands later; first he tells of this event and says that twelve men refuse to make bricks, including Abraham (Abram), Nahor, and Lot.[31] The people seize the twelve and bring them to their leaders, who ask why they refuse to contribute to the collective endeavor of all the people in the land. They reply, "We know only the Lord, and him do we worship. Even if you throw us into the fire with your bricks, we will not assent to you." Angered by their response, the leaders command that unless the men immediately reconsider, they are to burn in the fire together with the bricks. But the chief of the leaders, Joktan, who is also of the twelve men's tribe, allows for a seven-day period in order to give the twelve men time to repent. He locks them in the royal house, summons fifty warriors, and orders that they are to be brought to him; provisions will await them in the mountains. All of this is done surreptitiously, lest he too be cast into the fire.

When Joktan meets with the twelve men, he tells them of his plan; he has commanded fifty men to take provisions from his house, and fifty other men will accompany them on their way. They are to stay there for thirty days, "until the anger of the people of the land ceases and until God sends his wrath upon them and breaks them." Eleven of the twelve respond, "Your servants have found favor in your eyes, in that we are rescued from the hands of these arrogant men." Abraham, however, keeps silent. When asked why he has not responded, Abraham replies, "Behold, today I flee to the mountains. If I have escaped the fire, the wild beasts will come forth from the mountains and devour us; or we will lack food and die of famine. We will be found to have escaped the people of the land, but to have fallen because of our sins. And now, as surely as God in whom I trust lives, I will not move from my place where they have put me. If there be any sin of mine such that I should be burned, let the will of God be done." Thus Abraham refuses to go with the others because of his unwavering trust in God.

Joktan locks Abraham up, and when the seven days pass and the people request that the men be delivered to them, Joktan says that they broke out at night, although one remains. Two men speak up, Fenech and Nimrod: "This one who alone was found, let us burn him." They build a furnace, light it with fire, and throw bricks into it. Joktan, dismayed, throws Abraham into the fiery furnace along with the bricks.

Most versions of the story mention that God saves Abraham, or sends Gabriel (Jibril) to save him, or that the fires cool, but in this version we read that God stirs up a great earthquake, and then fire leaps out of the furnace and causes sparks and flames to scorch all those standing in front of it. The fire consumes 83,500, yet Abraham is unscathed. He arises from the furnace and joins the eleven men who were secluded in the mountains.

As Howard Jacobson notes, there is a great deal of evidence in *Biblical Antiquities* of the non-Jewish Greco-Roman world as well as the "Canaanite-Palestinian" one.[32] In this rendition of Abraham's near-death experience, he alone faces his enemies and is prepared to martyr himself, although there are others in his family who believe. *Biblical Antiquities* seems to whitewash the notion in Joshua 2:24 that Abraham's family worshipped other gods, and exalts Abraham from among them. Abraham is the prototypical man of faith who displays unwavering faithfulness to his God. In light of the fact that this work dates from the middle of the first century to the middle of the second, one can appreciate the depiction of Abraham as a leader who does not succumb to the widespread idolatry of his surroundings— who refuses to walk along with the other eleven in the ways of the people of the land.

In light of one of the predominant themes of this work—that despite the hardships faced by the Jewish people, God will never abandon them—Abraham triumphs over persecution. Here God takes an active role in their salvation. He stirs up an earthquake that leaves Abraham untouched. He reunites with the eleven, who have been hiding in the mountains, and they all come down together, "rejoicing in the name of the Lord. No one who met them frightened them that day."[33] Indeed, the story of Abraham in this work fits well into the broader theme of victory over oppression.

The casting of Abraham into the pyre is recorded in several rabbinic sources,[34] and in every instance Abraham is rescued, whether by God's indirect or direct action. *Genesis Rabbah* 38:13 on the verse "And Haran died in the presence of [or in the lifetime of] his father Terah" (Genesis 11:28) is an elaborate tale:

> R. Hiyya said: Terah was a manufacturer of idols. He once went away and left Abraham to sell them in his place. A man came and wished to buy one. "How old are you?" Abraham asked him.

"Fifty years," the man replied, to which he exclaimed, "Woe to such a man! You are fifty years old and would worship a day-old object!" The man became embarrassed and left. On another occasion a woman came with a plateful of flour and requested that Abraham take it and offer it to them. So he took a stick, broke them, and put the stick in the hand of the largest. When his father returned he demanded, "What have you done to them?" "I cannot conceal it from you," he answered. "A woman came with a plateful of fine meal and requested me to offer it to them. One claimed, 'I must eat first,' while another claimed, 'I must eat first.' Thereupon the largest arose, took the stick, and broke them.'" His father cried out, "Why do you make sport of me? Have they then any knowledge?" Abraham replied, "Should not your ears listen to what your mouth is saying?" Thereupon Terah seized him and delivered him to Nimrod, who proposed, "Let us worship the fire!" "Let us rather worship water, which extinguishes the fire," replied Abraham. "Then let us worship water," agreed Nimrod. Abraham suggested, "Let us rather worship the clouds which bear the water." "Then let us worship the clouds!" "Let us rather worship the winds which disperse the clouds." "Then let us worship the wind!" "Let us rather worship human beings, who withstand the wind." "Your words are meaningless." Nimrod exclaimed, "we will worship only the fire. Behold, I will cast you into it, and let your God whom you adore come and save you from it." Now Haran was standing there undecided. If Abram is victorious, [thought he], I will say that I am of Abram's belief, while if Nimrod is victorious I will say that I am on Nimrod's side. When Abram descended into the fiery furnace and was saved, he [Nimrod] asked him, "Of whose belief are you?" "Of Abram's," he replied. Thereupon he seized and cast him into the fire; his innards were scorched and he died in his father's presence. Hence it is written, "And Haran died in the presence of (*'al pene*) his father Terah, in the land of his birth, in Ur of the Chaldeans."[35]

The rabbis translate *'al pene*, "in the presence of," as "because of": "because of his father Terah." They also pun on the meaning of *ur*, fire. In other words, Haran died as in *Jubilees* 12:12–14, in the fire of the Chaldeans.[36] As Kugel observes, the two motifs, "Haran perished in the fire" and "Abraham is saved from the fire," are brought together in *Genesis Rabbah* 38:13.[37]

Several of the stories examined do not deal explicitly with what seems to be a problematic timeline in the Genesis narrative. According to Genesis 11:31, Terah and his family are already in Haran in Mesopotamia before God commands Abraham to leave for Canaan just two verses later, to go forth from "your country" and "from your kindred and your father's house." Furthermore, in Genesis 12:4–5, Abraham is seventy-five years old when he departs from Haran. In other words, if Ur was Abraham's ancestral homeland, why is he told to leave it when, according to the narrative chronology, he and his family were already elsewhere in Haran? One solution is to assert that Genesis 12:1–4 takes place while Abraham is still in Ur, as if God addressed Abraham while he was in Ur.[38] Another exegetical matter to consider is that according to Genesis 12:4, Abraham is seventy-five years old when he goes out from Haran. If Terah was seventy when he fathered Abraham in Chaldea and 205 years old when he died in Haran, how does one account for the 135 years that passed from Abraham's birth up to his father's death? Haran dies in Genesis 11:32 and then immediately we read in Genesis 12:1: "Now the Lord said to Abram . . ." According to *Genesis Rabbah* 39:7, God records Terah's death before Abraham's departure, lest he be considered in error for leaving his father in his old age. Thus, Abraham actually departs before his father dies in Haran, and God exempts Abraham from the commandment to honor one's parents.

Jerome also notices the chronological discrepancy and draws on the Jewish story of Abraham's survival in the fire of the Chaldeans to resolve the matter:

> Therefore that tradition of the Hebrews, which was related above, is true; that Terah with his sons went out from the fire of the Chaldeans, and that Abram, when surrounded by the Babylonian fire because he refused to worship it, was set free by God's help; and from that time onwards the days of his life and the measure of his age are reckoned for him, namely from that

time when he acknowledged the Lord and despised the idols of the Chaldeans.[39]

That is to say, Abraham's recorded age is not his actual age. His recorded age reflects the years between his departure from Chaldea, when he became a monotheist, and his departure from Haran. Jerome does not deal with the question whether Abraham was called from Ur or Haran but nonetheless notes attempts to explain the discrepancy.

Islamic Depictions of Abraham's Discovery of God and His Battle against Idolatry

The foregoing motifs are found in the Islamic tradition as well. Indeed, the tales of the prophets are replete with accounts detailing Abraham's perilous birth, his discovery of God, and his public renunciation of his people's idolatry, to say nothing of his fearless attempts to preach about the one true God. Al-Tha'labi, for example, in his *Tales of the Prophets ('Arā'is al-Majālis fī Qiṣaṣ al-Anbiyā')*, begins his account of the life of Abraham with a genealogy going back to Noah and mentions that the given name of Abraham's father was Terah, but says that during the time of Nimrod (Namrud), king of Chaldea, who is also considered the first tyrant on earth and the son of Canaan, Terah became the guardian over the treasure of Nimrod's gods and thus was called Azar, as we find in the Qur'an. Because in Qur'an 9:14 Azar appears as an enemy of God, some Islamic exegetes create greater distance between him and Abraham and claim that he is actually Abraham's uncle and is referred to as his father because he is a close relation. That is to say, while some exegetes conflate Azar and Terah, others maintain that they are not one and the same person.[40]

Like the births of Moses and Jesus, the birth of Abraham is divined as a threat to a ruthless leader. In his case Nimrod has a dream: a star depletes the brilliance of the sun and moon until they have no light. Disturbed by the dream, he summons magicians, diviners, and prognosticators, who predict that a child will be born in his region in a year and that this child will be the source of his and his family's demise. To prevent this, Nimrod orders the slaying of every boy born in that region that year and commands that men and women refrain from intercourse. An overseer is placed in charge of every ten men. When a woman menstruates, the husband is given permission to reunite with his wife, for surely they would not copulate during her menstrual cycle. When Azar returns home, he discovers that his wife is actually purified, and he has intercourse with her. She becomes pregnant with Abraham.

Al-Tha'labi records several other accounts that diverge in details but all illustrate how Abraham is protected from Nimrod's attempts to kill him by being inside a cave. According to al-Tha'labi, when Abraham's mother begins to feel labor pains, she goes into a cave and gives birth to Abraham. She supplies him with all the necessary provisions, seals him in the cave, and departs for home. When she later returns to the cave, she finds him sucking his thumb, and indeed whenever she returns to the cave she finds him doing so. When she examines his fingers, she notices that from one finger he sucks water, from another he sucks milk, from another honey, and from yet another clarified butter.[41]

Abraham grows up there and asks to be released from the hiding place. On observing camels, horses, and cows, he concludes that they must have a master who created them. Then he turns his attention to the creation of the heavens and earth and concludes: "Verily He Who created me and sustained me, fed me and gave me drink, is my Master. I have no god beside Him."[42]

In the next section, on Abraham's battle against idolatry, qur'anic verses are woven into the narrative and serve as an integral part of the story. As in other renditions, Abraham's father, in this case Azar, is an idol maker who sends Abraham to sell his gods. Expressing something akin to the sarcasm shown in the *Apocalypse of Abraham*, Abraham is depicted as mocking the idols' ineffectuality. He cries out, "Who will buy what is harmful and of no value?" Because no one buys them, they are of no profit to him. Here again we recognize an image from the *Apocalypse of Abraham*, where he casts the gods into the water. In this case, he strikes their heads off and says to them, "Drink your fill. You are worthless!" When news travels among his people that Abraham has derided and denigrated their gods, the people grow argumentative. He teaches the oneness of God and preaches against the notion of *shirk*, associating the one true God with other beings: "How can you argue with me about God when he has guided me? I fear nothing you associate with him unless he wills it. My Lord encompasses everything in His knowledge. Will you not take heed? Why should I fear what you associate with Him? . . . Tell me, whose way is the way of peace, if you have knowledge? They alone have peace who believe and do not mix belief with denial, and are guided on the right path" (Q. 6:80–83). He debates them until he wins the dispute. He then turns to his father, but, alas, the father refuses to follow the son's call: "My father, why do you worship that which can neither hear nor see, nor benefit you in the least?" (Q. 19:42). But Abraham's words make no impression on Azar. As in the Jewish texts, Abraham concludes on his own, through his observation of reality, that there must exist a higher being who has created all that is observable in nature.

When Abraham publicly announces his renunciation of his people's idols and declares that he worships the Lord of all the worlds (Q. 26:75–77), the news travels to Nimrod, who summons him and inquires about Abraham's God, to which he replies, "My Lord is the giver of life and death." Nimrod responds that on the contrary *he* is the giver of life and death: "I take two men who in my judgment deserve to die. I let one free, thus I give him life, and I kill the other, thus I cause him to die." Abraham retorts, "God makes the Sun rise from the East, so you make it rise from the West." Nimrod is dumbfounded and remains silent.[43]

The next episode al-Tha'labi recounts is an expansion of two passages in the Qur'an where Abraham confronts his father and his people, condemns their idolatry, exhorts them to worship the one true God, and mocks their idols (Q. 21:55–71, 37:83–98). In one of these instances, while the people are away he breaks their idols into pieces but leaves the biggest one intact. On their return, when they see their gods all smashed up, they accuse Abraham, but he responds, "No, the biggest one did it. Ask them if they can talk." They reply, "You know very well these gods can't speak," and Abraham asks why would they worship that which can be of neither benefit nor harm to them. They ignore both their idols' impotence and his remonstrations and decide to cast him into a fire, but God protects him by cooling the fire. In the other qur'anic passage Abraham feigns illness, and when the people depart he strikes the idols with his right arm. Here again they plan to throw him into a pyre, but God thwarts their endeavors.

The story of Abraham's birth and battle against idolatry is recounted in several collections of the tales of the prophets. The general arc of the stories is the same; the details vary, however. In the collection of Muhammad ibn 'Abd Allah al-Kisa'i *(Tales of the Prophets)*, Terah is the consummate idol worshipper who sacrifices animals and offers food and drink to the idols. While in the temple (Ka'bah), he lies with his wife, and she conceives Abraham, at which point the Ka'bah falls down and says, "There is no god but God alone who has no partner." The idols topple, and the "beasts beat the ground with their tails at the conception of Abraham."[44] As in stories told of the Prophet Muhammad's birth, light is associated with Abraham's birth. At conception, his star shone like the sun and moon together, and over time his light increased in his mother's womb. When his mother's birth pangs began, an angel took her to the Cave of Light, where Idris (Enoch) and Noah were also born. When his mother, Usha, delivered Abraham, he stood up and shouted, "There is no god but God alone who has no partner!" When he rubbed his mother's breast, it flowed with milk and honey. When he sucked his fingers, each provided nourishment: milk, honey, cream, and water. He remained in the cave for four years, until the angel Gabriel commanded him to go forth. When Abraham turned forty, Gabriel came to him with the message that God was sending him to Nimrod.

Not all the tales of the prophets go into great detail about Abraham's encounters with Nimrod. For example, in Ibn Kathir's collection we find hardly any mention of him. Muqatil's is probably the earliest Islamic account of Abraham's encounters with Nimrod. And al-Tabari's *History of the Prophets and Patriarchs (Ta'rīkh al-rusul wa'l-mulūk)* furnishes background about Nimrod, but references to the battles between him and Abraham are absent. On the other hand, al-Kisa'i's account of Abraham's battle with the tyrant is rather extensive and filled with tales of miraculous events and comical episodes. In one of them, Abraham kills a white cock, a black raven, a green dove, and a peacock, cuts off their heads, mixes up the blood and feathers, and scatters their flesh on four mountaintops.[45] He then calls them, and each head goes out of his hand and to its own body, saying, "There is no god but God; Abraham is God's apostle to Nimrod and his people." In another episode, Abraham, while imprisoned, meets a fellow prisoner who asks Abraham if he can reunite him with his three brothers, held captive in the east, in the west, and in Yemen. Abraham performs the ablutions and prays to God. Suddenly two of the brothers appear. When news reaches Nimrod, he calls the two brothers and asks them how they were reunited. They respond, "Our God did this through the intercession of Abraham." Nimrod, astonished, commands his sorcerers to bring the other brother from Yemen, but they admit their limitations. Nimrod turns to Abraham, saying, "Bring back the brother who is in Yemen the same way you brought these two." God informs Abraham that the third brother is dead. Nevertheless, Nimrod wants to see the grave, at which point the earth beneath their feet opens and the grave is exposed. Nimrod tells Abraham to pray to his God to bring him back to life, and when Abraham does so, the grave splits open and the man steps forth, blazing in flame, saying, "This is the retribution of him who worshipped idols and was ungrateful to his Lord."

Not one of the marvelous acts of the Lord convinces Nimrod of God's greatness. He persists in attempting to defeat the God of Abraham until he is vanquished in a rather comical, irony-laden manner. A gnat enters one of his nostrils and crawls up to his brain, gnawing at his flesh and blood and praising God. Nimrod cannot sleep, eat, or drink for forty days. In order to alleviate the pain, he has his assistants strike his head with an iron rod, which causes the gnat to keep still. They continue to strike his head until one day a man of tremendous strength hits his head so hard that his skull cracks in two. Out comes the gnat, like a chick hatching from an egg, claiming, "There is no god but God; Abraham is the apostle of God and His Friend." The tyrant of tyrants is taken down by a tiny insect.[46]

As noted, Pseudo-Philo's *Biblical Antiquities* recounts Abraham's encounter with Nimrod. The motif, while not widespread in the

first century CE, developed over time such that we find extravagant
tales of the tyrant's defeat in medieval legends. Jewish sources of the
eleventh to thirteenth centuries, such as *Sefer ha-Yashar*, the *Chronicles of Jerameel*, and *Midrash ha-Gadol*, include accounts of Abraham's victory over his nemesis, Nimrod.

In the Islamic texts the great iconoclast Abraham battles against
the infamous tyrant Nimrod, who is depicted at times as submitting
to the will of God, other times as a steadfast polytheist to his death.
But in every instance his paganism proves no match for Abraham's
monotheism. The epitome of arrogance is defeated by the apostle
of God.

Observations

Now that I have examined several stories concerning Abraham's
rejection of idol worship, let me step back and make some observations. In most of the accounts we find him opposed not only to
his people but also to his family. In *Jubilees* 11:16–17, for example,
Serug, who dwells in Ur, practices astrology and divination and
worships idols. Abraham rejects his family's practices, but in *Biblical
Antiquities* the family of Serug remains loyal to God. Abraham is
like his family in their rejection of idolatry. *Biblical Antiquities* para-
phrases Joshua 24:2 so as to absolve Abraham's family from the wrongdoing of the other inhabitants of the land, and Judith exonerates them
as well.

In contrast to Philo and Josephus, Pseudo-Philo does not portray
Abraham as the first to make monotheistic pronouncements. Rather,
he is set apart for his willingness to sacrifice his life for the sake of
his unflagging faithfulness to the one true God. In most instances
Abraham rejects his family's ways, although in *Jubilees* Abraham's
father is also portrayed as someone who also acknowledges God
but, unlike his son, is afraid for his life.

The idea that Abraham went against his father troubles some
interpreters. As noted, the rabbis indicate that Terah repented, and
some Islamic sources refer to him as Azar, not Terah, in order to
create distance between Abraham and Terah. Yet the notion is not
exceptionally troubling for Jerome, who likens Abraham's departure

from Terah's home to Jesus' call to leave one's family behind and follow him.

In the Qur'an, *tafsīr*, and *qiṣaṣ al-anbiyā'*, Abraham's break from the practices of his father is understood in the context of a different notion of family, one based not on blood ties but on belief. Abraham's family is that of believers, as one can see in the qur'anic story of Noah. Not all members of Noah's family are saved from the Flood, only the believers. In fact, if we compare the biblical and qur'anic narratives about Noah, we discover a fundamental Islamic understanding of family—that it is a lineage of believers. In Genesis, Noah's family is understood in biological terms: the immediate members of Noah's family are saved in the biblical account. In the Qur'an, however, one of Noah's sons is not saved. When Noah pleads with God to save his son, God responds that the son is guilty and thus not a member of Noah's family (Q. 11:46). Members of Noah's family are those who share his righteousness, not his blood. This is illustrative of the qur'anic meaning of "family," which is confessional, not biological, a distinction that sketches the contours of the Islamic tradition with its emphasis on the *ummah*, community of believers. Although Abraham is described as "your father" (Q. 22:78), his fatherhood plays a less significant role in Islam than in Judaism or even Christianity.

The notion of family as that of believers is also expressed in Matthew 12:46–50:

> While he was still speaking to the crowds, his mother and his brothers stood outside, wanting to speak to him. Someone told him, "Look, your mother and your brothers are standing outside, wanting to speak to you." "But to the one who had told him this," Jesus replied, "Who is my mother and who are my brothers?" And pointing to his disciples, he said, "Here is my mother and my brothers! For whoever does the will of my Father in heaven is my brother, and sister and mother."

As believers of Jesus, all belong to the family of Abraham, heirs to the promise: "For in Christ Jesus you are all children of God, through faith. As many of you as were baptized into Christ have clothed yourselves with Christ. There is no longer Jew or Greek, there is no longer slave or free, there is no longer male and female; for you are all one in Christ Jesus. And if you belong to Christ, then you are Abraham's offspring, heirs according to promise" (Galatians 3:26–29).

The stories about Abraham's rejection of idolatry demonstrate an interest in amplifying his life in Mesopotamia, with an eye toward addressing why God singled him out for a covenant. What was so special about Abraham? Our sources tell us that it was his rejection of idolatry, and in some cases his willingness to rail against idolatry, that set him apart from his father and his kinsfolk. Whether by means of rationally deducing God's existence or of observing natural phenomena, Abraham is depicted as someone who discovers God and therefore merits God's call to him.

The portrayal of Abraham as the first monotheist in works from the second century BCE to the first century CE (and retained in later sources) is multidimensional. While some works highlight his intellectual and spiritual discovery of the one true God, others underscore his violent physical and verbal assault on idolatry. Depictions of both his discovery of God and his rejection of gods come together in rabbinic and Islamic literature. Extant Christian writings, it is true, give little attention to the story of the smashing of idols. It does not figure prominently in sermons, although in his Genesis commentary Jerome makes reference to Abraham having been cast into the Chaldean pyre, a story that was widely known in various circles, as the *Cave of Treasures* attests. Christian preachers who referred to Abraham's journey from his father's household by and large discussed it in terms of a spiritual journey, as did Philo. The focus in the Christian sources I have discussed is on faith in God.

The overriding image of Abraham in the Qur'an is of someone who professes the oneness of God to all people. A precursor to Muhammad, who denounces idolatrous ways, including belief in a triune God, Abraham the iconoclast is the Abraham who tends to appear in the Qur'an and later traditions. People are commanded to follow Abraham (Q. 6:123), who actively rails against polytheism and leads people to the straight path. Images of Abraham's missionizing are also found in rabbinic sources. In *Sifre Deuteronomy 32*, for example, Abraham converts people, gathering them "under the wing of the divine presence *(Shekhinah)*."[47] But such images are indeed comparatively less prominent in rabbinic literature and early Christian writings. To be sure, the image of Abraham preaching the word of God is not readily detected in the writings of the church fathers; it was his faith that Christians invoked when spreading the gospel message. In Islam he is the paradigmatic Muslim, who renounces polytheism and proclaims the greatness of God.

The biblical story of the call of Abraham raises questions for ancient and modern readers alike. Why was Abraham chosen from all the peoples of the earth? What did he do to merit such distinction? It is true that he proves his worthiness when God commands him in Genesis to sacrifice Isaac as a burnt offering, but that is after the fact. Later interpreters portray him as one who stood apart from his environs by refusing to engage in idol worship, and, as noted, he is also depicted as having endured ten trials.

In Judaism, Christianity, and Islam, Abraham is depicted as one who recognizes the greatness of God and is obedient to God's word, yet the characterization of that obedience differs. Because of his recognition of God and rejection of idolatry, Abraham—along with his offspring—merits a covenant with God. In Judaism, the inheritors of this covenant are his progeny, the Israelites, that is, the Jewish people. For Christians, his seed are those who, like Abraham, believe—but not only in God; they believe in God's only begotten son, Jesus, as well. In Paul's writing, the Jews are included as children of Abraham, but by 150 CE, with the writings of Justin Martyr, a decisive shift takes place, and the Jews, merely by virtue of being Jews and physically descended from Abraham, are no longer considered his heirs. Rather, only those, Jews or Gentiles, who behave like Abraham in their belief are considered his true descendants.[48]

The stories of Abraham's valorous rejection of idolatry in the face of perilous consequences may have been widespread among Christians, but it is not a prominent theme in the writings of the church fathers. The Qur'an, as well as Islamic extrascriptural sources, emphasizes his role of one who calls people to abandon their practices and to follow the one true God. Unlike Muhammad, who exhorts humanity to reform its ways and follow in Abraham's steps, Abra-

ham is the discoverer of God and the founder of a new way of worship, revealed to him by God and professed to all who will listen.
He sets humanity on its proper course to love and serve God accordingly. Given that Islam is not wedded to the story of Abraham
in the book of Genesis, the concern is not in justifying his election.
The narrative sequence that transitions from the Tower of Babel to
Abraham's calling has none of the significance for Muslims that it
has for Jewish and, to a lesser extent, Christian exegetes. In this instance, therefore, the exegetical issues taken up by Jewish writers
are not the concern of Muslim interpreters, even though they, too,
portray Abraham as the discoverer of the one true God.

∎ 4

The Wives of Abraham

ABRAHAM'S WIVES Sarah and Hagar have historically received far less attention than their husband and sons, and Keturah, whom Abraham married after Sarah's death in Genesis, even less so. Exegetes nonetheless have recognized the need to interpret specific verses and storylines as well as define the role played by Abraham's wives in broader theological and moral narratives.[1] How are these women depicted? What role do Sarah and Hagar play as matriarchs in the founding family of Abraham?

Early Jewish Interpretations of Sarah and Hagar

Most interpreters extol Sarah's virtues, from her astounding beauty to her impeccable character and devotion to her husband, and whitewash her behavior toward Hagar and Ishmael. In his obituary of Sarah, Philo pays the matriarch unprecedented homage. Abraham's dearest wife, "most noble in all things," demonstrated her love for him in countless ways. Philo reminds readers of Sarah's stoical behavior, for Abraham was not the only one who endured tribulations.[2] She abandoned the comfort, certainty, and protection of her family in order to accompany Abraham during his peregrinations on foreign soil. Sarah was with him on war campaigns, was always beside her husband—a true life partner, deeming it right to share the good with the bad. She could have complained like other spouses, but instead she withstood challenges and accepted her fate with equanimity.[3]

Most striking in Philo's idealization of Sarah is the way her offer of Hagar to Abraham becomes the clearest proof of her virtuous character. In the Bible, Sarah says that Abraham should consort with her maid because she herself cannot bear children; in Josephus's telling, she makes the suggestion only at God's prompting. In Philo, in contrast with those accounts, Sarah graciously and humbly offers an elaborate rationale for her motives. Since as a couple they cannot fulfill the purpose of their union, Abraham should not suffer on account of her infertility. She exhorts him to allow himself to become a father. Abraham should not hesitate on her account: "But do not let the trouble of my barrenness extend to you, or kind feeling to me keep you from becoming what you can become, a father, for I shall have no jealousy of another woman, whom you will take not for unreasoning lust but in fulfillment of nature's inevitable law. And therefore I shall not be backward to lead to you a bride who will supply what is lacking in myself. And if our prayers for the birth of children are answered the offspring will be yours in full parenthood, but surely mine also by adoption" (*On Abraham*, 249–250).[4]

In her comments to her husband, which reflect Abraham's sensitivity toward his wife, Philo's Sarah expresses the importance of becoming a mother, if not biologically then through adoption. She is rational in her resolve to ensure her husband's parenthood.[5] Philo exonerates Sarah of untoward emotions and explicitly addresses the question of jealousy and resentment toward Hagar and Ishmael. Far be it from the paragon of virtue to display a lack of control over emotions. Rather than describing Sarah's feelings, Philo lets her voice them herself. His Sarah strikes a very sympathetic, sensitive note. Other early biblical interpreters, such as the rabbis, adjudicate on behalf of the Israelite matriarch and address the moral issues at stake in the biblical story. Sarah is vindicated; Hagar is vilified.

Ignoring the moral dimensions of the story, Philo develops an elaborate allegorical reading whereby "Hagar" stands for the soul's sojourning, specifically the academic subjects with which the soul must engage on its way to wisdom.[6] Hagar appears fifteen times in Philo's work, not including the twelve times she is mentioned in *On the Preliminary Studies (De Congressu Eruditionis Gratia)*, an entire treatise devoted to the story of Hagar and Sarah. In this by and large word-for-word commentary on Genesis 16:1–6, Abraham is a symbol of the soul in search of wisdom, and as he prepares to be in full possession of wisdom, he must study the "preparatory disciplines." In his quest for knowledge, Abraham marries Sarah and along the way unites with Hagar, who represents the preliminary studies, the profane sciences *(enkyklios paideia)* that are necessary—grammar, rhetoric, geometry, astronomy, and music, for example. Sarah—virtue, in Philo's allegorical reading—is served by the handmaiden Hagar: "When, then, you hear of Hagar as afflicted or evil-entreated by Sarah, do not suppose that you have here one of the usual accompaniments of women's jealousy. It is not women that are spoken of here; it is minds—on the one hand, the mind which exercises itself in the preliminary learning, on the other, the mind which strives to win the palm of virtue and ceases not till it is won" (*De Congressu*, 180).[7]

Philo completely effaces the literal and presents Hagar with relative neutrality and even a modicum of favor, noting that "he . . . who gains wisdom by instruction, will not reject Hagar, for the acquisition of these preliminary subjects is quite necessary" (*De Congressu*, 24).[8] Elsewhere (*Quaestiones in Genesim*, 3.29) he explains that Hagar's flight in Genesis 16:8 is caused by feelings of "reverential awe." In the presence of wisdom and virtue she felt so unworthy that she was impelled to flee.

Josephus, in contrast, justifies Sarah's treatment of Hagar. His accounts of Genesis 16 and 21 illustrate the tendency to interpret the story in Sarah's favor and at Hagar's expense. In his retelling in *Jewish Antiquities*, when she becomes pregnant Hagar turns insolent toward her mistress Sarah, putting on "queenly airs as though the dominion were to pass to her unborn son" (*Jewish Antiquities*, 1.187–90).[9] Humiliated by Sarah's treatment of her, she flees to the wilderness, where she meets an angel of God. In the Bible passage, Hagar is a sympathetic character who heeds the advice of the angel and subordinates herself to Sarah, her mistress. Josephus's angel, however, rebukes Hagar for her insolent and thoughtless behavior, attributes her present plight to her arrogance, and advises her to exert greater self-control, lest her actions continue to cause her greater suffering. Hagar obediently returns, is forgiven, and gives birth to Ishmael.[10]

Similarly, in his account of Genesis 21, Hagar is treated in a matter-of-fact fashion. Josephus omits entirely Hagar's plea to God and embellishes the story by noting that shepherds aided them in the wilderness and hence helped her escape her miseries (*Jewish Antiquities*, 1.215–19). Here, too, Josephus silences the moral issues the biblical text raises.

Josephus thus softens Sarah's image while also somewhat diminishing her importance. After all, she initially loved Ishmael, and it was to protect her biological son, Isaac, that she demanded his expulsion. Josephus also justifies her actions by playing up Hagar's arrogance. Thus, while it may be argued that the matriarch's importance is attenuated in his retelling of the Genesis story, he nonetheless whitewashes her behavior to avoid compromising her moral character.

Jubilees omits any reference to tension between Sarah and Hagar but is unusually explicit about Sarah's reason for casting Ishmael out. At the celebration of Isaac's weaning, Sarah sees how happy Abraham is watching his son Ishmael playing and dancing. Pangs of jealousy overwhelm her, and she requests that Abraham drive them both out. Ishmael, not Hagar, is the source of her discomfort.

Hagar and Keturah in Rabbinic Literature

Rabbinic approaches to biblical figures must take into account philological as well as theological factors; it is not simply a matter of exonerating Jewish ancestors. Perhaps predictably, given the different textual and extratextual factors at play, the rabbinic attitude toward Hagar is inconsistent and nuanced. That is, her depiction in rabbinic literature does not fit neatly into a dyadic framework that deems her entirely good or completely wicked.

Like her son, Ishmael, Hagar is a marginalized biblical figure. Although she is usually portrayed as a nonmember of the Israelite/

Jewish people, she does not represent a specific ethnic group. Rather, like other marginalized biblical figures, including Esau and the children of both Keturah and Ishmael, Hagar serves as a marker of Otherness. In rabbinic literature Esau is often a cipher for Christianity as well as the Roman Empire, and the *pesharim* of the Dead Sea Scrolls employ "Kittim" as code for Rome, but it would be misleading to understand such stand-ins as reflections of or references to a specific people or community.

Keturah and her children are regarded as antipodes of the self-conceived rabbinic notion of Israel, that is, a conceptualization based on an idealized understanding of Israel as the righteous heir of the Abrahamic covenant. In the book of Genesis, the children Abraham has with Keturah are given gifts and sent away from Isaac. They are Abraham's children, yet they are not part of the Abrahamic covenant. We see the difficulty of this situation in *Genesis Rabbah* 61:6, where Abraham is faced with the conundrum of whether to bless Isaac. If he blesses Isaac, his other children must be included. If he does not bless the others, how can he bless Isaac? What should he do? In the end, he blesses none but rather gives them gifts. According to the midrash, when Abraham dies, God blesses Isaac. It is God, not Abraham, who chooses Isaac. (See discussion of this midrash in chapter 5.)

Although the conceptual framework of wisdom literature, which maintains a polarized division of humanity into the righteous and the wicked, the wise and the foolish, in some instances also characterizes rabbinic exegesis, one is hard pressed to detect it readily with respect to liminal figures such as Hagar, who are at times portrayed as positive or neutral characters. Rabbinic engagement with Scripture is more pliable than rigid forms of exegesis. Thus the rabbinic commentary contains a great variety of depictions of biblical characters and interpretations of verses.

Rabbinic literature identifies Hagar in multiple ways. In *Genesis Rabbah* 45:1 Hagar is the daughter of Pharaoh:[11]

R. Shimon b. Yohai said, "Hagar was Pharaoh's daughter. When Pharaoh saw what was done to Sarah in his house, he took his daughter and gave her to Sarah. [See discussion of this below under "Sacrificing Sarah."] He said, 'It is better for my daughter to be a maidservant in this house than a mistress in another,' as it is written, 'And she had a maidservant, an Egyptian, and her name was Hagar.' This is your reward [here there is a play on the Hebrew word for reward, *agar*, and Hagar]."[12]

We also read in *Genesis Apocryphon*, a first-century CE document found among the Dead Sea Scrolls, that Pharaoh gave Hagar to Sarah, although it does not state explicitly that Pharaoh was Hagar's father. Sarah's hatred of Hagar is explained in terms of her feelings toward Nimrod. According to *Targum Pseudo-Jonathan*, Hagar is Nimrod's granddaughter. This association may be attributed to *Pseudo-Jonathan*'s emphasis on the idolatry of Hagar and Ishmael. She is also identified as Nimrod's daughter in Islamic sources.

According to the rabbis, Genesis 16:3—"And gave her to Abram her husband to be a wife to him"—should be read literally. That is, Hagar was Abraham's wife, not his concubine, hence was meant to enjoy all the rights of a wife. The rabbis make Hagar's status of wife more explicit when they interpret Genesis 24:62, "After the death of Abraham, God blessed his son Isaac. And Isaac settled near Be'er-lahai-ro'i." Located in southern Palestine, Be'er-lahai-ro'i is associated both with Hagar's encounter with the angel after she flees from Sarah and with Ishmael's birth. In *Genesis Rabbah* 60:14, the rabbis ask, "Why was Isaac coming from Be'er-lahai-ro'i?" and they answer, "To fetch Hagar." In other words, according to some rabbis, Hagar is Keturah, whom Abraham marries five verses later in Genesis 25:1. Isaac seeks Hagar, who is Keturah, for his father. Given Hagar's association with Be'er-lahai-ro'i, the biblical text lends itself to the interpretation that Isaac was in Be'er-lahai-ro'i to fetch Hagar; however, nowhere in the text are we told explicitly that Hagar and Keturah are the same person. The image of Abraham bringing her back from the desert and making her his wife counteracts the impression of Abraham as insensitive. While Sarah was alive, he listened to her at God's behest, and reluctantly granted her request, but now that she is no longer alive, he is free to bring her back.[13] This story also mitigates against the notion that Abraham had multiple wives.

The identification of Keturah as Hagar is also found in *Genesis Rabbah* 61:4:

Abraham took another wife, whose name was Keturah (Gen. 25:1). R. Yudah said, "This refers to Hagar." R. Nehemiah disagreed. He said to R. Yudah . . . "But the verse says, 'And her name was Keturah [not Hagar].'" R. Yudah replied, "She was perfumed[14] with mitzvot and good deeds."[15] [That is, the word "Keturah" functions as a descriptor.] He [R. Nehemiah] said to him, "Scripture says, 'But to the sons of his concubines, Abraham gave gifts'" (Gen. 25:6). [In other words, Abraham had many concubines.] R. Yudah said to him, "It is written *pei-yud-lamed-gimel-shin-mem: pilagsham*, the one who sat down by the well and said to The Life of all ages, 'See my sorrow.'"

Because of the Hebrew wordplay, the passage is difficult to understand in English and calls for a close look. According to R. Yudah, the biblical verse "Abraham took another wife" refers to Hagar. R. Nehemiah, however, maintains that she is an additional concubine, since Genesis 25:6 refers to concubines. R. Yudah, on the other hand, contends that Genesis 25:1 refers to Hagar, using the misspelling of the Hebrew word for "concubines" in Genesis 25:6 to prove his point. Since one of the letters, the yod of the plural indicative, is missing from *pilagsh'im*, "concubines," *pilagshm* begs for rabbinic interpretation. Using wordplay, R. Yudah interprets the irregularity to indicate that indeed Abraham had only one concubine. He reads *pilagshm* as *pilegesh* (concubine) plus *sham* (there), thereby deriving another meaning from the word *pilagshm*—that is, *pilegesh* (a concubine) was *sham* (there) at the well. And who is the concubine who sat by the well? None other than Hagar.

The dispute between R. Nehemiah and R. Yudah has as much to do with scriptural clarification as it does with certain extratextual concerns. Although *Jubilees* 19:11 explicitly states that Abraham took a third wife, Keturah, this idea was obfuscated by Philo and others, including Christian writers such as Jerome. R. Yudah's argument that Hagar and Keturah are the same person perhaps hinges on the idea that having several concubines does not reflect well on Abraham. This concern may underlie R. Berekiah's interpretation in the same chapter: "Because it is said, 'And she went and wandered' (Gen. 21:4), you might say that she [Hagar] was suspect of immorality: Scripture says, 'Her name was Keturah,' [from the verb form *qal* (*qatar*), to tie up] meaning one who is a seal of a treasure and he finds her with its seal." Here R. Berekiah assumes that Hagar and Keturah are the same person. Like R. Yudah, who claims that she was perfumed with good deeds, he avers that she is "a seal of a treasure." Notice, too, that R. Berekiah anticipates a negative interpretation of "And she went and wandered" and preemptively offers an alternative favorable reading.

Thus the rabbinic depiction of Hagar is fairly neutral or, in the case of Hagar as Keturah, rather positive. As Abraham's wife who is entitled to rights, and as Keturah who is praised for her character, she is a seal of a treasure, "perfumed with mitzvot and good deeds." Again, this portrayal of Hagar speaks to its ramifications regarding Abraham's character. If the rabbis demeaned Hagar and turned her into an unsavory figure, what would that say about Abraham, or even about Sarah, for that matter—Sarah who "gave her to Abram her husband to be a wife to him" (Gen. 16:3)?

For the redactor of *PRE*, this issue is of no concern. Hagar is depicted rather unfavorably there. The sharp contrast drawn in *PRE* between Sarah and Hagar is based on their relationship to Abraham: Sarah has superior status as his wife, and Hagar is only his maidservant:[16] "That same night, the Holy One, Blessed be He appeared to Abraham our father. He said to him, 'Abraham, do you know that Sarah was fit for you as wife? She is your companion and wife of your youth. Hagar is not called your wife nor is Sarah called your maidservant.'" The midrash in *Genesis Rabbah* has the rabbis asserting Hagar's status as Abraham's wife; here, in contrast, the author delineates a clear boundary between the wife and the maidservant. Furthermore, *PRE* tells us that when Hagar arrived in the desert, she began to go astray after worshipping idols in the house of Pharaoh, and because she did so, her water bottle became empty. Here the phrase "she departed and wandered" means that she engaged in idol worship. There is a distinct difference between this interpretation and R. Berekiah's cautionary comment in *Genesis Rabbah* not to interpret "wander" as "immorality."

As in *Genesis Rabbah*, *PRE* 30 regards Hagar as Keturah.[17] Genesis 25:1 reads, "And Abraham again took a wife and her name was

Keturah." Why, *PRE* asks, does Scripture say, "And Abraham again"? The response: "Because the first time she was his wife and again he had sex with her. Her name was Keturah because she was perfumed with all kinds of spices. Another explanation: her name was Keturah because her deeds were as beautiful as incense, and she bore him six children." Thus in *PRE* we find both favorable and unfavorable images of Hagar.

Hagar, associated with sweet-smelling Keturah, is also described as stinking like a donkey. *Aggadat Bereshit*, a tenth-century collection of homilies on the Book of Genesis, includes a midrash that upends the tradition in *Genesis Rabbah* and *PRE* 30. Far from being perfumed with incense, Hagar stinks like a donkey. The context for the midrash is as follows: Genesis 25:12 states, "This is the line of Ishmael, Abraham's son, whom Hagar the Egyptian, Sarah's slave, bore to Abraham," and verse 19 mentions Isaac as the son of Abraham. Does this make Ishmael and Isaac similar? According to the midrash, "God forbid! As Scripture says, 'For the Lord cherishes the way of the righteous, but the way of the wicked is doomed' (Ps. 1:6)." A comparison is made in order to highlight the distinction:

> This may be compared to the fat of a donkey that fell into rose oil. Even though its smell became pleasant from the rose oil, it ended up stinking as it had before . . . The fat of the donkey is Hagar the Egyptian, as it says of the Egyptians (Ezek. 23:20) "whose members were like those of asses . . ." Hagar cleaved to Abraham and gave birth to Ishmael . . . but in the end she returned to her stench as it is written, "And his mother took for him a wife from the land of Egypt" (Gen. 21:21). And this is why [the Bible] says that Abraham gave birth to Isaac whereas it says that Hagar gave birth to Ishmael (37:4).[18]

The midrash is reminiscent of a reference attributed to Abu Nuwas, a Persian classical Arabic poet of the mid-eighth to early ninth century, who describes Hagar as "the putrid-smelling woman." The association of Hagar with odors may have been familiar throughout the Near East. Be that as it may, what then are we to make of these competing images of her? On the one hand Hagar is Abraham's idol-worshipping Egyptian maidservant; on the other she is his wife. She was "perfumed with all kinds of spices" and her "deeds were as beautiful as incense," but she "returned to her stench" as well. In *PRE* when Hagar is away from Abraham she is an idol worshipper, but when she is his wife she is depicted in a more favorable light. It is not surprising that rabbinic works compiled around or after the rise of Islam tend to portray Hagar, as well as Ishmael, more negatively.

In the rabbinic imagination, Hagar is doubly Other. She represents non-Jews generically and is identified as Keturah, another biblical figure. But perhaps to describe her as having a double identity is misleading. Rather, the rabbinic treatment of Hagar is a double effacement of her character. She is Keturah and at the same time represents the nonelect. To be sure, in midrash one finds numerous examples of the use of one biblical figure to identify another: Iscah is Sarah, Ezra is Malakhi, Pinchas is Elijah, Nehemiah is Zerubabel, Melchizedek is Shem. In rabbinic literature Hagar is neither fully a member of Abraham's household nor completely ostracized, and Keturah, similarly, is not discussed in negative terms. After all, these are women associated with Abraham. Even though they do not play as pivotal a role as Sarah in the Jewish metanarrative, their association with Abraham, the patriarch of the Jewish people, places them in a liminal position between acceptance and rejection, between being part of and being apart from the family of Abraham.

Christian exegetes who took their allegorical lead from Philo, including Origen and Ephrem, read Abraham as representing wisdom and learning. That he takes a wife at the advanced age of one hundred signifies the limitless vitality of wisdom. As Origen notes, Abraham was at least 137 years old when he took Keturah as his wife. Scripture uses language relating to "wife," implying long-term fidelity, to indicate his continued learning.[19] In his *Commentary on Genesis*, Ephrem claims that by marrying Keturah and having many sons with her, Abraham spread the worship of God: "through the uprightness of his many sons who were to be scattered in lands throughout the entire earth, knowledge and worship of the one God would be spread."[20] Augustine, however, reads the verse literally and uses it as evidence that it is not a sin to marry a second time after the death of the first wife.[21]

In the Islamic tradition, Keturah is considered Abraham's third
wife. When Sarah died, he married the Canaanite woman Keturah,
who bore him six children. According to al-Tha'labi's *Tales of the
Prophets*, Abraham also married another woman, the Arab woman
Hajun, daughter of Ahib (Uhayb), who gave him five sons.[22] That
Abraham had more than one wife is a nonissue in the Islamic sources,
as it was acceptable to do so.

The Christian Sarah and Hagar

The Christian interpretation of the Sarah-Hagar narrative finds its
roots in the writings of Paul and Philo.[23] Like Philo, Paul allego-
rizes both women, one the mother of Abraham's free descendants,
the other the mother of his enslaved progeny. In Galatians 4:21–5:1
Paul identifies Sarah as heavenly Jerusalem and Hagar as earthly
Jerusalem:

> Tell me, you who desire to be subject to the law, will you not
> listen to the law? For it is written that Abraham had two sons,
> one by a slave woman and the other by a free woman. One, the
> child of the slave, was born according to the flesh; the other,
> the child of the free woman, was born through the promise.
> Now this is an allegory:[24] these women are two covenants. One
> woman, in fact, is Hagar, from Mount Sinai, bearing children
> for slavery. Now Hagar is Mount Sinai in Arabia and corre-
> sponds to the present Jerusalem, for she is in slavery with her
> children. But the other woman corresponds to the Jerusalem
> above; she is free, and she is our mother. For it is written, "Re-
> joice, you childless one, you // who bear no children, // burst
> into song and shout, you // who endure no birth pangs; // for
> the children of the desolate woman are more numerous than
> the children of the one // who is married." Now you, my friends,
> are children of the promise, like Isaac. But just as at that time
> the child who was born according to the flesh persecuted the
> child who was born according to the Spirit, so it is now also. But
> what does the scripture say? "Drive out the slave and her child;
> for the child of the slave will not share the inheritance with

the child of the free woman." So then, friends, we are children, not of the slave but of the free woman. (Gal. 4:21–5:1)

Paul's reading plays a significant role in building a basis on which later exegetes forge a hostile antipodal relationship between Judaism and Christianity. Not surprisingly, in *City of God*, 15:2, Augustine writes that Hagar symbolizes "earthly city," or the sinful condition of humanity. Paul's interpretation displaces the Jews as heirs of the promise and establishes those who follow his teachings as "children of the promise, like Isaac." (Chapter 5 discusses Paul's interpretation at length.)

Paul was referring to the immediate situation in Galatia, where his opponents' interpretation of the Torah created tension between Jewish and Gentile Christians.[25] Later Christian writers transpose the analogy to maintain an opposition between the church and the synagogue, Judaism and Christianity. Hagar and Sarah become codes for "synagogue" and "church," the former fallow, the latter fertile with Gentile believers. The church fathers deployed the narrative for theological and ecclesiastical purposes; its deleterious effects left an indelible mark on Jewish-Christian relations. This interpretation of Sarah and Hagar has fed—and continues to feed—anti-Semitic sentiment.

One of the earliest references to Paul's reading of the story is found in Tertullian's *Adversus Marcionem*, which dates from around 200–211 CE and attempts to refute Marcion's gnostic understanding of Christianity. According to Tertullian, the "one from Mount Sinai" refers to the synagogue of the Jews, which leads to bondage, whereas the other is the holy church. Through the use of allegory, Paul undoubtedly shows that Christianity had a noble birth: from Isaac, Abraham's son born of the free woman. From Ishmael, the son of the bond maid, came the legal bondage of Judaism (*Adversus Marcionem*, 5.4.8).[26] Christian writers turned the Jewish lineage to Abraham via Isaac on its head.

Philo's writings had a ripple effect on Christian writers such as Clement of Alexandria, Didymus of Alexandria, Justin Martyr, Tertullian, and Origen. Clement explicitly credits Philo, the etymological expert, for his interpretation of Hagar as a symbol of Greek learning and culture (*Stromateis* 1.5.28–32).[27] Hagar, a symbol of Greek philosophy, is preliminary to the attainment of wisdom—Sarah. A major difference between Clement and his predecessor is that Philo connects wisdom to law while Clement associates wisdom with Christ.[28]

The work of Origen, Clement's successor as head of the catechetical school in Alexandria, is indebted to Philo. Origen did not merely incorporate the works of others, however, but had insights of his own. In his treatment of Abraham's polygamy, for instance, Origen reads "wives" allegorically to refer to virtues, thus encouraging Christians to take as many wives, that is, virtues, as possible.[29] In his sermon on Genesis 21, Sarah is identified with Christianity and Hagar with Judaism, yet instead of using Hagar to represent the law, Origen turns to the bottle of water Abraham gave Hagar when he sent her off into the wilderness and maintains that the bottle failed to provide sufficient water because those born according to the flesh drink from it: "The bottle of the Law is the letter, from which that carnal people drinks, and thence receives understanding. This letter frequently fails them. It cannot extricate itself; for the historical understanding is defective in many ways. But the Church drinks from the evangelic and apostolic fountains which never fail, but 'run in its streets' [Proverbs 5:16], because they always abound and flow in the breadth of spiritual interpretation. The Church drinks also 'from wells' when it draws and examines certain deeper things from the Law" (*Genesis Homilies*, 7.5). Origen continues his homily with a reference to the Samaritan woman in John 4. Hagar's eyes open to Christ, the true well of living water.[30]

In Origen's hands, Hagar is both Judaized and Christianized; she is synagogue and church. In this instance he takes his lead from Philo, not from Paul, who presents Hagar as the forebear of enslaved children. Origen transforms her into a freeborn child of Sarah. His affirmation of Hagar moves beyond both Philo and Paul, presenting us with a rehabilitated and Christianized Hagar who in the biblical passage received a revelation of comfort and promise from God.

Origen's reading of Hagar is complicated—allegorical yet anchored in the literal. While she is rehabilitated and Christianized, she is also identified with the synagogue. This linkage plays out in the description of Hagar's inability to locate the well in the desert. She represents the synagogue that remains in darkness, blind to the truth, until the angel of God removes "the veil of the letter" so the synagogue can see the "living water." Origen writes: "For the Jews lie around the well itself, but their eyes are closed and they cannot drink from the well of the Law and the prophets" (*Genesis Homilies*, 7.6).[31] And his reading of Hagar's expulsion on account of the persecution of Isaac, "the spirit," at the hands of her son, "the law," implicates her in her son's behavior. Furthermore, Origen uses the Sarah-Hagar allegory to illustrate a difference between Jewish and Christian exegetical understandings of Scripture. Bound to the literal reading of Scripture, Jews have an unquenchable thirst—the bottle does not suffice. Christians, in contrast, drink from flowing fountains of wisdom and insight. Needless to say, Origen's caricature of the multifaceted Jewish interpretive traditions of the ancient period leaves much to be desired.

Cyril of Alexandria, too, reads Hagar as the mother of the Jews whose eyes are closed, but in this case her eyes remain shut: "So, when the mother of the Jews was sent away, she wandered for a long time in the wilderness, and there was some danger of her becoming wholly destroyed. But if she should begin to weep in time and cry out to God, she will be shown mercy abundantly. For God will open the eyes of their understanding, and they too will see the fountain of living water, that is, Christ" (*Glaphyra on Genesis*, 3.10).[32]

Allegory was used also to asceticize the story. Clement of Alexandria (d. ca. 215 CE), among others, portrays Sarah and Abraham as an asexual couple. By harking back to Abraham's claim to Abimelech, king of Gerar (Gen. 20:1–2), that Sarah is really his sister, Clement makes a case for the chastity of wives. That Sarah "laughed" when the visitors told her that she would bear a son (Gen. 18:12) is not, according to Clement, a sign of her disbelief but rather a reaction of shame to having engaged in sexual intercourse.[33] In his literal reading, Didymus explains that Scripture teaches that saints married not for the purpose of pleasure but for procreation.

Other church fathers, however, eschewed such ascetically inclined interpretations. One such exegete was Ambrose of Milan. Despite his several treatises extolling virginity, he points to the wives of the patriarchs as exemplars of the virtues of marriage. Others, too, such as John Chrysostom, refer to this narrative in order to illustrate not only proper wifely but also husbandly behavior. Chrysostom offers a sympathetic image of Sarah as the reasonable wife who questions her husband's excessive affections for Ishmael. Her request that he cast out Ishmael and Hagar is not severe, for example. In explaining why God intervenes on Sarah's behalf, Chrysostom praises her steadfast commitment to her husband, a commitment demonstrated on more than one occasion. She surrendered herself to save his life and ensure his prosperity. She saved him in Egypt, and she was responsible for the great esteem Abimelech bestowed on him as well.

Chrysostom and Ephrem the Syrian explain her behavior with respect to the inheritance. In fact, Ephrem tells us explicitly that her reaction had nothing to do with jealousy:

> Then Sarah, who showed no envy in any matter that concerned herself, became envious in this matter concerning her son. She was not envious of Hagar . . . Since it was a matter of God's promise, and the son of the concubine thought that he would be coheir with the son of the freewoman, Sarah said, "Cast out the slave woman and her son, because it is not just that a son of handmaid should have any inheritance together with that son of the promise, to whom it was promised by God. It is not right that you be opposed to God and make an heir him whom God has not made an heir."[34]

According to Ephrem, Hagar is haughty because she thought her seed would enter and possess the land promised to Abraham. When Hagar flees out of fear, she receives a vision that Ishmael will dwell at the boundary of his kinsmen. She goes back to Sarah and Abraham to tell them about it. Sarah is relieved.[35] The women of Abraham's household are reconciled.

The church fathers' use of the narrative of Sarah, Hagar, and Abraham demonstrates ways writers attempted to exert Christianity's superiority over Judaism through interpretation. The negative statements about Judaism found throughout the works of the church fathers reflect a desire to distinguish Christianity from Judaism. While Christians often locate the break between the two in the works of Paul, the actual separation did not occur overnight, certainly not during Paul's life. He furnished the scriptural anchoring for the theological differences, but on the ground Judaism remained very attractive to those who followed the teachings of Jesus, so much so that the church fathers went to great lengths to disparage Jewish traditions. Origen, who lived in Caesarea, near a thriving Jewish community, was undoubtedly aware of the fact that many Christians took part in Jewish services and festivals. It is thought, too, that Christians and Jews may have competed for pagan converts.[36]

As in Jewish sources, Sarah and Hagar in early Christian writings are often presented as opposites, but also as in Jewish sources, Hagar is not always envisioned unfavorably. Origen's nonliteral reading, for example, includes her among the children of Sarah. In the family of Abraham, Sarah plays a far more important role than Hagar, who when included is placed at its margins. Abraham's wives exchange positions in Islam, Hagar playing a more central role than Sarah, but in Islam the less important wife, Sarah, is still a full member of Abraham's family.

Sarah and Hagar (Hajar) in the Islamic Tradition

Both women are respected matriarchs in Islam. Sarah gives birth to Isaac, the father of many prophets, and through Hagar's son Ishmael, the Seal of Prophecy, Muhammad, will issue forth. The Qur'an alludes to Sarah and Hagar but does not mention them explicitly. For instance, Q. 51:25–30, about the honored guests of Abraham, echoes Genesis 18:1–15, the episode in which three men visit Abraham's tent. In both the Bible and the Qur'an, Abraham feeds the men, who give him good tidings of a son; according to the Qur'an, the son will be "gifted with knowledge." In light of her barrenness, Sarah is incredulous. Although the Qur'an does not explicitly name her, it is evident that the mention of Abraham's wife is a reference to Sarah, who in Genesis laughs at the prospect of conceiving at her advanced age. The only implicit reference to Hagar in the Qur'an is at Q. 14:37, where it is indicated that Abraham has settled some of his offspring in the vicinity of the Ka'bah. The Islamic commentary tradition makes the connection between Hagar and Ishmael's resettlement and the building of the Ka'bah more explicit by amplifying their story.

Extraqur'anic sources extol Sarah's beauty and virtue. According to a report in al-Tabari's *History of the Prophets and Patriarchs (Ta'rīkh al-rusul wa'l-mulūk)*, she was obedient to Abraham and was one of the best human beings who ever existed.[37] In one tradition, disguised as a man, Satan visits Sarah and tells her that Abraham is going to sacrifice Isaac:

> Sarah said, "There is no truth to that, he would not sacrifice his own son." Satan said, "By God, it is true." Sarah said, "And why would he sacrifice him?" He replied, "He claims that his Lord ordered him to do it." Sarah replied, "If his lord ordered him to do that, it is best that he obey." Then Satan left Sarah and went to Isaac.[38]

Al-Tha'labi reports that al-Suddi, Ibn Yasar, and others transmit accounts claiming that Sarah became pregnant with Isaac after Hagar was already pregnant but that the women gave birth at the same time. According to this report, the boys grew up together. One day when they were competing in archery, Abraham took on the role of judge and determined that Ishmael was the winner. With Sarah watching, he seated Ishmael on his lap and Isaac by his side. One cannot help but recall the image in *Jubilees* 17:2 with Ishmael seated in front of his father, a placement that made Sarah jealous. On this occasion, the day of the archery competition, she spoke to Abraham bitterly: "You have turned to the son of the servant-girl and have seated him in your bosom, whereas you have turned to my son and seated him at your side, while you have vowed that you would not injure me or do any evil to me."[39]

Al-Tha'labi gives reasons for the sending away of Hagar and her son—Sarah's envy and her fear that Ishmael might physically threaten her son, as well as her fear that he would inherit over Isaac. Her jealousy was so fierce and overwhelming that "she swore to cut off a piece of Hagar's flesh and deface her appearance," but she thinks twice about it and settles on piercing her ears. Al-Tabari's history also mentions that the boys fought. Sarah becomes angry and jealous toward Hagar, who is sent away and brought back, only to be sent away again and brought back yet again. In this rendition, however, Sarah does more than pierce Hagar's ears: "She said to herself, 'I shall cut off her nose, I shall cut off her ear—but no, that would deform her. I will circumcise her instead.' So she did that, and Hagar took a piece of cloth to wipe the blood away. For that reason women have been circumcised and have taken pieces of cloth down to today."[40]

Ibn Kathir's rendition of the birth of Ishmael in his *al-Bidāyah wa'l Nihāyah fī al-Ta'rīkh* most closely parallels the biblical story and does not, like other renditions, simply note Sarah's jealousy. Rather it places some blame on Hagar for Sarah's jealousy: "When she [Hagar] became pregnant her soul was exalted and she became proud and arrogant to her mistress, so Sarah became jealous of her."[41]

One day Isaac and Ishmael fought, as boys do, and Sarah became angry at Hagar, according to al-Tha'labi. While the biblical word is not used, this Islamic tradition explains the idea of "playing" as boyish rough-and-tumble. Sarah confronts Hagar, saying to her, "You will not live in the same town as I." It is at that point that she commands Abraham to send her away. In some renditions, God commands that Abraham build a house for him, and Abraham sets out with Hagar and Ishmael. The altercation between the wives is absent. In any case, the cause of the departure has to do with the sons and not the mothers. In fact, when Sarah gives Hagar to Abraham, she does so because she considers her pure.

According to several accounts, God inspires Abraham to take Hagar and her son to Mecca: "Lord, I have settled some of my offspring in a barren valley near your sacred house, so that they may be constant in devotion. Put in the hearts of men kindness towards them, and provide them with the earth's fruits, so that they may give thanks" (Q. 14:37). Abraham settles them in Mecca and its environs, rather than bringing them into the wilderness in the vicinity of Palestine. (The location is important in light of the later episode of the building of the Ka'bah and the pilgrimage.) Unlike the biblical account, in which Abraham sends them away with only a bottle of water that runs out,[42] in the Qur'an he prays for their safety and future well-being. He accompanies them to Mecca, thus fulfilling his responsibility and displaying his love.

In al-Tha'labi's account, sending Hagar and Ishmael away into the wilderness is not Abraham's doing but God's; Abraham behaved according to God's will. In this rendition, then, the moral ambiguity often associated with the biblical episode becomes moot. To be sure, in the biblical account God intervenes and tells a reluctant husband to listen to his wife, but God does not tell Abraham to cast them into the wilderness. Moreover, in al-Tha'labi's account, Abraham accompanies them. That is to say, the Islamic account makes clear that God plans for them to go to Mecca, a place of "thorny shrubs, acacia, and thistles," with the purpose of establishing ritual prayer. This is not an expulsion but a resettlement. They are not cast out with few provisions; rather, Abraham settles them in the vicinity of Mecca. God, as Abraham tells Gabriel, commanded him to place them in that location.

Once Abraham fulfills his duty he departs, but Hagar follows him and asks, "To whom have you entrusted us? Did God command you to do this?" He replies, "Yes." Hagar responds, "Then He will not let us perish," and Abraham goes back to Syria.[43] The incident reflects Abraham's obedience to God's command and Hagar's trust in divine providence. Both demonstrate submission to the will of God.

The narrative in al-Tha'labi mentions that Hagar carried with her an old skin with water that was soon used up, but it does not indicate that Abraham gave it to her. In al-Tabari's history, there is no reference to the bottle, but just as in al-Tha'labi and the Bible, Ishmael becomes thirsty. In the Islamic tradition, Hagar's search for water becomes woven into the Hajj rituals. While looking for water she encounters the Angel Gabriel and discovers the well of Zamzam. Here, too, she explains to Gabriel that Abraham has entrusted her to God, to which he replies, "Then he has entrusted you to One, Generous and Sufficient." He then proceeds to foretell Abraham's return and his and Ishmael's building a House for God "whose place is here." Hagar then meets a band of Jurhum, who settle there with her and become the first inhabitants of Mecca. Al-Tha'labi's account not only depicts Abraham as obedient but portrays Hagar as trusting in divine providence also, and it associates her with Mecca and by extension the rituals associated with it.

Although there is no explicit reference in the Qur'an to when Hagar was given to Sarah, *Saḥīḥ al-Bukhārī* refers to it this way: "Allah's Apostle said, The Prophet Abraham migrated with Sarah.

The people (of the town where they migrated) gave her Ajar (i.e., Hajar). Sarah returned and said to Abraham, 'Do you know that Allah has humiliated that pagan and he has given a slave-girl for my service?'"[44] The background seems to be the occasion when Abraham traveled with Sarah and encountered a tyrant. In some instances she is considered Nimrod's granddaughter, a reference we find also in *Targum Pseudo-Jonathan*, which emphasizes her idolatry.

The mother of Ishmael, the prophet through whom Muhammad descends, does not play a serious role in the early doctrinal history of Islam. It is likely that over time she becomes more prominent in the Islamic metanarrative, as in the case of her son.[45] None of the early *muffasirūn*, such as Muqatil, al-Tabari, or al-Tha'labi, discusses or even alludes to Hagar's connection to al-Safa and al-Marwah (Q. 2:158), two small hills that are part of the Hajj ritual commemorating Hagar's search for water. In interpretations of Qur'an 2:158, the ritual is associated with Abraham and in some instances with Abraham and Ishmael, but not with Hagar. However, in explanations of Q. 14:37, she is explicitly linked to the ritual, and moreover it is in this episode that the ritual nexus between Abraham, Ishmael, and Muhammad is established.

Sarah and Hagar were employed in internecine ninth-century polemics between Persian Muslims claiming to be descendants of Isaac and Arab Muslims who traced their lineage through Ishmael and thus Hagar. Persian Muslims used Hagar's slave status to denigrate Arab Muslims who asserted superiority over non-Arab Muslims. The controversy is a reminder that in the ninth century Ishmael and Hagar's prominence within the tradition had not yet been established. One may in fact argue that they grew in importance over time as Arab Muslims attempted to assert their superiority over other Muslims and as Islam's conceptualization continued to evolve vis-à-vis Judaism and Christianity, in much the same way that Judaism and Christianity developed vis-à-vis broader sociocultural and religious contexts.

My survey of some of the ways Jewish, Christian, and Muslim writers interpreted the story of Sarah and Hagar renders a variety of depictions. As the wife of Abraham and the mother of Isaac, Sarah is often above reproach in her behavior, although we see some portrayals

that question her attitude toward Hagar. In the battle of the matriarchs, more often than not, Jewish and Christian sources shift the
blame onto Hagar, whereas Muslim sources do not whitewash Sarah's jealousy. As in contemporary depictions of both women, ancient
and medieval sources valorize them, holding them up as models of
resilience in the face of tragedy. Yet at times they are vilified, blamed
for the troubles that befall them. Hagar is an idol worshipper, but
she is also Abraham's wife. She is cast out of his household, but she
is brought back. Hagar is perfumed with incense, but she also smells
putrid. Beyond the contradictions and ambiguities, Sarah and Hagar
are always depicted as mothers who fiercely protect their sons.
Christian interpretations tend to uphold a dichotomy between the two,
such that one represents the heavenly and spiritual, the other the
earthly and physical. Muslim sources, however, do not view these
matriarchs in such terms, for both are the mothers of prophets and
the wives of Abraham. Sarah is allowed to be jealous and to demand
that Hagar and Ishmael be sent away. Muslim sources regard both
women as within the family of Abraham, whereas many of the Jewish
and Christian sources I have examined consider Hagar either a liminal figure or a non-Jew or non-Christian, and in some Christian
sources she is considered the non-Christian Jew.

Sacrificing Sarah

A famine in the land causes Abraham and Sarah to migrate to Egypt
(Gen. 12). As they are about to enter Egypt, Abraham says to his
wife, "I know what a beautiful woman you are. If the Egyptians see
you, and think, 'She is his wife,' they will kill me and let you live.
Please say that you are my sister, that it may go well with me because
of you, and that I may remain alive thanks to you" (Gen. 12:11–13).
As Abraham predicts, because of her beauty, Sarah is taken to the
Pharaoh's palace. In turn the Pharaoh treats Abraham well, bestow-
ing on him sheep, oxen, servants, donkeys, mules, and camels.

Jubilees mentions this episode in the passive voice, that is, Sarah
is torn away from Abraham after dwelling in Egypt for five years.
Pharaoh takes her, so his house is plagued. In other words, Abraham
does not tell Sarah to keep his cover. In *Genesis Apocryphon*, included

in the cache of the Dead Sea Scrolls, Abraham relates a dream he has had about a cedar and an especially beautiful palm tree. Humans came to chop down the cedar so that the palm tree can stand on its own, but the palm tree speaks up: "Do not chop down the cedar, for both of us are from one root!" Thanks to the palm tree's protection, the cedar is left standing. Abraham wakes up and recounts the dream: the Egyptians will seek to kill him but will spare her. He asks her to say that he is her brother so he shall remain alive by her protection. In this rendition, Abraham's character is not called into question. He interprets a divine message conveyed nocturnally and acknowledges that because of Sarah he was not slain (*Gen. Apoc.* 20:10).

In *Genesis Rabbah* 40:4, Abraham subordinates himself to Sarah by making her the principal actor and himself of secondary importance, for as Scripture says, "And because of her it went well for Abram" (Gen. 12:16). In another midrash, the rabbis offer details absent in the story. Genesis 12:14 reads: "When Abram entered Egypt, the Egyptians saw how very beautiful the woman was." Why does Scripture indicate that Abram entered Egypt without mentioning Sarah? Why doesn't the verse say she was with her husband? True to form, the rabbis fill in the narrative lacuna by explaining that he put her in a box and locked her in it. When he came to the customs house, the officer demanded that he pay custom dues. Abraham obliged. The customs officer told Abraham to open the box so he could see what was in it, and when Abraham did, the entire land of Egypt radiated with Sarah's beauty. The rabbis go on to explain that Eve's beauty was transmitted to each generation, but that actually Sarah was even more beautiful than Eve (*Gen. Rab.* 40:5).

According to the rabbis, Pharaoh took possession of Sarah for one night, and as a result he and his household were smitten:

> The entire night Sarah lay stretched out on her face, crying, "Sovereign of the Universe! Abraham went forth from his land with your assurance, and I went forth with faith; Abraham is outside the prison while I am within!" The Holy One, blessed be He said to her: "Whatever I do, I do for your sake, and all will say, "It is because of Sarah it went well with Abraham." (*Gen. Rab.* 41:2)

The rabbis give voice to Sarah's anger. Why is she imprisoned and her modesty imperiled while Abraham is free from harm? When Abraham left his homeland, God made a promise to him, but Sarah left on complete faith. God responds by letting her know that she will be rewarded—that is, that Abraham is saved by her deeds.

In *Genesis Rabbah* 41:2, Sarah tells Pharaoh that she is married, but nonetheless he attempts to violate her: "All that night an angel stood with a whip in his hand. When she commanded, 'Strike,' he struck, and when she commanded him to stop, he stopped. Why such severity? Because she told him [Pharaoh], 'I am a married woman,' yet he would not leave her." The midrashic unit ends by drawing a connection between this incident with Pharaoh and its parallel in Genesis 20, where Abraham tells Abimelech that Sarah is his sister and she tells him that Abraham is her brother: "R. Eleazar[46] said: 'We know that Pharaoh was smitten with leprosy and Abimelech with the closing up [of the orifices: Gen. 20:18, "For the Lord had closed fast every womb of the household of Abimelech because of Sarah, the wife of Abraham"]. How do we know that what is said here [in this verse] is to be applied there [in the other verse], and vice versa? Because "for the sake of" occurs in both places, thus an analogy may be drawn between the two.'" In other words, in this case, too, God acted on account of Sarah's faith in God and self-sacrifice for the sake of her husband.

In his commentary to Genesis 12:10, the great medieval Jewish philosopher and scholar Rabbi Moses ben Nachman (Ramban), also known as Nachmanides (1194–1270), who lived most of his life in Spain, offers a completely different understanding of the episode in Egypt. He does not unequivocally indict Abraham for placing his wife in harm's way, nor does he justify his action. Abraham, according to Nachmanides, inadvertently committed a great sin by taking his righteous wife out of the Promised Land and bringing her to Egypt. Because Abraham did not trust God would provide for him and Sarah during the famine, he left the Promised Land, which in turn resulted in the precarious turn of events. Where was Abraham's trust in God? After all, just a few verses earlier, God promises Abraham's descendants this very land.[47]

Early Christian sources, in comparison, betray little interest in this chapter of the lives of the matriarch and patriarch. Didymus of

Alexandria regards Abraham's suggestion that Sarah tell them that she is his sister and not also his wife an intelligent compromise. Abraham trusts that God will watch over his marriage, given how God guided him during his emigration from his own country (*On Genesis*, 226–227). In *On Abraham* (1.2.6), Ambrose defends Sarah's lying to the Egyptians: she is willing to risk her modesty in order to save her husband's life. Ambrose ignores the fact that Abraham suggests to Sarah that she lie—note that although Didymus does not consider this a lie, Ambrose does—but Augustine attempts to exonerate Abraham by claiming that he told no lie in calling Sarah his sister (*City of God*, 16.19). According to Augustine, because Sarah is a kinswoman, she is considered his sister. He uses Lot as an example— Lot, who is Abraham's nephew, is also called his brother in Genesis 14:14 and 14:16. Abraham did not deny that Sarah was his wife; he simply omitted this fact, and thus did nothing wrong. Abraham trusted in God, and indeed it ended well for him and Sarah. According to Augustine, she was not defiled by Pharaoh, who suffered such afflictions as to make cohabitation impermissible.

There is nothing surprising in early Christian responses to the episode, but in a 180-line Syriac narrative poem attributed to Ephrem (although likely an anonymous work of the fifth century) Sarah is given a striking role.[48] She journeys to Egypt in order "to teach Egypt of her Lord, and like the Samaritan woman telling the Samaritans, she showed them the truth" (lines 35–36).[49] Here, she and Abraham travel to Egypt not only because of famine but also because of religious persecution.

When they arrive, Sarah tries unsuccessfully to conceal her beauty, and as in *Genesis Rabbah* 40:5, she is hidden in a chest. Noticing that her husband is distraught, she asks him to share his concerns with her so that she may be a comfort to him. When she hears of his fears, she too is horrified at the prospect of Abraham's death and suggests that they return to Canaan, but Abraham refuses and asks her to say to the Egyptians that he is her brother, and on her account perhaps he might be saved and his "honour will grow in Egypt" (line 65). She refuses even to consider the prospect of being anyone else's wife. She conceals herself in rags and puts dust on her head—all for naught. They are taken to Pharaoh, and Abraham tells him that Sarah is his sister, at which point she complies with her husband's stratagem.

At the "joyful wedding feast" for Sarah and Pharaoh, Sarah be-
seeches the dumbstruck Abraham to do something, to implore God,
to supplicate and cry out for deliverance. As the Egyptians come for
her, she rebukes her beloved:

> Alas, my lord, how much you have tested me, and how
>   much I have loved you:
> when I recognized God to be with you, I went forth from
>   my parents,
> and to wherever it pleased you, willingly I went with
>   you.
> But now you have laid for me a trap, while knowing that
>   it would be to me a stumbling block,
> for here I stand, about to go off today as a wife for a
>   pagan.
> Perhaps it was because I did not have any children that
>   you have separated me today from your side.
> But I know, by God, that I am more sad than you.
> Alas, that news of you is going out in the land, how you
>   have sold me for the bread of your youth!
> O my fair wedding crown, farewell, for the unbelievers
>   are mocking at me.[50]

Abraham's silence is deafening, and his immobility as Sarah embraces him before Pharaoh snatches her away unsettles the reader.
Just as Pharaoh enters the bridal chamber, Sarah's prayers, along
with Abraham's, reach God, who intervenes.[51]

Sarah's prominence and her role of benefiting her husband to this
degree are quite unusual in ancient and early medieval sources, to
say nothing of Abraham's pronounced impotence in the face of such
peril. The poem depicts her sympathetically and subverts Abraham's
valor, which is noteworthy in light of his characterization as fearless,
whether against Nimrod or during his military campaign to rescue
Lot (Gen. 14) or even when questioning God for his decision to destroy Sodom and Gomorrah (Gen. 18). When Sarah suggests that
they go back to Canaan, he not only refuses but hopes that his honor
in Egypt will grow. Moreover, she kneels in obeisance at his feet,

begging him to comprehend what is about to happen to her, but Abraham remains silent and still. He puts her in harm's way, and when she pleads with him, he is incapable of providing assistance.

Such a display of Abraham's severely compromised character is rare in extrascriptural sources. More often than not, Abraham's questionable behavior is whitewashed, the blame reassigned. Interpreters ask, for example, why Abraham, a gracious, wealthy man, would cast out Hagar and his firstborn with merely "some bread and a skin of water" (Gen. 20:14), for such an act would surely be tantamount to passing a death sentence. In *Genesis Rabbah 33:13*, the rabbis ask how Hagar could put Ishmael on her back, since according to their reckoning he was twenty-seven years old. To explain how it was possible for the father to send off the mother and child into the wilderness with an insufficient supply of water, the rabbis point to Sarah, who cast an evil eye on Ishmael. He became ill and feverish, and thus drank all the water. Sarah is blamed. Abraham did in fact give ample provisions; it was Sarah who was responsible for the changed circumstances.

Ibn Ezra (ca. 1089–1167) shifts the blame squarely onto Sarah:[52] "They ask, how could Abraham chase his son out of his house? How could he send away mother and child empty-handed? Where was his kindness? However, I am amazed at those who are amazed at Abraham, for Abraham acted according to God's dictates. Had he acted contrary to Sarah's wishes and given money to Hagar then he would have transgressed God's command. However, ultimately, after Sarah's death, he gave gifts to Ishmael's children."[53] Abraham would have given Hagar money, Ibn Ezra argues, but he did not want to go against his wife's wishes; doing so would have been a transgression of God's command to do as Sarah tells him. Ibn Ezra then tells us that Abraham may have given Hagar gold or silver. Be that as it may, Abraham made sure her provisions would last her until she arrived in Beersheba. The supplies did not in fact last, but that was because she got lost. Thus the blame is turned on Hagar, in this case, not on Abraham's stinginess. When Sarah died, the generous Abraham provided for his grandchildren.

While the Abraham of the Qur'an behaves righteously, the Muslim tradition—the *Saḥīḥ al-Bukhārī* (a compendium of ḥadīth about the prophet Muhammad) and elsewhere—does take up the matter of

Abraham's three prevarications. Abu Huraira narrates: Abraham did not tell a lie except on three occasions. Twice for the sake of Allah when he said, "I am sick" (Q. 37:89) and when he said, "No, it was done by the biggest of them (the idols)—this one" (Q. 21:63), and third while Abraham and Sarah were journeying and passed by a tyrant. According to al-Tha'labi, someone informs that tyrant that Abraham is accompanied by the most beautiful of women and describes her beauty and comeliness. The tyrant sends for Abraham, who appears before him, and the tyrant says to him: "What is this woman to you?" He replies, "She is my sister," fearing that if he said, "She is my wife" the tyrant would kill him. The tyrant says to Abraham, "Adorn her and send her to me so that I may lay eyes on her." Abraham returns to Sarah and says to her, "This tyrant asked me about you and I told him that you were my sister, so do not make a liar out of me with him. For you are indeed my sister in the book of God, and in this land there is no other Muslim besides you and me." She goes to the tyrant, who begins to stretch out his hand toward her, but his hand remains stuck to his chest, paralyzed. When the tyrant sees what has happened (some accounts claim that this happens three times), he shows her great esteem, requests that she ask her Lord to release his hand, and promises not to harm her. In some accounts the tyrant unsuccessfully attempts to reach for Sarah three times, after which point he returns her to Abraham and gives her a Coptic (Egyptian) slave-girl. When Abraham asks what happened, Sarah responds, "May God avert from (me) the cunning of the adulterer (who covets what he sees), and may He take Hagar away from me as a servant."[54]

Present-Day Readings of Sarah and Hagar

Early interpretive traditions exhibit an interest in portraying Sarah as a woman of piety and attempt to justify her feelings toward Hagar. At the same time, she is depicted as envious and vulnerable. In the hands of Jewish and Christian writers, Hagar's character is compromised vis-à-vis the matriarch. Sources vary: some consider her Abraham's wife; others emphasize her status as maidservant. Islamic texts speak of both women as Abraham's wives, and Hagar demonstrates complete trust in God—but not only Hagar, for Sarah too is a believer in God. Both women are honored matriarchs—polemical writings against Hagar notwithstanding—who gave birth to a line of prophets.

Even contemporary readers and interpreters take an interest in interrogating how their story addresses current social and political concerns from a theological perspective. The biblical story focuses on Sarah and casts Hagar off to the margins, but as some writers argue, Hagar is the first person visited by an angel in the Bible (Gen. 16:7) and the first to receive an annunciation (16:11–12). She attempts to liberate herself from an oppressive situation, and in Genesis 16:13 she bestows the name of God: "And she called the LORD who spoke to her, 'You are El-ro'i.'"[55] Because of the power she possesses, despite having been shunted to the sidelines, Hagar becomes a symbol for the disenfranchised. Hers is the voice of oppressed women. According to Dolores Williams, for well over two hundred years African Americans have appropriated the biblical figure of Hagar.[56] Williams notes the narration's efficacy in the construction of womanist theology, the primary audience of which is the African-American community, although others are invited into the dialogue. In this interpretive framework, Hagar is an analogue for African-American womanhood. "Like Hagar," Williams writes, "some African American slave women experienced upper-class white women taking their children away from them."[57] She understands the narrative as a convergence of religion and politics that has empowered African-American women whose confession of faith in God's sustaining power is passed orally from one generation to the next. Hagar's story is seen also as a story of survival in light of economic disparity, of God's sustaining power and love for the lowly slave.

Williams employs interdisciplinary methods to analyze references to Hagar in African-American culture from slave time to the present. An elaborate method of exegesis, protogesis takes as its starting point African-American cultural deposits in order to uncover "some of the ideas and beliefs about women and religion that African American culture has carried in its stream over time."[58] Other than the fact that protogesis focuses solely on the African-American experience, it is unclear how it differs from other interdisciplinary forms of exegesis, especially those pressed, as in this case, into the service of constructive theology. Be that as it may, Williams's approach high-lights ways the biblical story is appropriated and how that in turn shapes a community's consciousness about God.

Some scholars understand the struggle between Sarah and Hagar as a struggle against patriarchal oppression.[59] As one scholar writes:

> I have often found myself conflicted and guilty over this story from Genesis and the enmity it has symbolized through the ages. I could see the way that Sarah and Hagar were trapped into competition because of oppressive patriarchal social struc-tures. Yes, I also knew that Sarah's actions in casting out Hagar mirror many of the ways that I, as a white, North American, Christian woman have shared in patterns of privilege that use stereotypes of difference to oppress my sisters of color as well as my Jewish and my Muslim sisters.[60]

While one respects the candid introspection, the interpretation seems laden with ideology, for perhaps it was feelings of jealousy, inadequacy, and powerlessness on both sides that gave rise to the tragic situation. It is true that Sarah wielded power over Hagar, yet Hagar, fertile and pregnant, had power over the barren Sarah.[61] The fraught dynamic between the women, as well as the broader story's emotional depth and potency, is sideswiped when the focus remains strictly on "patriarchal social structures." This is not to suggest that social power dynamics are inoperative but to caution against heavy-handed, one-dimensional readings of the narrative. Hagar is regarded as a victim of patriarchy, of class- and race-conscious culture, as a pawn in the family dynamics of Sarah and Abraham, and at the same time as a victor who, on her own initiative and with the help of God, transforms her oppressive situation into a form of liberation. The biblical story of Hagar attests to God's concern for those who are marginalized yet attests also to the centrality of the Abrahamic covenant. Indeed, it is not difficult to understand the empowering effect of the story of Hagar for those who are oppressed and have been denied their share of power. At the same time, however, while God comforts Hagar, she and Ishmael, along with his progeny, are nonetheless relegated to the periphery of the main narrative. When Hagar first flees from Sarah's harsh treatment, God gives her assurances and consoles her with the promise of the birth of Ishmael. But then she and her son are cast out of Abraham's household, sent into the wilderness, where she endures the pain of watching Ishmael nearly die of thirst.

Like their sons, Sarah and Hagar are often understood metonymically—one representing Judaism, the other Islam; one the chosen, the other the rejected, marginalized unchosen. Even today, they are often portrayed in oppositional terms. Contemporary readers are interested in how the story of Sarah and Hagar speaks to political and social issues; how it might illumine power dynamics, the clash of classes, the power of victimhood; how it might reveal the anxieties of mothers-in-waiting. Modern readers are moved by the desire for the children of Sarah and Hagar—Arabs and Jews, Israeli Jews and Palestinians, Jews and Christians and Muslims—to live in peaceful coexistence. What those who use the story politically seem to ignore is that the narrative's framework does not support their desideratum. The very paradigm of rivalry between the women, as well as the power dynamic undergirding the storyline, undermines a reading whereby the two women live together happily ever after. If, however, we adopt an alternative reading of the story that allows us to appreciate the personal struggles each woman faces in her particular station, a reading that does not focus on the enmity between them but rather on the emotions that led to fear and loathing, a reading that highlights the common challenge and individual sacrifices each mother faces in order to secure her son's survival, and if we understand the story of Ishmael and Isaac as one of reconciliation, then perhaps we can begin to move beyond the ideological strictures imposed on the story's past and present interpreters.

Pre-postmodern exegetes, with the exception of some Muslim writers, by and large reiterate Hagar's lowly status and advocate overwhelmingly on Sarah's behalf. Far be it from them to regard Hagar as having experienced "use, abuse, and rejection." This is not to say that ancient and medieval sources show no sympathy for Hagar; on the contrary. But they do not generally employ a strategy of reading against the grain in such a way that they would take issue with

Hagar's relegation to the margins, or that they would find her banishment into the wilderness with little provisions so troubling as to call into question God's command. Reading with the Jewish metanarrative in mind, or in a Christian theological framework, scriptural exegetes whitewashed Sarah's and Abraham's behavior and to varying degrees perpetuated Hagar's marginality. Even though the biblical story is far more nuanced than that, ancient biblical interpreters, and most medieval ones, stripped the story of its complexity in order to justify the matriarch's behavior toward her handmaiden and the patriarch's treatment of his surrogate wife.[62] Disparaging comments made in internecine debates within Islamic circles notwithstanding, in Muslim sources Hagar as the wife of Abraham and mother of Ishmael is regarded as a woman of valor who, despite having been exiled, exhibits steadfast faithfulness to God.

■ 5

Sibling Rivals

REFERENCES to the siblings Ishmael and Isaac populate ecumenical as well as political discourse. Since the medieval period, Ishmael and Isaac have represented, respectively, Arabs and Jews (or Muslims and Jews, or Islam and Judaism). More often than not, underlying the rhetoric of the siblings—as with the use of the term "Abrahamic religions"—is a genuine desire to foster the notion of confraternity of religious and political communities. At the same time, however, the rhetoric brings a relationship marked by strife to the surface; ironically, the evocation of the biblical brothers subverts the peacemaking intention. Allusion to the biblical narrative whereby Abraham's firstborn son Ishmael is banished from his father's household, to say nothing of later Jewish and Christian depictions of him, does little to further mutual understanding and appreciation. If anything, it maintains deeply entrenched misconceptions of Islam and on some level aggravates the very antagonism it hopes to ameliorate.

In ancient and medieval literature, the relationship between the brothers is marked by opposition and long-standing strife, but neither the Qur'an nor the Bible portrays them as rivals. As a result of the strain between herself and Hagar, Sarah creates an implicit atmosphere of competition and fraternal conflict between their sons. That an explicit rivalry existed between Ishmael and Isaac is biblically unsubstantiated. That said, rivalry between them in the Bible exists to the extent that they participate in the larger narrative structure of Genesis that sets one line of Abraham's descendants apart from others. The promise made to both Hagar and Abraham as to Ishmael's fate, that he will be father of twelve nations, does not put him in direct conflict with Isaac, nor is there anything in the story that would lead one to believe that the brothers engaged in interpersonal conflict. To be sure, the prophecy in Genesis 16:12, "His hand will be against everyone and everyone's hand against him," portends a fate for Ishmael riddled with struggle, but it is not exclusively with Isaac. In fact, there is no mention of competition or warfare between them.

After a period of separation, when Ishmael is sent out of Abraham's house, they reunite when they bury their father: "And Isaac and Ishmael his sons buried him in the cave of Machpelah" (Gen. 25:9). The text reverses the birth order by mentioning Isaac before Ishmael. This reversal is significant when comparing the narrative to that of the more contentious siblings Esau and Jacob. Unlike the burial notice of Isaac (Gen. 35:29), where Esau and Jacob bury their father, in this notice the younger son is mentioned first. If we compare Genesis 25:9 and 35:29, the reversal "Isaac and Ishmael" seems to portray the brothers acting in unison as well as in accordance with God's preordained plan whereby the younger sibling supplants the older.

Moreover, sibling rivalry between Ishmael and Isaac is neither divinely ordained nor explicit in the narrative, unlike the Jacob-Esau prenatal struggle, for the Lord tells Rebecca: "Two nations are in your womb . . . The elder shall serve the younger" (Gen. 25:23). That is, Isaac is the son of the covenant, yet Ishmael is recognized as a great nation. Since there is no portent of domination in the case of Ishmael and Isaac, the reversal of names at Abraham's burial may be symbolic of acceptance of the divine displacement of the primogeniture.

In fact, one may go so far as to argue that the biblical account implicitly refers to Ishmael and Isaac's positive interpersonal relationship. In Genesis 24:62 we read that Isaac had just come back from the vicinity of Be'er-lahai-ro'i, "for he was settled in the region of the Negeb." This is the site of God's promise of a son to Hagar (Gen. 16:14), which is associated with Ishmael. In his commentary on Genesis 25:11, "And Isaac settled near Be'er-lahai-ro'i," N. Sarna suggests that Isaac's settling in this area "may be a symbolic assertion of hegemony over his brother,"[1] but to my mind the idea of hegemony over Ishmael is unwarranted. Given the preceding analysis of Genesis 16 and 17, there is no indication in the promises to Hagar and Abraham that augurs a fate riddled with fraternal strife for Ishmael. If anything, it is plausible that they dwelt "alongside" each other under relatively peaceful conditions. And certainly, unlike the other siblings and relations in the Genesis genealogies, Ammon, Moab, Edom, and for that matter Aram and Midian, the Ishmaelites never figure as conspicuous enemies of the Israelites.

Although the biblical story does not speak of enmity between the siblings, the Jewish and Christian interpretive traditions place them in direct opposition. In the Jewish tradition, Ishmael represents the generic non-Jew as well as the real Arab. He is pitted against Isaac, the chosen—that is, the Jewish people—and in early Christian sources Isaac is the spiritual, new covenant as opposed to Ishmael, who represents the flesh, the old covenant, sin, and darkness.

Two rabbinic texts explicitly pit them against each other as rivals. The first is a reading of Genesis 22:7, "And Isaac said to Abraham his father, Father." The verse is part of the episode concerning the binding of Isaac. Given the economy of biblical language, the doubling of words always grabs the rabbis' attention. Why does Scripture say "Abraham his father, Father"? What is the reason for "father, Father"? According to the rabbis, it is in order to make Abraham reconsider his zeal:

Samael [a demon] came to our father, Abraham, and said to him, "What is the reason your heart is despairing? Are you really going to slaughter the son given to you at the age of a hundred?" Abraham said to him, "Indeed so." He [Samael] said to him, "If God tests you even more, will you be able to stand it?" "If a thing

be put to you as a trial, will you be wearied?" (Job 4:2). He
[Abraham] said to him, "Even more so." He [Samael] said to him,
"Tomorrow he will say to you that you are a murderer and that
you are culpable." Abraham again replied, "Indeed so." When
Samael saw that his efforts were of no avail, he went to Isaac.
He said to him, "Oh son of an ill-fated mother, he is going to
slaughter you." Isaac replied, "This is so." He said to him, "If so,
all those lovely cloaks that your mother made will be the inheritance of Ishmael, the hated one of her house." If a word is not
entirely effective, it enters in part, as it is written, "And Isaac said
to his father Abraham, 'My father'" (Gen. 22:7) . . . It was so that
Abraham should be filled with mercy for him. (*Gen. Rab.* 56:4)[2]

The rabbis weave an elaborate narrative involving Samael, Abraham, and Isaac. After Samael tries unsuccessfully to dissuade Abraham from obeying God's command, he goes to Isaac, who initially
accepts his fate. When Samael tells him that his inheritance will go to
Ishmael, however, his resolve flags. Thus, he says "My father" so that
Abraham will reconsider and not carry through as planned. It is not
death that threatens Isaac but the thought that Ishmael will inherit
what is his.

The second example of sibling rivalry in rabbinic literature is in
Genesis Rabbah 55:4. In the dialogue between Isaac and Ishmael, Isaac
is depicted as a willing victim, a depiction that justifies the choice of
Isaac over Ishmael:

Isaac and Ishmael were arguing with one another. One said, "I
am more beloved than you because I was circumcised when I
was thirteen years old." The other said, "I am more beloved than
you because I was circumcised on the eighth day." Ishmael said
to him, "I am more beloved than you because I could have
refused but did not." At that moment Isaac said, "Would that
the Holy One, Blessed be He, appear to me and tell me that He
will cut off one of my limbs, I would not tarry!" The Holy One,
Blessed be He, said to him, "On account of your willingness to
sacrifice yourself and not tarry"—Thus, "After these things, God
put Abraham to the test." (Gen. 22:1)

The dialogue has a twofold function: it justifies the choice of Isaac over Ishmael, and it answers the question, What is meant by "After these things"? As it reads, the reader does not know why God tests Abraham. What are "these things" or "these words" (the Hebrew *devarim* can mean either things or words) that cause God to test Abraham? The rabbis expand the narrative by adding a pissing contest, to put it crudely, between the brothers. Ishmael is ready to fulfill God's command: his circumcision was one of choice, not of coercion. Isaac, however, makes a greater offer: an entire limb. Both are portrayed as being ready to fulfill God's command, but Isaac wins. He is the chosen victim.

Rabbinic literature affirms the special status of Isaac over Ishmael. Chapter 31 of *PRE* recounts a conversation between Ishmael and Abraham's faithful servant, Eliezer, on their way to Mount Moriah. In the midrash Eliezer and Ishmael, who are not even mentioned in Genesis 22, know in advance that Abraham is intending to sacrifice Isaac:

> Rivalry entered between Eliezer and Ishmael. Ishmael said to Eliezer, "Now Abraham will offer Isaac his son for a burnt offering kindled upon the altar, and I am his first born son and I will inherit Abraham." Eliezer replied, and said to him, "He has already driven you out like a woman divorced from her husband, and he sent you away to the wilderness, but I am his servant, serving his house day and night and I shall be the heir of Abraham." The Holy Spirit replied to them and said to them, "Neither this one nor that one will inherit."[3]

The author of *PRE* asserts Israel's status as the true inheritor of the covenant between God and Abraham's offspring. When they reach Zophim, Abraham sees the Shekhinah standing on the top of the mountain. He turns to Isaac and asks, "My son, do you see anything on one of these mountains?" Isaac responds, "Yes, I see a pillar of fire standing from the earth to the heavens." Abraham then turns to Ishmael and Eliezer and asks, "Do you see anything on one of these mountains?" They respond, "No." Since they cannot see, they are instructed to remain with the donkey.

Whether Eliezer and Ishmael are references to Christianity and Islam, or other groups vying for the biblical heritage, is up for debate. If indeed the midrash reflects theological contention, neither Eliezer nor Ishmael will inherit because Isaac is the chosen child. It is not Isaac who claims his position vis-à-vis Ishmael and Eliezer; rather it is the *Shekhinah*—divine ordinance—that affirms Israel's chosenness. The ability to "see," or better yet, to understand, is reserved exclusively for Israel. Emphasis is placed on Isaac's worthiness over and against Eliezer and Ishmael, a notion that plays out in depictions of the sacrifice of Isaac.

With the exception of *Genesis Rabbah* 56:4 and 55:4, rivalry between Abraham's sons is not found in rabbinic sources of late antiquity. It is, however, found more frequently and emphatically in midrashim of the medieval period, where Ishmael is characterized as hating his brother. The increase in interpretive sources that denigrate Ishmael should come as no surprise, given that the Near Eastern cultural, political, and religious landscape changes with the emergence of Islam.

In Christian sources, Ishmael and Isaac are discussed in antipodal terms, in some instances similar to the terms of the Jewish readings. Depiction of Ishmael and Isaac as rivals is by and large absent in the Islamic tradition with its understanding of both sons of Abraham as prophets. But we do encounter the use of Isaac and Ishmael in internecine debates between Arab and Persian Muslims.

Qur'anic Prophets, Rival Forefathers

In the Islamic tradition, genealogy as a conceptual metaphor had great impact on the patterning of historical narrative in which both biblical figures, Ishmael and to a lesser degree Isaac, play a role. The biblical lineage of these brothers factors into medieval Arab and Persian debates, for Persian Muslims assert their superior descent from Isaac. Such claims serve ideological and polemical purposes, but here the distinction does not exclude one from being a member of the prophetic lineage. That is to say, neither Arabs nor Persians dispute the Muslim lineage of the other.

The absence of any reference to Ishmael as the progenitor of the Arabs in the Qur'an is most curious. In verse 2:133, he, Abraham, and Isaac are referred to as the "Fathers" of Jacob, but in extraqur'anic sources Ishmael becomes more prominent. This is detected in genealogical writings that trace the Prophet Muhammad to Abraham via Ishmael.

The emphasis on genealogy evolves over time as Islam expands beyond the reaches of the Arabian Peninsula. There seems to be no indication that the Qur'an makes an attempt to identify the early Muslim community along national lines. The focus is on belief and submission (*aslama*) to the prophetic message delivered by Muhammad and his followers, not on genetic descent or peoplehood. Interactions with peoples beyond the Arabian pale with ancient traditions, peoples with their own history and characteristics, in part give rise to the development of the genealogical tradition in Islam.

By all accounts the Islamic genealogical tradition is of great importance. Qur'an 49:13, stating that men should know their genealogies so that they may recognize how they are related to one another, places some significance on genealogy. "Know concerning your genealogies that by which you may make your ties of blood kinship close," a *ḥadīth* from the collection of al-Tirmidhi states, "for the close tie of kinship is a cause of love among family, a creator of wealth and a means to prolong one's life."[4] And as several of the commentators point out, if men ignored genealogies they would be unable to follow the shari'ah (divine law) in distributing inheritance and avoiding forbidden kinds of marriage.[5] Genealogy, furthermore, deploys history as a series of biographies linked by the principle of hereditary succession, and the fundamental function of genealogical systems is to order society, to situate the individual or corporate entity, such as the tribe, accordingly. Competing genealogies provide a means for understanding tensions in a given society, as is the case with *shu'ūbiyya*, a type of literature that Persian Muslims produced in the medieval period and that first appeared in the eighth century as a reaction to the exclusive Arab hegemonic right in Islam.

Sociopolitical factors played a role in the transmission of genealogy, and while great pains were taken to preserve genealogy, the genealogists themselves were often under attack. Be that as it may, the conceptualization of ancestry was significant in the self-understanding of both the Arab and the non-Arab Muslims.

Whereas the Qur'an makes no explicit mention of Ishmael's Arabness, genealogies and later traditions certainly do. The biblical genealogy of Arabs became widely accepted, as adduced in the charged exchange between Arabs and non-Arabs (*'ajamī*) or Persians in *shu'ūbiyya* literature.[6] As Sarah Savant has argued, the Persians of the ninth and tenth centuries tailored genealogies of the prophets in order to assimilate themselves into the Muslim metanarrative and to identify themselves in it.[7] In fact, Ishmael's Arabness is taken for granted by non-Arab Muslims, who in response to Arab boasts of superiority disparage Ishmael's birth from a slave-girl and pronounce their own descent from Isaac, born of a free woman. As part of the ongoing polemics that took place in the ninth century, we notice that by this time Ishmael plays a more prominent role in Arab self-identity in the context of intra-Muslim debates.

During the ninth and tenth centuries, Shu'ūbīs—elite, mostly Persian littérateurs—criticized Arabs for their view that non-Arabs were equal to the Arabs or even better.[8] The Shu'ūbīs, whose name derives from *shu'ūb*, "peoples" (Q. 49:13),[9] claimed that the Persians, as a people with a prophet—Isaac—were better than the Arabs. Isaac was their "father," a prestigious prophet to whom they could trace their lineage and in whom they could take pride.[10] An example is taken from Yahya ibn 'Ali al-Munajjim (d. 912), an esteemed companion of the powerful 'Abbasid prince al-Muwaffaq (d. 891). He writes as recorded in al-Masudi (Murūj [1.282]): "O sons of Hagar: I explained it to you. What is this conceit and haughtiness? Was your mother not in ancient times a slave belonging to our mother, the beautiful Sarah? Kingship flows in us and the prophets belong to us. You cannot deny that, except unfairly."

Yahya denigrates the Arab descendants of Ishmael. Harking back to Hagar, who served Sarah, he at once dismisses them as sons of a slave and exalts the Persians for their preferred pedigree as sons of Isaac, whose mother was the mistress of the house. Other Shu'ūbī attempts to oppose the Arabs' pride of place among the community of believers insult Hagar, who, as many traditions attest, is considered the mother of the Arabs, of "the children of the water of Heaven."[11] Ibn Nuwas refers to her as "the putrid-smelling woman."[12] This further disparages Ishmael, hence the Arabs and, by extension, the

Prophet Muhammad. As the 'Abbasid prince Ibn al-Mu'tazz (d. 908)
claims, as preserved in al-Masudi: "Better than Isaac is the Seal of
the Messengers, exposing the darkness with his light."

The Arabs' affiliation with Ishmael widened the scope of Arab self-
understanding to transcend Arabia potentially creating a distinction
among Muslims, between Arabs and *'ajamī*. The extent to which
the controversies played out beyond the confines of the social elite,
however, remains uncertain. Be that as it may, Islamic sources convey an interest in including Persians within the span of prophetic
history. After all, Abraham is portrayed as the common ancestor
linking Arabs, descendants of Ishmael, and Persians, descendants of
Isaac. As Savant observes, al-Tabari, for example, places Persians
"within the story of Islam at an early stage, and in ways that respect
and preserve some of their native traditions, for which Persians and
Zoroastrians are given significant credit."[13] The mythic dimensions
of the family of Abraham serve to incorporate Persians into an
expanding Muslim community.

Let me step back and make some observations. The link between
Ishmael and Arabs, an association that is not found in the Qur'an
but emerges as Islam develops as a socioreligious institution, is a very
different link from the one we find in Jewish and Christian sources.
(See Chapter 6.) Thus while Islam merges Arab and biblical genealogies, while it tailors traditions to suit social and historical exigencies, it nonetheless does so in a manner reflective of that which is
distinctly Islamic.

This very brief survey of the rabbinic use of Isaac and Ishmael
and their use in intra-Muslim debates calls attention to the ways in
which the biblical story is refashioned to address theological, political, and cultural concerns. The Bible depicts Ishmael and Isaac in
antipodal but not antagonistic terms. Isaac is the chosen son, through
whom the covenant with Israel is realized. Ishmael is the marginalized son, who, although blessed, is cast to the periphery of Jewish
theological history.

In Muslim sources, both Ishmael and Isaac are prophets. They
are set in opposition to each other with respect to internecine antagonism. Yet the Persians' claim to Isaac works in the Abrahamic
familial paradigm. Persians who claim lineage from Isaac envision

themselves as descendants of the same line as the Prophet Muhammad. In other words, contrary to fashioning an opposition between Ishmael and Isaac that privileges one, Isaac, over the rejected Other, Ishmael, as in Jewish and Christian sources, in Islam both Ishmael and Isaac remain in the family of believers. Even as the Arab Ishmael is denigrated in the eyes of some Persians in order to establish and secure a place for themselves in Islamic genealogical history, and even as Ishmael comes to play a more prominent role in Islam than Isaac, both are members of Abraham's family of believers.

Constituting Family

Who constitute the children of Abraham in Jewish and Christian traditions is less straightforward. To illustrate the point, I will consider the ways *Genesis Rabbah* conceptualizes the family of Abraham. Given that this work is a corpus of midrashic literature, structured as a verse-by-verse exegetical commentary on Genesis, there is, relatively speaking, a great deal of material on Abraham and his family, a family that at times includes Ishmael and Isaac and the children of Keturah and at other times excludes all but Isaac. It is exceedingly difficult to cull the compilation in order to create a portrait of the patriarch and his family, for the concept of Abraham as father in *Genesis Rabbah* is anything but homogeneous. One discovers a pastiche of images that are at times in tension. This may be attributed to the fact that while an irregularity in a biblical verse or a discrepancy between verses gives rise to an interpretation, the midrashic process is always made up of factors that exceed the bounds of the biblical text. How an irregularity or discrepancy is resolved has as much to do with the verse or verses as it does with the rabbis' weltanschauung, with their predilections and presuppositions, and with "the burning issues of the day."[14] As Joseph Heinemann writes, "the rabbis looked back to back into Scripture to uncover the full latent meaning of the Bible and its wording, at the same time, they looked forward into the present and the future. They sought to give direction to their own generation, to resolve their own religious problems, to answer their own theological questions." In some cases extratextual factors are more discernible than in other examples and play a more significant role in the interpretation. But even, or perhaps especially, in the case of exegetical midrashim such as *Genesis Rabbah*, with its sustained attention to verses of a narrative seriatim, we do have some license to make observations about the attitudinal nature of interpretations, and when specifically discussing the depiction of a story or biblical figures, we can consider portrayals in the aggregate and note which portrayals are in fact prevalent or at least possible.

Genesis Rabbah reinforces the notion that Abraham's family extends beyond Isaac and even Ishmael. True to the story in Genesis, *Genesis Rabbah* portrays Abraham as the father of Ishmael, Isaac, and the children of Keturah. There is no attenuation of Abraham's role as father of non-Israelites or non-Jews. He is the progenitor of a multitude of nations. As we read in *Genesis Rabbah* 38:10, on Genesis 11:8: "So it came about that the Lord scattered them [*wayyafets*] from there over the face of the entire world and they stopped building the city." The thirty families swept away in the midrash are replaced by the progeny of Abraham, who are scattered family throughout the world. While his family includes non-Jews, not all non-Jews are from the line of Abraham.

The midrash places Abraham's progeny on equal footing. There is no qualitative distinction made among the three lines, one from Keturah, one from Hagar, and the other from Sarah (by way of Rachel). All are members of his family. That Abraham is the father of non-Jews as well is underscored throughout *Genesis Rabbah*. Ishmael, for example, despite a few disparaging comments, is depicted favorably, or at least neutrally. He remains, even if expelled and disinherited, Abraham's son.[15]

Genesis tells us that Isaac inherited all of Abraham's belongings but that he also gave gifts to the sons of his concubine (Gen. 25:5). What did Abraham give Isaac? What does it mean that he gave all that he had to him, if the rest of the verse states that he gave the sons of his concubines gifts? According to R. Yehudah, he gave Isaac the birthright, but R. Nehemiah maintains it was the power of blessing, and the rabbis claim that it was neither blessing nor birthright but rather the family vault and a disposition of property, for blessing and birthright are God's alone to bequeath. The *mashal* in *Genesis Rabbah* 61:6 illustrates the position that Abraham did not bless Isaac:

> A king had an orchard, which he entrusted to a steward. Now this orchard contained two trees which were intertwined, one yielded life-giving fruit and the other a deadly poison. The steward said: "If I water the life-bearing tree, the death-bearing one will flourish with it; while if I do not water the death-bearing tree, how can the other exist?" On reflection, he decided: "I am a steward; I will do my duty, and whatever the owner of the orchard wishes to do, let him do." So, too, Abraham argued: "If I bless Isaac, the children of Ishmael and of Keturah are included; while if I do not bless the children of Ishmael and of Keturah, how can I bless Isaac?" On reflection, however, he decided: "I am but flesh; I will do my duty, and whatever God wishes to do in His world, let Him do it." Consequently, when Abraham died the Holy One, blessed be He, appeared to Isaac and blessed him. Thus it is written, "And it came to pass after the death of Abraham, that God blessed Isaac his son" (Gen. 25:11).

In this *mashal*, Abraham is likened to a steward who is in charge of two intertwined trees, one poisonous and the other fruitful. In order to act responsibly, he must water the death-bearing tree lest the life-bearing tree wither and be destroyed. Parenthetically, the apposition between the steward and Abraham breaks down, for the steward must act; he must water both trees, whereas Abraham must refrain from acting; he must not bless. When he dies, God blesses Isaac; thus preferential treatment of Isaac is providential. Israel's covenantal status, its role as inheritor of land, nation, and blessing, means that promises made to Abraham are divinely ordained and not contingent on decisions that take human agency into account. Here, by the way, a qualitative distinction is made between the sons, yet both belong to the king, their father. The election of Israel is ultimately God's fiat.

Genesis Rabbah 61:6 deals with the blessing and emphasizes God's role in Isaac's distinction vis-à-vis Abraham's other sons. *Genesis Rabbah* 61:7 addresses the Ishmaelites' claim to the birthright and justifies Abraham's decision to give all to Isaac:

> "But to the sons of his concubines, Abraham gave gifts [and while he was still living, he sent them away from his son Isaac eastward, to the east country]" (Gen. 25:6). In the days of Alexander of Macedonia the Ishmaelites came to dispute with Israel about the birthright and with them came two wicked families, the Canaanites and the Egyptians. They said, "Who will go and dispute with them?" Gebiah, son of Qosem, said, "I will go and dispute them." They said to him, "Be careful lest you forfeit the land of Israel to them." He replied, "I will go and argue with them" . . . He went and disputed with them. Alexander of Macedonia said to them, "Who is laying claim against whom?" The Ishmaelites responded, "We are the claimants and we base our claim on their Torah," for it is written, "But he shall acknowledge the firstborn, the son of the hated . . ." (Deut. 21:17), and Ishmael was the first born." Gebiah, son of Qosem said, "My lord, the king, cannot a man do as he likes with his sons?" "Yes," answered Alexander. Thus, it is written, "Abraham gave all that he had to Isaac" (Gen. 25:2). "But how is he a legator?"[16] He replied, "But to the sons of the concubines, Abraham gave gifts." Shame-faced, they departed.

As in *Genesis Rabbah* 61:6, the rabbis offer a justification for Abraham's decision to leave all he has to Isaac, even though, according to Deuteronomy 21:17, the firstborn shall inherit. In this case, Abraham is a king who can do as he pleases and is therefore free to give all to Isaac. But one cannot accuse him of inequity, for he bestows gifts on the children of his concubines. Moreover, an unbiased king arbitrates in Israel's favor, adding a layer of legitimacy. Isaac—that is, Israel—is rightfully given the birthright, and Abraham in this instance ensures God's promise that it is through Isaac that Abraham's seed is named. In the preceding midrash, God effects his covenantal promise; here, Abraham enacts it.

The midrashim in *Genesis Rabbah* by and large acknowledge Abraham's fatherhood in concrete terms, as in this narrative expansion. His family includes all his progeny, even those whom he sends away. That is to say, although in this midrash they are cast away, they remain in the scope of the narrative. They are not entirely effaced; rather, they are marginalized. It is interesting to note that *Tanhuma Toledot* 1 (Buber) emphatically conceives of Abraham as the father of Isaac and only Isaac: "Did he father no one but Isaac? It is written, 'Hagar bore a son to Abram' (Gen. 16:15) and also, 'These are the sons of Keturah: Zimran, Yokshan . . .' (Gen. 25:2). But it does not say that Abraham fathered anyone else but Isaac, because Isaac was righteous. It is therefore written, 'Abraham fathered Isaac' (Gen. 25:19)." This late midrash goes beyond the *mashal:* there the blessing of Isaac is by divine fiat, but here we see that it was given because Isaac was righteous. The covenant is promised through Isaac, but he also merits it through his righteousness.

In addition to images of Abraham's family that to varying degrees include all his sons, another image of the family emerges: one that portrays Abraham as the father of Israel. *Genesis Rabbah* 40:6 makes a direct correlation between Abraham and Israel. The midrash enumerates several appositions. By means of philological correlation and other associations between verses in the life of Abraham and the Exodus story, the rabbis draw a connection between Abraham and his descendants, the Israelites; between Abraham and the Exodus. Israel's destiny mirrors that of its forefather, Abraham. Abraham is the father of the Israelites not only in biological but also in metaphysical terms. His history recapitulates itself in the lives of his children.

This image of Abraham as the spiritual patriarch of the Jews contradicts the image of Jacob as their spiritual forefather. The notion that Abraham and Isaac produced blemished, unfit offspring is fairly common in rabbinic literature of both the tannaitic (the first—third century CE) and amoraic periods (the third—six century CE).[17] In *Genesis Rabbah*, Abraham's family includes the children of Sarah and Hagar, yet Abraham is singled out as the father of Israel in *Genesis Rabbah* 40:6. *Genesis Rabbah* reflects two genealogies, one theological and the other biological. At times they operate separately, and at other times they come together in the conceptualization of Israel as both the physical and spiritual descendant of Abraham.

Let me now briefly turn to notions of Abraham's family in New Testament writings, which also reflect two genealogies. That Paul speaks of Abraham differently in the letter to the Galatians continues to challenge Pauline scholars attempting to reconcile these letters. In the letter to the Galatians Paul presents a way non-Jews may legitimately enter the family of Abraham through faith.

Paul thus establishes the identity of the sons of Abraham, the sons of the promise in Galatians 3:7–9: "So you see, those who believe are the descendants of Abraham. And the scripture, foreseeing that God would justify the Gentiles by faith, preached the gospel beforehand to Abraham saying, 'All the Gentiles shall be blessed in you.' For this reason, those who believe are blessed with Abraham who believed." Put succinctly: "And if you belong to Christ, then you are Abraham's offspring [*sperma*] heirs according to the promise" (3:29). Paul's letter to the Romans, in contrast, offers a more complicated image of Abraham's family. In Romans 4, all those who share in the faith of Abraham are his descendants; in them resides the promise of grace, even to those who adhere to the law.

Believers are children according to the spirit, and Jews, children according to the flesh, are also his children, but "it is not as though the word of God had failed," Paul writes in Romans. "For not all Israelites truly belong to Israel, and not all of Abraham's children are his true descendants; but 'It is through Isaac that descendants shall be named for you' (Gen. 21:12). This means that it is not the children of the flesh who are the children of God, but the children of the promise are counted as descendants" (Rom. 9:6–8).

Romans also portrays Abraham as the man of faith whose descendants are believers, children of the promise, as the father of Jews. According to Paul, God has not abandoned unbelieving Jews: "As regards the gospel they are enemies of God for your sake; but as regards election they are beloved, for the sake of their ancestors; for the gifts and the calling of God are irrevocable" (Rom. 11:28–30). In other words, even though they oppose the gospel message, the election

of the Jews is immutable. In Romans Paul contends that righteousness is reckoned on the basis of faithfulness and that Abraham
is the quintessential example. Two genealogical schemas—one physical and the other spiritual—are operative in Paul's thinking. It may
be that the spirit determines who really is Israel, but the Jews—Israel
after the flesh—are not being written off and will always be given
the chance to adopt the faith, precisely because of their specialness
in being Israel after the flesh. Fleshly Israelness will not save them,
but it will ensure them a forever open invitation to be saved. Whereas
a spiritualized genealogy undergirds the allegory in Galatians 4:22–
31, in Romans Paul employs both genealogies, thus creating confu-
sion. In Galatians, Abraham's family is through Isaac, but in Romans
Paul acknowledges Abraham's legitimate family of the flesh as well
as the spiritualized family that includes non-Jews.[18] Roughly speaking, in Romans Paul the exegete and Paul the theologian meet.

Furthermore, Galatians seems to imply that unbelieving Jews
have no standing before God, but Romans demonstrates God's enduring concern for them. Despite the differences between the two
letters—in terms of not only tone and intended audience but also
who is identified as Abraham's heirs[19]—in both epistles Abraham is
typical of all who have faith, Gentiles and Jews alike.

The images of the family of Abraham emanate from two genealogies that at times are intertwined, at other times are in competition, and sometimes simply coexist. In later Christian sources, such
as the Gospel of John, the Jews are displaced as biological children
of Abraham. That said, one still finds in Christian writings interpretations that regard Jews as the descendants of Abraham, if not
through Isaac, then through Ishmael.

By the second century, the place of Gentiles in the family of Abraham is no longer an issue; it is assumed that they alone are his heirs.
Barnabas, an early disciple mentioned in Acts of the Apostles, for
example, refers to Abraham as "the father of the Gentiles" (*Letter of
Barnabas* 13:6–7).

As with Sarah and Hagar, Ishmael and Isaac are employed dichot-
omously in Jewish and Christian sources, and at times the children
of Keturah are segregated with Ishmael. The sons represent the line

of separation between who is in and who is out. That is not the case in Islam, however, where both sons, along with their mothers, live in the abode of Abraham. Even when the sons are brought into competition with each other in rhetorical debates, both are nonetheless regarded as members of the family.

■ 6

Firstborn Son

PERHAPS NO OTHER biblical figure evokes a sense of liminality quite like Ishmael. He is Abraham's firstborn, circumcised with Abraham, yet he is not the son of the covenant but the son of a promise. He is a full-fledged member of the family, yet he is sent away, and Genesis 22:2 can speak of Isaac as Abraham's "only" son.[1] His presence is felt, yet his actions are few. He is spoken about yet never speaks. God hears his voice, but the reader hears silence. He will be a great nation, but "his hand will be against everyone, and everyone's hand against him." He is loved, and although expelled from Abraham's house, he is not rejected.

Ishmael evokes a variety of associations from nomads to *Moby-Dick*, from Arabs to Islam. The metonymic use of Ishmael to represent Islam or Arabs, however, is heavily fraught with misunderstanding. Many non-Muslims consider Ishmael the rejected son of Abraham, the one who according to popular Jewish interpretations tried to fornicate with Isaac, who practiced idol worship and was a shedder of blood.[2] Attempts to bring about peace and understanding between Palestinians—the Arab descendants of Ishmael—and Jews, who count Isaac among the patriarchs, often evoke Ishmael as the sibling of Isaac. But such attempts do not take into account the accretion of negative associations with Ishmael. And while such endeavors to recognize the Semitic heritage of Arabs and Jews are well-intentioned and indeed commendable, they result, ironically, in a distancing of Ishmael and a privileging of Isaac. After all, Isaac is the chosen son and Ishmael is sent away. Even the more nuanced taxonomy that categorizes biblical figures as chosen, antielect, and nonelect does not attenuate the fact that Ishmael resides among the nonelect. And even though God hears Ishmael, blesses him, and makes him the father of twelve nations, one son is privileged over another. One son inherits the Promised Land; the other is cast off into the wilderness. Within a Jewish-Christian religious frame of reference, who really wants to be called Ishmael?

Because one son is chosen over another, the assumption, based more on interpretive sources than on the Bible, is that Ishmael and Isaac were rivals. As noted in Chapter 5, this sense of sibling strife is found neither in Genesis nor in the Qur'an, which portrays Abraham's sons with equal reverence. Rabbinic sources, however, evoke a conflict in order to underscore Isaac's chosenness over and against Ishmael and designate Ishmael a marker of the outsider, the non-Jew, the Other, and in early Christian writings he represents the old covenant as well as the nonbeliever. That Ishmael and Isaac are biblical and qur'anic brothers does not mitigate the negative images associated with Ishmael. It behooves us to reconsider the extent to which evocations of confraternity serve a meaningful purpose in advancing ecumenical aspirations. If anything, they whitewash the interpretive traditions and misconstrue the biblical narratives.

In the Qur'an Ishmael plays a more prominent role than Isaac, in that he assists Abraham in building the Ka'bah, but the depiction of both sons betrays no sign that one is chosen at the expense of the other. Other Muslim sources do juxtapose the brothers in the context of intra-Muslim tensions between Arab Muslims and the 'ajam, non-Arab Muslims. But in the internecine polemics between Arab and Persian Muslims in the ninth and tenth centuries, Ishmael and Isaac represent two branches of the Abrahamic lineage. In intra-Muslim polemics, each group, one identifying with Ishmael, the other with Isaac, claims superiority over the other but nonetheless recognizes the legitimacy of the other in the family of Abraham. That is to say, the issue is not chosenness but rather claims of ethnic superiority. Ishmael was pressed into service for political, cultural, and religious purposes. There is a need to liberate the image of Ishmael from the stronghold of polemical discourse and the accretion of negative readings of the biblical story, but superficial, vacuous references to his relationship to Isaac do not advance his resuscitation.

The Jewish Ishmael

Since antiquity, Ishmael has been considered the progenitor of the Arab people, and since the medieval period he has symbolized Islam. The earliest datable occurrence of the term "Arab" is an Assyrian inscription of the ninth century BCE, and the designation is eventually associated with Ishmaelites in the Hellenistic period. The different theories of the identity and genealogical history of Arabs are many, and are by their very nature exceedingly complicated.[3]

Biblical references to Arabs seem to imply a collectivity much like "Israel." The Bible does not provide a genealogy for Arabs, as it does for Israel; the designation nonetheless adduces a sense of peoplehood and not a geographic entity. In a biblical reference in Isaiah 13:20, and another in Jeremiah 3:2, the promiscuous Judahites are admonished for their ravenous harlotry: "Look up to the bare heights, and see: Where have they not lain with you? You waited for them on the roadside, Like an Arab[4] in the wilderness." We also know of an individual Arab, Geshem (Neh. 2:19, 4:7), Nehemiah's long-standing enemy, and there is mention in the Bible of several Arabian regions (Jer. 25:23–25), including Dedan, Tema, Buz, Sheba, and Midian. Furthermore, a close affiliation exists between Arabian groups and the genealogical list in Genesis 25 of Abraham's descendants with Keturah.[5]

In nonbiblical sources of the biblical period, no connection is made between Ishmael (or the Ishmaelites) and the Arabs, nor, moreover, does the Bible itself offer information concerning how they are related. As scholars have argued, there is no historical basis for the Ishmaelite-Arab identity. It is based, rather, on the ethnological midrash in Genesis 25 that links the sons of Ishmael with tribes known as "Arabs" in Assyrian sources.[6] "But since it existed in the Bible," Eph'al writes, "the idea of such an association became established in Jewish tradition and consequently, among those in non-Jewish circles which in some way drew upon Jewish traditions."[7] The Greco-Roman categorization and identification of Arabs as a distinct people did not take place until the first century BCE.[8] Instances of this association are found in Josephus, the early rabbinic sources of the tannaitic period, *Targum Onkelos*, the Babylonian and Palestinian (Talmud Yerushalmi) Talmuds, and the works of the church fathers. Sozomenus, for example, a Christian writing in the early fifth century, identifies Ishmael as the ancestor of the Saracens (*Ecclesiastica Historia* Book 6, chapter 38). The identification of Ishmael and the Ishmaelites with Arabs seems to have taken hold in the first century BCE as an expression of the Greek tradition of identifying mythical founders of peoples as a way to locate their origins.[9]

The figure of Ishmael is introduced in Genesis 16, when the messenger of God appears to Hagar. He informs her that God will multiply her seed exceedingly, that she is with child, and that she shall call him Ishmael, which means "God hears," because the Lord has heard her affliction. Moreover, in Genesis 16:12, one learns that he will be a wild ass of a man *(pere' adam)* whose "hand shall be against everyone, and everyone's hand against him; and he shall dwell alongside [*'al penei*] all his kinsmen."[10] The Hebrew *'al penei* literally means "in the face of." Scholars do not agree on how it should be translated—"in defiance or disregard of," "in confrontation with," "over and against," or perhaps the more neutral "in the presence of." Since the narrative does not necessitate using a negative, hostile term, I have chosen the Jewish Publication Society translation, "alongside."[11] The context seems to suggest that the Ishmaelites will live near other tribes.[12] The church father Jerome explains that Ishmael's descendants will dwell in the desert and refers to Saracens who are nomadic, invade nations bordering on the desert, and in turn are attacked by all.[13] Another interpretation might be that despite constant mutual depredation, Ishmael will live among his kinsmen, which could well be a curse, since his fate would depend on his relatives.

There is no scholarly consensus on the meaning of the verse. For some, the roaming bedouin existence is uncouth and unconventional; for others, an unshackled lifestyle unencumbered by social

convention and unrestricted by geography is desirable. The characterization of Ishmael is neither inherently negative nor pejorative;
it merely presents him as the antithesis of the "civilized," sedentary
Israelites and suggests that he will dwell in the wilderness (Gen.
21:21). The notion that "his hand will be against everyone and everyone's hand against his" does depict tension between sedentary and
nomadic tribes in the Near East, but this tension need not be understood as disparagement of Ishmael.

What about his descendants, the Ishmaelites? It is true that although they are not depicted as Israel's archenemies, they are among
the list of enemies mentioned in Psalm 83:6–9: "Unanimous in their
counsel they have made an alliance against You—the clans of Edom
and the Ishmaelites, Moab and the Hagarites, Gebal, Ammon, and
Amalek, Philistia with the inhabitants of Tyre; Assyria too joins
forces with them; they give support to the sons of Lot." The psalmist entreats God to rescue Israel from its surrounding enemies. As
psalms rarely provide historical information, it is unlikely that the
list refers to an actual military campaign against Israel. More likely
than not the list is a composite of all the tribes encircling Israel
that are traditionally deemed her enemies. The Ishmaelites are also
mentioned in Genesis 37:25–28 (concerning the selling of Joseph to
the Ishmaelites), Genesis 39:1, and Judges 8:24, where they are in-
terchanged with Midianites. That they are substituted for the Midianites may be indicative of the generic way they designate nomadic
traders rather than an ethnic group.

Ancient and modern commentators have also grappled with Genesis 21:9: "And Sarah saw the son of Hagar the Egyptian, whom she
had borne to Abraham playing [metsaḥeq]."[14] Why did Sarah, who
provided Abraham with Hagar, now want her and her son "cast
out"? What does metsaḥeq mean? In what horrendous act was Ishmael engaged? Aramaic translations of the verse in *Targum Onkelos*
and *Neofiti* render the word as "idolatrous behavior," and rabbinic
interpretations include additional negative behavior. Even in Galatians (4:28–29) we read: "Now you, my friends, are children of the
promise, like Isaac. But just as at that time, the child born of the
flesh persecuted the child who was born of the Spirit, so it is now
also." Paul's presentation of Ishmael as the son of the flesh is taken

up in several writings of the early church that depict him as Isaac's antipode.

More often than not, negative connotations are imputed to the verse, yet it need not be understood as an indictment of Ishmael's character. Because Sarah's character is on the line, interpreters went to great lengths to justify her request. Moreover, why is Isaac, not Ishmael, the son of the promise? That is, interpreters also justify God's choosing of Isaac over Ishmael, for, after all, Abraham in a sense chooses Ishmael (Gen. 17:18, 21:11).

Metsaheq, derived from the same root as Isaac's name, "to laugh" *(tshq)*, can mean "playing," "sporting,"[15] or "laughing." Its meaning in the verse is impossible to determine. The piel form of the verb, that is, the active form used for expressing greater intensity, has many meanings, some that connote positive activities such as laughing, playing, and rejoicing and some that refer to negative, abusive behavior such as mocking and deriding.[16] But the negative meanings usually require the addition of the preposition *be-*, which is missing in Genesis 21:9, so it is argued from a purely grammatical point of view that without the preposition, *metsaheq* "cannot mean 'to mock' or the like."[17] And in translating the verb as either "playing" or "laughing," modern commentators are choosing activities that are in fact neither the same nor mutually exclusive.[18] Another interesting avenue to consider is that the word has sexual connotations, among them masturbation.[19] Since the verb *tshq* in this verse is used also in Genesis 39:17, where Potiphar's wife accuses Joseph of trying to seduce her, the rabbis also consider the notion that Ishmael's behavior was sexually immoral.

One explanation for Sarah's ire is that Ishmael may have been "Isaac-ing," acting like Isaac, an idea based on a typical biblical pun: Isaac in Hebrew is Yitzhaq, from the same root, *tshq*. As JoAnn Hackett contends, "this is perhaps what Sarah is complaining about in the next verse, that she noticed he was doing something to indicate he was just like Isaac, that they were equals, and it is this that threatens her so."[20] If this is the case, then Ishmael's "Isaac-ing" is perceived as negative, and his intentions are left ambiguous. Of course, what Sarah perceives as ill-intentioned and threatening may have been an innocuous gesture on Ishmael's part.[21] Another possibility, put forward by Ovadiah Seforno, an Italian rabbi of the late fifteenth century, is that Ishmael is engaged in mockery and his target is Sarah.[22] Perhaps she perceives him to be ridiculing her as his mother does; Sarah complains in Genesis 16:4–6, "I am lowered in her [Hagar's] esteem."

It is difficult to conclude from the biblical narrative that Ishmael's behavior was reprehensible and warranted Sarah's reaction. Perhaps rather than performing evil acts on Isaac, Ishmael may have displayed love and affection. A bond between her own son and Hagar's could be deemed a threat to Sarah. After all, the picture of them peacefully playing with each other on equal footing could be enough to feed Sarah's jealousy and fear that he would be a rival to Isaac.[23]

There is nothing in the text to suggest that Ishmael was abusing his younger brother. Rather, this motive is deduced by many troubled readers in their effort to account for Sarah's consternation.[24] As noted, the "playing" itself is not necessarily negative but has been read negatively by some rabbis in order to vindicate Sarah. In any case, Ishmael's actions, innocent or not, provoked her swift and uncompromising response.

Ishmael's fate is predicated not on his own behavior but rather on Sarah's: "She said to Abraham, 'Cast out that slave-woman and her son, for the son of that slave shall not share in the inheritance with my son Isaac'" (Gen. 21:10). Sarah herself provides the reason for her demand that Ishmael be cast out—she fears that he will inherit along with Isaac. It is not a stretch to say that it is Ishmael's presence alone that makes Sarah feel threatened.

The biblical text presumes that Ishmael has a portion in the inheritance. According to the Code of Hammurapi, a Babylonian law code dating back to the eighteenth century BCE, if the father of children of a slave-wife legitimates the children by claiming them as his own, then they have an equal share in the inheritance (paras. 170 and 171). If he does not claim them as his children, they have no share in the inheritance. Furthermore, both the slave and her children are given their freedom.[25]

Although we do not know whether legitimization would be required if the wife supplied the slave to provide a son, as in the case of Sarah and Hagar, the heir would doubtless not have been inferior to the children of an ordinary slave. And in the case of Ishmael, Abraham explicitly recognized him not only as a member of his household but also as his son.[26]

Indeed, several verses in Genesis underscore his unequivocal sonship: "Then Abraham took his son Ishmael . . . and his son Ishmael was thirteen years old when he was circumcised . . . Thus Abraham and his son Ishmael were circumcised" (Gen. 17:23, 25, 26). When Sarah demanded the eviction of Hagar and Ishmael, "the matter distressed Abraham greatly, for it concerned a son of his" (Gen. 21:11), and Abraham was buried by both sons: "His sons Isaac and Ishmael buried him in the cave of Machpelah" (Gen. 25:9). Finally, Ishmael's genealogy begins: "This is the line of Ishmael, Abraham's son, whom Hagar the Egyptian, Sarah's slave, bore to Abraham" (Gen. 25:12).

The Code of Lipit-Ishtar also throws light on the issue. Predating Hammurapi by about 150 years, Lipit-Ishtar stipulates that the progeny of a slave-wife relinquish their inheritance rights in exchange for their freedom.[27] The question, however, still remains whether, or to what degree, the Bronze Age Mesopotamian laws were applied in the (proto) Israelite legal system. Was primogeniture an ancient phenomenon, let alone a universal practice? Scholars offer a variety of perspectives on the matter. Near Eastern texts demonstrate that indeed Ishmael had inheritance rights as a member of the household, but his expulsion abrogated these rights.[28]

Given the legal codes of Near Eastern societies and the narrative structure of the Genesis story, it is reasonable to believe that Ishmael, as Abraham's legitimate son, absent any special circumstances (such as God's direct involvement) would have inherited along with Isaac. Even if no rigid laws of inheritance are mentioned in the Bible that obliged the father to treat the firstborn preferentially, in the case of Ishmael it seems likely that inheritance was an issue for Sarah. She assumed he would inherit with her son—if not legally then worse yet, by Abraham's choice. Fearing that Abraham's affection for Ishmael would lead to his inheriting with her son, and unwilling to have him share in the family fortune, Sarah sought Ishmael's eviction. Because Ishmael was Abraham's legitimate son and thus entitled to a share of the inheritance, Sarah's request that they be given their freedom would result in forfeiture of their stake in the inheritance.

As primogeniture he is afforded the status of Abraham's chief heir, and thus his very existence jeopardizes Isaac's entitlement to full inheritance.

Philo applies Roman provincial law to the interpretation of Ishmael's status as illegitimate.[29] By highlighting Hagar's menial status, Philo disqualifies Ishmael as Abraham's legitimate son. He seems to apply Greek-Hellenistic and Roman law whereby the off-spring of concubines are deemed illegitimate; children born by slave mothers de facto inherited slave status, not that of their father.[30] Philo's interpretation of *metsaheq* makes this quite clear: "and he was banished with his mother, because he being illegitimate was mocking the legitimate son, as though he were on terms of equality with him."[31]

Perhaps for Sarah the threat is of material and emotional inheritance, in the sense that Abraham's affections toward Ishmael might lead to favoritism. Whatever Ishmael's intentions might have been, his actions elicited a strong, visceral response from Sarah. In one rabbinic tradition (discussed in Chapter 4), *Genesis Rabbah* 53:13, Sarah places an evil eye on Ishmael, causing him to become sick and to drink all the water in the skin his father has given Hagar, so that mother and child are then in danger of dying in the desert. The midrash at once portrays Abraham as abundantly providing for Ishmael and Hagar and captures Sarah's resentment of the firstborn of Abraham.

Ancient and early medieval sources by and large cast Ishmael's behavior in a negative light. One exception is *Jubilees*, in which there is no hint of foul play on Ishmael's part. On the contrary, the impression of him is endearing, warm, and touching:[32]

> In the first year of the fifth week, in this jubilee, Isaac was weaned. Abraham gave a large banquet in the third month, on the day when his son Isaac was weaned. Now Ishmael, the son of Hagar the Egyptian, was in his place in front of his father Abraham. Abraham was very happy and blessed the Lord because he saw his own sons and had not died childless . . . He was very happy because the Lord had given him descendants on the earth to possess the land. With his full voice he blessed the creator of

everything. When Sarah saw Ishmael playing and dancing and Abraham being extremely happy, she became jealous of Ishmael. She said to Abraham: "Banish this girl and her son because this girl's son will not be an heir with my son Isaac." In Abraham's opinion the command regarding his servant girl and his son—that he should banish them from himself—was saddening. (*Jubilees* 17.1–6)[33]

Abraham rejoiced and expressed full-throated thanksgiving; "with his full voice" he blessed God. He was elated not because Isaac was weaned but because "he saw his own sons," because "the Lord had given him descendants," Ishmael as well as Isaac. Furthermore, Abraham is portrayed as being very much involved with Ishmael, who is seated "in his place in front of his father," whose "playing and dancing" delight Abraham, so much so that Sarah grows envious. What is somewhat tacitly conveyed in the Genesis story is made explicit in *Jubilees*. It is Abraham's affection for Ishmael and his position as the older son that Sarah finds threatening. Could it be that the son of the maidservant who has looked down on Sarah is equally beloved in her husband's eyes? After all, Abraham is thrilled by Ishmael's playing and dancing. It is not hard to imagine why Sarah would find this so threatening, or why, out of panic, she would demand Ishmael's banishment.

The scene at Isaac's weaning provides a compelling explanation for Sarah's demand and for Abraham's reaction, namely, that the matter "was grievous in his eyes," so much so that God intervened. Although the biblical account does not explicitly place Ishmael at the feast with his father, it is reasonable to infer this from the flow of the narrative: "And the child grew, and was weaned. And Abraham made a great feast on the day that Isaac was weaned. And Sarah saw the son of Hagar the Egyptian, whom she bore for Abraham, making sport" (Gen. 17:8–9).

In Josephus's *Jewish Antiquities*, Sarah initially felt affection toward Ishmael, "showing no less affection than if it were her own son, for he was being nurtured for the succession to the rule" (1.215).[34] Her feelings changed, however, when she gave birth to Isaac; she did not deem it proper for Ishmael, "who was older and was able to cause him harm after his father had died, to be reared with him."[35] In this reading, Sarah's request to banish Ishmael and his mother have nothing to do with what she saw, whether it was at the weaning banquet between Abraham and Ishmael, as depicted in *Jubilees*, or the encounter between Ishmael and Isaac in Genesis. The reason Josephus gives is Sarah's fear of what he might do once Abraham dies. Jealousy is not the motivating factor, as it was in *Jubilees*; here it is the maternal instinct, the wish to keep her child from harm, that compels Sarah to request Ishmael's expulsion.

The tradition with the most staying power is the one we find in rabbinic sources, promulgating the image of Ishmael as an idol worshipper, shedder of blood, and fornicator. Found in the earliest rabbinic texts, it made its way into medieval commentaries, such as Rashi, and continues to shape the way many think of Ishmael today.

Rabbinic Sources on *Metsaheq*

The earliest extant midrashim about Abraham's firstborn attempt to resolve the ambiguity of *metsaheq* in Genesis 21:9. *Tosefta Sotah*, a tannaitic source of Palestinian provenance probably codified in the middle of the third century, gives an explanation for Sarah's harsh request: "'Cast out this maidservant and her son'—This teaches that our mother Sarah saw Ishmael building altars, hunting locusts, making offerings, and burning incense for idol worship. She said, 'Perhaps Isaac, my son, will learn to do thus and will go and worship thus and the Name of Heaven will be profaned by this'" (*Tosefta Sotah* 5:12). The meaning is derived from Exodus 32:6: "Early next day, the people offered up burnt offerings and brought sacrifices of well-being; they sat down to eat and drink, and then they rose to revel [*letsaheq*]." The reason for Sarah's harsh dismissal is fear that Isaac might adopt Ishmael's idolatrous ways.[36]

Tosefta Sotah 6:6 presents a more elaborate exposition of Genesis 21:9. In addition to idol worship, Ishmael is thought to have engaged in forbidden sexual acts and the shedding of blood. What makes this midrash interesting is R. Shimon's position. He disagrees with these negative readings and proffers his own interpretation, exonerating Ishmael of objectionable behavior:

R. Shimon b. Yohai said, "There are four things which R. Aqiba used to expound and my words are more fitting than his. R. Aqiba expounded, 'Sarah saw the son of Hagar the Egyptian, whom she had borne to Abraham, making sport.' 'Making sport' [*tsehoq*] here means nothing other than idol worship, as it is said, 'Early next day, the people offered up burnt offerings and brought sacrifices of well-being; they sat down to eat and drink, and then they rose to revel [*letsaheq*]' (Exod. 32:6). This teaches that our mother Sarah saw Ishmael building altars, hunting locusts, and making offerings for idol worship." R. Eleazar b. R. Yosi the Galilean said, "Here 'making sport' means nothing other than forbidden sexual acts, as it is said, '. . . the Hebrew servant, whom you have brought among us, came to dally with me [*letsaheq*]' (Gen. 39:17). This teaches that our mother Sarah saw Ishmael womanizing and forcing himself on women."[37] R. Ishmael said, "'Making sport' is nothing other than the shedding of blood, as it is said, 'Abner said to Yoab, Let the young men, I pray you, arise and play before us [*vishaqu*] . . . Each one grasped his opponent's head and thrust his dagger into his opponent's side; thus they fell together' (2 Sam. 2:14–16). This teaches that our mother Sarah saw Ishmael take a bow and arrows and shoot at Isaac, as it is said, 'Like a madman who casts deadly firebrands, arrows so is the one who deceives his neighbor and says, I was only kidding *(metsaheq)*' (Prov. 26:18–19)."[38]

R. Shimon, however, is troubled by the notion that the son of Abraham behaved immorally:

> But I (R. Shimon) say, "Heaven forbid that such [behavior] should take place in the house of a righteous person. Can this be said of Abraham, of whom it is written, 'For I have singled him out, that he may instruct his children and his posterity [to keep the way of the LORD by doing what is right, in order that the LORD may bring about for Abraham what He has promised him]' (Gen. 18:19)? In his house is it possible there would be idol worship, forbidden sexual acts and the shedding of blood?

Rather, the word 'making sport' [*metsaḥeq*] here refers only to inheritance. For when our father Isaac was born to Abraham our father, everyone was happy. They said, 'A son has been born to Abraham! A son has been born to Abraham! He will inherit the world and take two shares.' Ishmael played [*metsaḥeq*] with the idea in his mind and said, 'Don't be fools. I am the firstborn, and I shall take the double portion.' From the answer to the matter, you learn . . . 'for the son of this slave woman shall not inherit with my son, with Isaac' (Gen. 21:10)."[39]

R. Shimon's interpretation is the only one that considers *metsaḥeq* neutrally. Whereas the other opinions put Ishmael—and thus, by extension, Abraham—in an unfavorable light, R. Shimon's position not only portrays Ishmael neutrally but also takes into account the implications of attributing such behavior to Ishmael: "In his (Abraham's) house is it possible there would be idol worship, forbidden sexual acts and the shedding of blood?"

How could the son of righteous Abraham, who is to keep the way of the Lord, engage in sinful activities? The earlier opinions are based on the use of a scriptural verse to illuminate the meaning of *metsaḥeq* and are very likely to vindicate Sarah and to compare Ishmael unfavorably with Isaac, thereby justifying God's choice of the latter. R. Shimon, in contrast, does not quote Scripture; instead he creates an internal monologue by which *metsaḥeq* is understood in light of Sarah's comment about inheritance (Gen. 21:10).

R. Shimon's interpretation of Genesis 21:9 takes Abraham's character into account. While the other interpretations adhere to the rules of rabbinic exegesis (although they, too, are probably not motivated by exegesis alone), they inadvertently impute to Abraham guilt by association (like father, like son) that is unacceptable to R. Shimon, who considers Genesis 18:19: "For I have singled him out, that he may instruct his children." In other words, the interpretation of *metsaḥeq* is about not only Ishmael's behavior but also Abraham's ability to instruct his children in the way of Torah. In addition, it is a justification of Sarah's questionable demand. R. Aqiba's interpretation explains and justifies Sarah's actions, but at the cost of besmirching Ishmael's character and diminishing Abraham's parental prowess, whereas R. Shimon justifies Sarah's actions while preserving the character of both father and son.

R. Shimon's neutral depiction is consistent with other tannaitic and amoraic portrayals of Ishmael such as *Tosefta Qiddushin* 5:17–19, *Genesis Rabbah* 59:7, and *Genesis Rabbah* 30:4. These sources convey the notion that Abraham was blessed in his old age and that one of those blessings has to do with Ishmael's repenting during Abraham's lifetime. Although the exact nature of his wrongdoing is unclear, his repentance is regarded as a blessing to his father. No father could die happily if he had a wicked son, and surely the son of righteous Abraham would repent. Abraham has not completely shunned his son or become indifferent toward him.

By the early medieval period, concern that Ishmael's disreputable behavior might reflect badly on Abraham is no longer a consideration:

> Thus we find in the case of Ishmael; he and Abraham had affection for one another and he did not chastise him and he came to be bad so Abraham hated him and cast him out of his house empty-handed. What did Ishmael do? When he was fifteen years old he began to bring an idol from outside and he worshiped it, as it says, "And Sarah saw the son of Hagar the Egyptian, whom she had bore Abraham, making sport *(metsaḥeq)*" (Gen. 21:9). (*Exod. Rab.* 1:1)[40]

In this instance, the indictment of Ishmael overshadows how it might reflect on his father.

An investigation of the retailoring of earlier midrashim on Ishmael in later rabbinic corpora demonstrates how the emergence of Islam affected portrayals of Ishmael. Before the emergence of Islam in the seventh century, the rabbis treated Ishmael as a metonym for Arabs and as a symbol of the non-Jew. Like his mother, Hagar, he is portrayed in various ways—neutrally, favorably, and negatively—but by the later medieval period he becomes a full-fledged antagonist.

In rabbinic compilations of the period of the rise of Islam and after, earlier sources are reworked and new midrashim portray Ishmael unfavorably, with about fifteen negative depictions in the later rabbinic works. Most important is that the animus intensifies with the passage of time. Midrashim that contrast Isaac the chosen one with Ishmael the rejected are fairly common in earlier literature, whereas the rabbinic literature of the early medieval period includes substantially harsher, more disparaging portrayals of Ishmael. There are more instances of Ishmael as metonym for Islam as well as Arabs. With the exception of rabbinic anthologies such as *Midrash ha-Gadol*, an anonymous fourteenth-century compilation of midrashim, and *Yalkut Shim'oni*, another medieval collection of midrashim, as well as the depiction in *PRE*, there are by my count only three positive portrayals, all of which are found in earlier, pre-Islamic sources.

The story of Abraham's visit to Ishmael in *PRE* is the most elaborate medieval midrashic narrative focusing on the relationship between Abraham and Ishmael.[41] Three years after Ishmael's expulsion, Abraham goes to the wilderness of Paran to visit him. Arriving at midday, he is greeted by Ishmael's wife, who tells Abraham that he and his mother have gone out to gather fruit. Abraham is fatigued from the arduous journey and asks her for some bread and water, but she offers him no hospitality. Before returning home, Abraham tells her: "When Ishmael comes home tell him that a certain old man came from the land of Canaan to see you, and he said, 'Exchange the threshold of your house, for it is not good for you.'" When Ishmael comes home, his wife conveys the message, and he understands his father's coded language. His mother sends and gets him a wife named Fatimah from her father's house in Egypt.[42]

Another three years go by, and Abraham revisits Ishmael, again promising Sarah beforehand that he will not descend from the camel in the place where Ishmael dwells. The reader is not told why she makes this request of him, but it may very well be that she fears he will reside with Ishmael or take Hagar as his wife. Again he arrives at midday and is greeted by Ishmael's wife. He inquires as to his son's whereabouts; she replies that he is with his mother in the wilderness, feeding the camels. He asks for bread and water, which she readily provides. Abraham rises and prays before God for his son, and thereupon Ishmael's house is replete with all good things. When he returns and his wife relates what happened, Ishmael knows that his father's love is still upon him.

The narrative, also found in several Islamic exegetical sources, captures the affection between father and son and portrays Abraham as taking an interest in his son's well-being after his departure from Abraham's household. Other portrayals of Ishmael in *PRE* are also sympathetic. Unlike his mother, who strays after idols, Ishmael remains faithful to God, and when he faces death he cries out to God not out of anger for his lot in life but out of sheer desperation. God so cares for Ishmael that he opens the well that he created on the eve of the first Sabbath in the week of Creation. While it is true that *PRE* upholds the chosenness of Isaac over Ishmael, it nonetheless presents him favorably. The Ishmaelites on the other hand are discussed in eschatological terms and not as sympathetically as their forefather.[43]

Changes in the portrayal of Ishmael and his relationship to Abraham are best elucidated in light of the rise of Islam. The success of Islam as a real presence in the Middle East presented theological, social, and political challenges for Judaism. The conflicts arising from these challenges, particularly the theological, differed fundamentally from those Christianity had presented several centuries earlier, for unlike Islam, Christianity established its identity at the expense of Judaism.[44] Nonetheless, Judaism was now confronted with another viable monotheistic religion in part rooted in the stories recounted in the Hebrew Scriptures, a religion that also exercised its political hegemony beyond the Near East. Jews attempted to make sense of the rise of Islam and the role this new empire played in their understanding of its sweeping success across the Near East and North Africa in the seventh century.

Ishmael and the Ishmaelites in the Apocalyptic Imagination

In the early Middle Ages, as Islam emerged as a force on the global religious and political stage, the metonymic use of Ishmael for Islam became de rigueur. The advent of Islam ushered in a new era that to some meant a change in the world order. For many Jews of the mid-seventh century, the emergence of Islam was anything but a tragic event.[45] As in times of yore, following the classical use of foreign kings as a "rod" against Israel's enemies, God would avenge the Jews by destroying their sworn adversaries. In this case, Ishmael, Islam, would conquer Esau, Christendom,[46] and Israel would no longer be subject to foreign rule.

The first few centuries of Islamic rule rekindled the flames of messianic fervor.[47] The Messiah would come and end the suffering of the faithful and the dominion of their opponents. The long-awaited establishment of the kingdom of God on the earth would finally become a reality. It is therefore no surprise that we have a relative surge of apocalyptic texts, which attempt to render a traumatic situation meaningful; cultural and political oppression by a foreign force is understood within the trajectory of salvation history.[48] In attempting to console the oppressed with hopes of imminent triumph, to justify the ways of God to Jews who might have wondered whether their suffering was for naught, earlier apocalyptic writings were adapted to accommodate new exigencies. Prophecies were retailored, traditions recast, revised, and expanded. Visions were attributed to some great figure of antiquity, to Elijah, Zerubbabel, or Rabbi Shimon ben Yohai.[49]

The rabbis turned to the Bible in order to engage the burning issues of the day. Through the creative exegetical process they made Scripture relevant to contemporary needs.[50] They found comfort and consolation as well as responses to current concerns. For the rabbis the Bible was more than a repository of the past; it was a blueprint for the trajectory of triumph and tragedy, tragedy and triumph. Enemies conquered and were vanquished by the hand of God. The die was cast. New players on the world stage filled familiar roles. Thus the Jews and Romans (later the Byzantines) were avatars of Jacob (Israel) and Esau, the Jews and Muslims avatars of Isaac and Ishmael. The Bible provided a host of prototypes and story arcs, including—but by no means limited to—the power struggle between Esau and Jacob and the redemptive Exodus narrative.[51] These stories were adapted to contemporary political exigencies by means of extending the Jewish metanarrative into the future. That is to say, the Jewish national narrative, which finds its culmination in the fulfillment of God's promise to God's chosen people, is given a teleology that reaches into the future in such works as apocalypses, visions, and eschatological midrashim. For the Jews of the early medieval period these genres of literature provided an alternative narrative for depicting historical reality, one that appropriated biblical imagery but also extended the biblical narrative into the future in order to confront the present. Roman occupation of the Promised Land, the destruction of the Second Temple, the debacle of the Bar Kokhba Revolt, Christian hegemony, and the emergence of Islam were understood and explained in light of Israel's salvation history.

In the early seventh century, as the Persians achieved astonishing successes against the Byzantines, as the latter staged a stunning, perhaps even miraculous, comeback, and as the Arabs decisively defeated both, apocalyptic feelings could not but proliferate. Already in the late sixth century many were convinced that "the end of the present world is already near and that the never-ending kingdom of the saints is about to come," as Pope Gregory I would write in 601 to the English king Ethelbert.[52] Indeed, the increasing intolerance of Byzantine Christians from the mid-sixth century onward further encouraged many Jews to see in the invading Arab armies a sign of their imminent deliverance. In the ensuing two centuries, such speculation intensified and was rife among all the communities of the Middle East.

Near Eastern Jewish, Christian, and Muslim apocalypses of late antiquity and the early medieval era exhibit a series of remarkable structural correspondences that transect permeable boundaries of ethnic and religious affiliation. Along with the inevitable individual doctrinal variations, these apocalypses reveal a number of common motifs, dramatis personae, and discursive sequences. And despite the history embedded in this literature, apocalypses employ what John Reeves has called "a distinctively formulaic set of conventions, tropes, and figures."[53]

Apocalyptic texts, regardless of differing religious backgrounds and periods, possess similar earmarks, such as the notion that the trajectory of human history is divinely ordained from beginning to end. They also display a fatalistic foreboding of imminent crisis that will ultimately result in the triumph of good over evil. "For a brief moment at the end of antiquity," Steven Wasserstrom writes, "the dialectic between Messianic myth and Messianic social movements, between apocalypse and apocalypticism, developed along patterns that were structurally parallel within Judaism and Islam. Jewish Messianic anticipations could become Muslim myths, and even movements, but not by 'influence' or by 'borrowing.' Rather, the family resemblance of idea and organization was due to a shared inheritance. And this common cultural milieu encompassed more than the expected economies, cuisines, architecture, head gear, and jurisprudence."[54]

With this background in mind, let me now turn to the *Nistarot (The Secrets)*, a work credited to the second-century rabbi Shimon ben Yohai, a rejecter of all that was Roman. "His strident opposition to foreign imperial hegemony," Reeves notes, "made him an ideal figure around which to cluster literary expressions of nationalist hopes for ultimate vindication and deliverance."[55] At the opening of the apocalypse, we are introduced to Shimon, who has been hiding from the emperor, the king of Edom, in a cave. Fasting and praying for forty days, he calls on God to enlighten him:[56]

"Lord God, how long will you spurn the prayer of your servant?" Immediately there were revealed to him the secrets of the eschaton [last things or end of the world] and [various] hidden things. When he perceived that the kingdom of Ishmael would come (and exercise dominion over Israel), he exclaimed: "Is it not sufficient that the wicked kingdom of Edom has done to us that we should also suffer the dominion of the kingdom of Ishmael?" Immediately Metatron [the chief of the angels in rabbinic literature], the prince of the Presence answered him and said: "Do not be afraid, mortal, for the Holy One blessed be He is bringing about the kingdom of Ishmael only for the purpose of delivering you from that wicked one [i.e., Edom]. He shall raise up over them a prophet in accordance with His will, and He will subdue the land for them; and they shall come and restore it with grandeur. Great enmity will exist between them and the children of Esau." "How are they understood as our deliverance?" He [Metatron] said to him, "Did not Isaiah the prophet say, 'And he saw a chariot with a couple of horsemen, one riding an ass, and one riding a camel' (Isa. 21:7)?"[57] Why did he put the "rider of the ass" before the "rider of the camel"? Should he not instead have said, "rider of a camel, rider of an ass"? [No, the textual sequence means that] when the one who rides on the camel [Ishmael or Muhammad] emerges, the kingdom ruled by the "one mounted upon an ass" (Zech. 9:9) has manifested [lit. sprouted] by his [i.e., Ishmael or Muhammad's] agency. Another opinion: "rider of an ass" means at the same time when "he rides upon an ass" (Zech. 9:9). Consequently they [Ishmael] are a deliverance for Israel like the deliverance [associated with] the "one mounted upon an ass."[58]

The mention of a prophet is noteworthy. Metatron says: "He shall raise up over them a prophet in accordance with his will, meaning Muhammad is an agent of God." *Nistarot* includes other passages like this containing a number of messianic interpretations of the Arab conquerors. Here is another example of how the Muslims were considered not the instrument of salvation but rather its harbinger, as one stage in the process toward final redemption:

> As soon as he saw the Kingdom of Ishmael was coming, he began to say: Was it not enough for us what the wicked Kingdom of Edom has done to us; now [there comes] also the Kingdom of Ishmael? Immediately Maṭaṭrōn . . . retorted, saying to him: do not fear, man, the Almighty only brings the Kingdom of Ishmael in order to save you from this wicked one, and he appoints over them a prophet of His wish, and will conquer the Land for them; they will restore it to its grandeur; and a great fear will befall the Children of Esau.[59]

It should be no surprise that the Jewish communities of the Byzantine Empire would hail the Arab conquerors as deliverers. During the late sixth and early seventh centuries they were subject to increasing hostility from Christians, culminating in Emperor Heraclius's decree ordering their compulsory baptism in Northern Africa and exile from Jerusalem.[60] Yet, over time, the anticipation certain sectors of the Jewish population felt at the prospect of liberation from "the wicked kingdom"—Byzantium—at the hands of the invading Arabs is tempered. Islam, which was once heralded as a liberator by Jews, is seen as another oppressive empire. Passages from *PRE* accentuate the invective against Islam.

Dated to the second half of the eighth or early ninth century, *PRE*,[61] a rabbinic pseudepigraphic work, unlike the *Nistarot*, is not an apocalypse. Yet one readily comes across apocalyptic imagery

woven into its midrashic exegesis. In chapter 44, for example, the
children of Ishmael are depicted as a nation, which the Son of David
will destroy in the future because the other nations "intermixed"
with them. All will fall: "The tents of Edom and the Ishmaelites,
Moab and the Hagarites, Gebal and Ammon and Amalek, Philistia
with the inhabitants of Tyre, Assyria also is joined with them" (Ps.
83:6, 7, 8). The hand of the Son of David will fell them, as it is said,
"O my God, make them like the whirling dust" (Ps. 83:14). Whatever hopes Jews might raise that the Islamic empire would vanquish
the Byzantines, Israel, too, would suffer the demise that all her enemies faced. So the welcome the Arabs will receive is expedient, for
ultimate victory is reserved for the Messiah.

Chapter 28 of *PRE* uses Genesis 15:9 to reconstruct the actual
historical succession of foreign dominance over Israel during the
first eight centuries of the Common Era:

> R. Eliezer said: The Holy One, Blessed be He showed Abra-
> ham our father the four kingdoms between the pieces ruling
> and perishing, as it is said, "And He said, Take me a heifer of
> three years old" (Gen. 15:9). This is the fourth kingdom, that is
> the kingdom of Edom [Rome] which is like a threshing heifer.
> "And a she-goat of three years old" (ibid.) refers to the Greek
> kingdom, as it is said, "And the he-goat magnified himself ex-
> ceedingly" (Dan. 8:8). "And a ram of three years old" (Gen.
> 15:9) refers to the kingdom of Media and Persia. "And a turtle-
> dove" (ibid.)—these are the sons of Ishmael.[62] It does not say
> "tor," "turtle-dove" in the language of the Torah, but rather in
> Aramaic where "tor" means the "ox." When the male ox is har-
> nessed to the female, they will open and break all the valleys.
> "And a young pigeon" (ibid.)—this is Israel who is compared to a
> young pigeon, as it is said, "O my dove you are in the clefts of
> the rock" (Song of Songs 2:14) . . . R. Ze'era said, "These
> kingdoms were created only as fuel for Gehinnom."

We have a recalibration of the standard formulaic sequence of
four world empires, but this new schema, unlike its Hellenistic and
Roman prototypes, begins with the toponym Edom for the western

or Latin principate, and in this case "Greece" represents eastern or Byzantine suzerainty. It is noteworthy that this midrash, an embellishment of *Genesis Rabbah* 44:15, includes the Ishmaelites.[63]

Chapter 30 of *PRE* concludes with a statement attributed to R. Ishmael outlining the fifteen things that the Ishmaelites will do in the land of Israel at the "end of days." In the end, they will fight three great battles, and the son of David will "sprout up [from Rome], and he will come to the Land of Israel and behold the destruction of both these and those," indicating Christians and Muslims. What Ishmaelites will do is mentioned also in *PRE*, chapter 32: "In the future, the Holy one, Blessed be He will hear the voice of the groaning of the people from what in the future the Ishmaelites will do, therefore his name is Ishmael, as it is said, 'God hears and afflicts them' (Ps. 55:2)."

As noted, the rise of Islam ignited messianic fervor among Jews, and it is therefore of no surprise that we find the Ishmaelites depicted throughout *PRE*, except for one midrash, in eschatological terms whereby in the future the son of David will rise against them:

> R. Ishmael said: "The five fingers of the right hand of the Holy One, Blessed be He, all of them are the secret of redemption . . . with the thumb and the entire hand in the future the Holy One, Blessed be He will destroy the people of Esau who are the foes of the Israelites and likewise the Ishmaelites who are their enemies, as it is said, 'Your hand shall prevail over your foes, and all your enemies shall be cut down'" (Mic. 5:8). (*PRE*, chapter 38)

The Christians and Muslims will be destroyed in the end as part of the redemptive process. To be sure, one can detect an initial excitement about the rise of Islam in several Jewish texts of this period, but over time this excitement turns into disappointment, and eventually the disappointment turns into hope for a future time when all of Israel's enemies will be destroyed.

The "apocalyptic imagination" is an incredibly fluid and fertile mentality, operating more or less continuously within more expansive ethnic or religious frameworks of the wider Near East. These Jewish apocalypses are part and parcel of broader tendencies of this period and region.[64] There seems to have been a surge in such works during the centuries that most historians identify as marking the gradual transition from late antiquity to the medieval era. But how widespread was these works' readership? Was the apocalyptic genre cultivated exclusively by dissidents, marginalized "sects," or disenfranchised "minority" groups? Scholars of apocalyptic texts, regrettably, situate their genesis and their perennial appeal in a localized malaise or disillusion spawned by the social and historical realities of cultural oppression and subjection, and do not take into account that while some apocalypses might display cultural hostility, others communicate the "ideological supremacy of the ruling powers."[65]

Early medieval texts referring to Ishmael as Islam display a sense of expectation, renewal, and retribution. We find this not only in apocalypses but, as mentioned above, in *PRE*, a work that is replete with rabbinic precedent but at the same time displays apocalyptic fantasy, a genre of midrash that uses Scripture to predict both historical and eschatological events. The historical interpretation seeks predictions of future events in scriptural texts that refer to past events. This is surely the case with chapter 30, where we learn of the fifteen things the Ishmaelites will do in the future, which they actually did in the past. The eschatological interpretation on the other hand seeks nonliteral references that may be applied to the events occurring in the end days, such as the coming of the Messiah.

The rise of Islam fueled the apocalyptic impulse. Ishmael becomes synonymous with Islam and is depicted in ways that accommodate cultural and religious needs that arose as Jews negotiated the arrival and ascent of Islam as a dynamic political and religious contender in the world arena. Some Jews experienced the emergence of the Arabian empire as a harbinger of a political or religious sea change. Given the paucity of evidence, however, it would be enormously difficult to gauge the readership and impact of these works. Be that as it may, Jewish literature of this period reflects reactions to the changing landscape of the Near East. Contemporary historical events are experienced through the biblical past.

Christian References to Ishmael

Like Jewish sources, Christian references to Ishmael also posit him in a less than flattering light. The notion that Isaac is the chosen son, the son through whom God will maintain his covenant, is the lens through which early Christian readers interpreted verses pertaining to Ishmael. For both Jews and Christians, Ishmael is the nonchosen son sent away, cut off from the family of Abraham. Paul interprets the Genesis story in which the younger sibling supplants the older in terms of the new community of believers, those represented by the son born of the spirit. That he is the older son is especially important for Paul, whose explanation of the story of Hagar and Sarah, Ishmael and Isaac, in Galatians establishes a platform for later Christian readings of Genesis 21.

At the heart of its symbolism are the antitheses of slavery versus freedom, earthly versus heavenly, fleshly versus spiritual.[66] The allegory both maintains the Genesis narrative and traduces it; it builds on the story of Abraham's two sons and upends its literal meaning. That is, true descent from Abraham is of the spirit (born of the promise). According to the allegory, believers in Christ are the spiritual descendants; observers of Torah are represented by Hagar and Ishmael, for they are slaves to the Mosaic law.[67] Sarah, the heavenly Jerusalem, is free from the bondage of Torah observance, and her children, children of the promise, are also liberated from its yoke.[68]

Paul explicitly states that the story is meant to be understood allegorically. Hagar and Ishmael stand for one covenant, the covenant given at Mount Sinai, and Sarah and Isaac for the other. The slave Hagar and her son represent those who are shackled to the yoke of the Mosaic covenant, whereas Sarah, the free woman, and her son are heirs to the new and everlasting covenant established by Jesus. Hagar represents earthly Jerusalem, Sarah the Jerusalem above.

According to Paul, there are two forms of sonship—one a function of the flesh, the other of the promise. The son of a slave represents the former; the son of the free woman represents the latter. The free sons of Abraham are those who live in freedom under the new covenant and are members of the new Jerusalem. By contrast,

the former are enslaved by the old covenant and dwell in the present
Jerusalem. Familiar with Jewish readings of "playing," Paul writes
that the older son "persecuted" Isaac, and with this word he drives
home a major point of the letter: that those demanding adherence
to circumcision are persecuting non-Torah-observant Christians. It
is important to make clear here that those "persecuting" the Christians were fellow Christians, not Jews, and not necessarily Jewish
followers of Jesus.[69] These anti-Pauline apostles were posing a
threat to his authority, demanding that the male, Gentile converts
undergo circumcision in order to be saved. Later Christian writers
decontextualized the allegory and applied it to Jews, although not
exclusively. Rather, the brothers embody good and evil, spirit and
flesh. Paul's allegorical reading of the brothers establishes an antipodal relationship that forms the foundation of Christian interpretations of the story. In turn, they are used to interpret contemporary
situations and to instruct Christians on moral behavior, as well as to
provide spiritual guidance.

Christian interpreters also had to contend with the meaning of
Ishmael's play. On a prima facie level, Sarah's demand seems harsh,
as it is unclear what, exactly, she saw. Keeping in mind that the early
Christian interpreters sought to draw lessons from Scripture and
often read the Old Testament stories typologically, as well as allegorically, many take their cue from Galatians 4. Origen asks, "How
did he injure or harm him if he was playing? As if this ought not to
be pleasing even at that age, that the son of the bondwoman played
with the son of the free woman" (*Homilies on Genesis*, 7:3).[70] Moreover, he marvels at Paul's understanding of Ishmael's actions as a
form of "persecution." What does Paul mean that Hagar's son persecuted Isaac, "he who was after the spirit" (Gal. 4:29)? Jerome, true
to form, mentions two Jewish interpretations of Ishmael's actions:
"he made a game of idols" and "he arrogated to himself by means of
a jest and a game the rights of the first-born in opposition to Isaac,
on the grounds that he was the elder."[71]

Sarah, who represents virtue, is offended that Ishmael, born of
the flesh, entices and seduces Isaac, who is of the spirit. This is what
Origen claims Paul means by "persecution." He writes: "And you,
therefore, O hearer of these words, do not suppose that alone is per-

secution whenever you are compelled by the madness of the pagans
to sacrifice to idols. But if perhaps the pleasure of the flesh allures
you, flee these things, as the greatest persecution if you are a child
of virtue. Indeed, for this reason the apostle also says, 'Flee fornica-
tion' (1 Cor. 6:18)." That is to say, physical temptations are a form of
persecution for the virtuous. Furthermore, Ishmael embodies the
allurements of the flesh, which through their very temptation persecute the spirit. For Origen, the matter is not about Jews, or anti-
Pauline apostles who demand adherence to the law but the seduc-
tion that impedes spiritual well-being.

Paul's depiction of Ishmael and Isaac is echoed throughout the
writings of the early church exegetes and homilists. In his commentary on Galatians, Augustine draws a connection between Ishmael
and the Jews who are the older sibling and who are of "the flesh":
"Thus the Apostle says that *we, like Isaac, are sons of the promise* (Gal.
4:28), and just as Isaac had been persecuted by Ishmael, so those
who had begun to live spiritually were being persecuted by carnal
Jews. Yet this persecution is in vain, since according to the Scripture the slave woman is cast out and her son cannot be an heir
alongside the free woman's son."[72]

Augustine's *Treatises on John (In Iohannis Evangelium Tractatus)*,
11, on John 2:23–25 and 3:1–5, is a good illustration of how Ishmael
and Isaac are taken out of their scriptural context and employed
metaphorically. He uses the Isaac–Ishmael dyad to refer to the opposition between Donatists, members of a schismatic church in the
Roman provenance of Africa in the fourth and fifth centuries, and
Catholics.[73] Augustine's occupation with Donatism began with his
ordainment and spanned thirty years. In brief, Donatism was a dynamic social force in Africa. In some regions it had greater appeal
and membership than the Catholic Church. Its attraction may in
part be attributed to the fact that many Africans regarded the Catholic Church's alliance with Roman power as a sign of its corruption.
The schism went back to the persecutions under Diocletian in the
early fourth century, when Christians were asked to hand over their
Scriptures. Once the persecutions were over, those who had aposta-
tized were deemed sinners, *traditores*, by Donatists, whereas the rest
of the church was more forgiving of their apostasy. Donatists regarded

sacraments as invalid and therefore believed that rebaptism was in
order, but Augustine rails against this notion:

> 12. There is a great mystery here. Ishmael and Isaac were play-
> ing together; Sarah saw them playing, and said to Abraham,
> "Cast out the slave-girl and her son; for the son of the slave-girl
> shall not be heir together with my son Isaac" [Gen. 21:9–12].
> And when Abraham showed his distress at the idea, the Lord
> backed up his wife's demand. Already the mystery is beginning
> to show itself here, because this episode was somehow laden
> with some future event. She saw them playing, and said, "Cast
> out the slave-girl and her son." What is this all about, brothers
> and sisters? For what harm had Ishmael done to the boy Isaac
> by playing with him? That playing was mocking; that playing
> signified deception. Now attend, beloved, to this great mys-
> tery. The apostle calls it persecution; that playing, that game,
> he calls persecution: for he says, "But just as at that time the
> child who was born according to the flesh persecuted the child
> who was born according to the Spirit, so it is now also"; that is,
> those who have been born according to the flesh persecute
> those who have been born according to the Spirit. Who are the
> ones born according to the flesh? Lovers of the world, lovers of
> this life. Who are born after the Spirit? Lovers of the kingdom
> of heaven, lovers of Christ, longing for eternal life, worship-
> ping God freely. They are playing together and the apostle
> calls it persecution. For after he said these words, "But just as at
> that time the child who was born according to the flesh perse-
> cuted the child who was born according to the Spirit, so it is
> now also," the apostle went on, to show what persecution he
> was talking about: "But what says the Scripture? 'Drive out the
> slave-girl and her child; for the child of the slave-girl will not
> share the inheritance with the child of the free woman'" (Gal.
> 4:30). We search where the Scripture says this, to see whether
> any persecution on Ishmael's part against Isaac preceded this;
> and we find that this was said by Sarah when she saw the boys
> playing together. The playing which Scripture says that Sarah
> saw, the apostle calls persecution. Hence, they who seduce you

by playing, persecute you the more. "Come," say they, "Come, be baptized here, here is true baptism for you." Do not play, there is one true baptism; that other is play: you will be seduced, and this persecution will weigh heavily on you. It would be better for you if you could gain Ishmael for the kingdom but he is not willing because he wants to play. Hold on to the inheritance of your father and listen: "Drive out the slave-girl and her child; for the child of the slave-girl will not share the inheritance with the child of the free woman." 13. These men, too, dare to say that they are used to suffering persecution from Catholic kings, or from Catholic rulers. What persecution do they endure? Physical suffering—but if they suffered at some point or suffered in some way, it is up to them to know and to examine their own consciences; still they suffered only physically. Yet, the persecution they inflict is more grievous. Beware when Ishmael wishes to play with Isaac, when he flatters you, when he offers another baptism. Tell him, 'I have already been baptized.' For if this baptism which you have received is genuine, anyone wishing to give you another one seeks to deceive you. Beware of the persecution of the soul. For though the party of Donatus has at times suffered somewhat at the hands of Catholic rulers, it was a bodily suffering, not the suffering of spiritual deception.[74]

For Augustine, Ishmael's play points to the Donatists' persecution of Christians. That is, the Donatists deceive other Christians into believing that they must be rebaptized. While Catholic rulers have inflicted physical pain on Donatists, they themselves inflict spiritual suffering through their deception. For Augustine, the meaning of the story of Genesis is given full expression in the contemporary situation between Catholics and Donatists. In Augustine's other works, Ishmael represents the old covenant, Isaac the new.[75] In his discussion of Psalm 120, Augustine again reads them in opposition to each other—not to illustrate divisions between Christians, or between Jews and Christians, but rather as representations of darkness and light, of that which is earthly, fleshly, and that which is of the spirit. The psalmist portrays his suffering as exile from the divine presence in distant regions: "Woe to me that I dwell in Meshekh, that I live

among the tents of Qedar. Too long have I lived among those who
hate peace. I am for peace; but when I speak, they are for war" (verses
5–7). Meshekh refers to a people in the far north, in Anatolia. Qedar
are the southern desert dwellers. The terms are therefore likely mer-
ismatic, representing the extremes of the world. The Qedarites are
a northern Arab tribe, descendants from Ishmael (Gen. 25:13). The
Hebrew term *qedar*, as "gloom," also stands for the lowly, depressed
state of the psalmist.[76] Psalm 120 evokes imagery of oppression, of
living in contention among those who seek war, "among the tents of
Qedar." The well-known connection between Ishmael and Qedar
allows Augustine to explain the psalm in light of Isaac and Ishmael.
The psalm, much like Paul's allegorized reading of Abraham's two
sons in Galatians, is read in the context of the Church—the spiritual body of believers who dwell among the unrighteous, "among
the tents of Qedar," among descendants of Ishmael, those that are
fleshy, and dark, for *qedar* is a reference not only to southern desert
dwellers but also to darkness, as it is rendered in Latin *(tenebrae):*

> Now you know that Abraham had two sons, whom indeed the
> Apostle mentions, and declares them to have been types of the
> two covenants . . . Ishmael therefore was in darkness, Isaac in
> light. Whoever here also seeks earthly felicity in the Church,
> from God, shall belong to Ishmael. These are the very persons
> who oppose spiritually-minded persons who are making prog-
> ress and disparage them. They have deceitful tongues and
> unrighteous lips. Our psalmist on his upward journey prayed
> against them, and he was supplied with destructive coals and
> sharp arrows of a mighty warrior, for he still has to live among
> such people until the whole threshing-floor is winnowed. This
> is why he complained, "I have been dwelling among the tents
> of Qedar." The tents of Ishmael are called those of Qedar. Gen-
> esis indicates this, for it tells us that Qedar belonged to Ishmael
> (Genesis 25:13). Isaac therefore is with Ishmael: that is, they
> who belong to Isaac, live among those who belong to Ishmael
> (Galatians 4:29). Those belonging to Isaac wish to ascend, but
> those belonging to Ishmael press them downwards: the former
> wish to fly to God, but the latter try to pluck their wings.[77]

Taking his cue from Galatians 4, Augustine interprets Psalm 120, a song of ascent, for instructional purposes, that is, to offer guidance to those Christians, ideally all Christians, who have committed themselves to a spiritual journey. For Augustine, the psalm speaks of the soul's spiritual ascent, its abandonment of temporal objects and the pursuit of vanity. Here Ishmael is an allegory of Christians of the flesh who persecute Isaac, Christians who strive to elevate themselves above carnal desires. Ishmael represents those who gainsay spiritual progress. He distracts them, in a sense "plays" with them, by offering deceitful words.

Christians and Jews depicted Ishmael and Isaac in antipodal terms as a means to address contemporary situations of political, social, or religious nature. Moreover, Christian writers drew on the biblical story in order to encourage Christians to remain upright and resilient against the temptations of the flesh.

Ishmael in the Islamic Tradition

Ishmael's presence in the Qur'an is relatively unremarkable. With the exception of his building the Ka'bah with Abraham (Q. 2:127), little is said about his life. Ishmael is mentioned only twelve times in the Qur'an itself as a prophet (*nabī*) or messenger (*rasūl*), and more often than not these mentions simply list him among several other prophets. It is beyond the bounds of the Qur'an that Ishmael grows in importance. We read that Ishmael was "a man of his word, an apostle and a prophet," that he "enjoined prayer and almsgiving on his people, and his Lord was pleased with him" (Q. 19:54–54). But even here there is also mention of Idris, a saint and prophet honored and exalted by God. In verse 21:85 Ishmael, Idris (commonly identified with Enoch), and Dhul-Kifl (Ezekiel) are praised for their patience and uprightness. Even Shi'ite sources only assign significance to Ishmael's birth insofar as they give meaning to the births of all prophets.[78] Unlike the biblical birth of Isaac, Ishmael's birth in the Qur'an is not linked to the covenantal promise of children who number the stars of the sky or sands of the earth. When he was born, al-Kisa'i tells us, his face radiated the Light of the Prophet Muhammad like the moon.[79] The reference to light in association with his birth links him with Abraham and Muhammad, who radiated light either on conception or in the mother's womb.

One of the most popular stories about Ishmael is actually about Abraham's visit to him. (Told briefly in Chapter 5, the story bears repeating.) It appears in many extraqur'anic texts—it is in these texts that we find Ishmael's importance growing—with various details sprinkled throughout the various renditions. In most sources, Ishmael and Hagar remain in Mecca after Abraham settles them there. Longing for his son, Abraham, with Sarah's permission, visits Ishmael. In some versions Gabriel brings him a horse from Paradise that he rides to the Sacred Land.[80] When he enters his son's abode, he greets the woman, but she behaves rudely toward this unexpected visitor. "What do you want?" she inquires. When she informs Abraham that the master of the house is away, he replies, "When your husband comes back, tell him to change the threshold of his house." When Ishmael returns from hunting, his wife informs him of the visitor and conveys Abraham's message. Ishmael knows immediately the meaning of Abraham's words, and commands his wife to rejoin her people. Ishmael remarries, in this version marrying a woman from the Jurhum.

Abraham revisits his son. He greets Ishmael's second wife, "Peace be with you, O people of this dwelling," to which she replies, "And with you peace, O noble man. Come in for the master of the house is away but will be back shortly." Abraham asks, "Do you have any food?" The wife replies in the affirmative and brings him an assortment of food: bread, meat, some roast fowl, and a cup of water. Then she washes his head and anoints it with oil. Before he departs, Abraham says, "When the master of the house returns, tell him to keep the threshold of his house." Ishmael's wife greets him on his return and tells him what happened. Ishmael knows that he should keep his wife, for she is an honorable woman.[81] Some versions include a third visit, and at that point father and son build the sacred house of God (Ka'bah).[82]

The question whether the story originated in Jewish or Islamic circles continues to capture the attention of scholars. But can we ever know for sure the relationship between the various renditions? That the narrative is found in both Islamic and Jewish sources calls

our attention to the ways folkloric texts function in any given culture
and reminds us of the rich circulatory system of stories that migrated
throughout the Near East. This phenomenon of the appearances of
parallel narratives allows us to appreciate the crosscultural fertiliza-
tion that doubtless took place in the medieval period. It is surprising, then, that studies of the striking similarities have been significantly overshadowed by the debate as to whether or not the Jewish
version predates the Muslim and vice versa. The attempt to locate
the original source of the narrative is indeed highly speculative and
ignores their oral nature. The story might have originated in rabbinic
circles and been later reworked by Muslims, and then later refashioned in *PRE*, the earliest extant Jewish version of the story.[83] On the
other hand it is also quite possible that the story originated in the Muslim tradition, which used both Arab folklore and Jewish legends. Given
both the nature and the paucity of the sources, we are left with mere
conjecture as to originary claims and concerns.

Moreover, this line of inquiry reduces the dynamic of intercul-
tural relations to facile alternatives. To say that the story was either
original or borrowed is to belie the complex web of interchange—
oral, written, social, and cultural—between Muslims and Jews. Indeed, it is futile to posit a unidirectional influence, and thus the model
of influence should be abandoned altogether.[84] We are better served
by trying to understand how the story functioned in each tradition,
sustaining the tradition's metanarratives—and in the case of the
Jewish tradition, trying to understand how the story functions in the
context of a shifting political and religious landscape. The story as
related in *PRE* highlights Ishmael's liminal status as a beloved member of Abraham's household who is also the father of the Arabs, the
Ishmaelites. The Islamic versions merge the expulsion of Hagar and
Ishmael and the building of the Ka'bah, and they Arabize Ishmael
through marriage.

One striking feature of the development of Ishmael's identity in
the Islamic tradition is its biblical as well as Arabian base. According
to traditional genealogists, all Arabs are derived from one of two
great ancestors, Qathan or 'Adnan, the former associated with the
true or original Arabs, a designation that includes the Jurhum tribe.
At least one genealogical system, that of Ibn al-Kalbi, whose form

was finalized around the beginning of the ninth century CE, regards Ishmael as the progenitor of the northern Arabs, identified with 'Adnan, the great ancestor of the Arabized northern tribes (*al-'Arab al-musta'riba* or *al-'Arab al-muta'arriba*). Ishmael marries a noble woman from the Jurhum tribe, one of the legendary pre-Islamic Arab tribes affiliated with the holy city of Mecca, and he adopts their language. His marriage to a Jurhumite woman legitimizes him as an Arab, since the Jurhum are from Qathan, the original Arabs of the south (*al-'Arab al-'Ariba*). It furthermore establishes him as the patriarch of the northern tribes and thus the progenitor of Muhammad, who is of the Quraysh, one of the northern tribes.

In other words, the pre-Islamic Arab and the biblical genealogical systems are conflated by means of grafting one onto the other in order to Arabize Ishmael and make him the progenitor of Muhammad, but not the progenitor of all Arabs, since he is from one main tribe, the tribe of 'Adnan. The complete Arabization of Ishmael was possible through marriage and not by birth, in comparison to Muhammad, who is an Arab by birth. In an attempt to end the antagonism between the northern and southern tribes, Muhammad became the embodiment of the full-blooded Arab, whereas Ishmael's Arabness, although crucial, mattered less.

In a tradition attributed to Ibn Abbas, the Jurhumite taught Ishmael Arabic, as noted. True, who would be a better teacher of Arabic than the Jurhum? The notion that Ishmael was taught Arabic, however, calls attention to his Arabization and in a sense subverts his role as *pater eponymus*. Yes, Arabs descend from him, but he is assimilated into the true line of Arabs through marriage, a situation that to some degree attenuates his postbiblical role as father of the Arabs. And yet it was when Islam traversed the borders of the Arabian peninsula and established itself in Persia that Ishmael's prominence as the father of the Arabs became more intricately incorporated into the Islamic metanarrative.

Ishmael, the progenitor of Arab Muslims, the firstborn of Abraham, the son willing to be sacrificed according to God's will, is also the son who assists Abraham in raising the foundations of the holy sanctuary, the Ka'bah (Q. 2:127).[85] In pre-Islamic Arabia, the Ka'bah served as the central shrine in Mecca that housed the 360 idols of tribal patron deities. It was also the site of the annual fair and pilgrimage that brought Mecca significant revenue. A tradition attributed to Ibn Abbas, as preserved in al-Tha'labi, describes the Ka'bah as one of the jewels of Paradise created before Adam descended to earth. God sends Adam down to the place of the Ka'bah and promises Adam that one of Adam's offspring, Abraham, will ensure its prosperity. God will instruct him on the pilgrimage stations and on what is lawful and what is prohibited in the sanctuary.

There are many different versions of the details of the story, including the way God reveals the place of the Ka'bah to Abraham, and Ishmael's role in building it.[86] But whether Ishmael only helps to lay the foundations or whether he plays a larger role in the whole project, he wholeheartedly agrees to assist his father in doing the will of God. In al-Tha'labi Ishmael hands Abraham the stones for the House. "While Abraham was a Hebrew, Ishmael was an Arab, God instilled in each of them the language of the other."[87] Together they build the Ka'bah and recite Q. 2:127–128: "Our Lord, accept this from us, for you are the all-hearing, the all-knowing . . . Teach us the way of worship and forgive our trespasses, for You are compassionate and merciful." God hears their prayer and sends Gabriel to teach them about the rituals associated with Pilgrimage (Hajj).

Tradition also relates that when Muhammad returned victoriously to Mecca he immediately cleansed the Ka'bah of idols and restored it to the rightful worship of one God. Today the Ka'bah is the focus of the Hajj, the obligatory trip to Mecca during the twelfth month, Dhūl al-Ḥijja. In addition to this tradition, another tradition, associating *Maqām Ibrāhīm* (also known as the station of Abraham) with Abraham's visit, reports that Abraham's footprints were imprinted on the stone while he was building the Ka'bah with Ishmael.

Ishmael is portrayed as a dutiful son who demonstrates a steadfast willingness to carry out God's command. When Abraham grows weary from the labor, or in some renditions when the building becomes too high for him to reach to its top, Ishmael brings him a large rock (*Maqām Ibrāhīm*), on which Abraham stands. That Ishmael assists his father in building the Ka'bah and together with him is taught the pilgrimage ceremonies establishes a basis for his importance in Islam. Yet, even though Ishmael assists Abraham in raising the foundations of the House of God, his role is secondary to that of Abraham, who is explicitly commanded to build it and is shown where to place it, as well as commanded to call all humanity to take part in the Hajj. While the qur'anic Ishmael is considered a prophet and messenger of God, one of the righteous who submits to God, extraqur'anic sources throw light on interactions between Arab and non-Arab Muslims and illustrate the importance of his identity as the Arab son of Abraham. During the period when Arab hegemony expands to Persia, Ishmael is given a more prominent position in the Islamic metanarrative.

Concluding Remarks

Ishmael plays different roles in each religious tradition's explanation of who constitutes the family of Abraham. His expulsion along with his mother from Abraham's house serves as the indelible image of him in Jewish and Christian circles. Jewish and Christian reasons for his rejection contribute to an irremediable image of a naughty, licentious, evil son and brother. The Jewish Ishmael is relegated at best to the margins, cast aside and displaced by Isaac, through whom God establishes his Abrahamic covenant. While not all Jewish portrayals are negative or neutral—some are even positive—the accretion of negative traditions overwhelms whatever more favorable references are found in ancient and medieval sources. So, too, Christian sources paint Ishmael in negative tones and locate him outside the family of Abraham. In the hands of some Christian writers Ishmael morphs into Judaism, God's firstborn, rejected people, who are replaced by Isaac, believers in Christ. The Christian Ishmael is fleshly, earthly, and dark. He represents wrong teaching and temptation. The Jewish-Christian Ishmael is also the father of the Arabs and comes to represent Islam.

Islam's Ishmael, in contrast, is a full-fledged member of Abraham's family, the devoted son, messenger, and prophet of God. The Qur'an does not tell us a great deal about him, but he builds the Ka'bah with his father, and in nonqur'anic Islamic sources he marries an honorable woman of the Jurhumite tribe and fathers the line of the Prophet Muhammad. He willingly offers himself for sacrificial slaughter, and his deed is commemorated in the Muslim tradition. Even when early traditions debate whether he or Isaac was the sacrificial son, or when he is denigrated in Persian and Arab polemics, he resides well within the center of Abraham's family.

This survey of how the Jewish, Christian, and Muslim traditions treat the figure of Ishmael demonstrates the way scriptural interpretation serves a number of theological as well as political purposes. The variety of images and impressions of Ishmael across the three monotheisms complicates one's understanding of what is meant by Abrahamic religions. And yet, whether Ishmael dwells within or outside the Abrahamic family, whether we refer to him as Yishmael, Isma'il, or Ishmael, he resides within the larger Abrahamic penumbra of traditions that identify him as the firstborn of Abraham, born of Hagar, brother of Isaac.

■ 7

The Sacrifice of Isaac and Ishmael

GOD'S COMMAND to Abraham that he sacrifice Isaac (Genesis 22) is one of the best-known episodes in the patriarch's life, perhaps one of the most read and discussed stories in the entire Bible. One cannot overestimate its significance in Jewish and Christian theological musings or the role it plays in the liturgical life of each religious community. The story was told on funerary objects in ancient times, has been represented in paintings throughout history, and was reimagined in religious as well as secular writings.[1] It is recounted on Rosh Hashanah; it is mentioned in Christian Eucharistic prayers and read on Good Friday or the Easter Vigil. Muslims commemorate the near sacrifice of Ishmael on the great feast (Eid al-Adha) that marks the end of the Hajj period.

Consisting of fewer than two dozen lines, it is a terse tale, told with mounting apprehension.[2] That God would test Abraham by commanding him to sacrifice the son of the covenant has troubled not only biblical scholars and theologians but also ethicists and moral philosophers such as Immanuel Kant, who rejects altogether the command as morally incongruous. Even for Søren Kierkegaard, who valorizes Abraham—he refers to him as the father of faith, the knight of faith—the event is haunting: "The ethical expression for what Abraham did is that he was willing to murder Isaac; the religious expression is that he was willing to sacrifice Isaac, but in this anguish lies the contradiction that can indeed make one sleepless."[3] Modern readers are not the only ones unnerved by the account. Within the interstices of the narrative of Abraham's unwavering faith and the son's assent echo the dissenting voices of angels, bodies, fathers, sons, and mothers.[4]

The scholarship on the binding of Isaac (also known as the Aqedah) is exceedingly vast and varied, from studies on child sacrifice in the ancient Near East to its imprint on twentieth-century secular Israeli literature.[5] I will limit this discussion to the ways Jews, Christians, and Muslims read the story in light of Abraham's constant faithfulness despite the trials God puts him through, and I will focus on the sacrificial son. The traditions of Judaism, Christianity, and Islam emphasize the son's willingness to sacrifice himself. Especially in Judaism and Islam, the sacrificial son gains merit for complying. We will also consider examples of how the tradition acknowledges and critiques the sacrificial command.

Christian writings generally read the story typologically. Isaac is a figure of Jesus who willingly sacrifices himself. So, too, the ram is understood as a type for Jesus, the ransom for all. Depictions of the Aqedah in works of art dating back to the ancient period emphasize the different ways in which the story is understood. The sacrifice of Isaac in the Jewish tradition celebrates God's steadfast commitment to his covenanted people; however, the event often depicted on Christian sarcophagi and funerary art is that of the salvific power of Jesus' sacrifice.

The Trials of Abraham

The theme of God testing human beings is not prevalent in the Bible, but there are nevertheless examples of God doing so in order "to know" or "to see" how certain groups or individuals will act.[6] In many instances he makes his purpose known, but in Genesis 22 this is not revealed until verse 12, when the angel of the Lord calls out to

Abraham, "Lay not your hand upon the lad, nor do anything to him;
for now I know that you fear God, seeing that you did not withhold
your son, your only son from me." Extrascriptural traditions amplify
the meaning of the test. It becomes the culminating test in a series
of trials and tribulations that Abraham confronts over the course of
his lifetime, beginning with the command to leave the safety of his
homeland and the shelter of his father's house.

The list of ten trials seems to date back to the second century BCE.[7]
We find mention of seven trials in *Jubilees:*

> Now the Lord was aware that Abraham was faithful in every
> difficulty which he had told him. For he had tested him through
> his land and the famine; he had tested him through the wealth
> of kings; he had tested him again through his wife when she
> was taken forcibly, and through circumcision; and he had tested
> him through Ishmael and his servant girl Hagar when he sent
> them away. In everything through which he tested him he was
> found faithful. He himself did not grow impatient, nor was he
> slow to act; for he was faithful and one who loved the Lord
> (17:17–28).[8]

The notion of ten trials is explicitly stated in *Mishnah Avot* 5:3, where
we find a litany of tens—ten generations from Noah to Abraham,
ten plagues, and the ten things created on the eve of Shabbat at twilight. The Qur'an also refers to the trials and tribulations that Abraham endures (Q. 2:124) and the blessings bestowed on him for having
overcome them, although there is no explicit reference to ten specific
trials.

All three traditions regard God's command to Abraham to sacrifice his son as the greatest trial Abraham endured. It highlights the
extent of Abraham's faithfulness. As we read in *Jubilees* 18:16, "I [God]
have made known to all that you are faithful to me in everything
which I say to you," and in Pseudo-Philo's *Biblical Antiquities* 32:4,
"it made you [Abraham] known to those who do not know you."
Similarly, in the Qur'an Abraham is praised by succeeding generations (Q. 37:108).[9] Indeed, this notion that Abraham was an emblem
of faithfulness pervades all three traditions.

The rabbis play with the term *nissah* (tested) in order to make this point. In rabbinic fashion, a verse from Psalms is brought to bear on the verse: " 'You have given a banner [*nes*] to those who fear you that it may be displayed [*lehithnoses*] because of the truth' (Ps. 60:6). Trial after trial [*nissayon ahar nissayon*], exaltation upon exaltation so that they may be exalted in the world like a ship's flag [*nes*]" (*Gen. Rab.* 55:1). By means of philological associations, the rabbis draw a connection between trial *(nissayon)* and banner *(nes)*. As the righteous overcome trials, they are set apart from others, serving as a ship's banner set high above all else. Punning on *nes*, the rabbis make a theological claim: Abraham's hardship, his *nissayon*, is proof of his exaltation, his *nes*. God did not capriciously choose Abraham but singles him out because of his righteousness.[10] *Genesis Rabbah* 50:2 emphasizes this point:

> " 'The Lord tries the righteous . . .' " (Ps. 11: 5). Rabbi Jonathan said: "A potter does not examine defective vessels, because he cannot give them a single blow without breaking them. What then does he examine? Only the sound vessels, for he will not break them even with many blows. Similarly, the Holy One, blessed be He, tests not the wicked but the righteous, as it says, 'The Lord tries the righteous.' " R. Jose b. R. Hanina said: "When a flax worker knows that his flax is of good quality, the more he beats it the more it improves and the more it glistens; but if it is of inferior quality, he cannot give it one knock without it splitting. Similarly, the Lord does not test the wicked but only the righteous," as it says, 'The Lord tries the righteous.' " R. Eleazar said: "When a man possesses two cows, one strong and the other feeble, upon which does he put the yoke? Surely upon the strong one. Similarly, God tests none but the righteous," as it says, 'The Lord tries the righteous.' "

The notion that good deeds are rewarded and bad deeds punished, much like the laws of karma (we reap what we sow), pervasive in several books of the Hebrew Bible, does not apply to this midrash. In fact, the converse is true: it is the righteous who suffer, and in their suffering they are exalted. The rabbinic interpretation of the binding of Isaac, the Aqedah, addresses queries as to why Abraham, out of all the people who roamed the earth at that time—or the Israelites, out of all the nations of the world—was called into a covenantal relationship with God, was chosen by God. Abraham was chosen because of his righteousness, or rather because of his capacity to endure suffering, to overcome trial after trial. He is made an emblem of obedience and righteousness, and in turn a sign of God's justice to the extent that he was rewarded for his suffering.

The list of Abraham's trials culminates with the call to sacrifice Isaac. This most difficult of tests is understood as the ultimate sign of his obedience, proving his unconditional devotion to God. Abraham's silence in light of what he is asked to sacrifice is rather perplexing. How is it that he advocates on behalf of Sodom and Gomorrah yet when commanded to sacrifice Isaac he utters nary a word of protest? Why does he equivocate when Sarah demands Ishmael's expulsion? Perhaps an answer emerges when reading together the parallel commands, one to sacrifice Ishmael and the other to sacrifice Isaac.

Because the Aqedah looms so large in the life of Abraham, the harrowing sacrifice of Ishmael in Genesis 21 usually goes unnoticed. Although Ishmael is not mentioned in the entire chapter, it is manifestly clear that the "son of that slave" is Ishmael. In Genesis 16:6, when Sarah complains to her husband about feeling lowered in Hagar's esteem, he tells her to do as she wishes with Hagar, even at the possible cost of his son. But in Genesis 21 he does not acquiesce to her request. In fact, the matter gravely distresses Abraham. It could be that by now, in Genesis 21, Abraham has forged a bond with Ishmael. Whatever the case, God must intervene, reiterating that his offspring will continue through Isaac but also promising to make Ishmael a nation. He thus ensures the covenant through Isaac and assures the safety of Ishmael.

Putting his trust in God, Abraham gets up "early in the morning,"[11] takes some bread and a skin of water, and gives them to Hagar. He places them on her shoulder, "together with the child,"[12] and sends her away, sacrificing them to the wilderness of Beer-sheba, where their water runs dry. Unable to watch her son die, Hagar leaves him under one of the bushes, sits away from him, and bursts into tears. God hears the cry of the boy, and an angel of God calls to her from heaven and informs her that God has heard his cry and will make a great nation of him. God opens her eyes, and she sees a well of water. The child is saved and grows up to be a father of twelve nations.

It is worth considering the possibility that casting Ishmael off into the wilderness is the hardest trial Abraham suffers. Only after God promises Ishmael's prosperity does he go through with the command. Now that he has put his full faith in God, he can withstand anything else God asks of him, even the command that he offer Isaac as a burnt offering. On that occasion Abraham is silent, unflinching, and obedient, possibly because he already went through a similar test. Of course, there is more at stake when Abraham is asked to give up the son of the promise, and to do so with his own bare hands, but once he is able to do the seemingly impossible act of sacrificing Ishmael, it might not be as difficult for him to give up Isaac. The unbinding of Ishmael leads to the binding of Isaac.

A medieval Hebrew poem draws a portrait of Abraham that is reminiscent of many aspects of the story of Abraham, how he was chosen, endured ten trials, and attempted to obey God's command to sacrifice Isaac:

> Abraham, the steadfast one, made You
> Known, before You were known by the
> World; he revealed to all creatures the
> Path which they should take.
>
> He was designated from among twenty
> generations and withstood every trial,
> Lord, you put him to the test ten
> times; You granted him offspring in
> his hundredth year.
>
> Benign One, when You said to him:
> 'I desire your child as a fragrant
> offering'—he rushed to fulfil the
> command, he lost no time at all.
>
> Quickly he split the wood, took up the
> fire and knife, loaded his favoured
> one, Isaac, with the faggot for the burnt offering.[13]

Jewish and Christian writers found themselves defending the near sacrifice of Isaac against pagans who assailed the idea that God required human sacrifice. Josephus emphatically states that the command arose from God's desire not for human blood (*Ant.*, 1.133) but to test Abraham's mind to see if he would obey the command. Other early writers, like Philo, also defend the test as a sign of his faith and obedience. This notion carries through to later Christian and Jewish writers who portray Abraham as an exemplar.

Addressing the question why God had to test Abraham at all, some traditions point to Mastema, one of the angels. Much like the challenge Satan poses to God in the book of Job is Mastema's provocation: "Behold, Abraham loves Isaac his son, and he delights in him above all else. Tell him to offer him as a sacrifice on the altar. Then You will see if he will carry out this command, and You will know if he is faithful in everything through which You test him" (*Jub.* 17:16).[14] *Jubilees* is explicit that God knew Abraham's faithfulness, for he had tested him through "his land and the famine," through "the wealth of kings," through the taking of his wife captive, through circumcision, and through the sending away of Ishmael and Hagar. In all these matters, Abraham is found faithful (17:17–18).

Passages such as 4Q225, *Biblical Antiquities*, 32:1–2, *Genesis Rabbah* 55:4, and *b.Sanhedrin* 89b somewhat ameliorate God's role in the Aqedah. As in *Jubilees*, Prince Mastema casts doubts about Abraham in 4Q225, and in *Biblical Antiquities*, 32:1–4, the angels envy Abraham. In the Talmud (*b.Sanhedrin* 89b), Satan marshals objections against Abraham, for when he made a feast, he did not sacrifice to God, not even a turtledove or young bird. By presenting the test as proving Abraham's worthiness to the world at large, and here to Mastema in particular, the passage shifts the focus away from God. Satan instigates the test: "Abraham made a great banquet on the day that Isaac was weaned" (Gen. 21:8). At that time Satan said to God, "Master of the Universe, you have blessed this old man at the age of one hundred with offspring. Yet amidst this banquet that he prepared, he has not sacrificed a pigeon or fowl for you!" God replied, "All that he did he did only for the sake of his son. Still, were I to say to him, 'Sacrifice your son before Me,' he would sacrifice him at once." Hence it says (Gen. 22:1), "And after these words, God tested

Abraham." It is not only the ministering angels who raise the question of his faithfulness; Abraham voices the same concern about himself in *Genesis Rabbah* 55:4. God consoles him: "I know if I were to ask that you sacrifice your only son to Me, you would not refuse."

The biblical verse introducing the Aqedah is rather vague, given that there is no connection between what directly precedes it in Genesis 21, namely, Abraham's covenant with Abimelech and his peregrinations in the land of the Philistines. Thus, the dialogue between God and Satan places blame on Satan for instigating the test and at the same time explains what the verse means by "these things" or "these words."[15]

In Judaism, the binding of Isaac is interpreted in light of God's abiding love for his covenanted people. Through the actions of their forefather Abraham, the Jewish people are rewarded. The notion of the merit of the fathers, *zekhut avot* (vicarious atonement), has its roots in the Bible. In Exodus 20:5–6 God visits the iniquity of the fathers upon the children unto the third and fourth generations and shows mercy unto the thousand generations that love him and keep his commandments. The same idea appears in Deuteronomy 12:28: "Observe and hear all these words which I command you, that it may go well with you, and with your children after you forever, when you do that which is good and right in the sight of the Lord your God." The end of the Aqedah also exemplifies this notion: "For because you have done this thing, and have not withheld your son, your only son that in blessing I will bless you, and in multiplying I will multiply your seed as the stars of the heaven and the sand which is on the sea shore; and your seed shall possess the gate of his enemies. And in your seed shall all the nations be blessed because you have obeyed my voice" (Gen. 22:16–18).

In Exodus 32:13–14 Moses reminds God of his covenant: "Remember your servants Abraham, Isaac, and Israel, how you yourself swore to them and said to them, 'I will make your offspring as numerous as the stars of heaven, and I will give to your offspring this whole land of which I spoke, to possess forever.' And the Lord renounced the punishment planned for God's people." According to the rabbis, the entire world would be suspended in its position on account of the deeds of each of the forefathers (Abraham, Isaac, and Jacob).[16] Israel relies on the merits of its forefathers. The rabbis also interpret God's parting of the Red Sea as reward for Abraham's willingness to sacrifice his son: "Because of the merit of the deed which their father Abraham did, I will divide the sea for them, for it is said, 'and he split [*wayyebaqqa*] the wood of the burnt offering' (Gen. 22:3). And here it is written, 'And the waters were divided [*vayyibbaqe'u*]' (Exod. 14:21)."[17] The rabbis anchor their interpretation by means of a philological connection (split, cleave, or divide) between the two verses. God saves the Israelites from the Egyptians because their forefathers obeyed his commandment.

In another midrash, the rabbis ask why God's command was not "Take Isaac" but rather "Take your son, your only son, the one you love." It was to ensure that Abraham was rewarded for every word spoken, they tell us. Similarly, when Abraham was commanded to leave his father's house, he was not told immediately where to go, so that he would be rewarded for every step he took (*Gen. Rab.* 35:7). His reward in turn was to redound to the benefit of his progeny. The rabbis give expression to this idea of the merit of the fathers in their exegetical work, but they do not use it as an excuse for irresponsibility in the sons. In an example directly related to Abraham's binding of Isaac, *Leviticus Rabbah* 29:9 expresses the expiatory value of Abraham's act. Abraham asks God to look favorably on his act, an act that required Abraham to suppress his compassion for his son and act accordingly. God is implored to similarly suppress his feelings, in this case his anger against the "children of Isaac" on account of their evil deeds, and to remember the binding of their father, so that he will turn away from judgment toward mercy. Although *Genesis Rabbah* 56:10 does not explicitly mention the Israelites' wrongdoing, God is nevertheless called to show compassion for them when they are in trouble. Later generations also gain merit through Isaac, the perfect sacrifice, whose ashes "store up merit for atonement generation after generation."[18]

Late antique and medieval reflections on the binding of Isaac promote the idea that Isaac's blood was shed, and in some cases he was sacrificed and brought back to life. Abraham "concedes nothing to the tie of relationship," Philo says, "but his whole weight is thrown into the scale on the side of acceptability with God . . . [H]e did not incline partly to the boy and partly to piety, but devoted his whole soul through and through to holiness and disregarded the claims of their common blood."[19] According to the rabbis, Abraham was so focused on the task at hand that he did not hear the angel call out to him the first time—hence "Abraham, Abraham" (Gen. 22:11).[20] He was so zealous to perform the mitzvah (command) to sacrifice Isaac that when the angel called out to him, Abraham considered strangling him, and asked to bring forth a drop of Isaac's blood (*Gen. Rab.* 56:7).[21] The midrash depicts Abraham as ardent to prove his devotion to God and answers the question why the verse says, "Do not lay your hand on him, nor do anything to him." If Abraham is told not to put his hand on Isaac, why does Scripture add "nor do anything to him"? The rabbis suggest that in his eagerness to prove his devotion to God, Abraham insists that he shed Isaac's blood; hence "Nor do anything to him."[22]

The Aqedah is commemorated on Rosh Hashanah and is not associated with Yom Kippur (Day of Atonement); its expiatory significance is thus underplayed. There is, however, evidence connecting it to Passover.[23] Indeed, in an early midrashic collection, *Mekhilta de Rabbi Ishmael* (7:78–82), the blood spread on the lintels of the doors of Israelites evokes the blood of Isaac, who according to extrabiblical traditions was a willing victim. According to Judith, God tested not only Abraham but Isaac also: "Remember what thing he did to Abraham and how he tried Isaac" (8:26–27).

In *Targum Neofiti* and *Pseudo-Jonathan*, as well as in *Genesis Rabbah* 56:8, for example, Isaac requests to be tied, for fear that upon seeing the knife he might flinch and thus render the sacrifice unfit. He consents fully to his own sacrifice, a notion found also in 4 Maccabees 13:12 and 16:20, Pseudo-Philo's *Biblical Antiquities,* 32:2–3, and Josephus (*Ant.,* 1.232), where the twenty-five-year-old son builds the very altar toward which he hastens when Abraham reveals to him what is about to take place. As discussed in Chapter 5, the brothers compete over who is more beloved, and Isaac "wins" the contest. In another rabbinic text, Isaac states explicitly, "If God were to command my father, 'Slaughter your son Isaac, I would not stop him.'"[24] This idea of the son's willingness to be sacrificed is prevalent in Jewish, Christian, and Muslim sources.

The narrative recited on Rosh Hashanah, the Day of Remembrance, when the ram's horn (shofar) is blown, reminds the descendants of Abraham, Isaac, and Jacob of God's rule over all creation, and of their relationship with the sovereign of the universe. The Torah reading on the first day of Rosh Hashanah recounts Hagar and Ishmael's exile, conceivably Abraham's hardest trial, leading up to the reading of the Aqedah on the second day. The sound of the ram's horn evokes not only the ram sacrificed in Isaac's stead but also the horn that sounded as Moses received revelation on Sinai. It is thus a reminder of the covenantal relationship between God and the children of Abraham and a reminder of their obedience to the God of Israel.

Christian Writings on the Sacrifice of Isaac

In Christianity, the binding of Isaac occupied the attention of the church fathers, from Origen and Ambrose to Gregory of Nyssa and John Chrysostom, to Cyril of Alexandria and Augustine. Many other church writers commented on this narrative, and it came alive in frescoes and on sarcophagi. About the binding of Isaac, Augustine writes, "The deed is so famous that it recurs to the mind of itself without any study or reflection, and is in fact repeated by so many tongues, and portrayed in so many places, that no-one can pretend to shut his eyes or his ears from it."[25]

The biblical story is understood typologically as the sacrifice God the father made by ransoming his only son to atone for the sins of all. Abraham serves as a type for God, who sacrifices his only son, and Isaac serves as a model *(typos)* for Jesus, who also carries the wood on his shoulders,[26] silently and willingly accepting his fate. In some cases the church fathers emphasize the ways in which the story foreshadows Christ's crucifixion; in other instances they note the contrasts between Isaac and Jesus. The *Epistle of Barnabas*, one of the earliest works to draw a typological connection between the Aqedah and the crucifixion, suggests that God "was going to offer the vessel of the spirit as a sacrifice for our sins, in order that the type established in Isaac, who was offered upon the altar, might be fulfilled" (7:3). Melito of Sardis, a middle to late second-century Christian writer, draws on many parallels between the two narratives: "A ram appeared for slaughter on behalf of Isaac the righteous one so that Isaac might be loosed from bonds. That ram when slain redeemed Isaac thus also the Lord when slain saved us and when sacrificed redeemed us."[27] The ram represents Jesus, for the ram redeemed Isaac, and Jesus redeems humanity. Irenaeus writes: "Since indeed Abraham, having followed, in keeping with his faith, the commandment of God's word, did with a ready mind give up his only begotten and beloved son, for a sacrifice unto God, that God again might be well pleased to offer unto Abraham's whole seed His only begotten and dearly beloved son to be a sacrifice for our redemption" (*Against the Heresies*, 5.4.5). And Augustine evokes the image of the crucifixion:

> And on this account Isaac carried the wood on which he was to be offered up to the place of sacrifice, just as the Lord Himself carried His own cross. Finally, since Isaac himself was not killed—for his father had been forbidden to kill him—who was that ram which was offered instead, and by whose foreshadowing blood the sacrifice was accomplished? For when Abraham had caught sight of him, he was caught by the horns in a thicket. Who then did he represent but Jesus, who, before He was offered up, had been crowned with thorns.[28]

Christian sources testify abundantly to the typological reading of the binding of Isaac, although in some instances Isaac is the type of Christ and in others the ram is Christ. Ephrem, for example, construes the ram as Christ, saying that the mountain "spit out the tree and the tree the ram, so that in the ram that hung in the tree and had become the sacrifice in the place of Abraham's son, there might be depicted the day of Him who was to hang upon the wood like a ram and was to taste death for the sake of the whole world."[29] In his *Homilies on Genesis*, Origen suggests a dual analogy whereby the ram represents Christ in the flesh that suffered and Isaac represents Christ in the spirit (8.9). So, too, Cyril of Alexandria (*Paschal Homilies*, 5) describes Isaac as the Word sacrificed to the Father, and the ram represents Christ the human offered on the cross and altar.[30]

According to 1 *Clement* 31:3,[31] Isaac willingly and joyfully sacrifices himself, but some church fathers distinguish between Isaac and Jesus in order to emphasize the uniqueness of Jesus' offering. Melito says, "But Christ suffered, whereas Isaac did not suffer for he was the model of the Christ who was going to suffer" (frag. 9). Melito is not alone in depicting Isaac as not having suffered. Clement of Alexandria, Cyril of Alexandria, and Athanasius also distinguish between Isaac and Jesus: it is Jesus alone who conquers death. In his sixth *Festal Letter* Athanasius writes: "However, the one who was sacrificed was not Isaac but he who was foretold in Isaiah; 'he shall be led as a lamb to the slaughter, and as a sheep before her shearers he shall be speechless' (Isa. 53:7), but he who took away the sins of the world."[32]

Chrysostom's typological reading relates the father and son in Genesis to God the Father and Jesus the Son: "Just as in our text the sheep was offered in place of Isaac, so here the rational Lamb was offered for the world. You see, it was necessary that the truth be sketched out ahead of time in shadow. Notice, I ask you, dearly beloved, how everything was prefigured in shadow: an only-begotten son in that case, an only-begotten son in this. 'This is my beloved Son,' Scripture says in fact, 'in whom I have found satisfaction.' The former was offered as a burnt offering by the father, and the latter his Father surrendered." The focus on Chrysostom's reading is not the willing son, but the willing Father who offers up his only-begotten son to the world: "Paul too shouts aloud in the words, 'He who in fact did not spare his own Son but handed him over for the sake of us all' [Rom. 8:32]."[33]

In both Jewish and Christian traditions of this period, the story is read through the lens of corporate reward as well as individual salvation. For the church fathers, the story serves to illustrate the redemptive power of Christ's death for all humanity: through his death, life is restored to all who believe. For the rabbis, it is through Abraham's actions, as well as Isaac's, that Jews are merited; all of Israel is rewarded on account of Abraham's willingness to sacrifice his son. The notion of vicarious merit or redemption through the near sacrifice is absent in classical Islamic sources, in which father and son are exemplars of complete submission to the will of God. The obedience of Abraham and his son rewards others only insofar as they benefit from Abraham's and Isaac's model behavior.

The Christian Greek and Syriac homiletic traditions of the fifth and sixth centuries amplify the biblical text through the use of dialogue and speeches. The semidramatic renditions of Genesis 22 give Sarah a leading role. Two Syriac verse homilies *(memre)* are especially noteworthy. Both include extended dialogues between Sarah and Abraham. In the first, Sarah, suspicious, is reluctant to let Isaac go with him, for fear that he will meet an untimely death: "For I am being unjustly deprived of the single son to whom I have given birth. Let not the eye of his mother be darkened, seeing that after one hundred years light has shone out for me. You are drunk with the love of God—who is your God and my God—and if He so bids you concerning the child, you would kill him without hesitation" (lines 35–38).[34] Memra I ends with Sarah welcoming Isaac back.

Memra II draws directly on Memra I and develops it in striking ways. Surprisingly, Sarah wants to join Abraham in the offering: "Let me see my only child being sacrificed; if you are going to bury him in the ground I will dig the hole with my own hands, and if you are going to build up stones, I will carry them on my shoulders" (lines 25–26).[35] Sarah turns to Isaac and tells him to listen to his father, "and if he should actually bind you, stretch out your hands to the bonds, and if he should actually sacrifice you, stretch out your neck before the knife; stretch out your neck like a lamb, like a kid before the shearer" (lines 34–36).[36] In tears, she embraces and kisses him, and then she hands him over to Abraham.

When father and son return home in Memra II, Abraham holds back his son in order to test Sarah's reaction. She welcomes Abraham and asks how Isaac behaved. Abraham assures her that he died bravely and that on the pyre he remembered her. She speaks movingly about her beloved son and yearns to see where he was sacrificed. With a sorrowful heart and "a mind dazed as she grieved," she gets up, and suddenly the child returns to her safe and sound. She welcomes him back and utters thanksgiving to the "Good One who returned her only child" (line 135).[37] In this extraordinary homecoming, it is Sarah who is the heroine. As Sebastian Brock observes, "Whereas Abraham only underwent a single trial at the Aqedah, Sarah had to endure two, the first shared with her husband, the other imposed upon her by him; in this way her faith in, and love of, God, can be said to have actually excelled that of Abraham."[38]

Islamic Traditions on the Near Sacrifice
of Abraham's Son

Unlike Genesis 22, the qur'anic account of Abraham's sacrifice (Q. 37:102–111) lacks details such as the three-day journey, the wood and the knife, and the son's question about the sacrificial lamb. In the Qur'an, the unnamed son knows of God's command to Abraham. When Abraham tells him of the dream, the son responds, "Father, do as you are commanded, and God willing, you will find me steadfast." Thus there are no surprises, no mounting tension. Father and son willingly fulfill the command, but only Abraham is rewarded: future generations will praise him.

The Qur'an (2:124) states that God tests Abraham with many commandments but does not specify what these commandments are. The list of trials Abraham faces in some Islamic texts are associated with Islamic ritual practices: rinsing the mouth, clearing the nostrils with water, trimming the mustache and nails, using the toothstick, plucking the armpit, shaving pubic hair, washing between fingers, cleansing the rear and vulva, and being circumcised. Opinions vary. Some maintain that six of the commands have to do with the person and four with the cultic stations: walking around the Ka'bah, running between al-Safa and al-Marwah, stoning the pillars, and hurrying. And still others understand the trials in terms of Abraham's appointment as a leader for humankind and in terms of pilgrimage rituals. There is indeed mention of other trials, including his emigration and the sacrifice of his son. Abraham's rejection of the stars, sun, and moon is considered a test, as is his trial by fire at the hands of Nimrod. And in every instance Abraham displays his singular devotion to the one true God.

Both al-Tha'labi and al-Tabari preserve a poem that explains the reason Abraham was commanded to sacrifice his son. The following is al-Tabari's rendition:

> Abraham, the one who carries out the vow
> > to satisfaction, and the bearer of easy-burning
> > firewood

For his firstborn, could not desist from him
or see himself in the company of enemies.

'O my son! I have consecrated you to God
as a slaughtered kid, but be steadfast; a ransom for you is
ready.

Bind the fetters; I shall not turn from the knife
the head of the manacled captive.'

For he has a knife which is quick in the flesh
a cutting edge curved like a crescent moon.

While he was taking his garments from him
his Lord ransomed him with the best of rams.

'So take this and release your son; verily I
do not dislike what you now have done.'

A God-fearing father and the other, his offspring;
they fled from him [Satan] on hearing, 'Do it!'

People often are unhappy about a thing
which brings relief, like the untying of bonds.[39]

According to the poem Abraham was commanded to sacrifice his son in order to fulfill a vow. In the act of Abraham fulfilling his vow, his son also shows himself to be obedient. They both "surrendered" (Q. 37:103), that is according to a report in al-Tabari, "The boy was satisfied to be the sacrifice, and the father was content to sacrifice him."[40]

As in Jewish sources, Satan (al-shaytan) attempts to tempt them to disobey God and thwart the sacrifice. After Satan (also known in Arabic as Iblīs) visits Sarah and is unable to make any headway with her, he goes to Isaac, who also responds that if God ordered his father to sacrifice him, he should certainly obey. Then God says to Isaac, "I will grant you any prayer you choose to make now." Isaac replies, "My God! I pray to You that I be granted this, that You give entry into paradise to any worshipper, past or present, who encounters You and does not make anything a partner with You."[41] In every version, both Abraham and his son are resolute in obeying God's command.

In al-Kisa'i's rendition of the near sacrifice of Isaac, Abraham's determination, as well as his son's, is on full display. Isaac asks his father to fasten his shoulders lest he squirm and cause Abraham pain. As he is about to slaughter his son, a voice from heaven calls to him: "O Friend of God, how can you not be compassionate for this small child who speaks to you with such words?" Abraham thinks that it is the mountain speaking to him, so he tells it to quit distracting him from the mission at hand. Abraham takes off Isaac's shirt at his son's request (Isaac does not want his mother to see his blood-soaked shirt), and again he takes knife to throat, but the knife turns over and says, "There is no might nor power save with God the Most High and Magnificent!" Abraham then sharpens the blade on the stone until it is red-hot; but when he returns to Isaac, the knife again turns away and, speaking with God's permission, says, "Do not blame me, O prophet of God, for thus am I commanded to do!" Abraham then hears a voice crying, "O Abraham, you have [already] fulfilled the vision" (Q. 37:105) . . . "We redeemed him with a magnificent ram" (Q. 37:107). The voice cries, "Abraham, take this ram and ransom your son. Offer it in sacrifice, for God has made this day a holy day for you and your children." The ram says, "O Friend of God, sacrifice me instead of your son, for it is more fitting for me to be sacrificed than him." Abraham praises God for ransoming Isaac. When he goes to untie Isaac, he notices that the bonds were already loosened. "Who untied you, my son?" Abraham asks. Isaac responds, "The one who brought the ram for sacrifice." Abraham sacrifices the ram, and a white smokeless fire from heaven descends and consumes the ram whole, except for the head, which Abraham and Isaac take home. When Sarah hears what happened, she falls prostrate in thanks to God.[42]

The story captures Abraham's unwavering resolve in executing the will of God. Even when a voice cries out to him, he is steadfast. Even when the knife refuses to comply, he is undaunted. Isaac, too, is prepared to sacrifice himself. His only concern is the pain he might cause his parents in the process.

Muslims today celebrate Eid al-Adha, the Feast of the Sacrifice, to commemorate Abraham's obedience to God to sacrifice Ishmael

and Ishmael's willingness to be sacrificed. Both father and son submit to God; however, the Qur'an does not state explicitly the identity of the son. Modern qur'anic commentators assume that Ishmael
was the intended son, but early exegetical sources indicate that
opinions differed on the matter.[43] Al-Tabari explicitly writes that
the earliest sages disagreed about which son Abraham was commanded to sacrifice: "Both views are supported by statements related on the authority of the Messenger of God. If both groups of
statements were equally sound, then—since they both come from
the Prophet—only the Qur'an could serve as proof that the account
naming Isaac is clearly the more truthful of the two."[44]

According to Muqatil ibn Sulayman and al-Kisa'i, the victim is
identified as Isaac, but al-Tha'labi is one of many sources that report
a range of opinions on the matter. He explicitly comments that preceding generations disagreed about which of the two sons Abraham
was commanded to sacrifice.[45] For example, when the angel Gabriel
tells Sarah, advanced in age, the news of Isaac's birth, Sarah asks
Gabriel, "What is God's sign?" Then, according to al-Tha'labi, "he
takes a dry piece of wood in his hand and twists it between his fingers, at which point it stirs and becomes verdant. Abraham says, 'He
will therefore be a sacrifice to God.'"[46] In another tradition we read
that when Moses asks the Lord why people refer to Him as the God
of Abraham, Isaac, and Jacob, he replies, "Abraham considered
nothing to be My equal but chose Me over all else, and Isaac freely
offered himself to Me as a sacrifice, and even without this willingness
he would be beyond reproach."[47]

Another account suggests that claiming descent from Isaac was
prestigious: "a man was boasting to 'Abdallāh b. Mas'ūd, saying that
he was so-and-so, son of so-and-so, son of the 'noble elders.' 'Abdallāh
explained that the man was saying in effect: 'I am a descendant of
Joseph, son of Jacob, son of Isaac, the *Dhabīḥ* [sacrificial offering]
to God, son of Abraham, the Friend of God." Even Joseph while in
Egypt refers to his own pedigree when speaking to the king of Egypt:
"Do you want to eat with me? For, by God, I am Joseph son of Jacob
the prophet of God, son of Isaac the *Dhabīḥ* of God, son of Abraham,
the Friend of God!"[48] And others note that it was Ishmael, claiming
to have seen firsthand the horns of the ram suspended in the Ka'bah.

In defense of Ishmael, some allege that the Jews who hold Isaac as the intended son are liars. In one particular account, a Jew who was considered one of the Jewish sages becomes Muslim. When asked which of the two sons of Abraham was intended for sacrifice, he responds, "Ishmael." Then he says, "By God, Commander of the Faithful, the Jews know this fact, but they envy you Arabs, that it was your forefather whose sacrifice God commanded, he being the son with superior ability to endure what God had ordered for him. But they deny all this, claiming that it was Isaac, because Isaac is their forefather."[49] Some draw support for Isaac by turning to the Qur'an. Verse 11:71 mentions that Abraham received news of Isaac and then Jacob. Since God gave that promise, he would not then command Abraham to sacrifice Isaac.

Even later medieval collections of *tafsīr* consider the identity of the intended son. The fourteenth-century Ibn Taymiyya, a proponent of using the Qur'an to interpret the Qur'an, actually turns to the Torah to support his argument for Ishmael. His argument is as follows: Abraham is ordered to sacrifice his only son (Gen. 22:2), but Jews and Christians ("People of the Book") added Isaac. The contention that it was Isaac made its way into Muslim circles, but it is a distortion *(taḥrīf)*. Isaac, to begin with, was born after the test; we know that because the story of the sacrifice (Q. 37:102–111) is followed by the announcement of the birth of Isaac: "And We gave him the glad tiding of Isaac, a Prophet, one of the Righteous" (Q. 37:112). Moreover, on the three occasions when the Qur'an mentions Isaac's birth, it does not refer to sacrifice. And the descriptions of the two sons in the Qur'an are further evidence that the son intended for sacrifice is Ishmael, Ibn Taymiyya argues. Isaac is described (Q. 15:53) as a "knowledgeable boy" *(ghulām 'alīm)*, in contrast to Ishmael, who is listed in Qur'an 21:85 among the patient prophets *(min al-ṣābirīn)*. The intended son declares, "God willing you [Abraham] will find me of the patient" *(min al-ṣābirīn)* (Q. 37:102).[50]

Ibn Kathir, too, makes a case for Ishmael. Like Ibn Taymiyya, he cites qur'anic verses to support his position. In addition to noting that Isaac is described as a "knowledgeable boy," he refers to Qur'an 11:71: "we gave her (Sarah) glad tidings of Isaac and after him, of Jacob." If the Qur'an states that Isaac will have progeny, then why would God command his slaughter? Therefore, it must have been Ishmael. Ibn Kathir delves further into al-Tabari's *tafsīr* in order to demonstrate how in fact it supports his claim for Ishmael.[51]

Exegetes were eager to add details to the qur'anic episode. They sought to address a variety of unresolved issues, such as the extent of Abraham's resolve, the age of the intended victim, and what was sacrificed in his stead. Identifying the intended son took on another dimension vis-à-vis Judaism and Christianity. In Judaism and Christianity, Isaac is the seed through whom God maintains his covenant; he is glorified above his siblings, Ishmael, and the children of Keturah. In the Islamic tradition, of course, Ishmael plays a more prominent role. As the account of the Jewish convert to Islam attests, there was competition among various religious adherents who relied on the identity of the sacrificial son to buttress claims of superiority.

Countervoices

The sources examined here reflect ways in which the traditions reread the near sacrifice of Abraham's son. Some shifted the cause from God to Satan, or even the ministering angels (*Gen. Rab.* 55:4); they read it as Abraham's ultimate trial that resulted in a reward for generations to come. They focused on Abraham's steadfast faith and the son's willingness to fulfill God's commandment.

Whether in the Jewish, Christian, or Islamic tradition, the near sacrifice of Abraham's son is understood as the paradigmatic act of Abraham's obedience, and of his son's: the sacrificial victim also wholeheartedly accepts the command. Obedience to God as depicted through interpretations of this scriptural episode takes on a different complexion in each tradition. But if we step back from the differences, we can also appreciate the ways in which all three traditions interpret the command to sacrifice his son as a sign of Abraham's exceptional faith, a faith that is in turn worthy of merit and emulation. So, too, the sons who readily offer themselves as sacrifice do so in order to do the will of God. The three traditions infuse the scriptural narrative of God's command to Abraham with meaning that reverberates in the different liturgical celebrations of Rosh Hashanah, the Eucharist, and Eid al-Adha. The near sacrifice of Ishmael,

like that of Isaac in the Jewish tradition, is ritually enshrined. Sacrificing an animal on the tenth day of Dhūl al-Ḥijja, whether on pilgrimage or not, is to remember both Abraham's resolve and Ishmael's
willingness to obey God's command.

The traditions also carry with them voices, cries, whimpers, and
shouts, muffled by the sweep of time, that resist the ungodly Godly
command. Expressions of horror and sorrow present themselves in a
variety of Jewish, Christian, and Muslim sources. So while each tradition justifies the story of near sacrifice, exalts Abraham for his faith
and obedience, hails the son for his valor in the face of death, and
understands the event in theological terms, late antique and medieval sources disclose a sense of anxiety about it. Although they do
not explicitly critique or question God's command, they challenge it
and voice reactions that run counter to conventional religious views.

One important element of the scriptural expansions is that Abraham resists Satan's temptations and remains constant. But the rabbis seem to be overreaching when they ask and answer the question,
Where was Isaac when Abraham built the altar? (Gen. 22:9). R. Levi
says, "He had taken and hidden him, lest anyone who sought to seduce him throw a stone at him, maim him and thus disqualify him
from serving as a sacrifice" (Gen. Rab. 56:5). In al-Kisa'i, not even a
voice from on high could keep Abraham from slaughtering his son.
And yet the interpretive traditions implicitly evince uneasiness; one
senses some equivocation on their part with respect to Abraham's
enactment of the unthinkable command.

Al-Kisa'i opens with Abraham misinterpreting the dream (Q.
37:102). God commands him to make a sacrifice. He takes a fat bull,
slaughters it, and distributes it among the poor. The next night he
hears a voice that says, "Abraham, God commands you to make a
greater sacrifice than a bull." When he awakens, he takes a camel,
slaughters it, and distributes it among the poor. On the third night,
he again hears the voice: "God commands you to make a sacrifice
greater even than a camel." Abraham asks, "What can be greater
than a camel?" When there is a motioning toward Isaac, Abraham
wakes up frightened.

The narrative expansion emphasizes Abraham's eagerness to obey
God. He slaughters a fat bull and then a camel, yet he is frightened

at the prospect of slaughtering his son. The story echoes midrashim that interpret "after these things [words] God put Abraham to the test" (Gen. 22:1) as indicating that Abraham had misgivings.[52] God commands, "Take your son," and Abraham replies, "I have two sons." "The one you love." Abraham replies: "This one is the only son of his mother and this one is the only son of his mother." God says, "The one you love," but Abraham retorts, "I love them both." God says, "Take Isaac" (Gen. Rab. 55:7). As noted, the verse does not say simply "Take Isaac"; extra words are added to the effect that Abraham will be rewarded for this bitter test. At the same time, like the story in al-Kisa'i, the text reveals Abraham's anxiety.

Even Sarah, who is portrayed as being as steadfast as her husband and son, displays fear in two Shi'ite sources (al-Qummi and al-Tabarsi). Satan goes to Sarah while she is engaged in the 'umra pilgrimage to the Ka'bah and tells her that he saw her husband laying her son down and taking up a knife to sacrifice him.[53] She says: "You lie! Abraham is the gentlest of men. Why would he sacrifice his own son?" When Satan tells her that the Lord commanded him, she replies, "It is true that he would obey his Lord." When she completes her ritual duties, she runs toward Mina with her hand on her head, saying, "O Lord! Do not punish me for what I did to the mother of Ishmael!"[54] The thought that her husband is about to kill her son terrifies her.[55] Even though in one of the two Syriac verse homilies Sarah is eager to participate along with Abraham in the slaughtering of Isaac, in the other she collapses from shock when told that Isaac had been sacrificed.

In one of the rabbinic texts, when Abraham comes to slaughter Isaac, he says, "Father, bind my hands and feet, lest my soul be intimidated when I see the knife. Perhaps I will tremble and the sacrifice be made unfit. Please, do not make a blemish that will disqualify me from being a fit sacrifice." Immediately Abraham stretches out his hand and takes the knife to slaughter his son. Isaac says to him, "Father, do not tell mother when she is standing at the well, or on the roof, because she might throw herself down and die." The two of them build the altar, and Abraham binds Isaac on it. He takes the knife, until a quarter of his blood flows from him. Then Satan comes and pushes away Abraham's hand. The knife falls, and as he is about to pick it up, an oracle comes forth from heaven: "Do not lay your hand on the boy" (Gen. 22:11).[56]

The midrash portrays Isaac as eager to ensure that the sacrifice is proper, lest it be nullified. That is, his body might reflexively flinch at the sight of the knife—the spirit is willing, but the flesh is weak. Isaac's words emphasize his acquiescence, but they also heighten the horror of what is about to take place. His request that Abraham be careful when telling his mother reminds us of her sorrow. The news could kill her. And indeed, in some Jewish interpretations, knowledge of the near sacrifice is linked to her death. In *Leviticus Rabbah* 20:2, Isaac tells his mother that had it not been for the angel calling on his father to stop, he would have been slain. When she hears this, she utters six cries that correspond to the six shofar blasts (of Rosh Hashanah). She has barely finished speaking when she dies.[57] As Yvonne Sherman observes, "Supremely, *Leviticus Rabbah* and the *Pirke de Rabbi Eliezer* say that the six blasts of the shofar on Rosh Hashanah *also* memorialize the final three long cries and three short howls of Sarah in her death-throes, so making the proclamation of redemption and its subversion collide in the very same breath."[58] The same idea is found in al-Tabarsi: "When Sarah came and was told the story, she went to her son and saw the sign of the knife scratched into his throat. She was terrified and was stricken with a paroxysm of sickness that killed her."[59]

Satan's role in attempting to undermine Abraham is noteworthy. He questions Abraham's worthiness and thus incites God to test him. He and the angels try to foil God's plan—the angels because they are jealous of Abraham, Satan because he wants to defeat God— yet at the same time they represent a counterweight to the Aqedah. Does Satan push the knife from Abraham's hand to prevent him from executing the command or to keep him from murdering his son? Is it an attempt to pervert God's plan or to prevent a horrific act?

Like Satan, the ministering angels serve to instigate the test: "This Abraham," they complain, "made others rejoice but didn't so much as offer a bullock to God."[60] And yet it is the ministering angels whose tears in another passage melt the knife away. The tears of the angels fall and dissolve the knife (*Gen. Rab.* 56:7). In another rabbinic passage (*Gen. Rab.* 56:5), at the moment of slaughter, tears of compassion streaming from the father's face flow into the son's. The angels then break into loud weeping and exclaim: "It is unnatural that Abraham should slay his son with his own hand! Where is the reward of Abraham, he who took the wayfarers into his house, gave them food and drink, and went with them to bring them on the way?" In the first of the two Syriac verse homilies, Memra I, the angels supplicate: "Abraham has ministered well, let his child bound on the pyre serve as a pledge of his reward, let there be joy for Sarah at her offering, let it not pain her; let the child go back in peace, let him become thousands beyond number" (lines 95–100).[61] Whether they instigate or sabotage the test, they serve to remind the reader of the disturbing elements associated with the story.

The binding of Abraham's son plays such a significant ritual role in Judaism, Christianity, and Islam that premodern interpretations voicing discomfort at the thought of Abraham's determination to kill his son because "God said so" are repressed. But those living in the ancient and medieval worlds did indeed express fear, disquiet, and horror. Their critique is unlike that of modern-day secularists who attack the narrative with passionate dispassion; it is a more subtle yet provocative resistance that does not altogether reject the story but rather deepens and complicates it.

The ways in which the story was interpreted and told in the ancient and early medieval periods remind us that the sacrifice of Abraham's son is not only about Abraham. It is about his family; it is about the mother and son who participate in the momentous event. Perhaps in this way, too, the story as well as these religious traditions is more than Abrahamic.

Conclusion

OVER THE COURSE of these chapters I have investigated the ways in which Jewish, Christian, and Muslim writers of the ancient and early medieval periods depicted the story of Abraham. I have considered how they understood and wrestled with scriptural stories about the members of his family, stories that at times raise questions about the character of the patriarch and his wife Sarah. In this inquiry I have shown how biblical and qur'anic narratives were retailored in ancient and medieval sources in order to address concerns in the scriptural narrative, highlight certain aspects, and make them meaningful for contemporary readers and listeners.

I focused on conceptualizations of Abraham and his family in Jewish, Christian, and Muslim literary traditions of the ancient and early medieval periods and considered the extent to which they share fundamental attitudes, as well as the way those attitudes and notions have been manifested and integrated into a historically embedded, complex nexus of narratives, beliefs, and practices. They are not denominations of the same religion but distinct religions with similar rhythms and commonalities. They are religious traditions with multiple Abrahams, and different historical and theological trajectories that resonate with traditions beyond the "Abrahamic" pale.

Abraham is the unflinching, obedient, supremely righteous Friend of God, the sage philosopher and (according to Josephus) military commander, who brings monotheism into the world. Philo, Josephus, the rabbis, Paul, the church fathers, al-Tabari, al-Tha'labi, al-Kisa'i, Ibn Kathir, and other Muslim interpreters tailored his image to suit variegated religious, political, theological, didactic, and social agendas. The same is true of modern thinkers and religious leaders who draw on the idealized Father Abraham for a variety of purposes, some more irenic than others. They turn to his wives and sons as well in order to promote a host of competing agendas related to identity and cultural politics.

It is my hope that by looking at the ways in which ancient and medieval Jewish, Christian, and Muslim exegetes examined and storytellers told the story of the family of Abraham, readers have come to appreciate recurring threads and concerns as well as differences among and within the traditions. Constant attentiveness is required in order to move beyond stereotypes and generalities and to see both the common rhythms of all three religions and the richly hued textual and cultural traditions of each. As we try to understand the extent to which Judaism, Christianity, and Islam are members of the family of Abraham, we must come to grips with *how differently* the three religions belong within and outside that family and, even more important, with *how differently* the notion of the "family" is constructed.

Judaism, Christianity, and Islam share the notion of a spiritual family. *Am Yisrael*—the People or Children of Israel—is the covenanted family in Judaism. Christians also claim that the community of believers—the church—is the new Israel, a community based not on physical descent from Abraham but rather on spiritual affinity. In Islam, the universal community of believers is the *umma*. Abraham is the father of the faithful in Islam, in that Muslims follow the religion of Abraham and all his descendants in the Qur'an are faithful to the word of God. In Judaism and Christianity, however, the notion of Abraham's fatherhood carries a different sense: specific offspring of Abraham are heirs of a promise. In other words, Abraham is a father of nations in Islam, but his fatherhood does not play a pivotal role in the community's theological understanding of itself. In Qur'an 2:124 God makes Abraham a leader of humankind. Abraham inquires with respect to his descendants, to which God replies, "My covenant does not apply to the evil-doers." In Islam, it is not biological descent from Abraham that bestows membership, as in Judaism; rather, one must follow the path set out by the prophets, and membership is available to all who do so, not just to Abraham's descendants. As I have observed, the Gospel of John similarly rejects this notion of genealogical descent and instead proclaims that those considered children of Abraham are so regarded on account of their behavior. The church is the family of believers in Jesus, the new and everlasting covenant, the promised seed of Abraham.

Other members of Abraham's biological family, such as his father, Terah, are interpreted in various ways. Some exegetes were concerned with the image of Terah as an idol worshipper and with the implications for Abraham. But what was of utmost concern to the exegetes was the depiction of Abraham's unique discovery and devotion to the one true God that ultimately results in God's choosing him from among all the peoples of the world.

A working assumption of many contemporary Jews and Christians vaguely familiar with the biblical story is that the relationship between Ishmael and Isaac is marked by sibling rivalry. The biblical and qur'anic narratives, however, do not portray a competitive and antagonistic relationship. The rivalry that emerges in extrascriptural sources has more to do with attempts to employ the two figures for theological and political purposes. Jewish, Christian, and Muslim exegetes may anchor the rivalry in the Bible and Qur'an, but the competition is enacted in several inter- and intrareligious arenas that obfuscate the scriptural narratives. Negative Jewish and Christian interpretations of Ishmael are so pernicious and prevalent that the evocation of Ishmael and Isaac in contemporary parlance may contribute more to the tension between the groups the siblings metonymically represent than to a peaceful bond. What are the implications of evoking Ishmael and Isaac to demonstrate the confraternal bonds between Jews, Christians, and Muslims? Does it only serve to widen the distance between members of other faith traditions and ourselves? Meanwhile, the complex relationship between Abraham's wives Sarah and Hagar continues to be deployed for political purposes.

Even today, as the existence of the term "Abrahamic religions" makes clear, Abraham and his family claim the imagination of religious and secular poets, musicians, and artists, whose understanding of these characters often resides in the narratives' interpretive layers, many of which I have explored—layers of philological inquiry, flights of fancy, theological rigor, and political polemic. Like interpreters of yore, we turn to Scripture in order to make sense of the world around us, to explain current events, political upheavals, and human relationships. For many it is a guidebook to the present and a blueprint for the future.

Eager to draw closer to one another, to bridge fundamental theological gaps, Jews, Christians, and Muslims committed to interfaith dialogue turn to Abraham. At times they envision him as the father of these three monotheistic faiths; at other times he is considered the father of all peoples. But as Sidney Griffith writes, "while western thinkers in recent times have thus made much of the Qur'an's idea of the 'religion of Abraham' and of its potential as a theological foundation for dialogue between Muslims and Christians, the Christian writers in Syriac and Arabic who lived in the world of Islam in the heyday of its classical culture, by way of contrast, made use of the Abraham theme largely to highlight the clash between Christian and Muslim theologies."[1] Christian writers presented Islam as a religion of Abraham in order to emphasize that it was primitive, that it possessed little in the line of innovation. One example comes from Gregory bar Hebraeus, a thirteenth-century cleric of the Syriac Orthodox Church:

Chroniclers say that Heraclius, when the Arab armies overtook him and seized his lands, assembled all the bishops and the head priests and the rest of the satraps, and interrogated them about the matter of who and what these people were. Once each of them had replied as best as his knowledge permitted, the subject then lay open for him and he gave his answer thus: "As far as their way of life, manners and belief" he said, "I see this people as the faint glimmer of first dawn, when it was no longer completely dark, but at the same time it is not yet completely light." They asked him for an explanation of his words, and he continued, "Yes, they have indeed left darkness far behind in that they have rejected the worship of idols and worship the one God, but at the same time they are deprived of the perfect light in that they still fall short of complete illumination in the light of our Christian faith and orthodox confession."[2]

The adherents of the seventeenth-century revivalist Kadizadeli movement rejected the notion that Islam was the religion of Abraham (*millat Ibrāhīm*) and emphasized that it was the religion of Muhammad.[3] They took issue with the widespread use of "religion of Abraham," and scholars debated the theological implications of the phrase. Is "the religion of Abraham" the same as the religion of Muhammad? Does it include Christians and Jews? Today, for a host of different reasons, one asks more or less the same questions: What do we mean by Abrahamic religions? Is Judaism—or Christianity, or Islam—a religion of Abraham?

One may question, even dismiss, the use of "Abrahamic," but a great deal is lost if we ignore the historical, cultural, and religious reasons that allow us to make ready comparisons and complex distinctions. Looking at the different ways Jews, Christians, and Muslims constitute the family of Abraham, and how they interpret the scriptural narratives, gives us reason to reconsider the usefulness of the "Abrahamic" category. The category at best simplifies, at worst distorts, the relationship between these religions. "Abrahamic" is based on a contemporary, ecumenical interpretation of the story of Abraham by those who would see Judaism, Christianity, and Islam as sibling religions with a common forefather—that is, those who want to underscore their common scriptural heritage for irenic purposes.

In the process of exploring Jewish, Christian, and Muslim traditions about Abraham's discovery of God, the relationship between Sarah and Hagar, and Ishmael and Isaac, I have introduced readers to the rabbis, church fathers, and Muslim exegetes whose writings address a host of issues such as Abraham's questionable behavior, Sarah's treatment of Hagar, Ishmael's status within the family of Abraham, and God's command to sacrifice his son. Each tradition reflects a variety of interpretations and concerns that often, but not always, resonate in the other traditions. This is not to suggest that Christians, Jews, and Muslims of the ancient and medieval periods read the same way—on the contrary!—but it does remind one that despite different competing underlying principles (the church fathers' christocentric reading, for example), other principles are at play, namely, the unity and truth of Scripture. These principles in turn lead to readings that are common among all three traditions, or at least are strikingly similar and therefore cut across "Jewish," "Christian," and "Muslim" demarcations. This, however, does not make them "Abrahamic."

My exploration of how the exegetical traditions about the family of Abraham intersect and differ complicates the relationship between these religions and exposes the illusory nature of the Abrahamic category. And yet I hope that it will give one a deeper appreciation of why we are sometimes—not always—well served by locating them within the same frame of reference, why even though "Abrahamic" is inaccurate and insufficient, we nonetheless seek ways to describe their commonalities and interrelatedness while acknowledging their vast differences.

Notes

Introduction

1. "One God, One Revelation, One People: On the Symbolic Structure of Elective Monotheism," *American Academy of Religion* 69 (2001): 757.

2. Ibid., 760. "Phenomenologically" is emphasized in the original.

3. Ibid., 774.

4. See Massignon, "Les trois pières d'Abraham, père de tous les croyants," *Dieu Vivant* 13 (1949): 13–28, translated into English as "The Three Prayers of Abraham," in *Testimonies and Reflections: Essays of Louis Massignon,* selected and introduced by Herbert Mason (Notre Dame, Ind.: University of Notre Dame Press, 1989), 3–20. See also Neal Robinson, "Massignon, Vatican II and Islam as an Abrahamic Religion," *Islam and Muslim Christian-Relations* 2.2 (1991): 182–205, and Sidney Griffith, "Sharing the Faith: The 'Credo' of Louis Massignon," *Islam and Christian-Muslim Relations* 8 (1997): 193–210. More recently see Hughes's discussion of Massignon's influence in *Abrahamic Religions: On the Uses and Abuses of History* (New York: Oxford University Press, 2012), 60–65, as well as Jon D. Levenson, *Inheriting Abraham: The Legacy of the Patriarch in Judaism, Christianity and Islam* (Princeton: Princeton University Press, 2012), 210–212.

5. Abraham's Vision, Spring 2009 Newsletter.

6. Available online at http://charterforcompassion.org/our-partners/partner/5, accessed November 11, 2013.

7. Available online at www.abrahamfund.org, accessed May 2011, and www.jspace.com/org/the-abraham-fund/221, accessed November 11, 2013.

8. Bruce Feiler, *Abraham: A Journey to the Heart of Three Faiths* (New York: HarperCollins, 2002), 218.

9. Ibid., 9.

10. For references to the religion (*milla,* translated variably as religion, law, and community) of Abraham, see Q. 2:130, 2:135, 3:95, 4:125, 6:161, and

16:123. See Hawting, "The Religion of Abraham and Islam," in *Abraham, the Nations, and the Hagarites: Jewish, Christian, and Islamic Perspectives on Kinship with Abraham*, ed. Martin Goodman, George H. van Kooten, and Jacques T. A. G. M. van Ruiten (Leiden; Boston: Brill, 2010), 479–483, who concludes that the religion of Abraham *(millat Ibrāhīm)* should be understood as a product of the religious and social conditions brought about by the Arab conquests of the Middle East. In other words, he calls into serious question the notion that Abraham introduced monotheism into Arabia. See Sidney Griffith's discussion in *The Church in the Shadow of the Mosque: Christians and Muslims in the World of Islam* (Princeton: Princeton University Press, 2008), 164–166. See Chapter 2 for a discussion of the term *milla*.

11. See discussion of Karl-Josef Kuschel's *Abraham: Sign of Hope for Jews, Christians and Muslims* (New York: Continuum, 1995) in Levenson, *Inheriting Abraham*, 183–193.

12. This was not always the case. See Chapter 4 on the ninth- and tenth-century Persian claims to ancestry from Isaac.

13. As Alon Gershon-Gottstein avers: "The designation 'Abrahamic' emerges carrying in it the suggestion not only of a shared story, but also of an ideal harmonious relationship that should characterize adherents of the three faiths, emanating, as it were, from a common branch." Alon Gershon-Gottstein, "Abraham and 'Abrahamic Religions' in Contemporary Interreligious Discourse," *Studies in Interreligious Dialogue* 12 (2002): 165–183.

14. For Wittgenstein's notion of family of resemblance, see his *Philosophical Investigations:* the German text, with a revised English translation by G. E. M. Anscombe (Oxford; Malden, MA: Blackwell, 2001). Its application to understanding the relationship between Judaism, Christianity, and Islam may shed some insight, but it also comes with its own set of problems.

15. Gottstein, "Abraham and 'Abrahamic Religions' in Contemporary Interreligious Discourse," probes the hidden assumptions and the attendant problems of using "Abrahamic." By emphasizing aspects of a tradition's understanding of the figure of Abraham, those interested in interreligious dialogue can choose to construct Abraham along parallel lines. The description of the religions as "Abrahamic," however, Gershon-Gottstein argues, is vacuous and distorting. The term does not refer to any fact or set of beliefs that unites the three religions. If anything, it distorts fundamental differences between them.

16. Levenson, "The Idea of Abrahamic Religions: A Qualified Dissent," *Jewish Review of Books*, no. 1 (Spring 2010), http://www.jewishreviewofbooks. com/publications/detail/the-idea-of-abrahamic-religions-a-qualified-dissent, accessed November 11, 2013.

17. *Inheriting Abraham*, 207.

18. Ibid., 214. Emphasis in original.

19. *Abrahamic Religions*, 5.

20. Ibid., 98.

21. Nancy Calvert-Koyzis, *Paul, Monotheism and the People of God: The Significance of Abraham Traditions for Early Judaism and Christianity* (London: T & T Clark International, 2004), 1.

22. Excerpt taken from the booklet *The Faith of Abraham: Bond or Barrier? Jewish, Christian and Muslim Perspectives* (New York: Fordham University

Press, 2011), 19, based on the symposium at which Patrick J. Ryan, S.J., delivered the annual spring McGinley Lecture. Other articles include brief responses by Rabbi Daniel Polish and Professor Amir Hussain. Here he mentions the "polyvalence of Abraham."

23. And as Smith observes, "The 'afterlife' of a canonical text is as significant as the origins of the text—after all, the notion of 'the Bible' is, itself, a postbiblical phenomenon." Smith, "Religion and the Bible," in *Journal of Biblical Literature* 128.1 (2009), 21.

1. *Scriptures and Interpreters*

1. Traditionally, in Judaism, Christianity, and Islam, references to God use the masculine pronoun.

2. See A. C. Sundberg, "Toward a Revised History of the New Testament Canon," in *Studia Evangelica*, iv/1, ed. F. L. Cross (Berlin: Akademie Verlag, 1968), 452–461, who made a sharp distinction between the two terms that set the stage for later research on the subject. See, too, H. von Campenhausen, *The Formation of the Christian Bible* (Philadelphia: Fortress Press, 1972). For a discussion of the various meanings of canon, see Bruce M. Metzger, *The Canon of the New Testament: Its Origin, Development, and Significance* (Oxford: Clarendon Press, 1987), and for a concise summary, see Michael W. Holmes, "The Biblical Canon," in *The Oxford Handbook of Early Christian Studies*, ed. Susan Ashbrook Harvey and David G. Hunter (Oxford: Oxford University Press, 2008), 406–426. See William Graham, *Islamic and Comparative Religious Studies: Selected Writings*, Ashgate Contemporary Thinkers on Religion: Collected Works series (Burlington, VT: Ashgate, 2010), especially "Scripture," 195–216, and "Scripture as Spoken Word," 217–246.

3. "The distinctive characteristic of canon, in contradistinction to its generic partners, the list and the catalogue," Jonathan Z. Smith writes, "is its closure, that it is held to be complete, and that, therefore, a canon requires an interpreter, a practitioner of 'exegetical ingenuity,' to manipulate it in such a way that it 'covers' novel situations without adding new matter to the canon." Smith, "Religion and Bible," *Journal of Biblical Literature* 128.1 (2009): 22. See his "Sacred Persistence: Toward a Redescription of Canon," in *Approaches to Ancient Judaism: Theory and Practice*, ed. William Scott Green (Missoula, MT: Scholars Press, 1978), 11–28; reprinted in Jonathan Z. Smith, *Imagining Religions: From Babylon to Jonestown* (Chicago: University of Chicago Press, 1982), 36–52, 141–143. For a further treatment of canon, see his "Canon, Catalogues and Classics," in *Canonization and Decanonization*, ed. Arie van der Kooij and Karel van der Toorn (Leiden: Brill, 1998), 295–311.

4. I will use the terms "Hebrew Bible," "Jewish Bible," and "TaNaKh" interchangeably.

5. Some refer to the Old Testament as the First Testament and the New Testament as the Second Testament in order to attenuate the potentially offensive implications of "old" and "new."

6. From the New Revised Version. Chapter 4 in the English edition is 3:19–24 in the Hebrew. The Jewish Publication Society translation reads: "awesome, fearful day of the LORD" (3:23).

7. See also Zephaniah 1:14–18.

8. Christian interpretations render Elijah as a figure either of John the Baptist or of Jesus.

9. For background on apocalypses and apocalypticism, see volume 14 of *Semeia* and David Hellholm, ed., *Apocalypticism in the Mediterranean World and the Near East* (Tübingen: Mohr, 1983; reprinted 1989 with supp. bibliog.). See also Bernard McGinn, *Visions of the End: Apocalyptic Traditions in the Middle Ages* (New York: Columbia University Press, 1979); and John J. Collins, *The Apocalyptic Imagination: An Introduction to Jewish Apocalyptic Literature* (Grand Rapids, MI: Eerdmans, 1984).

10. The Fathiha, the first chapter, is the exception to the ordering from longest to shortest.

11. Although the word *taḥrīf* does not appear in the Qur'an, several verses include the verbal noun *yuḥarrifūna*, generally translated as "distort." Examples from the Qur'an include "Do you hope, O believers, that they would believe you while a part of them heard the word of God and then distorted it after they had understood it and we knowing?" (Q. 2:75); "Among the Jews are those who distort words from their place" (Q. 4:46); "They distort words from their places and have forgotten a portion of that which they were reminded" (Q. 5:13); and "They distort words beyond their places" (Q. 5: 41). See also Q. 6:91; 7:162. This assertion of alteration explains, inter alia, why Muhammad's mission is not explicitly mentioned in Jewish and Christian Scriptures. For a discussion of these arguments against the Bible, as well as others such as *naskh* (abrogation) and lack of reliable transmission (*tawātur*), see Hava Lazarus-Yafeh, *Intertwined Worlds* (Princeton: Princeton University Press, 1992), 19–49.

12. For a useful discussion of the concept, see Hava Lazarus-Yafeh, "Taḥrīf," in *Encyclopedia of Islam*, 2nd ed., ed. P. Bearman, Th. Bianquis, C. E. Bosworth, E. van Donzel, W. P. Heinrichs, Brill Online, 2013, http://referenceworks.brillonline.com/entries/encyclopedia=of=islam=2/tahrif=SIM_7317. See, too, R. Caspar and J.-M. Gaudeul, "Textes de la tradition musulmane concernant le taḥrīf (falsification) des Écritures," *Islamochristiana* 6 (1980): 61–104; and Camilla Adang, *Muslim Writers on Judaism and the Hebrew Bible: Ibn Rabban to Ibn Hazm* (Leiden: Brill, 1996), 23–109. Both Jews and Christians are given a special status as *ahl al-Kitāb*, "People of the Book," a term applied to pre-Islamic religious groups possessing sacred texts. Zoroastrians, Samaritans, and Mandeans are also included in this category. As Islam expanded eastward, the term also came to encompass Buddhists and Hindus who lived under Muslim rule.

13. See David Thomas, "The Bible in Early Muslim Anti-Christian Polemic," in *Islam and Christian-Muslim Relations* 7.1 (1996): 29–38; and Martin Accad, "Corruption and/or Misinterpretation of the Bible: The Story of Islamic Usage of Tahrîf," in *Christian Presence and Witness among Muslims*, ed. Peter F. Penner (Schwarzenfeld, Germany: Neufeld Verlag, 2005), 36–86. In a series of articles, "The Gospels in the Muslim Discourse of the Ninth to the Fourteenth Centuries: An Exegetical Inventorial Table (parts 1–4)," *Islam and Christian-Muslim Relations* 14.1–4 (2003), Accad provides well over one thousand references to the Gospels used by Muslims to argue against Christianity.

14. Walid Saleh, "A Fifteenth-Century Muslim Hebraist: Al-Biqāʿī and His Defense of Using the Bible to Interpret the Qurʾān," *Speculum* 83 (2008): 632. See also Sidney H. Griffith, *The Bible in Arabic: The Scriptures of the 'People of the Book' in the Language of Islam* (Princeton: Princeton University Press, 2013).

15. Sidney H. Griffith, *The Bible in Arabic*, 7.

16. See Roberto Tottoli, *Biblical Prophets in the Qurʾān and Muslim Literature* (Richmond, Surrey, England: Curzon, 2002).

17. See also Q. 4:163.

18. M. J. Kister, "Ādam: A Study of Some Legends in Tafsīr and Ḥadīth Literature," *Israel Oriental Studies* 13 (1993): 113; and C. Adang, *Muslim Writers*, 1.

19. As Sidney H. Griffith observes in *The Church in the Shadow of the Mosque: Christians and Muslims in the World of Islam* (Princeton: Princeton University Press, 2008), "it seems not improbable that Arabic-speaking, Christian priests, preachers, and teachers in pre-Islamic times may have had private notes or texts, even in Arabic, which would have served them as *aides de memoire*" (50). See also Griffith, *The Bible in Arabic*.

20. Adang, *Muslim Writers*, 2. According to Griffith (*Church in the Shadow of the Mosque*, 50), the earliest translations of the Bible into Arabic for which there is any clear documentary evidence come from the late seventh century. To date there is no comprehensive work on chronicling the translation of the Hebrew Bible into Arabic. See Lazarus-Yafeh, "Muslim Authors and the Problematics of Arabic Translation of the Bible," chapter 5 in *Intertwined Worlds*, 111–129. For an example of Muslim appropriation of the Bible as Scripture, see Walid Saleh, *In Defense of the Bible: A Critical Edition and an Introduction to al-Biqāʿī's Bible Treatise* (Leiden: Brill, 2008), and "A Fifteenth-Century Muslim Hebraist."

21. H. T. Norris, "Fables and Legends in Pre-Islamic and Early Islamic Times," in *Arabic Literature to the End of the Umayyad Period*, ed. A. F. L. Beeston et al. (Cambridge: Cambridge University Press, 1983), 374–384.

22. The term "source-hunting" was used by Jonathan Culler, "Intertextuality and Presupposition," *Modern Language Notes* 91 (1976): 1383.

23. See Gabriel Reynolds's recent work, *The Qurʾān and Its Biblical Subtext* (London; New York: Routledge, 2010). There is much to recommend the work, but I take issue with his use of the term "biblical subtext," by which he means not only the Bible but also apocrypha and Jewish and Christian exegetical works. He writes: "The Qurʾān expects its audience to be familiar with Biblical literature. Whereas both Islamic tradition and the tradition of critical scholarship have tended to separate Qurʾān and Bible, the Qurʾān itself demands that they be kept together" (2). As Marilyn Waldman demonstrates in a well-known study on the qurʾanic Joseph narrative, readers of the Qurʾan must reject the assumption that the Qurʾan depends on the Bible, that it is a "version" that was "passed on in altered, if not debased, form." "New Approaches to 'Biblical' Materials in the Qurʾān," *Muslim World* 75.1 (1985): 1, reprinted in *Studies in Islamic and Judaic Traditions*, ed. William M. Brinner and Stephen D. Ricks (Atlanta: Scholars Press, 1986), 47–64. She discusses in general problematic approaches to the study of scriptural material as "versions" of a story.

24. Hava Lazarus-Yafeh, "Judaism and Islam: Some Aspects of Mutual Cultural Influences," in Lazarus-Yafeh, *Some Aspects of Islam* (Leiden: Brill, 1981), 72–89, applies H. A. R. Gibb's theory that the absorption of foreign influences is a sign of the vitality of a religion or culture.

25. I am not using the terms "social" and "cultural" interchangeably. "Society" implies a set of interrelationships among people and institutional structures, whereas "culture" includes all those institutions but also implies a set of traditions about those very institutions. Culture is socially transmitted knowledge and behavior patterns shared by a group of people. It is the set of ideas, rituals, beliefs, and attitudes that underlie the various relationships that make up society.

26. Drawing on the work of Julia Kristeva, I define intertextuality as the notion that every text is constructed as a mosaic of citations—that is, intertexts—that are in the same instance absorbed and transformed. In his classic work *Intertextuality and the Reading of Midrash* (Bloomington: Indiana University Press, 1990), Daniel Boyarin writes that "every text is constrained by the literary system of which it is a part and . . . every text is ultimately dialogical in that it cannot but record the traces of its contentions and doubling of earlier discourses" (14). See, too, Jonathan Culler, *The Pursuit of Signs: Semiotics, Literature, Deconstruction* (Ithaca: Cornell University Press, 1981), 100–118, and Alice Jardine, "Intertextuality," in *Encyclopedic Dictionary of Semiotics*, ed. Thomas A. Sebeok (Berlin: de Gruyter, 1986), 1:387–389.

27. Reuven Firestone, *Journeys in Holy Lands: The Evolution of the Abraham-Ishmael Legends in Islamic Exegesis* (Albany: State University of New York Press, 1990), for example, explores the relationship between Jewish interpretations of the Bible and Muslim exegesis of the Qur'an in his focused study of Abraham-Ishmael traditions. Also, Jacob Lassner, in *Demonizing the Queen of Sheba: Boundaries of Gender and Culture in Postbiblical Judaism and Medieval Islam* (Chicago: University of Chicago Press, 1993), looks at how the Queen of Sheba legends were adapted into an Islamic context, that is, how Jewish cultural artifacts were "Islamicized." For Lassner, Muslim allusions to the Bible are understood as purposeful, and the absorption and transmission of Jewish artifacts carried intentionality. He locates the use of Jewish sources within a polemical context of the Jews' rejection of the prophet Muhammad in Medina. For a discussion of their work, see Brannon M. Wheeler, *Moses in the Quran and Islamic Exegesis* (London: RoutledgeCurzon, 2002), 3–6; and Shari Lowin, *The Making of a Forefather: Abraham in Islamic and Jewish Exegetical Narratives* (Leiden: Brill, 2006), 33–38. Lowin's work illustrates the shift in scholarship that deals with Jewish and Muslim texts.

28. An example of crosscultural intertextuality is found in a Judeo-Arabic retelling of the story of Joseph, "The Story of Our Master Joseph the Righteous." For a detailed analysis, see Marc S. Bernstein, *Stories of Joseph: Narrative Migrations between Judaism and Islam* (Detroit: Wayne State University Press, 2006). See also Steven Wasserstrom, *Between Muslim and Jew: The Problem of Symbiosis under Early Islam* (Princeton: Princeton University Press, 1995). Focusing on the eighth through the tenth centuries, Wasserstrom explores the concept of creative symbiosis by looking at the Judeo-Isma'ili interchange and the

ways in which Jews and Muslims shared both the imaginative world of apocalypse and the intellectual world of philosophy. In the same vein as Lazarus-Yafeh, Wasserstrom emphasizes that "the debtor-creditor model of influence and borrowing must be abandoned in favor of the dialectical analysis of intercivilizational and interreligious process" (11).

29. Especially relevant works from Neuwirth's massive scholarly output include "Qur'ān, Crisis and Memory: The Qur'ānic Path toward Canonization as Reflected in the Anthropogonic Accounts," in *Crisis and Memory in Islamic Societies*, ed. Angelika Neuwirth and Andreas Pflitsch, *Beiruter Texte und Studien* 77 (Beirut: Orient-Institut, 2001), 113–152; "'Oral Scriptures' in Contact: The Qur'ānic Story of the Golden Calf and Its Biblical Subtext between Narrative, Cult and Inter-communal Debate," in *Self-Referentiality in the Qur'ān*, ed. Stefan Wild (Wiesbaden: Harrassowitz, 2006), 71–92; *Studien zur Komposition der mekkanischen Suren: Die literarische Form des Koran—ein Zeugnis seiner Historizität?* (Berlin: de Gruyter, 2007); *The Qur'ān in Context: Historical and Literary Investigations into the Qur'ānic Milieu*, ed. Stefan Wild, Nicolai Sinai, and Michael Marx (Leiden; Boston: Brill, 2010); and, most recently, *Der Koran als Text der Säptantike: Ein europäischer Zugang* (Frankfurt: Verlag der Weltreligionen, 2010).

30. Michael Fishbane compellingly illustrates this point in his groundbreaking *Biblical Interpretation in Ancient Israel* (Oxford: Oxford University Press, 1985).

31. James VanderKam, *Book of Jubilees* (Sheffield, UK: Sheffield Academic Press, 2001), 21, argues convincingly for a possible 160–150 BCE date of composition. For recent works on *Jubilees*, see Michael Segal, *The Book of Jubilees: Rewritten Bible, Redaction, Ideology and Theology* (Leiden: Brill, 2007) and James Kugel, *A Walk through Jubilees: Studies in the Book of Jubilees and the World of Its Creation* (Leiden: Brill, 2012). Much is made of the composition of the work, whether or not it is the product of a single author. Whereas James Vanderkam argues for authorship, Segal argues for a creative author or composer, who used sources. Kugel on the other hand accounts for inconsistencies and discrepancies in attitudes toward law by contending that it is also the product of an interpolator. Furthermore, the current scholarly trend is to jettison the term "rewritten Bible," which Vermes coined in his *Scripture and Judaism* (Leiden: Brill, 1961).

32. On *Genesis Apocryphon*, see Daniel Michiela, *The Dead Sea Genesis Apocryphon: A New Text and Translation with Introduction and Special Treatment of Columns 13–17* (Leiden: Brill, 2009). For a discussion of the dating of *Biblical Antiquities*, see Howard Jacobson, *A Commentary on Pseudo-Philo's "Liber Antiquitatum Biblicarum": With Latin Text and English Translation*, vol. 1 (Leiden: Brill, 1996), 199–209.

33. For a summary of current scholarship on the *pesher*, see Shani Berrin, "Qumran Pesharim," in *Biblical Interpretation at Qumran*, ed. Matthias Henze (Grand Rapids, MI: Eerdmans, 2005), 110–133.

34. Since the discovery of the Dead Sea Scrolls in 1947, scholars have explored the relationship between exegetical techniques in Dead Sea documents and early rabbinic literature. To what extent are they linked diachronically? See Moshe J. Bernstein, "4Q252: From Re-written Bible to Biblical Commentary,"

Journal of Jewish Studies 45 (1994): 1–27, and "4Q252: Method and Context, Genre and Sources," *Jewish Quarterly Review* 85 (1994): 61–79. Bernstein's collected articles have been published as *Reading and Re-reading Scripture at Qumran*, 2 vols. (Leiden: Brill, 2013). See also Steven D. Fraade, "Looking for Legal Midrash at Qumran," in *Biblical Perspectives: Early Use and Interpretation of the Bible in Light of the Dead Sea Scrolls*, ed. Michael E. Stone and Esther G. Chazon (Leiden: Brill, 1998), 59–79; and Maren Niehoff, "Commentary Culture in the Land of Israel from an Alexandrian Perspective," *Dead Sea Discoveries* 19 (2012): 442–463.

35. For an introduction to the compilations of rabbinic literature, see Herman L. Strack and Günter Stemberger, eds., *Introduction to the Talmud and Midrash* (Minneapolis: Fortress, 1992) and Fergus Millar, Eyal Ben-Eliyahu, and Yehudah Cohn, eds., *Handbook of Jewish Literature from Late Antiquity, 135–700 CE* (Oxford: Oxford University Press, 2013).

36. This is true except for chapters 13, 15, 17, 18, 25, 35, and 37.

37. Unless stated otherwise, all translations of midrashic material are my own. My translations of *Genesis Rabbah* are based on the critical edition of J. Theodor and C. Albeck, *Bereshit Rabba*, 2 vols. (Jerusalem: Shalem Books, 1996). For an English translation of *Midrash Rabbah*, see Harry Freedman and Maurice Simon, eds, *Midrash Rabbah*, 10 vols. (London: Soncino Press, 1992). Refer to Strack and Stemberger for a guide to critical editions. My translations are based on available critical editions. References to them will be made throughout.

38. For an analysis of rabbinic parables, see David Stern, *Parables in Midrash* (Cambridge, MA: Harvard University Press, 1991).

39. For a general introduction to *PRE*, see Leopold Zunz, *Ha-Drashot beYisrael*, ed. and supp. H. Albeck (Jerusalem: Mossad Bialik, 1954), 134–140, 417–424; *Midrash Pirke de Rabbi Eliezer*, trans. Gerald Friedlander (London, 1916; reprint, New York: Sepher-Hermon Press, 1981), xiii–lvii; and Herman L. Strack and Günter Stemberger, eds., *Introduction to the Talmud and Midrash*, 332–333. On the use of narrative in *PRE*, see Ofra Meir, "Hasipur Hadarshani Bemidrash Qadum Ume'uchar," *Sinai* 86 (1980): 246–266; Yaakov Elbaum, "On the Character of the Late Midrashic Literature" (Hebrew), in *Proceedings of the Ninth World Congress of Jewish Studies* 3, 4 vols. (Jerusalem: World Congress of Jewish Studies, 1986), 57–62, "Rhetoric Motif and Subject-Matter: Toward an Analysis of Narrative Technique in Pirke de-Rabbi Eliezer" (Hebrew), *Jerusalem Studies in Jewish Folklore* 13/14 (1991–92): 99–126, and "From Sermon to Story: The Transformation of the Aqedah," *Prooftexts* 6 (1986): 97–117. On the folkloristic aspects of *PRE*, see Dina Stein, *Maxims, Magic, Myth: A Folkloristic Perspective of Pirkei de Rabbi Eliezer* (Hebrew) (Jerusalem: Magnes Press, 2005); Rachel Adelman, *The Return of the Repressed: Pirqe de-Rabbi Eliezer and the Pseudepigrapha* (Leiden: Brill, 2009); and Eliezer Treitl, "Pirke de-Rabbi Eliezer: Text, Redaction and a Sample Synopsis" (Ph.D. diss., Hebrew University of Jerusalem, 2010).

40. In *The Return of the Repressed*, Rachel Adelman contends that *PRE* preserves mythic narratives of the Pseudepigrapha of the Second Temple Period.

41. J. Rubenstein, "From Mythic Motifs to Sustained Myth: The Revision of Rabbinic Traditions in Medieval Midrashim," *Harvard Theological Review* 89.2 (1996): 131–159, quoted from 158. See Joseph Dan, *Hasipur Ha'ivri Bimei Habeinayim* (Jerusalem: Keter, 1974), esp. 21, 135–136. See, too, Anna Urowitz-Freudenstein, "Pseudepigraphical Support of Pseudepigraphal Sources: The Case of PRE," in *Tracing the Threads: Studies in the Vitality of Jewish Pseudepigrapha*, ed. J. C. Reeves (Atlanta: Scholars Press, 1994), 35–54. And see especially Avigdor Shinan, *Aggadatam shel meturgamnim* (Jerusalem: Makor, 1979), 162–165, and Yacob Elbaum, "Messianism in Pirke de-Rabbi Eliezer: Apocalypse and Midrash" (Hebrew), *Teudah* 11 (1996): 245–266. On the folkloristic aspects of *PRE*, see Dina Stein, *Maxims, Magic, Myth: A Folkloristic Perspective of Pirkei de Rabbi Eliezer* (Hebrew) (Jerusalem: Magnes Press, 2005), and most recently Steven Sacks, *Midrash and Multiplicity: Pirke de-Rabbi Eliezer and the Renewal of Rabbinic Interpretive Culture* (Berlin; New York: de Gruyter, 2009).

42. Quoted in Charles Kannengiesser, *Handbook of Patristic Exegesis: The Bible in Ancient Christianity* (Leiden: Brill, 2006), 171. Kannengiesser's tome is an indispensable tool for anyone interested in patristic literature.

43. Ibid., 175.

44. The interest in etymology harks back to Homer and Hesiod and generally speaking played a role in the development of allegorism. In Christian circles, although Origen (ca. 185–ca. 253 CE) believed in the significance of the original meaning of Hebrew names, unlike Jerome he did not compose an *onomastikon* (book of names).

45. Quoted by Jaroslav Pelikan, *Whose Bible Is It? A History of Scriptures through the Ages* (New York: Viking, 2005), 95.

46. Unless otherwise noted, translations of the New Testament are taken from the New Revised Standard Edition.

47. Not all gnostics took this approach. Others, such as the Valentinian Ptolemy, displayed a more nuanced position. See Simonetti's brief discussion of his *Letter to Flora* in *Biblical Interpretation in the Early Church: An Historical Introduction to Patristic Exegesis*, trans. John A. Hughes (Edinburgh: T & T Clark, 1994), 16.

48. See Kannengiesser, *Handbook of Patristic Exegesis*, and Simonetti, *Biblical Interpretation in the Early Church*, for a discussion of these terms.

49. As translated in Kannengiesser, *Handbook of Patristic Exegesis*, 250.

50. As Kannengiesser mentions (ibid., 249), traces of allegorism in Hellenistic Judaism are found in Aristobulos (mid-second century BCE). Fragments of his *Commentary on Pentateuch* are found in Eusebius of Caesarea's *Praeparatio Evangelica* (Preparation for the Gospel), 8.10, 12.2.

51. For a discussion of the use of allegory in ancient Alexandria, see David Dawson, *Allegorical Readers and Cultural Revision in Ancient Alexandria* (Berkeley: University of California Press, 1992).

52. For an excellent discussion of allegory in midrash, see Menahem Kister, "Allegorical Interpretations of Biblical Narratives in Rabbinic Literature, Philo, and Origen: Some Case Studies," in *New Approaches to the Study of Biblical Interpretation in Judaism of the Second Temple Period and in Early Christianity:*

Proceedings of the Eleventh International Symposium of the Orion Center for the Study of the Dead Sea Scrolls and Associated Literature, Jointly Sponsored by the Hebrew University Center for the Study of Christianity, 9–11 January, 2007, ed. Gary A. Anderson, Ruth A. Clements, and David Satran (Leiden: Brill, 2013), 133–184.

53. For an excellent overview of patristic studies, see Elizabeth Clark, "From Patristics to Early Christian Studies," in Hunter and Harvey, eds., *Oxford Handbook of Early Christian Studies*, 7–42.

54. Simonetti, *Biblical Interpretation in the Early Church*, 67.

55. See Francis Young, "The Rhetorical Schools and Their Influence on Patristic Exegesis," in *Making of Orthodoxy: Essays in Honour of Henry Chadwick*, ed. Rowan Williams (Cambridge: Cambridge University Press, 1989); Bradley Nassif, "Spiritual Exegesis in the School of Antioch," in *New Perspectives on Historical Theology: Essays in Memory of John Meyendorff*, ed. Bradley Nassif (Grand Rapids, MI: Eerdmans, 1996), 343–377; Demetrios Trakatellis, "Theodoret's Commentary on Isaiah: A Synthesis of Exegetical Traditions," in Bradley Nassif, *New Perspectives on Historical Theology*, 313–342; and Charles Kannengiesser, "A Key for the Future of Patristics: The 'Senses' of Scripture," in *In Dominicio Eloquio—In Lordly Eloquence: Essays on Patristic Exegesis in Honor of Robert Louis Wilken*, ed. Paul M. Blowers et al. (Grand Rapids, MI: Eerdmans, 2002), 90–106.

56. See Young's discussion of how Origen and Eusthatius of Antioch treat Saul's meeting with the witch of Endor in 1 Samuel 28.

57. See Frances M. Young, *From Nicaea to Chalcedon: A Guide to the Literature and Its Background* (Philadelphia: Fortress, 1983), and Camillus Hay, "Antiochene Exegesis and Christology," *Australian Biblical Review* 12 (1964): 10–23.

58. After Didymus, who lived to the end of the fourth century, the Alexandrian school's importance diminished.

59. Psalms 9.4, quoted in Kannengiesser, *Handbook of Patristic Exegesis*, 171.

60. "Teaching songs" is Andrew Palmer's apt description. See his "A Lyre without a Voice: The Poetics and the Politics of Ephrem the Syrian," *ARAM* 5 (1993): 371–399. For a general introduction, see E. G. Mathews, Jr., and J. P. Amar, *St. Ephrem the Syrian: Selected Prose Works* (Washington, DC: Catholic University Press, 1994), 3–56, and Sidney H. Griffith, "Ephraem the Exegete (306–373): Biblical Commentary in the Works of Ephraem the Syrian," in Kannengiesser, *Handbook of Patristic Exegesis*, 1395–1428.

61. Griffith, "Ephraem the Exegete," 1407.

62. Ibid., 1400. For an analysis of the relationship between late antique Hebrew and Aramaic poetry and Christian liturgical poetry in Syriac and Greek, and Samaritan liturgy, see Ophir Münz-Manor, "The Liturgical Poetry in the Late Antique Near East: A Comparative Approach," *Journal of Ancient Judaism* 1.3 (2010): 336–361. Münz-Manor provides compelling evidence for the rich cultural dialogue that took place among different religious communities.

63. Griffith, "Ephraem the Exegete," 1416.

64. Ibid., 1417.

65. Augustine's correspondence with him attests to his widespread reputation.

66. Pierre Jay in Kannengiesser, *Handbook of Patristic Exegesis*, 1114.

67. Ibid., 1104.

68. His *Glaphyra* (Elegant Comments), an exposition of passages in the Pentateuch arranged in the order in which they are located in the Bible (not topically), is found in volume 69 of Jacques Paul Minge, ed., *Patrologia Cursus Completus, Series Graeca* (Paris: Migne, 1864).

69. John J. O'Keefe, "Christianizing Malachi: Fifth-Century Insights from Cyril of Alexandria," *Vigiliae Christianae* 50.2 (1996): 139.

70. Robert L. Wilken, "Cyril of Alexandria (ca. 375–444), A Special Contribution," in Kannengiesser, *Handbook of Patristic Exegesis*, 865.

71. R. P. H. Green, *Saint Augustine: On Christian Teaching*, Oxford World Classics (Oxford: Oxford University Press, 1997), 86–87.

72. *De Doctrina*, 3.35.39, and *Confessions*, 12.30.41–12.31.42. He continues: "Even if the writer's meaning is obscure, there is no danger here, provided that it can be shown from other passages of the holy scriptures that each of these interpretations is consistent with the truth." Augustine also appreciated the rhetorical devices used in Scripture: "The literary-minded should be aware that our Christian authors used all the figures of speech which teachers of grammar call by their Greek name of tropes, and that they did so more diversely and profusely than can be judged or imagined by those who are unfamiliar with scripture or who gained their knowledge of figures from other literature."

73. Another related term is *ta'wīl*, exegesis, interpretation, from the verb *ta'awwala*, which originally meant "to apply a verse to a given situation." See Claude Gilliot, "Exegesis of the Qur'ān: Classical and Medieval," *Encyclopedia of The Qur'ān*, gen. ed. Jane Dammen McAuliffe (Washington, DC: Brill Online, 2013).

74. Jane Dammen McAuliffe, "An Introduction to Medieval Interpretation of the Qur'ān," in *With Reverence for the Word: Medieval Scriptural Exegesis in Judaism, Christianity, and Islam*, ed. Jane Dammen McAuliffe, Barry D. Walfish, and Joseph W. Goering (Oxford: Oxford University Press, 2003), 312.

75. For some literature on the debate as to the reliability of the chains of transmission, see G. H. A. Juynboll, *Muslim Tradition: Studies in Chronology, Provenance and Authorship of Early Ḥadīth* (Cambridge: Cambridge University Press, 1983); Harald Motzki, "The Muṣannaf of 'Abd al-Razzāq al-Ṣanʿānī as a Source of Authentic Ḥadīth of the First Century A.H.," *Journal of Near Eastern Studies* 50 (1991): 1–21; Fuad Sezgin, *Studies in Early Hadith Literature: With a Critical Edition of Some Early Texts*, 3rd ed. (Indianapolis: American Trust Publications, 1992); Fred Leemhuis, "Origins and Early Development of the *Tafsīr* Tradition," in *Approaches to the Early History of the Qur'ān*, ed. Andrew Rippin (Oxford: Clarendon Press, 1988), 13–30; Michael Cook, *Early Muslim Dogma: A Source-Critical Study* (Cambridge: Cambridge University Press, 1981); Herbert Berg, "Weaknesses in the Arguments for the Early Dating of Qur'ānic

Commentary," in *With Reverence for the Word*, 329–345, and *The Development of Exegesis in Early Islam: The Authenticity of Muslim Literature from the Formative Period*, McAuliffe et al. (Richmond, Surrey, England: Curzon, 2000); and Jane Dammen McAuliffe, *Qur'ānic Christians: An Analysis of Classical and Modern Exegesis* (Cambridge: Cambridge University Press, 1991), 23–26. See Claude Gilliot, "Les débuts de l'exégèse coranique," *Revue du monde musulman et de la Méditerranée* 58 (1990): 83–100, who examines the mythic dimensions of the Companion Ibn 'Abbās, considered by some the father of *al-tafsīr bi'l-ma'thūr*.

76. For a superb biography of al-Tabari, see Chase Robinson, "al-Ṭabarī," in *Dictionary of Literary Biography*, vol. 311, *Arabic Literary Culture, 500–925*, ed. Michael Cooperson and Shawkat Toorawa (Farmington Hills, CT: Thomson Gale, 2005), 332–343. See, too, *The History of al-Ṭabarī*, vol. 1, "General Introduction," *From the Creation to the Flood* (Albany: State University of New York Press, 1989), trans. Franz Rosenthal, 5–134. See also Hugh Kennedy, ed., *Al-Tabari: A Muslim Historian and His Work* (Princeton: Darwin Press, 2008); Claude Gilliot, "La formation intellectuelle de Tabari (224/5–310 / 839–923)," *Journal Asiatique* 276 (1988): 201–244, "Mythe, récit, histoire du salut dans le commentaire coranique de Tabari," *Journal Asiatique* 282 (1994): 237–270, and "Les oeuvres de Tabari (mort en 310/923)," *Mélanges de l'Institut Dominicain d'Etudes Orientales du Caire* 19 (1989): 49–90.

77. Ibn Kathir, *Tafsīr al-Qur'ān al-'azīm*, 1:5, quoted from Jane Dammen McAuliffe, *Qur'ānic Christians*, 20. McAuliffe notes that in the introduction to his commentary, *Jāmi' al-bayān 'an taw'il ay al-Qur'ān*, 1:77–79, al-Tabari enumerates variants on the Prophet's denunciation of *al-tafsīr bi'l-ra'y*.

78. See McAuliffe's discussion, 20–21.

79. See Walid Saleh, "Marginalia and Peripheries: A Tunisian Historian and the History of Qur'anic Exegesis," *Numen* 58 (2011): 284–313, for a discussion of *al-tafsīr bi'l ma'thūr*.

80. It is important to note the use of the terms was ideologically driven. It was a Sunni (of the Salafi type) endeavor to suppress "heretical" interpretations. For a discussion of the genealogy of the term, see Saleh, "Preliminary Remarks on the Historiography of tafsīr in Arabic: A History of the Book Approach," *Journal of Qur'anic Studies* 12 (2010): 6–40.

81. Muqatil b. Sulayman, *Tafsīr Muqātil ibn Sulaymān*, ed. 'Abdallah Mahmud Shihata, 5 vols. (Cairo: al-Hay'a al-Miṣriyya al-'Āmma lil-Kitāb, 1979–1989). See Fred Leemhuis, "Origins and Early Development of the Tafsir Tradition," in *Approaches to the History of the Interpretation of the Qur'an*, ed. Andrew Rippin (New York: Oxford University Press, 1988), 1–30.

82. Even though Ibn Kathir falls outside the designated temporal purview of this work, I have nonetheless included him because of the popularity of his *Qiṣaṣ al-anbiyā'*. For Arabic editions of his work, see Abu Fida' Isma'il ibn Kathir, *Qiṣaṣ al-anbiyā'*, ed. Dr. Sayyid al-Jamili (Beirut: Dar al-jīl, 1993), and ibid., *Tafsīr al-Qur'ān al-'azīm* (Beirut: Dar al-fikr, 1970). In addition to his *qiṣaṣ* and *tafsīr*, Ibn Kathir's *al-Bidāya wa-l-nihāya* (Beirut: Maktabat al-ma'ārif, 1990) is a major historical work of the Mamluk period. For Arabic editions of al-Tabari's work, see Muhammad b. Jarir al-Tabari, *Jāmi' al-bayān 'an ta'wīl ay*

al-Qur'ān (Cairo: Sharikat maktabat wa-maṭbaʿat Muṣṭafa al-Bābī al-Ḥalabī wa-awlādihi, 1954), and *Ta'rīkh al-rusul wa-l-mulūk*, ed. M. J. DeGoeje as *Annales* (Leiden: E. J. Brill, 1879–1901), and for al-Thaʿlabi, see Ahmad b. Muhammad al-Thaʿlabi, *Qiṣaṣ al-anbiyā' al-musammā ʿArā'is al-Majālis* (Beirut: Dar al-Kutub al-ʿImīyyah, 1985).

83. Claude Gilliot, "Exégèse, langue, et théologie en Islam: L'exégèse coranique de Tabari" (m. 311/923) (Paris: J. Vrin, 1990).

84. Claude Gilliot, "Exegesis of the Qur'an: Classical and Medieval."

85. *Asānīd* is the Arabic plural of *isnād*, from the root *sanad* meaning "support."

86. See Claude Gilliot, "Parcours exégétiques: De Ṭabarī á Rāzī (Sourate 55)," *Analyses, théorie* (1983): 87–116, and "Traduire ou trahir at-Ṭabarī?," *Arabica* 34 (1987): 366–370, and his monograph *Exégèse, langue et-théologie en Islam.*

87. McAuliffe, *Qur'ānic Christians,* 42.

88. Chase Robinson, "al-Ṭabarī," 337.

89. According to Rosenthal, trans., *The History of al-Ṭabarī,* vol. 1, 56, "His own views leaned toward moderation and compromise."

90. For a complete, annotated English translation of al-Tabari's works, with useful historical and philological notes, see the thirty-eight-volume *History of al-Ṭabarī,* gen. ed. Ehsan Yarshater (Albany: State University of New York Press, 1985–99). Volumes of special interest are vol. 1, *The History of al-Ṭabarī,* trans. Franz Rosenthal (1985); vol. 2, *Prophets and Patriarchs,* trans. William M. Brinner (1987); and vol. 3, *The Children of Israel,* trans. William M. Brinner (1991).

91. Here I summarize the useful outline in Tarif Khalidi, "Al-Ṭabarī: An Introduction," in *al-Tabari: A Medieval Muslim Historian and His Work,* ed. Hugh Kennedy (Princeton: Darwin Press, 2008), 4–5.

92. It would be worthwhile to compare the rabbinic rule of *kelal uperat, perat ukelal* (rules of inference between general and specific statements and vice versa) to al-Tabari's principle.

93. As Khalidi, 6, notes, when it comes to questions of human freedom, and anthropomorphic verse, al-Tabari is willing to "entertain a less than fully exoteric interpretation."

94. Compare with *gezera shavah,* the rabbinic hermeneutical rule of analogy in which a particular detail of a biblical law in one verse is derived from the meaning of the word or phrase in the other.

95. This is antithetical to the rabbinic penchant to fill in the lacunae of biblical verses. See discussion to follow.

96. Walid Saleh, "Hermeneutics: al-Thaʿlabī," in *Blackwell Companion to the Qur'ān,* ed. Andrew Rippin (Malden, MA: Wiley-Blackwell, 2009), 323. Saleh describes *al-Khasf* as an "epoch-making work," 324. See his *Formation of the Classical Tafsīr Tradition.*

97. Isaiah Goldfeld, *Qur'ānic Commentary in the Eastern Islamic Tradition of the First Four Centuries of the Hijra: An Annotated Edition of the Preface of al-Thaʿlabī's "al-Kashf wa'l-bayān ʿan tafsīr al-Qur'ān"* (Acre, Israel: Srugy, 1984).

98. For an introduction, see William Brinner, trans., *'Arā'is al-Majālis fī Qiṣaṣ al-Anbiyā'* or *"Lives of the Prophets": As Recounted by Abū Isḥāq Aḥmad ibn Muḥammad ibn Ibrāhīm al-Thaʻlabī* (Leiden: Brill, 2002), xi–xxxiii, and Tottoli, *Biblical Prophets in the Qur'ān and Muslim Literature.* For a flawed but useful compendium of legends associated with biblical and qur'anic personages, see Haim Schwartzbaum, *Biblical and Extra-biblical Legends in Islamic Folk-Literature*, Beiträge zur Sprach-und Kulturgeschichte des Orients, vol. 30 (Walldorf-Hessen: Verlag für Orientkunde Dr. H. Vorndran, 1982).

99. While I refer to the terms interchangeably, some scholars argue that the generic term *qiṣaṣ al-anbiyā'* covers three different categories: legends about creation, legends about prophets, and stories dealing specifically with the Israelites *(isrā'īliyyāt)* and their rulers, beginning with the death of Moses and their entry into the Promised Land. Others, however, are of the opinion that the *qiṣaṣ al-anbiyā'* are a subdivision of the *isrā'īliyyāt.* See discussion in Adang, *Muslim Writers.* For an introduction to the stories of the prophets, see Marianna Klar, "Stories of the Prophets," in Rippin, *Blackwell Companion to the Qur'ān*, 339–349.

100. On *isrā'īliyyāt*, see Roberto Tottoli, "Origin and Use of the Term *Isrā'īliyyāt* in Muslim Literature," *Arabica* 46 (1999): 193–210; Cornelia Schöck, *Adam im Islam: Ein Beitrag zur Ideengeschichte der Sunna* (Berlin: K. Schwartz, 1993), 39–54; Adang, *Muslim Writers*, 8–10; and Jane Dammen McAuliffe, "Assessing the Isrā'īliyyāt: An Exegetical Conundrum," in *Story-telling in the Framework of Non-fictional Arabic Literature*, ed. Stefan Leder (Wiesbaden: Harrassowitz, 1998), 345–369. McAuliffe comments that "perhaps the most felicitous translation is that provided by Jacob Lassner, who dubs the whole genre 'Jewish memorabilia,'" but the term, as she herself observes, is sometimes attributed to "the earlier *ahl al-kitāb*," even though "the association with Jews predominates" (346). In *Satan's Tragedy and Redemption: Iblīs in Sufi Psychology* (Leiden: Brill, 1983), Peter Awn, like some other scholars, points out: "The qiṣaṣ literature should not be viewed as wholly derivative from Jewish and Christian sources, for it underwent substantial Islamization at the hands of Muslim preachers and commentators. Cross-fertilization occurred, with details, nuances and embellishments traded back and forth among the various religious communities. Finally, the influence of these tales on indigenous non-Christian or Jewish pre-Islamic beliefs should not be discounted" (9).

101. Roberto Tottoli, "Narrative Literature," in Rippin, *Blackwell Companion to the Qur'ān*, 469.

102. Tottoli, "Origin and Use of the Term *Isrā'īliyyāt*," *Arabica* 46 (1999), 193–210; and Norman Calder, "Tafsīr from Ṭabarī to Ibn Kathīr: Problems in the Description of a Genre, Illustrated with Reference to the Story of Abraham," in *Approaches to the Qur'an*, ed. G. R. Hawting and Abdul-Kader A. Shareef (New York: Routledge, 1993), 101–140.

103. Tottoli, "Origin and Use of the Term *Isrā'īliyyāt*," 206.

104. Wahb ibn Munnabih (654 or 655–728 or 732), of Persian or Yemeni descent, is inextricably associated with *isrā'īliyyāt.* Later Muslim sources look down upon his writings because they appear to have been drawn heavily from Jewish and Christian sources. See Adang, *Muslim Writers*, 10–12, for a brief

discussion of his role in disseminating Jewish and Christian traditions. On Wahb b. Munabbih, see Raif Georges Khoury, *Wahb b. Munabbih* (Wiesbaden: Harrassowitz, 1972); Menahem Kister, "On the Papyrus of Whab b. Munabbih," *Bulletin of the School of Oriental and African Studies* 37 (1974): 547–571; and Nabia Abbott, "Wahb b. Munabbih: A Review Article," *Journal of Near Eastern Studies* 36 (1977): 103–112.

105. Compare G. Vajda, "Isrā'īliyyāt," in *Encyclopedia of Islam*, 2nd ed., P. Bearman, Th. Bianquis, C. E. Bosworth, E. van Donzel, W. P. Heinrichs, Brill Online, 2013, who subsumes *qiṣaṣ* under the broader *isrā'īliyyat* category. Adang adopts the term "to indicate the whole genre of Islamicized biblical legends," *Muslim Writers*, 9.

106. Adapted from *'Arā'is al-Majālis fī Qiṣaṣ al-Anbiyā'* or *"Lives of the Prophets"*: *As Recounted by Abū Isḥāq Aḥmad ibn Muḥammad ibn Ibrāhīm al-Tha'labī*, trans. and annot. William Brinner (Leiden: Brill, 2002), 3–5.

107. A great deal has been written on Islamic historiography. See Franz Rosenthal, *A History of Muslim Historiography*, 2nd rev. ed. (Leiden: Brill, 1968); Tarif Khalidi, *Arabic Historical Thought in the Classical Period* (New York: Cambridge University Press, 1994); Chase Robinson, *Islamic Historiography* (Cambridge: Cambridge University Press, 2003); R. S. Humphreys, *Islamic History: A Framework for Inquiry* (Princeton: Princeton University Press, 1991), and "Qur'anic Myth and Narrative Structure in Early Islamic Historiography," in *Tradition and Innovation in Late Antiquity*, ed. F. M. Clover and R. S. Humphreys (Madison: University of Wisconsin Press, 1989), 271–290. For a focused discussion of two of the major histories and the use of sources, see Khalil Athamina, "The Historical Work of al-Balādurī and al-Ṭabarī: The Author's Attitude towards the Sources," in *Al-Tabari: A Muslim Historian and His Work*, ed. Hugh Kennedy (Princeton: Darwin Press, 2008), 141–155. This triumph of collection over composition that prevailed during the emergence of Islamic historiography in the ninth century may be an oversimplification. Robinson, *Islamic Historiography*, describes three phases of the development of the genre of historiography and it is in the second phase, from ca. 730 to ca. 830, that we can speak of Islamic historiography: "By 830, biography, prosopography and chronology had all emerged in forms that would remain recognizable throughout the classical period" (24).

108. M. G. S. Hodgson, "Two Pre-modern Muslim Historians: Pitfalls and Opportunities in Presenting Them to Moderns," in *Towards World Community*, ed. John Ulric Nef (The Hague: W. Junk 1968), 53–68. Hodgson briefly discusses al-Tabari's method of selecting *ḥadīth* reports and illustrates how the process of selecting anecdotes is quite deliberate.

109. See James Kugel, "Two Introductions to Midrash," *Midrash and Literature*, ed. Geoffrey Hartman and Sanford Budick (New Haven: Yale University Press, 1986), 77–103.

2. *The Biblical and Qur'anic Abraham*

1. *Mishnah Avot* 5:2–3 sums up this notion rather neatly: "There were ten generations from Adam to Noah, in order to make known God's long

suffering. For all those generations had provoked God to anger, until he brought upon them the waters of the flood. There were ten generations from Noah to Abraham, in order to make known God's long suffering. For all those generations had provoked him to anger until Abraham came and received the reward of all."

2. Library shelves abound with works on Abraham. See Helmut Weidmann, *Die Patriarchen und ihre Religion im Licht der Forschung seit Julius Wellhausen*, 94 (Göttingen: Vandenhoeck & Ruprecht, 1968), for a survey of research on Abraham from Wellhausen to Alt. For references to works on Abraham in Islam, see the Oxford online bibliography: http://www.oxfordbibliographies.com /view/document/obo-9780195390155/obo-9780195390155-0164.xml.

3. Unless otherwise noted, all translations of the Hebrew Bible, except citations appearing in the New Testament, are from *Tanakh: The Holy Scriptures* (Philadelphia: Jewish Publication Society, 1985).

4. Jon D. Levenson, *Death and Resurrection of the Beloved Son* (New Haven: Yale University Press, 1993), 70.

5. Robert Alter, *The Art of Biblical Narrative* (New York: Basic Books, 1981), 6.

6. Joel Kaminsky, *Yet I Loved Jacob: Reclaiming the Biblical Concept of Election* (Nashville: Abingdon Press, 2007). See Gary Anderson and Joel Kaminsky, eds., *The Call of Abraham: Essays on the Election of Israel in Honor of Jon D. Levenson* (Notre Dame, IN: University of Notre Dame Press, 2013).

7. Will Herberg, "The 'Chosenness' of Israel and the Jew of Today," in *Arguments and Doctrines: A Reader of Jewish Thinking in the Aftermath of the Holocaust*, ed. Arthur Cohen (New York: Harper and Row, 1970), 280.

8. Unless otherwise specified, I have translated qur'anic passages in consultation with several English translations: Abdel Haleem, *The Qur'an* (Oxford: Oxford University Press, 2010); Marmaduke Pickthall, *Koran* (New York: Everyman's Library, 1992); and A. J. Arberry, *The Qur'an Interpreted: A Translation* (New York: Simon and Schuster, 1996 c. 1956).

9. For an overview of covenant in the Qur'an, see Gerhard Böwering, "Covenant," in *Encyclopedia of the Qur'ān*, gen. ed. Jane Dammen McAuliffe (Washington, DC: Brill, 2012), http://referenceworks.brillonline.com/entries /encyclopaedia-of-the-quran/covenant-SIM_00098, and Andrew Rippin, "God," in *The Blackwell Companion to the Qur'ān* (Malden, MA: Wiley-Blackwell, 2009), 229–230, and Reuven Firestone, "Is There a Notion of 'Divine Election' in the Qur'an?," in *New Perspectives on the Qur'ān: The Qur'ān in Its Historical Context 2*, ed. Gabriel S. Reynolds (New York: Routledge, 2011), 393–410.

10. Ur is an ancient Mesopotamian city, probably south of modern Baghdad. The Chaldeans (Hebrew *Kasdim*; Aramaic *Kasdayy*a) were an Aramaic-speaking people who infiltrated into Babylonia. By 600 BCE they had become rulers. The Neo-Babylonian rulers (Nebuchadnezzar, inter alia) were in fact Chaldeans, though they had been Akkadianized. From this time on (and even earlier starting from ca. 800 BCE), Akkadian was being replaced both in Assyria and Babylonia by Aramaic, which is why the Judaean exiles returned speaking Aramaic. Calling Ur, a very ancient city in Sumer, whose heyday was ca. 2000 BCE "Ur of the Chaldees" (*Ur Kasdim*) is an anachronism, though

Ur, as the city of the moon god Sin, became important again ca. 600. The last Neo-Babylonian king, Nabonidus, promoted the worship of the moon god Sin at Ur and especially at Harran. These are the two cities associated with the patriarchs in Mesopotamia. It has often been pointed out that Terah is also another form of the Hebrew word for moon, *yareaḥ* (pronounced *yeraḥ* in biblical times). The Bible claims that Abraham lived in Ur ca. 2000 BCE, about a thousand years before the Chaldeans even began to enter Mesopotamia. "Ur of the Chaldees" is therefore either an anachronism or evidence that the patriarchal stories, at least this aspect of the Abraham tradition, in their present form are fairly late—600 BCE or later. In the Bible, only the priestly source speaks of Ur of the Chaldees. The other sources know only of Harran as the homeland of the patriarchs. And the Septuagint speaks only of "the land of the Chaldeans '*erets kasdim*.'" I am grateful to Stephen Geller, who provided invaluable information on this subject.

11. The notion that all the nations of the earth will be blessed through Abraham figures prominently in Christian theological historiography. See discussion to follow.

12. In Genesis 11:31, Abraham's father, Terah, takes him, his wife, and his grandson, Lot, son of his brother Haran, from Ur of the Chaldeans to Canaan.

13. On the trials, see Chapter 7.

14. Abraham builds God a sanctuary in Mecca.

15. Compare Gen. 13:16 and 15:5.

16. The Islamic tradition also retains a version of this episode. See for example al-Tha'labi's tales of the prophets, in '*Arā'is al-Majālis fī Qiṣaṣ al-Anbiyā'* or "*Lives of the Prophets*": *As Recounted by Abū Isḥāq Aḥmad ibn Muḥammad ibn Ibrāhīm al-Tha'labī*, trans. and annot. William M. Brinner (Leiden: Brill, 2002), 136, where Sarah is considered Abraham's paternal sister. When the tyrant stretches out his hand toward Sarah, his hand becomes paralyzed, sticking to his chest. This occurs three times.

17. As Michael Fishbane, *Biblical Interpretation in Ancient Israel* (Oxford: Oxford University Press, 1985), suggests, there is a connection between this incident and the Exodus story such that "Abraham comes to serve as a prototype of Israel for later generations," 376. Abraham and Sarah's escape from the clutches of Pharaoh back to Canaan prefigures Israel's triumphal flight out of Egypt into the Promised Land. See, too, Levenson, *Death and Resurrection of the Beloved Son*, 86, who writes: "and so in Genesis 12 we have in the life of Abram and Sarai a prefiguration of the Exodus: famine forces the couple into Egypt, where they settle, but with Sarai taken into Pharaoh's palace, as Moses will later be (v 15; Exod 2:10)."

18. Melchizedek is also mentioned in the Letter to the Hebrews. He is understood typologically as a figure of Christ. See discussion in Chapter 3.

19. The name of the steward is sometimes translated as Eliezer of Damascus. The Hebrew is unclear.

20. This is an important verse in Christian conceptions of Abraham as the father of faith. See Galatians 13:6–9 and Hebrews 11:8–12.

21. The opening of the Decalogue (Exod. 20:2), "I am the Lord your God, who brought you out of the land of Egypt, out of the house of slavery," parallels Genesis 15:7.

22. This "curious oracle" is not only, as Levenson observes, the first mention in the biblical narrative of the Exodus event, but it is "an exquisitely artful interlacing of the story of Abram with that of his Israelite descendants. For their descent into the unspecified 'land not theirs' recalls nothing so much as Abram and Sarai's descent into Egypt three chapters earlier." *Death and Resurrection of the Beloved Son*, 88. On the same page he continues: "In the prophecy that interrupts the covenant-making ceremony, Abram's experience is shown to have been itself akin to a prophetic sign-act. It is a biographical pre-enactment of the providential design for the whole people Israel." See also Jon D. Levenson, *Inheriting Abraham: The Legacy of the Patriarch in Judaism, Christianity and Islam* (Princeton: Princeton University Press, 2012).

23. We find a similar prescription to a wife's barrenness in an ancient contract from Nuzi (Mesopotamia, fourteenth century BCE): "Kelim-ninu [a woman] has been given in marriage to Shennima [a man] . . . If Kelim-ninu does not bear, Kelim-ninu may not send the offspring away"; James B. Pritchard, ed., *The Ancient Near East: An Anthology of Texts and Pictures* (Princeton: Princeton University Press, 1969), 220.

24. See Levenson's discussion, *Death and Resurrection of the Beloved Son*, chapter 10, of Gen. 16 and the parallels between it and Gen. 22.

25. There is a parallel between God's promise to Abraham of offspring too numerous to count (Gen. 15:5 and 22: 17), and His promise to Hagar (Gen. 16:10).

26. This is similar to the feelings Abraham expresses toward Eliezer in Genesis 15:3.

27. For a stimulating reexamination of the issue of particularism and universalism in the Hebrew Bible, see Jon D. Levenson, "The Universal Horizon of Biblical Particularism," in Mark G. Brett, ed., *Ethnicity and the Bible* (Leiden: Brill, 1996), 143–169. See also Joel Kaminsky, *Yet I Loved Jacob*. The literature on chosenness and election is massive and broad in scope. See, for example, Michael Wyschogrod, *The Body of Faith: Judaism as Corporeal Election* (New York: Seabury Press, 1983), and the following articles in Daniel Frank, ed., *A People Apart: Chosenness and Ritual in Jewish Philosophical Thought* (Albany: State University of New York Press, 1993): David Novak, "The Election of Israel: Outline of a Philosophical Analysis," 11–50; Menachem Kellner, "Chosenness, Not Chauvinism: Maimonides on the Chosen People," 51–76; Norbert M. Samuelson, "Response to Menachem Kellner," 77–84, "Menachem Kellner, "Response to Norbert Samuelson," 85–90; and Ze'ev Levy, "Judaism and Chosenness: On Some Controversial Aspects from Spinoza to Contemporary Jewish Thought," 91–106.

28. R. Syren explains Genesis 17's dual message of inclusion and exclusion as arising from postexilic conditions. He writes, "After the upheavals of the exile, the Israelite community had to come to terms with radically changed conditions affecting its life and institutions. At the same time, however, its old beliefs and time-honoured practices had to be safeguarded. The new prospects opening up in the outside world had to be understood by looking back in its own traditions and religious inheritance." *The Forsaken Firstborn: A Study of a Recurrent Motif in the Patriarchal Narratives* (Sheffield, UK: Sheffield

Academic Press, 1993), 41; see also 62–63. It is not, however, a fully convincing argument. There is no scholarly consensus that Gen. 17 is postexilic, and furthermore, even if his assertions were correct, this alone does not explain an acceptance of groups. Can we assume that the postexilic period gave rise to openness to outsiders when in fact Ezra provides countervailing evidence? For a discussion of the attitude of postexilic writers toward foreigners during the time of restoration, see Daniel L. Smith-Christopher, "Between Ezra and Isaiah," in Brett, *Ethnicity and the Bible*, 117–142. Smith-Christopher outlines three distinct options coexisting in postexilic biblical thought—exclusion, transformation, and inclusion. See also M. Weinfeld, "The Universalist Trend and the Isolationist Trend in the Period of the Restoration to Zion" [Hebrew], *Tarbiz* 23 (1964): 228–242, who argues that Isa. 40–66 envisages a Judaism open to all during the period of restoration.

29. Abraham does not request that the guilty be punished and the righteous spared. The entire city should be acquitted for the sake of the righteous, a notion echoed in Jeremiah 5:1: "Roam the streets of Jerusalem, search its squares, look about and take note: You will not find a man, there is none who acts justly, who seeks integrity—that I should pardon her." Rabbinic literature gives expression to the idea that the world endures on account of the righteousness of thirty-six individuals.

30. Compare Abraham's dialogue with God in Gen. 18 and Abimelech's in Gen. 20.

31. For an illuminating comparison of Ishmael's expulsion from the Promised Land on the one hand and of Cain's expulsion from Eden on the other, see Levenson, *Death and Resurrection of the Beloved Son*, 91–92, and also 102, where he writes, "The terse narrative of Gen. 21:9–13 looks, Janus-like, both back to the story of the primal family and forward to the next generation of Patriarchs." Furthermore, Levenson astutely draws our attention to the "intertextual connection between the supernatural deliverance of Ishmael in Gen. 21 and another story of a first-born son whose life is spared, the story of Joseph," 108.

32. The question is addressed in Chapter 6.

33. We also read in Micah: "You [God] will keep faith with Jacob, loyalty to Abraham, as you promised on oath to our fathers in days gone by."

34. For an introduction to Ben Sira, see J. J. Collins, *Jewish Wisdom in the Hellenistic Age* (Louisville: Westminster/John Knox Press, 1997), 21–111. On chapters 44–50, the "praise of the fathers" section of the Wisdom of Jesus ben Sira, see Burton L. Mack, *Wisdom and the Hebrew Epic: Ben Sira's Hymn on the Praise of the Fathers* (Chicago: Chicago University Press, 1985).

35. For a thorough discussion, see Jeffrey Siker, *Disinheriting the Jews: Abraham in Early Christian Controversy* (Louisville: Westminster John Knox Press, 1991).

36. There is a great deal of scholarly literature on the Matthean genealogy. See Raymond E. Brown, *Birth of the Messiah* (New York: Doubleday, 1977), as well as his article on research on the birth narratives, "Gospel Infancy Narrative Research from 1976 to 1986: Part I (Matthew)," *Catholic Biblical Quarterly* 48 (1986): 468–483, "Gospel Infancy Narrative Research from 1976 to 1986:

Part II (Luke)," *Catholic Biblical Quarterly* 48 (1986): 660–680. See also Krister Stendahl, *Quis et Unde?: An Analysis of Mt 1–2* (Berlin: Alfred Töpelmann, 1960).

37. The Gospel of Luke also includes Jesus' genealogy (3:23–38) and mentions Abraham. Indeed, they are the only two Gospels that include a genealogy, and refer to Bethlehem as the city of Jesus' birth to a virgin, Mary, who is engaged to Joseph. His lineage in Luke, however, is traced back all the way to Adam, "son of God." Furthermore, the Gospel of Luke opens with the foretelling of the birth of John the Baptist and his preaching that "all flesh shall see the salvation of God" (3:6). When Jesus is baptized, a voice from heaven declares: "You are my son, the Beloved; with you I am well pleased" (4:22). The emphasis therefore is on Jesus' role in the salvation of humankind. Through his Jewish ancestry he is depicted as important for Jews and Gentiles alike.

38. The first fulfillment citation reads as follows: "All this took place to fulfill what had been spoken by the Lord through the prophet: 'Look, the virgin shall conceive and bear a son, and they shall name him Emmanuel, which means God is with us'" (Matt. 1:22–23). Another example: "So that what had been spoken through the prophet Isaiah might be fulfilled" (4:14–16). Other fulfillment citations include 2:6, 15, 17, 23; 8:17; 12:17–21; 13:14, 35; 21:4; 27:9–10. In many cases, a specific prophet is mentioned such as Isaiah or Jeremiah, and in other instances no specific prophet is named.

39. See Siker, *Disinheriting the Jews*, 79, who writes: "Overall, Matthew refers to David fifteen times in his Gospel . . . more than twice as often as he refers to Abraham. Thus Matthew subordinates Abraham to the figure of David, both in the genealogy and in the Gospel at large. Still, it is significant that Matthew grounds the genealogy of Jesus in Abraham, for it relates Jesus to the father of the Jews."

40. John Gager, *Reinventing Paul* (New York: Oxford University Press, 2004), 77–101; Daniel Boyarin, *A Radical Jew: Paul and the Politics of Identity* (Berkeley: University of California Press, 1994), 32–38, and 106–135; and Levenson, *Death and Resurrection of the Beloved Son*. Works that propound an alternative to the traditional view of Paul's renunciation of the law include Krister Stendhal, *Paul among Jews and Gentiles and Other Essays* (Philadelphia: Fortress Press, 1976); see therein especially his groundbreaking essay, "The Apostle Paul and the Introspective Conscience of the West," originally printed in *Harvard Theological Review* 56 (1963): 199–215, and Stendahl, *Final Account: Paul's Letter to the Romans* (Minneapolis: Fortress Press, 1995); Lloyd Gaston, *Paul and the Torah* (Vancouver: University of British Columbia Press, 1987); John G. Lodge, *Romans 9–11: A Reader-Response Analysis* (Atlanta: Scholars Press, 1996); Stanley Stowers, *A Rereading of Romans: Justice, Law and Gentiles* (New Haven: Yale University Press, 1994); and most recently Gager, *Reinventing Paul*. Current scholarship has focused on an assessment of Paul's Jewish context and thus addresses the Jewish origins of Christianity. See Brendan Byrne, "Interpreting Romans Theologically in a Post-'New Perspective' Perspective," *Harvard Theological Review* 94 (2001): 227–241; Gager, *Reinventing Paul*; James D. G. Dunn's introduction and "In Search of Common Ground," in *Paul and the Mosaic Law*, ed. James. D. G. Dunn (Grand Rapids, MI: Eerdmans, 2001),

1–5, 309–334, and introduction to *The Cambridge Companion to St. Paul*, ed. James D. G. Dunn (Cambridge: Cambridge University Press, 2003), 1–15, esp. 9–12. Those opposed to this new perspective on Paul included Seyoon Kim, *Paul and the New Perspective: Some Thoughts on the Origin of Paul's Gospel* (Grand Rapids, MI: Eerdmans, 2002), and "The Jesus Tradition in 1 Thess. 4.13–5.11," *New Testament Studies* 48 (2002): 225–242, and Charles H. Thalbert, "Paul, Judaism, and the Revisionists," *Catholic Biblical Quarterly* 63 (2001): 1–22, who writes: "Paul, then, fits into the Christian-Jewish messianic way of thinking about a new covenant that replaces the old, inefficacious one" (20). For an excellent treatment of Paul's "simultaneous Jewishness and non-Jewishness" in Christian writings of the fourth and fifth centuries, which in turn teases out the ramifications of approaches to Paul in light of the historical and theological debate about Christianity's Jewish origins, see Andrew S. Jacobs, "A Jew's Jew: Paul and the Early Christian Problem of Jewish Origins," *Journal of Religion* 86.2 (2006): 258–286. For a discussion of how to read Paul's argument for Gentile inclusion, see Caroline Johnson Hodge, *If Sons, Then Heirs: A Study of Kinship and Ethnicity in the Letters of Paul* (New York: Oxford University Press, 2007), and see Paula Fredrickson, "Judaizing the Nations: The Ritual Demands of Paul's Gospel," *New Testament Studies* 56 (2010): 232–252.

41. As Arland Hultgren, *Paul's Letter to the Romans: A Commentary* (Grand Rapids, MI: Eerdmans, 2011), 1, writes, "the constructive theological work and reforming activities of major figures in church history—such as Augustine, Martin Luther, John Wesley, and Karl Barth—cannot be explained except that those persons were ignited and affected deeply by the study of Paul's letter to the Romans." A great deal has been written on the Epistle of Paul to the Romans. See discussion in Chapter 5, and note 40 above. For a lucid and concise analysis, see Bart Ehrman, *The New Testament: A Historical Introduction to the Early Christian Writings* (New York: Oxford University Press, 1997), 299–310, and Hultgren, *Paul's Letter to the Romans*, which contains an extensive bibliography.

42. Gen. 15:6. The Jewish Publication Society translation: "And because he put his trust in the LORD, He reckoned it to his merit."

43. Unless otherwise specified, all quotations from the New Testament are taken from the New Standard Version Bible Translation.

44. Siker, *Disinheriting the Jews*, 70–71.

45. The dating of the letter is problematic, with opinions varying from 48 or 49 CE to the mid-50s. Scholarship on Paul is as varied as it is vast. For more detail on the letter, see Hans Deiter Betz, *Galatians: A Commentary on Paul's Letter to the Church of Galatia* (Philadelphia: Fortress Press, 1979); James D. G. Dunn, *A Commentary on the Epistle to the Galatians* (London: A & C Black, 1993); Frank Matera, *Galatians*, Sacra Pagina Series 9 (Collegeville, MD: Liturgical Press, 1992); Lloyd Gaston, "Israel's Enemies in Pauline Theology," *New Testament Studies* 28 (1982): 400–423, and *Paul and the Torah*.

46. Gager, *Reinventing Paul*, 79.

47. As Matera, *Galatians*, 1, notes, "the search for the identity, origin, and message of those who advocate circumcision has generated a veritable library of articles and monographs, but not a consensus." Matera claims there is

general agreement that the agitators were Jews from Judea who saw themselves as followers of Christ and who advocated observance of the law; however, this is not the case. On the agitators or so-called enemies of Paul, see Gerd Leudemann, *Opposition to Paul in Jewish Christianity* (Minneapolis: Fortress Press, 1989), and Wayne Meeks, *The Writings of Saint Paul* (New York: Norton, 1972), 176–184. See Gager, *Reinventing Paul;* and as Gaston, "Israel's Enemies in Pauline Theology," 401, writes, "it seems that the trouble makers who try to get the Galatians to Judaize are themselves Gentile Judaizers (the περιτεμνόμενοι, and most important, those who do not keep the law, 6. 13), so that Judaism is not an issue at all." See Siker, *Disinheriting the Jews,* who writes, "The most important observation regarding the Teachers is that they were Jewish *Christians* (emphasis his). There is no evidence in Galatians to suggest that they were non-Christian Jews" (31). Siker, however, continues: "Paul's fight is an intramural battle between rival *Christian* (emphasis his) understandings of the gospel and not in the first place an expression of conflict between Paul and non-Christian Judaism" (32). Even though Siker identifies the Teachers/agitators as Jewish Christians and others as Gentile Judaizers, they agree that the conflict is not between Paul and Judaism per se but about competing understandings of the gospel.

48. For a compelling reading of Galatians, see Lloyd Gaston, *Paul and the Torah* (Vancouver: University of British Columbia Press, 1987), and Gager, *Reinventing Paul,* 77–99. Taking his cue from Krister Stendahl, E. P. Sanders, and Marcus Barth, Gaston demonstrates that Paul's concern is the justification of Gentiles through Christ, who is not pitted against the Law. Nor is he the fulfillment of the Law, but the means through which Gentiles are made righteous before God.

49. See Romans 9–11. Discussion of the allegory in chapter 4 of Galatians is discussed in Chapter 3.

50. Siker, *Disinheriting the Jews,* 137. Compare John 1:12–13 and 8:33–40.

51. Traditionally Hebrews was attributed to Paul; however, even early Christians such as Origen (185–254 CE) recognized that the letter was unlike Paul's other letters in terms of style and rhetoric. While scholars have proposed other authors, there is no corroborating evidence sufficient to attribute the letter to a specific author. The letter casts Jesus as the Son and High Priest, which is unusual.

52. James Swetnam, *Jesus and Isaac* (Rome: Biblical Institute Press, 1981), 128.

53. Siker, *Disinheriting the Jews,* 92.

54. The idea that Abraham was a "friend of God" is a common notion in early Judaism, as well as in the Qur'an. See discussion below.

55. I will translate names in the Qur'an into English, but initially I will provide a transliteration of the Arabic in parentheses.

56. Q. 6:75–84; 14:37; 19:41–50; 21:51–75; 26:69–104. See *Jub.* 17:15–18; 18:14–16; 19:9; 21:2–4; 23:10; *Pseudo-Philo, Biblical Antiquities (Liber Antiquitatum Biblicarum),* 6.1; Apocalypse of Abraham.

57. Q. 4:125: "Who is better in religion than one who surrenders to God while being righteous and following the tradition of Abraham the monotheist. God chose Abraham as friend." See Isa. 41:8, and discussion below.

58. The term is associated especially with Abraham, who possesses a pure worship of God, as opposed to idolaters, *mushrikūn*. See, for example, Q. 2:129, 135; 3:67, 95; 4:125; 6:79, 161. On *ḥanīf*, see J. Wellhausen, *Reste arabischen Heidentums*, 2nd ed. (Berlin: De Gruyter Co., 1927), 234; W. Montgomery Watt, "Ḥanīf," *Encyclopedia of Islam* 2nd ed., 3:165–166; Uri Rubin, "Ḥanīf," *Encyclopedia of the Qur'an*, 2:402–404, and "Ḥanīfiyya and Kaʿba," *Jerusalem Studies in Arabic and Islam* 13 (1990): 85–112; N. A. Faris and H. W. Glidden, "The Development of the Meaning of the Koranic Ḥanīf," *Journal of the Palestinian Oriental Society* 19 (1939): 1–13; P. Crone and M. Cook, *Hagarism*, 13–14. See also J. Wansbrough, *The Sectarian Milieu: Content and Composition of Islamic Salvation History*, London Oriental Series, Volume 34 (Oxford: Oxford University Press, 1978), esp. 4, 6, Andrew Rippin, "RḤMNN and the Ḥanīfs," in *Islamic Studies Presented to Charles J. Adams*, ed. W. B. Hallaq and D. P. Little (Brill: Leiden, 1991), 153–168.

59. Patricia Crone and Michael Cook, *Hagarism: The Making of the Islamic World* (Cambridge: Cambridge University Press, 1977), 12–13.

60. Hawting, "The Religion of Abraham and Islam," in *Abraham, the Nations and the Hagarites: Jewish, Christian, and Islamic Perspectives on Kinship with Abraham*, ed. Martin Goodman, George H. van Kooten, and Jacques T.A.G.M. van Ruiten (Leiden; Boston: Brill, 2010), 480. See F. Buhl and C. E. Bosworth, "Milla," *Encyclopedia of Islam* 2nd ed., 7:61. Noteworthy is the appearance of the word *ḥanīf* in these passages.

61. Hawting, "The Religion of Abraham and Islam," 480. François de Blois, "Naṣrānī (Ναζωραλος) and Ḥanīf (ἐθνικός) Studies on the Religious Vocabulary of Christianity and Islam," *Bulletin of the School of Oriental and African Studies* 65 (2002): 1–30 (see esp. 16–25 on *ḥanīf*), suggests that the term derives from the Syriac *ḥanpā*, meaning non-Jew, Gentile, or one who is not subject to Jewish Law. For a more detailed discussion of the linguistic issue, see W. Montgomery Watt, "Ḥanīf," Encyclopedia of Islam, 2nd ed., 3:165–166, and Uri Rubin, "Ḥanīf," in McAuliffe, *Encyclopedia of the Qur'an*, 2:402–404; Cook and Crone, *Hagarism*, 13–14; and N. A. Faris and H. W. Glidden, "The Development of the Meaning of the Koranic Ḥanīf," *Journal of the Palestinian Oriental Society* 19 (1939): 1–13. Wellhausen, *Reste arabischen Heidentums*, 234, considers *ḥanīf* a purely literary construct. See A. Rippin, "RḤMNN and the Ḥanīfs," in *Islamic Studies Presented to Charles J. Adams*, ed. W. D. Hallaq and D. P. Little (Leiden: Brill, 1991), 153–168, and Hawting, "Religion of Abraham and Islam," 489, n. 23, for additional references to modern discussions and interpretations of *ḥanīf*. As Clare Wilde and Jane McAuliffe observe, "the tension between the apparent Quranic meaning and the close Syriac cognate has yet to be explained satisfactorily particularly with regards to its usage in a Muslim framework"; "Religious Pluralism in the Qur'an," in *The Encyclopedia of the Qur'ān* (Leiden: Brill, 2004), 4:402.

62. M. Sirry, "The Early Development of the Quranic Ḥanīf," *Journal of Semitic Studies* 41.2 (Autumn 2011): 345–366, argues that the meaning of the term in the Qur'an is not self-evident and the term is used differently in various contexts such that it possessed both the monotheistic and polytheistic senses, although he does not convincingly demonstrate this to be the case. He

also attempts to demonstrate that "in the post Ṭabarī tafsīr" the word "acquires a more stable, fixed meaning as the adherent of the straight and right religion and the equivalent of 'Muslim'" (366). Because he has not compellingly shown that the term was fluid in the Qur'an, his argument for fixity is not persuasive, as intuitively attractive as it may be. Rather than investigating the use of the term in exegetical works, Gabriel Reynolds, *The Qur'ān and Its Biblical Subtext* (New York: Routledge, 2010), takes another approach: to investigate its use in earlier Jewish and Christian sources. Drawing on the work of Blois, he argues (83–87) that the secondary meaning of the Syriac *ḥanpā*, "gentile," should be applied to the Qur'anic use of *ḥanīf*. In other words, Abraham was a *ḥanīf* in the ethnic, not the religious sense of the word. Abraham was not beholden to the People of the Book for his faith, but came to it as a Gentile who after rejecting worship of the stars, moon, and sun came to know the one, true God.

63. Hawting, "Religion of Abraham and Islam," 489.

64. See Reuven Firestone, *Journeys in Holy Lands: The Evolution of the Abraham-Ishmael Legends in Islamic Exegesis* (Albany: State University of New York Press, 1990), and Shari Lowin, *The Making of a Forefather: Abraham in Islamic and Jewish Exegetical Narratives* (Leiden: Brill, 2006).

65. See *Jubilees* 8:2–4 and 11:7–8. James Kugel, *How to Read the Bible: A Guide to Scripture Then and Now* (New York: Free Press, 2007), 93. As Kugel notes, in Greek and Aramaic, the word "Chaldean" became a synonym for "astronomer."

66. See *Jubilees*, where Abraham's celestial contemplation is discussed, and *The Apocalypse of Abraham*, trans. R. Rubinkiewitz, in *The Old Testament Pseudepigrapha*, ed. James H. Charlesworth (New York: Doubleday and Company, 1983), 1:689–690. Josephus, too, provides an account of Abraham's discovery of the one true God by way of rejecting heavenly bodies. See Philo (*Philo*, trans. F. H. Coulson [London: Heinemann, 1935], 6:41), and *Gen. Rab.* 39:1, where Abraham looks to the earthly realm for theological enlightenment. See Chapter 3 for a more detailed discussion of Abraham's discovery of the true God and his rejection of idolatry in several sources.

67. For a comparison of how Islamic and Jewish sources recount Abraham's rejection of idolatry, see Menahem Kister, "Observations on Aspects of Exegesis, Tradition, and Theology in Midrash, Pseudepigrapha and Other Jewish Writings," in *Tracing the Threads: Studies in the Vitality of Jewish Pseudepigrapha*, ed. John C. Reeves (Atlanta: Scholars Press, 1994), 1–34, and Lowin, *The Making of a Forefather*, 87–136.

68. In Islamic sources Abraham's revelation is brought about by God's own active participation, that is, Abraham is "rightly guided," whereas in Jewish sources Abraham is depicted as a seeker who through intellection discovers God. In rabbinic sources, however, Abraham is also led to discover God. See Lowin's discussion (*The Making of a Forefather*, 87–139) of the way the motif of the patriarch's discovery of God through celestial contemplation evinces intertextual influence. While it seems that she makes too sharp a distinction between Abraham's unaided discovery in Jewish sources and God's role in Islamic sources, her analysis nonetheless details the manner by which the motif is adopted and tailored to the values of each tradition.

69. According to Gerald R. Hawting, *The Idea of Idolatry and the Emergence of Islam: From Polemic to History* (Cambridge: Cambridge University Press, 1999), the Qur'an does not identify *mushrikūn* ("associators") as pre-Islamic Arab polytheists or idol worshippers, even though traditional materials present Islam as having emerged as "an attack on polytheism and idolatry." Furthermore, according to traditional accounts, "the polytheism and idolatry concerned was specific to the Arabs of central and western Arabia" (5) and arose "in a remote region which could be said to be on the periphery of the monotheistic world, if not quite outside it" (7). Rather, he contends, "as a religious system Islam should be understood as the result of an intra-monotheistic polemic, in a process similar to that of the emergence of the other main divisions of monotheism," (7) that is, Judaism and Christianity.

3. The First Monotheist

1. The Jewish Publication Society translation reads "in the lifetime of his father." Other translations include "in the presence of." As I shall observe later in the chapter, the rabbis play with *'al pene*, which also means "because of."

2. A Jewish pseudepigraphical, parabiblical recounting of the Hebrew Bible (Genesis to Samuel), specifically from Adam to the death of King Saul, dating from the first to second century and extant in Latin. As Howard Jacobson notes in *A Commentary of Pseudo-Philo's Liber Antiquitatum Biblicarum: With Latin Text and English Translation* (Leiden: Brill, 1996), the date of the work has been amply debated, but the general consensus places it between 50 CE and 150 CE. Jacobson reviews the debate among scholars as to whether the work is a pre-70 or post-70 work, and concludes: "There are no cogent arguments in support of a pre-70 date, while the arguments for a post-70 date seem to me overwhelming" (209). The work centers around themes found in the Book of Judges in which sinful people are redeemed by divinely appointed leaders. See Calvert-Koyzis, *Paul, Monotheism and the People of God: The Significance of Abraham Traditions for Early Judaism and Christianity*, Journal for the Study of the New Testament Supplement Series 273 (London: T & T Clark International, 2004), 42–44. On the story of Abraham in *Liber Antiquitatum Biblicarum*, see F. J. Murphy, "Retelling the Bible: Idolatry in Pseudo-Philo," *Journal of Biblical Literature* 107 (1988): 275–287, and Calvert-Koyzis, *Paul, Monotheism and the People of God*, 41–50.

3. Kugel, *How to Read the Bible: A Guide to Scripture, Then and Now* (New York: Free Press, 2007), 93.

4. On *Jubilees*, see James VanderKam, *The Book of Jubilees*, Guides to Apocrypha and Pseudepigrapha Series (Sheffield, UK: Sheffield Academic Press, 2001), Hindy Nijman, *Seconding Sinai: The Development of Mosaic Discourse in Second Temple Judaism* (Leiden: Brill, 2003), 41–69, and most recently the extensive commentary on and studies in the formation of *Jubilees*, see James Kugel, *A Walk through Jubilees: Studies in the Book of Jubilees and the World of Its Creation* (Leiden: Brill, 2012) and Michael Segal, *The Book of Jubilees: Rewritten Bible, Redaction, Ideology and Theology* (Leiden: Brill, 2007). See discussion of *Jubilees* in Chapter 2.

5. All translations from *Jubilees* are from James VanderKam, trans., *The Book of Jubilees, Corpus Scriptorum Christianorum Orientalium* vol. 511, Scriptores Aethiopici 88 (Louvain: Peeters, 1989), passage cited from page 67.

6. VanderKam, trans., *The Book of Jubilees*, 69. Compare the encounter between Abraham and his father in the Qur'an (Q. 19:42–50).

7. Ibid., 69–70. In *Gen. Rab.* 30:4, Terah merits a portion in this world and the world to come. The midrash explains Genesis 6:9: "These are the generations of Noah: Noah was a just man and perfect in his generation." What is the significance of the repetition of Noah's name? R. Abba b. Kahana said: "Whoever has his name repeated has a portion in this world and in the world to come." R. Abba contends that it is to demonstrate that the person, in this specific case Noah, has a portion in this world, and in the world to come. Each mention of the name corresponds to a portion. Turning to another verse, the rabbis raise an objection to him: "'Now these are the generations of Terah. Terah begot Abram . . .' (Gen. 11: 27). Does Terah have a portion in this world and in the future world?" But R. Abba retorts, "Even this does not contradict me, for R. Judan said in R. Abba's name, quoting Genesis 15:15, 'But you [Abraham] shall go to your fathers in peace.' God informed him that his father had a portion in the world to come." In other words, R. Abba's rule also applies with respect to the idol-worshipping Terah. It is unclear why this is the case. It may be because he too acknowledges God or he is rewarded in the world to come through the merit of his son Abraham. Scripture in any case tells us that Abraham will go to his fathers in peace, hence to Terah. Rashi on Genesis 15:15 notes that Terah was an idol worshipper who repented. On Terah acknowledging God, see also *Tanhuma Shemot* 18, and other medieval Jewish commentaries: Rashi 15:15, Ibn Ezra on Gen. 12:1, and Nahmanides on Gen. 11:32.

8. Gen. 11:28 mentions that Haran died before his father Terah in Ur, but does not tell us how. *Jubilees* amplifies the story with details of his death. There is a discrepancy between Gen. 11:31—"Terah took his son Abram, his grandson Lot . . . and they set out together from Ur of the Chaldeans for the land of Canaan; but when they came as far as Haran, they settled there"—and what we read two verses later in Gen. 12:1: "Go forth from your country and from your kindred and your father's house." Ur was Abraham's country, not Haran. See Kugel's discussion of how ancient exegetes solved the matter in *Traditions of the Bible: A Guide to the Bible As It Was at the Start of the Common Era* (Cambridge, MA: Harvard University Press, 1998), 264–266. See Jerome's commentary, *Saint Jerome's Hebrew Questions on Genesis*, trans. C. T. R. Hayward (Oxford: Clarendon Press, 1995), 43.

9. On Josephus's portrayal of Abraham, see especially Louis H. Feldman, *Josephus's Interpretation of the Bible*, Hellenistic Culture and Society Series (Berkeley: University of California Press, 1998), 223–289. See his following works: "Abraham the Greek Philosopher in Josephus," *Transactions and Proceedings of the American Philological Association* 99 (1968): 143–156; "Abraham the General in Josephus," in *Nourished with Peace: Studies in Hellenistic Judaism in Memory of Samuel Sandmel*, ed. F. E. Greenspahn, E. Hilgert, and B. L. Mack (Chico, CA: Scholars Press, 1984) 43–49; "Josephus as Biblical Interpreter: The Aqedah," *Jewish Quarterly Review* 75 (1984–85): 212–252; "Hellenizations in

Josephus' *Jewish Antiquities*: The Portrait of Abraham," in *Josephus, Judaism, and Christianity*, ed. L. Feldman and G. Hata (Detroit: Wayne State University Press, 1987), 133–153; *Josephus's Interpretation of the Bible* (Berkeley: University of California Press, 1998), 223–289; and, most recently, a detailed commentary on Josephus's *Jewish Antiquities* 1.148–256 in *Judean Antiquities 1–4*, vol. 3 of *Flavius Josephus: Translation and Commentary*, ed. Steve Mason (Leiden: Brill, 2000), 53–100. See also A. Y. Reed, "Abraham as Chaldean Scientist and Father of the Jews: Josephus *Ant. 1:154–168*, and the Greco-Roman Discourse about Astronomy/Astrology," *Journal for the Study of Judaism* 35 (2004): 119–154. In *Jewish Antiquities*, 1.166–168, Abraham is described as having taught arithmetic and knowledge of the stars to the Egyptians.

10. In *Jewish Antiquities*, 1.152, Josephus mentions that Terah hated Chaldea on account of the death of his son, Haran. There all of them moved to Haran in Mesopotamia where Terah died. See discussion to follow.

11. Taken from Feldman, *Judean Antiquities 1–4*, 57. Feldman observes that Josephus's argument, namely, that if the celestial spheres had their own independent power, then they would have arranged for their own uniformity. He challenges the view held by the Chaldeans that "it is the celestial phenomena that are the originating cause of all that happens and that they alone determine the future" (57).

12. *On the Virtues* (*De virtutibus*), 212. Philo, trans. F. H. Colson, Loeb Classical Library (London: Heinemann, 1938), 293–295. For a discussion of Abraham in the works of Philo, see Calvert-Koyzis, *Paul, Monotheism and the People of God*, 19–40.

13. *On the Virtues*, 212–213. This is also expressed in Philo's *Migration of Abraham (De Migratione Abrahami)* (179): "These men imagined that this visible universe was the only thing in existence, either being itself God or containing God in itself as the soul of the whole. And they made Fate and Necessity divine, thus filling human life with much impiety, by teaching that apart from phenomena there is no originating cause of anything whatever, but that the circuits of sun and moon and of the other heavenly bodies determine for every being in existence both good things and their opposites." Trans. F. H. Colson and G. H. Whitaker, vol. 4, Loeb Classical Library (London: Heinemann, 1932), 237.

14. Philo, *On Abraham (De Abrahamo)*, trans. F. H. Colson, vol. 6, Loeb Classical Library (London: Heinemann, 1935), 41.

15. Unless otherwise noted, all excerpts are adapted from R. Rubinkiewicz, trans., *The Apocalypse of Abraham*, in *The Old Testament Pseudepigrapha*, ed. James H. Charlesworth (New York: Doubleday, 1983), 1:689–705. Although the work is preserved in an Old Slavonic version of a Greek translation, scholars agree that it was most likely written in Hebrew or Aramaic. For background to the text, see the introduction to the translations by G. H. Box and J. I. Landman, *The Apocalypse of Abraham: Edited, with a Translation from the Slavonic Text and Notes* (London: SPCK, 1918), and published online: http://www.marquette .edu/maqom/box.pdf. For general background to apocalyptic literature, see Michael Stone, "Apocalyptic Literature," in *Jewish Writings of the Second Temple Period*, CRINT, 2.2 (Minneapolis: Fortress Press, 1968), 383–441; E. P. Sanders, "The Genre of Palestinian Jewish Apocalypse," in *Apocalypticism in the Mediterranean World and the Near East: Proceedings of the International Colloquium on*

Apocalypticism, ed. David Hellhom (Tübingen: Mohr Siebeck, 1989), 447–459; and John J. Collins, *The Apocalyptic Imagination: An Introduction to Jewish Apocalyptic Literature* (Grand Rapids, MI: Eerdmans, 1998).

16. According to Box, *The Apocalypse of Abraham,* the root is Hebrew, *meruma,* "deceit." Ginzberg, *Legend of the Jews,* 7 vols. (Philadelphia: Jewish Publication Society of America, 1937–1966), 5:217, n. 49, suggests that Marumath derives from the verb *ḥrm,* "to excommunicate" or "to dedicate."

17. According to Box, *Apocalypse of Abraham,* perhaps it is *bar 'ishta,* "son of fire."

18. Excerpt is adapted from George Box's translation, http://www.marquette.edu/maqom/box.pdf. See Rubinkiewicz, 686–688, for a discussion of the transmission of the *Apocalypse of Abraham.*

19. Examples of this notion are found in the Babylonian Talmud, tractate Sanhedrin, (*b.Sanhedrin* 89b) *b.Shabbat* 104a and *b.Makkot* 10b: "From the Torah, the Prophets, and the Writings, it can be demonstrated that one is led on the path one wishes to take."

20. Unless otherwise specified, all translations of rabbinic texts are mine. Translations of *Genesis Rabbah* are based on the critical edition of J. Theodor and Ch. Albeck, *Midrash Bereshit Rabba: Critical Editions with Notes and Commentary,* 3 vols. (Berlin, 1912–36; repr. Jerusalem: Shalem Books, 1996, with corrections) in consultation with MS Vatican 30.

21. See *b.Shabbat* 156a, where God commands Abraham to go forth from his horoscope.

22. Lowin, *The Making of a Forefather,* 130–135. The word "Torah" derives from the Hebrew root *yrh,* to teach or instruct.

23. I thank Stephen Geller for his assistance with the translation.

24. The story is adapted from *The Book of the Cave of Treasures: A History of the Patriarchs and Kings Their Successors from the Creation to the Crucifixion of Christ,* E. A. Wallis Budge (London: Religious Tract Society, 1927), 145–147. This is the only complete English translation of the work. See *La caverne des trésors: les deux recensions syriaques,* Corpus Scriptorum Christianorum Orientalium vols. 486–487 (Louvain: Peeters, 1987), Andreas Su-min Ri's two-volume French translation and edition based on nineteen different Syriac manuscripts, and his *Commentaire de la Caverne des trésors: etude sur l'histoire du texte et de ses sources,* Corpus Scriptorum Christianorum Orientalium vol. 581 (Louvain: Peeters, 2000).

25. I have translated all excerpts from Didymus's *On Genesis* from *Sur la Genèse: Introduction, Édition, Traduction et Notes,* vol. 2, ed. Pierre Nautin and Louis Doutreleau (Paris: Les Éditions du Cerf, 1978), 136–139 (*On Genesis,* 209).

26. *Fathers of the Church: A New Translation,* St. Caesarius of Arles Sermons, vol. 2 (81–186), trans. Mary Mueller, O.S.F. (Washington, DC: Catholic University of America Press, 1964), 4.

27. Ibid., 5.

28. *The Fathers of the Church, St. Ephrem the Syrian, Selected Prose Works,* trans. Edward G. Mathews and Joseph P. Amar (Washington, DC: Catholic University of America Press, 1994), 67.

29. For an excellent analysis, see Karel van der Toorn and Pieter W. van der Horst, "Nimrod before and after the Bible," *Harvard Theological Review* 83.1 (1990): 1–29. Many of the motifs found here are also found in other works, such as *Targum Pseudo-Jonathan* 11:28, that also mention Haran. And, as van der Toorn and van der Horst argue, the development of Nimrod as the arch-rebel against God was a gradual process that began in the second century BCE. Building on the work of Wilhelm Bousset, *Hauptprobleme der Gnosis* (Göttingen: Vanderhoeck & Ruprecht, 1907; reprint, 1973), esp. 369–378, they argue that even though Christian sources purport Nimrod to have been the originator of fire and star worship, especially Pseudo-Clementine, *Homiliae*, 9.45 (see *Recognitiones*, 1.30) and the *Cave of the Treasures*, 27, there can be no doubt that "the identification of Nimrod and Zoroaster had a Jewish origin" (27). See mention below of Nimrod in Islamic narratives.

30. *Targum Pseudo-Jonathan* identifies Nimrod with Amraphel, one of the potentates mentioned in Genesis 14. According to van der Toorn and van der Horst, "the real reason behind this identification, however, may have been that Amraphel is said in the biblical text to have been 'King of Shinar' in the days of Abraham. But, of course, the king of Shinar in Abraham's time was known to have been Nimrod. One could find corroborative evidence for this identification in the folk-etymological analysis of the name Amraphel: *'amar pil*, 'he said: "throw!" ' " (23). This etymological identification is also found in *b.'Eruvin* 53a: " 'And it came to pass in the days of Amraphel' (Gen. 14:1). Rav and Samuel disagree as to his name. One holds that his name was Nimrod. Why was he called Amraphel? Because he ordered our father Abraham to be cast into a burning furnace. But the other holds that his name was Amraphel; and why was he called Nimrod? Because in his reign he led the entire world in rebellion against himself (*she-himrid* [play on Nimrod and the verb *marad*, to rebel] *et kol ha'olam kullo 'alav bemalkhut*)." This passage from *b.'Eruvin* 53a is discussed in van der Toorn and van der Horst, "Nimrod before and after the Bible," 24. For other Talmudic references to Nimrod as the leader of a rebellion against God, and to the episode with Abraham, see *b.'Avod. Zar.* 53b, Ḥag. 13a, *b.Pesaḥim.* 118a, *b.Hullin* 89a. For other references, see van der Toorn and van der Horst, "Nimrod before and after the Bible," 25–28.

31. The account discussed is adapted from Jacobson, *Commentary of Pseudo-Philo's Liber Antiquitatum Biblicarum*, 97–100.

32. Ibid., 213.

33. Ibid., 100 (end of chapter 6).

34. *b.Pesaḥim* 118a, *b.'Eruvin* 53a, *Song of Songs Rabbah* 1:12, *Midrash Tanhuma* 1:58, and *PRE* 26. See also Jerome's reference in his *Hebrew Questions on Genesis*, on 11:28: "Moreover the Hebrews, taking the opportunity afforded by this verse, hand on a story of this sort to the effect that Abraham was put into the fire because he refused to worship fire, which the Chaldeans honour; and that he escaped through God's help, and fled from the fire of idolatry." Hayward, trans., *Saint Jerome's Hebrew Questions on Genesis*, 43.

35. *Gen. Rab.* 38:13 mentions that Abraham is saved, but *Gen. Rab.* 44:13 and *Song of Songs Rabbah* indicate another detail, namely, that the angel Michael came down and saved him from the fiery furnace. Rather than naming Michael, *b.*

Pesaḥim 118a states that it is Gabriel who offers to save Abraham's life: "When the wicked Nimrod cast our father Abraham into the fiery furnace, Gabriel said to the Holy One, blessed be He: 'Sovereign of the Universe! Let me go down, cool [it], and deliver that righteous man from the fiery furnace.' The Holy One, blessed be He said to him: 'I am unique in my world, and he is unique in his world: it is fitting for Him who is unique to deliver him who is unique. But because the Holy One, blessed be He does not withhold the [merited] reward of any creature, he said to him, 'Thou shalt be privileged to deliver three of his descendants.'"

36. *Targum Neophyti* to Gen. 11:28–31 reads: "And his father Terah was still alive when Haran died in the land of his birth, in the fiery furnace of the Chaldeans." The image of the furnace evokes the image in Daniel 3:19–23, in which Daniel's three young companions, Hananiah, Mishael, and Azariah, are cast into a fiery furnace by the Babylonian king, Nebuchadnezzar, and rescued by God. This motif is also found in *Targum Neophyti* to Gen. 11:31: "And Terah took his son Abram and his grandson Lot and his daughter-in-law Sarai, Abram's wife, and went out with them from the Chaldeans' fiery furnace to go to the land of Canaan." And Gen. 15:7: "I am the Lord who took you out of the fiery furnace of the Chaldeans to give you this land to inherit." In Jerome's Vulgate, we read: "It was you yourself, O Lord, who chose Abram and led him out of the fire of the Chaldeans" (Neh. 9:7). For a discussion of the fire of Daniel and its relationship to this fiery furnace motif, see Shari Lowin, *The Making of a Forefather*, 192–204, who also deals with the frog motif and its competition with the gecko in the same chapter.

37. Kugel, *Traditions of the Bible*, 269. See William Adler, "Abraham and the Burning of the Temple of Idols: Jubilees' Traditions in Christian Chronography," *Jewish Quarterly Review* 77 (1987): 95–117. See also Geza Vermes, *Scripture and Tradition in Judaism*, 2d rev. ed., Studia Post-Biblica (Leiden: Brill, 1973), 76–90. His "retrogressive," historical study, whereby an excerpt of a late text, *Sefer Ha-Yashar*, which he dates to the eleventh century but was probably composed at the beginning of the sixteenth century—according to Joseph Dan, *The Hebrew Story in the Middle Ages* (Hebrew) (Jerusalem: Keter, 1974), 137–138—is analyzed with an eye toward its "constitutive elements," is highly problematic. To begin with, even if one were to accept his early dating, his investigation ignores the ways stories circulate and the possible role that iterations of traditions of the early life of Abraham in Muslim and Christian circles may have played.

38. See Kugel's discussion of this in *Traditions of the Bible*, 264–266. See, for example, Judith 5:8–9 and *Apocalypse of Abraham* 8:4–6, which suggest that God spoke to Abraham in Haran. See Josephus 1:152 and 1:157. For example, we read in Acts 7:2–4, as Stephen, accused with prophesying against the temple and about to be martyred, speaks: "Brethren and fathers, hear me. The God of glory appeared to our father Abraham, when he was in Mesopotamia, before he lived in Haran, and said to him, 'Depart from your land and from your kindred and go into the land which I will show you.' Then he departed from the land of the Chaldeans and lived in Haran."

39. Adapted from Hayward, trans., *Saint Jerome's Hebrew Questions on Genesis*, 44.

40. See, for example, Norman Calder, "Tafsīr from Ṭabarī to Ibn Kathīr: Problems in the description of a genre illustrated with reference to the story of Abraham," in *Approaches to the Qur'ān*, ed. Gerald R. Hawting and Abdul-Kader A. Shareef (London: Routledge, 1993; reprinted 2002), 101–140.

41. On Abraham's early childhood and the finger-food motif, see Lowin, *The Making of a Forefather*, 140–173.

42. *'Arā'is al-Majālis fī Qiṣaṣ al-Anbiyā' or "Lives of the Prophets": As Recounted by Abū Isḥāq Aḥmad ibn Muḥammad ibn Ibrāhīm al-Thaʻlabī*, trans. and annot. William M. Brinner (Leiden: Brill, 2002), 128.

43. See Louis Ginzberg, *Legends of the Jews* 1:194.

44. Muhammad ibn 'Abd Allah al-Kisa'i, *Tales of the Prophets (Qiṣaṣ al-anbiyā')*, trans. Wheeler M. Thackston, Jr. (Chicago: Great Books of the Islamic World, 1997), 137. My retelling is based on Thackston's English translation and in consultation with the original, Muhammad b. 'Abdallah al-Kisa'i, Qiṣaṣ al-anbiyā', ed. Isaac Eisenberg, titled *Vita Prophetarum* (Leiden: E.J. Brill, 1922).

45. Ibn Kathir tells of a similar account. Abraham asks God to show him how to bring the dead back to life.

46. The Babylonian Talmud *Gittin* 56b preserves an account of Emperor Titus's travails inflicted by a gnat that enters one of his nostrils and bangs inside his head for seven years. It is interesting to note that Nimrod is identified as Titus's grandfather. Furthermore, Nebuchadnezzar, another villainous character, also dies in the same manner. For a treatment of the motif, see Shari Lowin, "Narratives of Villainy: Titus, Nebuchadnezzar, and Nimrod in ḥadīth and Midrash Aggadah," in *The Lineaments of Islam: Studies in Honor of Fred McGraw Donner*, ed. Paul M. Cobb (Leiden: Brill, 2012), 261–296.

47. For a discussion of the subject, see Moshe Lavee, "Converting the Missionary Image of Abraham: Rabbinic Traditions Migrating from the Land of Israel to Babylon," in *Abraham, the Nations and the Hagarites: Jewish, Christian, and Islamic Perspectives on Kinship with Abraham*, ed. Martin Goodman, George H. van Kooten, and Jacques T.A.G.M. van Ruiten (Leiden: Brill, 2010), 204–222. See also Jon D. Levenson, *Inheriting Abraham: The Legacy of the Patriarch in Judaism, Christianity and Islam* (Princeton: Princeton University Press, 2012), 134–138. In *Gen. Rab.* 30:10, Abraham is depicted as one who is summoned from Mesopotamia to glorify God in Israel. Other images of Abraham the proselytizer in rabbinic literature include *Gen. Rab.* 39:14, 39:16, 43:4, 46:2, 46:3, 46:10, 47:10, 48:2, and 53:9.

48. This notion is abandoned—but, alas, not altogether—in Christian thinking after the Holocaust.

4. The Wives of Abraham

1. There is a great deal of literature on the subject. Here I provide a brief selection of works: Elizabeth Castelli, "Allegories of Hagar: Reading Galatians 4:21–31 with Postmodern Feminist Eyes," in *The New Literary Criticism and the New Testament*, ed. Elizabeth Struthers Malbon and Edgar McKnight (Sheffield, UK: University of Sheffield Press, 1994), 228–250; Phyllis Trible,

Texts of Terror: Literary-Feminist Readings of Biblical Narrative (Philadelphia: Fortress, 1984), 9–36; Jo Ann Hackett, "Rehabilitating Hagar: Fragments of an Epic Pattern," in *Gender and Difference in Ancient Israel*, ed. Peggy L. Day (Philadelphia: Fortress, 1989), 12–27; J. Cheryl Exum, *Fragmented Women: Feminist (Sub)versions of Biblical Narratives* (Valley Forge: Trinity Press International, 1993), 130–147; and John L. Thompson, *Writing the Wrongs: Women of the Old Testament among Biblical Commentators from Philo through the Reformation* (Oxford: Oxford University Press, 2001), 17–99.

2. Niehoff's insightful discussion of Philo's portrayal of Sarah illustrates how the author perceived Sarah as a true partner, and an espouser of Mosaic law. See her article "Mother and Maiden, Sister and Spouse: Sarah in Philonic Midrash," *Harvard Theological Review* 97.4 (2004): 413–444. Niehoff explores the complex ways Philo reads Sarah as "the masculine daughter of a masculine God" (443). She contrasts his allegorical and literal exegesis of her in great detail.

3. Philo writes: "She showed her wifely love by numberless proofs, by sharing with him the severance from his kinsfolk, by bearing without hesitation the departure from her homeland, the continual and unceasing wanderings on a foreign soil and privation in famine, and by the campaigns in which she accompanied him." *On Abraham (De Abrahamo)*, 245–256. Excerpt from Philo, vol. 6, trans. F. H. Colson, Loeb Classical Library (London: Heinemann, 1935), 121.

4. Philo, *On Abraham (De Abrahamo)*, trans. F. H. Colson, vol. 6, Loeb Classical Library (London: Heinemann, 1935), 123.

5. Near Eastern texts demonstrate that indeed Ishmael had inheritance rights as a member of the household, but his expulsion abrogates these rights. See discussion of Nuzi text in Chapter 2, note 23, and for example, the Code of Hammurapi (pars. 170 and 171) states that if the father of children of a slave-wife legitimates the children by claiming them as his own, then they have an equal share in the inheritance (James B. Pritchard, ed., *The Ancient Near East: An Anthology of Texts and Pictures* [Princeton: Princeton University Press, 1958], 157). See also Deut. 21:15–17 where the firstborn son, even though he is from the unloved wife, receives double portion of the father's possessions. For a discussion of Ishmael's legal rights, see my *Ishmael on the Border: Rabbinic Portrayals of the First Arab* (Albany: SUNY Press, 2006), 52–54. According to Niehoff, Sarah's role as mother relies on an understanding of matrilineality that assumes that a child's status is determined by both the father and mother. According to Philo, Abraham's child by the Egyptian servant has a Jewish mother. See Niehoff, "Jewish Identity and Jewish Mothers: Who Was a Jew According to Philo?," *Studia Philonica Annual* 11 (1999): 31–54.

6. Philo etymologizes her name as "foreigner," "asylum-seeker." See Abraham Bos, "Hagar and the *Enkyklios* in Philo of Alexandria," in *Abraham, the Nations and the Hagarites: Jewish, Christian, and Islamic Perspectives on Kinship with Abraham*, ed. Martin Goodman, George H. van Kooten, and Jacques T. A. G. M. van Ruiten (Leiden; Boston: Brill, 2010), 163.

7. Trans. F. H. Colson and G. H. Whitaker, vol. 4, Loeb Classical Library (London: Heinemann, 1932), 551. See Adele Reinhartz and Miriam-Simma

Walfish, "Conflict and Coexistence in Jewish Interpretation," in *Hagar, Sarah, and Their Children: Jewish, Christian, and Muslim Perspectives*, ed. Phyllis Trible and Letty M. Russell (Louisville: Westminster John Knox Press, 2006), 101–125. For a brief discussion and a more detailed analysis see Alan Mendelson, *Secular Education in Philo of Alexandria*, Monographs of the Hebrew Union College, no. 7 (Cincinnati: Hebrew Union College Press, 1982).

8. Trans. F. H. Colson and G. H. Whitaker, vol. 4, Loeb Classical Library (London: Heinemann, 1932), 471. Philo mentions Hagar and Sarah in several treatises. See Dorothy Sly, *Philo's Perception of Women* (Atlanta: Scholars Press, 1990), esp. 125, n. 27.

9. *Jewish Antiquities*, vol. 4, Loeb Classical Library (Cambridge, MA: Harvard University Press, 1998), 93–95. See discussion in Chapter 6 on Ishmael below.

10. According to Brigit van der Lans, self-control is one of the "cardinal virtues and was a widespread ideal in Hellenistic ethical philosophy," van der Lans, "Hagar, Ishmael, and Abraham's Household," 185–199, in Goodman et al., *Abraham, the Nations and the Hagarites*, 187. See also B. Halpern-Amaru, "Portraits of Biblical Women in Josephus's *Antiquities*," *Journal of Jewish Studies* 39 (1988): 143–170.

11. In some Islamic collections, Hagar was not an Egyptian or a lovely servant but was of royal Arab blood.

12. The midrash draws a parallel between Pharaoh and the incident in Abimelech's house such that he, too, gives his daughter to Sarah because he witnessed miracles in his household on account of Sarah.

13. *Gen. Rab.* 45:6 depicts Abraham as washing his hands of the matter, and thus it is Sarah who must deal harshly with Hagar.

14. The feminine passive participle of the piel verb *qitter*, to offer incense.

15. See also *PRE* 30. In *Targum Neofiti* and *Targum Pseudo-Jonathan*, Keturah is another name for Hagar.

16. For a general introduction to *PRE*, see Leopold Zunz, *Hadrashot beYisrael*, ed. and supp. H. Albeck (Jerusalem: Mossad Bialik, 1954), 134–140, 417–424; *Midrash Pirke de Rabbi Eliezer*, trans. Gerald Friedlander (London, 1916; reprint, New York: Sepher-Hermon Press, 1981), xiii–lvii; and Herman L. Strack and Günter Stemberger, eds., *Introduction to the Talmud and Midrash* (Minneapolis: Fortress, 1992), 332–333. On the use of narrative in *PRE*, see Ofra Meir, "Hasipur Hadarshani Bemidrash Qadum Ume'uchar," *Sinai* 86 (1980): 246–266; Yaakov Elbaum, "On the Character of the Late Midrashic Literature" (Hebrew), in *Proceedings of the Ninth World Congress of Jewish Studies 3*, 4 vols. (Jerusalem: World Congress of Jewish Studies, 1986), 57–62, "Rhetoric Motif and Subject-Matter—Toward an Analysis of Narrative Technique in Pirke de-Rabbi Eliezer" (Hebrew), *Jerusalem Studies in Jewish Folklore 13/14* (Jerusalem: World Congress of Jewish Studies, 1991–92), 99–126, idem, "From Sermon to Story: The Transformation of the Aqedah," *Prooftexts 6* (1986): 97–117. On the folkloristic aspects of *PRE*, see Dina Stein, *Maxims, Magic, Myth: A Folkloristic Perspective of Pirkei de Rabbi Eliezer* (Hebrew) (Jerusalem: Magnes Press, 2005); Rachel Adelman, *The Return of the Repressed: Pirqe de-Rabbi Eliezer and the Pseudepigrapha*, Supplements to the Journal for the

Study of Judaism 140 (Leiden: Brill, 2009); and Eliezer Treitl, "Pirke de-Rabbi Eliezer: Text, Redaction and a Sample Synopsis" (Ph.D. diss., Hebrew University of Jerusalem, 2010).

17. See *Gen. Rab.* 47:2 and 61:4.

18. Solomon Buber, *Aggadah Bereshit* (New York: Menorah Institute for Research and Publishing of Manuscripts and Rare Books, 1959), 74. According to Lieve Tuegels, *Aggadat Bereshit: Translated from the Hebrew with an Introduction and Notes* (Leiden: Brill, 2001), 115, Ms. Oxford 2340 has a more extensive version: "Why does Scripture say, whom Hagar the Egyptian (. . .) bore? To teach us that all mix with their own kind, and at the end everyone returns to the stench of his mother, as is stated: And his mother got a wife for him from the land of Egypt. She returned to her roots: from the birthplace of her ancestors, he took himself a wife." Similarly, the midrash illustrates that Abraham ordered his servant Eliezer to go to Abraham's kindred to seek a wife for Isaac.

19. *Homilies on Genesis*, 11.1. Origen offers an etymological interpretation for Keturah from the Greek *thymiama*, which means incense or a pleasing fragrance. See *Gen. Rab.* 61:4 and *PRE* 30.

20. *St. Ephrem the Syrian: Selected Prose Works*, The Fathers of the Church, vol. 91, Edward G. Mathews, trans. 166–167. Commentary on Genesis 18:2, in *Fathers of the Church*, 91 (Washington, DC: Catholic University of America Press, 1994), 171.

21. *City of God* 16.34.

22. Al-Tha'labi, *'Arā'is al-Majālis fī Qiṣaṣ al-Anbiyā'* or *"Lives of the Prophets": As Recounted by Abū Isḥāq Aḥmad ibn Muḥammad ibn Ibrāhīm al-Thaʿlabī*, trans. and annot. William Brinner (Leiden: Brill, 2002), 164.

23. See David Runia, *Philo in Early Christian Literature: A Survey* (Minneapolis: Fortress Press, 1993), and John L. Thompson, *Writing the Wrongs*.

24. On Paul's use of the term see Richard B. Hays, *Echoes of Scripture in the Letters of Paul* (New Haven: Yale University Press, 1993), 116, and Daniel Boyarin, *A Radical Jew: Paul and the Politics of Identity* (Berkeley: University of California Press, 1994), 32–36.

25. See Chapter 2, nn.45–48 and Chapter 6 n.66 for sources on Galatians. See, too, Caroline Johnson Hodge, *If Sons, Then Heirs: A Study of Kinship and Ethnicity in the Letters of Paul* (New York: Oxford University Press, 2007). Johnson Hodge argues that contrary to views of Paul's theology as "universal," as ameliorating cultural and ethnic differences, such notions of peoplehood and lineage are not rejected or downplayed by Paul but in fact central to his teachings. See, too, Karin B. Neuel, " 'Neither Jew nor Greek': Abraham as a Universal Ancestor," in Goodman et al., *Abraham, the Nations and the Hagarites*, 291–306, and in the same volume, Brigit van der Lans, "Belonging to Abraham's Kin: Genealogical Appeals to Abraham as a Possible Background for Paul's Abrahamic Argument," 307–318, and Albert L. A. Hogeterp, "Hagar and Paul's Covenant Thought," 345–360.

26. For a discussion of Tertullian's interpretation of Paul, see J. Louis Martyn, "The Covenants of Hagar and Sarah," in *Faith and History: Essays in Honor of Paul W. Meyer*, ed. John T. Carroll, Charles H. Cosgrove, and Elizabeth Johnson (Atlanta: Scholars Press, 1990), 160–192.

27. See Thompson's discussion, *Writing the Wrongs*, 29–30. For an English translation of Clement of Alexandria's *Stromateis*, see *Clement of Alexandria: Stromateis, Books One to Three*, The Fathers of the Church, vol. 85, trans. John Ferguson (Washington, DC: Catholic University of America Press, 1991).

28. For a discussion of Clement's use of Philo, see Annewies van den Hoek, *Clement of Alexandria and His Use of Philo in the Stromateis: An Early Christian Reshaping of a Jewish Model*, Supplements to Vigiliae Christianae 3 (Leiden: Brill, 1988), especially 23–47, and "Mistress and Servant: An Allegorical Theme in Philo, Clement and Origen," in *Origeniana Quarta*, ed. Lothar Lies, Fourth International Colloquium for Origen Studies, Innsbruck, 1985; *Innsbruker Theologische Studien* 19 (Innsbruck: Tyrolia-Verlag, 1987). For a comparison of how Clement and Didymus read Gen. 16:1–6, see Johan Lemans, "After Philo and Paul: Hagar in the Writings of the Church Fathers," in Goodman et al., *Abraham, the Nations and the Hagarites*, 435–447.

29. Ambrose, *On Abraham*, 1.4.23, for example, like others, argues that because Abraham lived prior to the giving of the law of Moses and the gospel, he did not violate the law.

30. Origen writes: "On account of this mystery also, I think, our Lord and Savior said to the Samaritan woman, when, as if he were speaking with Hagar herself he said, 'Whoever shall drink of this water shall thirst again; but he who shall drink of the water which I give him shall not thirst forever' [Jn 4:13–14]. But she says to the Savior, 'Sir, give me this water, that I may not thirst, nor come here to draw' [Jn 4:15]. After this the Lord says to her, 'There shall come to be in him who believes in me a fountain of water springing up into life everlasting' [Jn 6:47]." Excerpts from Ronald E. Heine, trans., *Origen: Homilies on Genesis and Exodus* (Washington, DC: Catholic University of America Press, 1982), 133–134. In a Syriac poem discussed below, it is Sarah who is likened to the Samaritan woman.

31. Ibid., 134.

32. Mark Sheridan, *Ancient Christian Commentary on Scripture: Old Testament II: Genesis 12–50* (Downers Grove: Intervarsity Press, 2002), 99. See also Chrysostom, *Homilies on Genesis*, 46:7–8.

33. For a discussion of the subject, see Elizabeth A. Clark, "Interpretive Fate amid the Church Fathers," in Trible and Russell, *Hagar, Sarah, and Their Children*, 127–147.

34. *St. Ephrem the Syrian: Selected Prose Works*, trans. Edward G. Mathews, 166–167.

35. Ibid., 155.

36. See Seth Schwartz, *Imperialism and Jewish Society* (Princeton: Princeton University Press, 2001); Daniel Boyarin, *Border Lines: The Partition of Judaeo-Christianity* (Philadelphia: University of Pennsylvania Press, 2006), and "Rethinking Jewish Christianity: An Argument for Dismantling a Dubious Category," *Jewish Quarterly Review* 99.1 (2009): 7–36; and Steve Mason, "Jews, Judaeans, Judaizing, Judaism: Problems of Categorization in Ancient History," *Journal for the Study of Judaism* 38.4–5 (2007): 457–512. See Shaye Cohen, *The Beginnings of Jewishness: Boundaries, Varieties, Uncertainties* (Berkeley: University of California Press, 2001), 3.

37. Al-Tabari, *The History of al-Ṭabarī*, vol. 2, *Prophets and Patriarchs*, trans. William Brinner (Albany: State University of New York Press, 1987), 62.

38. Ibid., 85. In a medieval midrashic compilation, *Tanhuma* (Buber) *Vayera* 23, Satan also goes to Sarah, but according to the midrash, on hearing the news, Sarah's soul leaves her.

39. Al-Tha'labi, *'Arā'is al-Majālis fī Qiṣaṣ al-Anbiyā'* or *"Lives of the Prophets,"* trans. Brinner, 139.

40. *The History of al-Tabari*, vol. 2, *Prophets and Patriarchs*, trans. William Brinner (Albany: State University of New York Press, 1987), 72. According to Brinner, "This strange tradition probably reflects the antiquity of the practice of circumcision (both male and female) among the Arabs, which antedates Islam" (72, n. 204).

41. Ibn Kathir, *al-Bidāyah wa-al Nihāyah fī al-Ta'rīkh*, vol. 1 (Cairo: Maṭba'at al-Sa'ādah, 1933), 153.

42. Jewish sources go to some lengths to justify Abraham's generosity, or lack thereof. See *Gen. Rab.* 53:13, for example.

43. Brinner, *'Arā'is al-Majālis fī Qiṣaṣ al-Anbiyā'* or *"Lives of the Prophets,"* 139.

44. *Saḥīḥ al-Bukhārī*, bk. 47, no. 803.

45. For a survey of early Islamic sources about Hagar, see Fred Leemhuis, "Hājar in the Qur'ān and Its Early Commentaries," in Goodman et al., *Abraham, the Nations and the Hagarites*, 503–508.

46. The text adds that the same was also taught in the name of R. Eliezer b. Jacob.

47. See Levenson, *Inheriting Abraham: The Legacy of the Patriarch in Judaism, Christianity and Islam* (Princeton: Princeton University Press, 2012), 38, for a brief discussion.

48. See Sebastian Brock and Simon Hopkins, "A Verse on Abraham and Sarah in Egypt: Syriac Original with Early Arabic Translation," *Le Museon* 105.1–2 (1992): 87–146, and Brock, "Creating Women's Voices: Sarah and Tamar in Some Syriac Narrative Poems," in *The Exegetical Encounter between Jews and Christians in Late Antiquity*, ed. E. Grypeou and H. Spurling (Leiden: Brill, 2009). All quotations from the poem are taken from the Brock and Hopkins translation, 1992.

49. See *Gen. Rab.* 39:14, where Abraham converts the men and Sarah the women.

50. Brock and Hopkins, "Verse on Abraham and Sarah in Egypt," 122–124.

51. See the rabbinic text *Tanhuma* B *Ḥayye Sarah* 3, which seeks to enhance her role by associating her with Eshet Ḥayil, Prov. 31:11–12, the wife who benefits her husband. See also parallels with *Gen. Rab.* 41:2, where we hear Sarah's supplications. That Sarah's grievances against Abraham are expressed is not unusual. See *Targum Pseudo-Jonathan*, Gen. 16:5, and *Targum Neophyti*, Gen. 16:5: "And Sarai said to Abram: 'My judgment and my humiliation, my insult and the beginning of my affliction are given unto your hand. I forsook my country and the house of my birth and the house of my father, and I came with you with faith. I went in with you before the kings of the earth, before the Pharaoh king of Egypt and before Abimelech king of Gerar and I

said: "He is my brother," so that they may not kill you. And when I saw that I did not bear, I took Hagar the Egyptian, my handmaid, and gave her to you as wife, and I said: "She will bear children and I will rear (them). Perhaps I too will have children through her." But when she saw that she had conceived my honour was of little value in her sight. And, now, let the Lord be revealed and let him judge between me and you, and let him spread his peace between me and you and let the earth be filled from us and we will not need the son of Hagar the Egyptian, who belongs to the sons of the sons of the people who gave you to the furnace of fire of the Chaldeans.'" Translation by M. McNamara and M. J. Maher in *MS. Neophyti I, Genesis*, ed. Alejandro Diez Macho, Textos y estudios "Cardenal Cisneros" 7 (Madrid: Consejo Superior de Investigaciones Científicas, 1969), 534.

52. Rabbi David Luria offers the explanation that it was customary for slaves to carry pitchers of water and thus Abraham wanted to ensure that she retain her slave status lest Ishmael claim that he, not Isaac, was his freeborn heir and thus usurp Isaac's inheritance.

53. Ibn Ezra, *Commentary on the Pentateuch*, vol. 1, *Genesis*, trans. H. Norman Strickman and Arthur M. Silver (New York: Menorah, 1988), 218–219. Nachmanides, *Commentary on the Torah*, echoes this explanation.

54. Brinner, *'Arā'is al-Majālis fī Qiṣaṣ al-Anbiyā'* or *"Lives of the Prophets,"* 136, and also in *Saḥīḥ al-Bukhārī*, book 55, al-Anbiyā', chapter 9, number 578. In al-Bukhari's account we read: "He (the tyrant) asks Sarah, 'Pray to God for me, and I shall not harm you.' So Sarah asks God to cure him and he gets cured. He tries to take hold of her for the second time, but (his hand got as stiff as or stiffer than before and) is more confounded. He again requests of Sarah, 'Pray to God for me, and I will not harm you.' Sarah asks God again and he becomes all right. He then calls one of his guards (who had brought her) and says, 'You have not brought me a human being but have brought me a devil.' At that point, the tyrant gives Hajar as a slave-girl to Sarah. Sarah returns to Abraham while he is praying. Gesturing with his hand, he asks, 'What has happened?' She replied, 'God has spoiled the evil plot of the infidel (or immoral person).'"

55. Trible, *Texts of Terror*, 14–18 and 28.

56. Dolores Williams, "Hagar in African American Biblical Appropriation," in Trible and Russell, *Hagar, Sarah, and Their Children*, 171–184. The discussion of Williams's work relies heavily on my previously published review of *Hagar, Sarah, and Their Children*, in *Hebrew Political Studies* 4.1 (2009): 84–90.

57. Williams, "Hagar in African American Biblical Appropriation," 181.

58. Ibid., 180.

59. Letty M. Russell, "Children of Struggle," in *Hagar, Sarah, and Their Children*, 185–197.

60. Ibid., 186.

61. For an examination of two sixth-century Hebrew liturgical poems by Yannai that treats the barrenness of Sarah (and Abraham) from the perspective of literary and contemporary gender studies, see Ophir Münz-Manor, "All about Sarah: Questions of Gender in Yannai's Poems on Sarah's (and Abraham's) Barrenness," *Prooftext* 26.3 (Fall 2006): 344–374.

62. For a discussion of the views of several medieval Jewish commentators on Sarah's treatment of Hagar, see "Conflict and Coexistence in Jewish Interpretation," in Trible and Russell, *Hagar, Sarah, and Their Children*, 112–115.

5. Sibling Rivals

1. N. Sarna, *Understanding Genesis* (New York: McGraw Hill, 1966), 174.

2. See *Yalkut Shim'oni Wayyera* 101, *b. Sanhedrin* 89b, *Tanhuma Wayyera* 23, and *Pesikta Rabbati*, chap. 40. See Chapter 7 for an Islamic account of Satan's endeavors to thwart God's plan.

3. See *Lev. Rab.* 20:2 and *Eccles. Rab.* 9:6. See *Gen. Rab.* 56:2, *Pesikta de Rav Kahana*, *Tan. Wayyera* 46, and *Midrash ha-Gadol*, where the names are not mentioned. See also *Seder Eliyyahu Rabbah* 25.

4. Also found in the Musnad of Ibn Hanbal. Quoted from Roy Mottahedeh, "The Shu'ûbîyah Controversy and the Social History of Early Islamic Iran," *International Journal of Middle East Studies* 7 (1976): 167.

5. According to the Qur'an, there are degrees of prohibited marriage: mother, daughter, sister, paternal aunt, maternal aunt, brother's daughter and sister's daughter (4:23). The verse continues: "and your foster-mothers [who suckled you], and your foster-sisters, and your mothers-in-law, and your step-daughters who are under your guardianship [born] of your women unto whom you have gone in—but if ye have not gone into them, then it is no sin for you [to marry their daughters]—and the wives of your sons who [issue] from your own loins. And [it is prohibited] that you should have two sisters together, except what has happened already in the past. Indeed! God is ever Forgiving, Merciful."

6. See Mottahedeh, "The Shu'ûbîyah Controversy and the Social History of Early Islamic Iran," 161–182, who argues that the controversy was primarily literary and not political, as others have argued. Earlier studies include Ignaz Goldziher, *Muslim Studies*, 2 vols., ed. S. M. Stern, trans. C. R. Barber and S. M. Stern (Chicago: Aldine, 1967), 1:137–163; and H. A. R. Gibb, "The Social Significance of the Shuubiya," in *Studies in the Civilization of Islam*, ed. Stanford J. Shaw and William R. Polk (Boston: Beacon Press, 1962), 62–73.

7. Sarah Bowen Savant, "Isaac as the Persians' Ishmael: Pride and the Pre-Islamic Past in Ninth and Tenth-Century Islam," *Comparative Islamic Studies* 2.1 (2006): 5–25.

8. Savant, "Isaac as the Persians' Ishmael," 16, n. 3, and most recently *The New Muslims of Post-Conquest Iran: Tradition, Memory and Conversion* (Cambridge: Cambridge University Press, 2013).

9. The verse reads: "We have made you peoples [shu'ūb] and tribes that you may know one another. The most noble among you before God is the most pious."

10. See René Dagorn, *La Geste d'Ismaël d'aprés l'onomastique et la tradition arabes*, Hautes Études Orientales 16 (Geneva: Librairie Droz, 1981), 220–234.

11. Al-Tha'labi, *'Arā'is al-Majālis fī Qiṣaṣ al-Anbiyā'* or *"Lives of the Prophets": As Recounted by Abū Isḥāq Aḥmad ibn Muḥammad ibn Ibrāhīm al-Tha'labī*, trans. and annot. William Brinner (Leiden: Brill, 2002), 136. Al- Tha'labi

preserves a tradition about Abu Hurayrah who would transmit a tradition about the Prophet Muhammad, who used to say, "This is your mother, children of the water of Heaven." The moniker may derive from the fact that Hagar was miraculously given the water of Zamzam, which nourished Ishmael, the Arab progenitor, or it might refer to the fact that Arabs depended on rain for their agricultural sustenance. See also *Ṣaḥīḥ al-Bukhārī*, book 55, the Anbiyā', chapter 9, number 578. For an English translation, see *Ṣaḥīḥ al-Bukhārī*, trans., Muhammad Muhsin Khan (Lahore: Kazi Publications, 1983), 368–370.

12. See discussion in Chapter 4.

13. Savant, *The New Muslims of Post-Conquest Iran*, 43.

14. "The Nature of Aggadah," *Midrash and Literature*, ed. G. Hartman and S. Budick (New Haven: Yale University Press, 1986), 49.

15. Moreover, the notion that Abraham produced unfit children, as in the case of Ishmael and the sons of Keturah, whereas Jacob produced only righteous sons, hence he, not Abraham, is named Israel, is remarkably absent, with one exception, in *Genesis Rabbah*, even though we find it in several tannaitic texts (*Sifre* Deut. 312 and 343) as well as in the Babylonian Talmud (*Pesaḥim* 119b), as well as other texts (*Lev. Rab.* 36:5). To be sure, I do not want to build an argument on silence, but this fact is to my mind noteworthy.

16. Vatican 30 *loqa tor* and other variants: *loqtor* and in the *Yalkut* we read: "And how could he have given gifts to the sons of Keturah?" (That is, if he has already given all he has to Isaac, then what is left for him to give them?) Printed editions and the Yemenite manuscript of Elhanan Adler have: "Where is the proof, or deed of expulsion that separates the sons?" See the critical edition of J. Theodor and C. Albeck, *Bereshit Rabba*, vol. 2 (Jerusalem: Shalem Books, 1996), 666–667.

17. The only midrash that refers to this in *Gen. Rab.* that I am aware of is 68:11. On a textual level, *Gen. Rab.* 68:11 is concerned with reconciling two verses, Gen. 28:11 and verse 18 of the same chapter. Genesis 28:11 reads: ". . . Taking *one* of the stones of the place, he put it under his head and lay down in that place to sleep," while Gen. 28:18 reads: "Early in the morning, Jacob took the stone . . ." That is, in verse 11, reference is made to stones, but in verse 18 there is only one stone. According to the rabbis, the stones by miraculous means became one. In explaining the meaning of Gen. 28:11, the rabbis emphasize Israel's election. Jacob produced the twelve tribes. Abraham did not produce them because he fathered Ishmael and the children of Keturah. Isaac did not produce them because of Esau. Unlike his forefathers, all of Jacob's children will be righteous or at least will constitute Israel. Jacob, not Abraham, is the progenitor of righteous Israel.

18. See Paula Fredrickson, "Judaizing the Nations: The Ritual Demands of Paul's Gospel," *New Testament Studies* 56 (2010): 232–252, especially 243–244 on her discussion of *kata sarka* (according to the flesh) and *kata pneuma* (according to the spirit).

19. See Rom. 9–11. The allegory in chapter 4 of Galatians is discussed in Chapter 6.

6. Firstborn Son

1. Jewish Publication Society translates this as "your favored one," but literally *yaḥid* means "only, unique."

2. See discussion below.

3. See Jan Retsö, *The Arabs in Antiquity: Their History from the Assyrians to the Umayyads* (London: RoutledgeCurzon, 2003); James Montgomery, *Arabia and the Bible* (New York: Ktav, 1969); I. Eph'al, "'Ishmael' and 'Arab(s)': A Transformation of Ethnological Terms," *Journal of Near Eastern Studies* 35 (1976): 225–235; ibid. *The Ancient Arabs: Nomads on the Borders of the Fertile Crescent, 9th–5th Centuries BC* (Hebrew) (Jerusalem: Magnes Press, 1984); F. V. Winnett, "The Arabian Genealogies in the Book of Genesis," in *Translating and Understanding the Old Testament: Essays in Honor of Herbert Gordon May*, ed. H. T. Frank and W. I. Reed (Nashville: Abingdon Press, 1970); I. Shahîd, *Rome and the Arabs: A Prologomenon to the Study of Byzantium and the Arabs* (Washington, DC: Dumbarton Oaks, 1984), and *Byzantium and the Arabs in the Fourth Century* (Washington, DC: Dumbarton Oaks, 1984); and the important work of René Dagorn, *La Geste d'Ismaël: D'aprés l'onomastique et la tradition ababes* (Geneva: Librairie Droz, 1981). A portion of this discussion is a revised version of sections of my monograph *Ishmael on the Border: Rabbinic Portrayals of the First Arab* (Albany: State University of New York Press, 2006).

4. NRSV translated Arab as "nomad," and Jewish Publication Society as "bandit." Ishmaelites/Arabs are often associated with both.

5. Montgomery, *Arabia and the Bible*, 42.

6. I. Eph'al, "'Ishmael' and 'Arab(s).'"

7. Ibid., 231.

8. F. Millar, "Hagar, Ishmael, Josephus and the Origins of Islam," *Journal of Jewish Studies* 44 (1993): 23–45.

9. Elias Bickerman, "Origenes Gentium," *Classical Philosophy* 47 (1952): 65–81.

10. See Exod. 20:3; Deut. 21:16; and Job 1:11.

11. For a lengthier discussion of Gen. 16:12, see my *Ishmael on the Border*, where I also deal with *pere' adam*, "wild ass of a man."

12. N. Sarna, *Understanding Genesis*, Jewish Publication Society Torah Commentary (Philadelphia: Jewish Publication Society, 1989), 121.

13. C. T. R. Hayward, *St. Jerome's Hebrew Questions on Genesis* (Oxford: Clarendon Press, 1995), 49, on Gen. 16:12.

14. Both the Septuagint and the Vulgate include "with her son Isaac," but the phrase is not in the Masoretic text.

15. As in the case of Exod. 32:6, "Early the next day, the people offered up burnt offerings and brought sacrifices of well-being; they sat down to eat and drink, and then rose to make sport." The Jewish Publication Society translates the term as "to dance."

16. Joshua Schwartz, "Ishmael at Play: On Exegesis and Jewish Society," *Hebrew Union College Annual* 66 (1995): 203–204. See especially 204, n. 2, where he gives a bibliographic listing of scholars dealing with this issue.

17. Claus Westermann, *Genesis 12–36: A Commentary*, trans. John J. Scullion, S.J. (Minneapolis: Augsburg, 1981), 339.

18. Schwartz, "Ishmael at Play," 204.

19. See Phyllis Trible, *Texts of Terror* (Philadelphia: Fortress, 1984), 33.

20. J. A. Hackett, "Rehabilitating Hagar: Fragments of an Epic Pattern," in *Gender and Difference in Ancient Israel*, ed. Peggy Day (Minneapolis: Fortress, 1989), 20. See Westermann, *Genesis 12–36*, who notes: "It is not to be assumed that the verb *(mezaheq)* is a play on the name of Isaac, because Ishmael is its subject apart from the fact that all previous uses derive from the Qal [form of the verb]" (339). Westermann's argument is unconvincing. Most scholars claim that it is an allusion to the name Isaac—an obvious pun.

21. See Schwartz, "Ishmael at Play," 205, n. 5, where he makes a similar argument. See, too, G. W. Coats, "Strife without Reconciliation: A Narrative Theme in the Jacob Traditions," in *Werden und Wirken des Alten Testaments*, ed. R. Albertz et al. (Göttingen: Vandenhoeck & Ruprecht, 1980), 97, who also makes a similar argument; J. Kaminsky, "Humor and the Theology of Hope: Isaac as a Humorous Figure," *Interpretation* 54 (2000): 366; and L. H. Silberman, "Listening to the Text," *Journal of Biblical Literature* 102 (1983): 21. And Esther Fuchs, *Sexual Politics in the Biblical Narrative: Reading the Hebrew Bible as a Woman*, *Journal for the Study of the Old Testament Supplement* 310 (Sheffield, UK: Sheffield Academic Press, 2000), 150–152, compares the strife between Sarah and Hagar with that of Rachel and Leah and categorizes these stories under "contest type-scene."

22. Jon D. Levenson, *Death and Resurrection of the Beloved Son* (New Haven: Yale University Press, 1993), 101.

23. Gerhard von Rad, *Genesis: A Commentary*, trans. John H. Marks (London: SCM, 1972), 232.

24. E. A. Speiser, *The Anchor Bible: Genesis* (Garden City: Doubleday, 1964), 155.

25. James B. Pritchard, ed., *The Ancient Near East: An Anthology of Texts and Pictures* (Princeton: Princeton University Press, 1958), 157.

26. Sarna, *Understanding Genesis*, 156. See Philo, who disqualifies Ishmael by highlighting the menial status of Hagar, a slave woman from Egypt. See M. Niefhoff, *Philo on Jewish Identity and Culture*, Texts and Studies in Ancient Judaism 86 (Tübingen: Mohr Siebeck, 2001), 24–27.

27. Sarna, *Understanding Genesis*, 156.

28. See also Deut. 21:15–17, where the firstborn son, even though he is from the unloved wife, receives double portion of the father's possessions. For a discussion of the special status of the firstborn male offspring and the law of Deut. 21:15–17, see Levenson, *Death and Resurrection of the Beloved Son*, chapter 7. See also F. Greenspahn, *When Brothers Dwell Together: The Preeminence of Younger Siblings in the Hebrew Bible* (New York: Oxford University Press, 1994), 57–59.

29. Maren Niehoff, *Philo on Jewish Identity and Culture* (Tübingen: Mohr Siebeck, 2001), in chapter 1, "Jewish Descent: Mothers and Mothercities," examines Philo's treatment of Hagar and its implications on Ishmael, especially 24–27.

30. See Catherine Hezser, *Jewish Slavery in Antiquity* (Oxford: Oxford University Press, 2005).

31. Philo, *De Sobrietate*, 8. Translation from *The Works of Philo*, trans. C. D. Yong (Peabody, MA: Hendrickson, 1993), 228.

32. For a comparison of the treatment of Ishmael and Isaac in *Jubilees*, see Roger Syren, "Ishmael and Esau in the *Book of Jubilees* and *Targum Pseudo-Jonathan*," in *The Aramaic Bible: Targums in their Historical Context*, ed. D. R. G. Beattie and M. J. McNamara (Sheffield, UK: JSOT, 1994), 310–315. For a summary of scholarly discussions of attitudes toward Ishmael in *Jubilees*, *Targum Pseudo-Jonathan*, and Josephus, see my *Ishmael on the Border*, 144, n. 34.

33. J. C. VanderKam, trans. and ed., *The Book of Jubilees: A Critical Text* (Louvain: E. Peeters, 1989), 102–103. The episode described in *Jubilees* echoes in Islamic sources. See my forthcoming study of parallels in *Jubilees* and tales of the prophets.

34. Feldman, *Judean Antiquities 1–4*, vol. 3 of *Flavius Josephus: Translation and Commentary*, ed. Steve Mason (Leiden: Brill, 2000), 81.

35. Ibid.

36. According to Josephus, Abraham's initial reluctance to consent to her request had nothing to do with his affections for Ishmael but was on account of it being "the most cruel of all things to send away a child and a woman destitute of the necessities of life" (*Josephus Antiquities* 1.216–217). Quote taken from Feldman, *Judean Antiquities 1–4*, 82. And, since Ishmael was too young to be cast off on his own, Hagar is sent along with him.

37. In *Ishmael on the Border*, 33, I translated the phrase *mekabesh et haganot* as "having homosexual intercourse." This was based on Lieberman's reading. Shamma Friedman, "Rabbinic and Colloquial Language" (Hebrew), *Leshonenu* (2011): 27–53, however, convincingly connects the verb *horesh* with homosexual intercourse, but the verb does not occur in this tosefta passage. Friedman argues that the phrase is best taken as a colloquialism for Ishmael's womanizing.

38. See *Gen. Rab.* 53:11: "R. 'Azariah said in R. Levi's name: Ishmael said to Isaac, 'Let us go and see our portions in the field'; then pretending to be playing, Ishmael would take a bow and arrows and shoot them in Isaac's direction." Thus it is written, "As a madman who casts firebrands, arrows, and death, so is the man who deceives his neighbor and says, 'I was only kidding'?"(Prov. 26:19).

39. The various renderings of *metsaheq* as well as understandings of the verse seem to form a single unit in *Tos. Sotah* 6:6 and *Gen. Rab.* 53:11, whereas in *Tos. Sotah* 5:12, we read only of Ishmael as an idol worshipper and in *Sifre Deuteronomy* 31 (see Finkelstein, *Sifre al Sefer Devarim* [New York: Jewish Theological Seminary, 1993], who sets it as a baraita), we have a shorter version of *Tos. Sotah* 6:6. In *Sifre Deuteronomy* 31, R. Shimon does not discuss the four examples where he and R. Aqiba differ, nor are R. Eleazar and R. Ishmael's interpretations of *metsaheq* included. The interpretation of Genesis 21:9 in *Tosefta Sotah* 5:12, that Sarah saw Ishmael building altars, hunting locusts, and offering them for idol worship, has no attribution.

40. *Exodus Rabbah* (*Shemot Rabbah*), like *Psalms Rabbah*, is composed of two parts, the first an exegetical midrash on Exod. 1–10, the second a homiletic midrash on Exod. 12–40. Leopold Zunz, *Die gottesdienstlichen Vorträge der Juden, historisch entwickelt. Ein Beitrag zur Alterthumskunde und biblischen Kritik, zur Literatur- und Religionsgeschichte* (Berlin: L. Lamm, 1919), 268–270, dates the entire work to the eleventh or twelfth century, whereas Herr considers the first part later than the second, thus dating it no earlier than the tenth century. For more on *Exodus Rabbah*, see Herman L. Strack and Günter Stemberger, eds., *Introduction to the Talmud and Midrash* (Minneapolis: Fortress, 1992 repr. 1996), 308–309.

41. See my discussion of the story in "Abraham Visits Ishmael: A Revisit," *Journal for the Study of Judaism* 38 (2007): 553–580.

42. The name Fatima is found in the *Yalkut* and in *Targum Pseudo-Jonathan*.

43. See discussion below.

44. For a discussion of "a rough parallel" between the rise of Islam and the rise of Christianity, see M. Cohen, *Under Crescent and Cross* (Princeton: Princeton University Press, 1994), 22–29.

45. Of course the situation for the Jews of Arabia was much more complicated. See, for example, S. D. Goitein, *Jews and Arabs: Their Contacts Through the Ages*, 3rd ed. (New York: Schocken, 1974); Gordon Newby, *A History of the Jews of Arabia* (Columbia: University of South Carolina Press, 1988); and Norman Stillman, *The Jews of Arab Lands* (Philadelphia: Jewish Publication Society, 1979), 3–21. For a general overview, see Shari Lowin, "Hijaz," *Encyclopedia of Jews in the Arab World*, executive editor Norman Stillman (Brill Online, 2013).

46. For a discussion of the use of Esau as Rome, and Christianity, see Gerson Cohen, "Esau as Symbol in Early Medieval Thought," in *Studies of the Variety of Rabbinic Cultures* (Philadelphia: Jewish Publication Society, 1991), 243–269; Adiel Schremer, "Eschatology, Violence, and Suicide: An Early Rabbinic Theme and Its Influence in the Middle Ages," in *Apocalypse and Violence*, ed. A. Amanat and J. J. Collins (New Haven: Yale Center for International and Area Studies, 2002), and "Rabbis, Christians and Romans," chapter 1 of *Brothers Estranged: Heresy, Christianity and Jewish Identity in Late Antiquity* (New York: Oxford University Press, 2010). See also Israel Yuval, *Shenei Goyim be bitnekh, Yehudim ve-Notsrim: Dimuyim hadadiyim* (Tel Aviv: Am Oved, 2000); Jacob Neusner, *Judaism and Its Social Metaphors* (Cambridge: Cambridge University Press, 1999), and *From Enemy to Sibling: Rome and Israel in the First Century of Western Civilization*, Ben Zion Bokser Memorial Lecture (New York: Queens College, 1986); Harry Freedman, "Jacob and Esau: Their Struggle in the Second Century," *Jewish Bible Quarterly* 23 (1995): 107–115; and my "Figuring (Out) Esau: The Rabbis and Their Others," *Journal of Jewish Studies* 58.2 (2007): 250–262, where I argue that several references to Esau evince a sense he represents an imagined Other, not Rome or Christianity, even though in many instances he is a sobriquet for Rome, and certainly in later rabbinic texts represents Christianity.

47. See the following: Jacob Mann, "Proceedings of the Society at Cincinnati," *Journal of the American Oriental Society* 47 (1927): 364; Bernard Lewis,

"An Apocalyptic Vision of Islamic History," *Bulletin of the School of Oriental and African Studies 13/2* (1950): 308–338; Michael Cook and Patricia Crone, *Hagarism: The Making of the Islamic World* (Cambridge: Cambridge University Press, 1977); Robert Hoyland, *Seeing Islam as Others Saw It* (Princeton: Darwin Press, 1997), 307–320; S. Wasserstrom, *Between Muslim and Jew: The Problem of Symbiosis under Early Islam* (Princeton: Princeton University Press, 1995); and Uri Rubin, *Between Bible and Qur'an: The Children of Israel and the Islamic Self-Image* (Princeton: Darwin Press, 1999), 11–34.

48. For a discussion of apocalypse and apocalypticism, see volume 14 of *Semeia* and David Hellholm, ed., *Apocalypticism;* David Hellholm, ed., *Apocalypticism in the Mediterranean World and the Near East* (Tübingen: Mohr Siebeck, 1983; reprint, 1989, with supp. bibliography); Bernard McGinn, *Visions of the End: Apocalyptic Traditions in the Middle Ages* (New York: Columbia University Press, 1998); and John Collins, *The Apocalpytic Imagination: An Introduction to Jewish Apocalyptic Literature* (Grand Rapids, MI: Eerdmans, 1984); and John J. Collins, ed., *Apocalypse: The Morphology of a Genre*, Semeia 14 (Atlanta: Society of Biblical Literature, 2003).

49. *Sefer Eliyahu* and the *Nistarot of Shimon ben Yoḥai* are edited with introduction and notes in Yehuda Even-Shmuel (Kaufman), ed., *Midreshey Ge'ullah*, 2nd ed. (Jerusalem: Mosad Bialik, 1954), 31–48 and 162–198, respectively. For an introduction to and excerpts from these works, see John C. Reeves, *Trajectories in Near Eastern Apocalyptic: A Postrabbinic Jewish Apocalypse* (Atlanta: Society of Biblical Literature, 2005).

50. J. Heinemann, "The Nature of Aggadah," in *Midrash and Literature*, ed. Geoffrey Hartman and Sanford Budick (New Haven: Yale University Press, 1986), 49.

51. Much has been written regarding the various uses of the Exodus story in Jewish and Christian narratives, be they literary or theological. To provide a few examples, see Michael Walzer's *Exodus and Revolution* (New York: Basic Books, 1985); Jon D. Levenson, "Exodus and Liberation," in his *The Hebrew Bible, Old Testament and Historical Criticism* (Louisville: Westminster/John Knox Press, 1993), 127–160, and "Liberation Theology and the Exodus," in *Jews, Christians and the Theology of Hebrew Scriptures*, ed. A. Ogden Bellis and J. S. Kaminsky (Atlanta: Scholars Press, 2000), 215–230; Arnaldo Momigliano, "Preliminary Indications on the Apocalypse and Exodus in the Hebrew Tradition," in his *Essays on Ancient and Modern Judaism*, trans. Maura Masella-Gayley (Chicago: Chicago University Press, 1994), 88–100; and Erich Gruen, "The Use and Abuse of the Exodus Story," *Jewish History* 12 (1998): 93–122. Most recently, and for present purposes, Oded Irshai, "Dating the Eschaton: Jewish and Christian Apocalyptic Calculations in Late Antiquity," in *Apocalyptic Time*, ed. A. Baumgarten (Leiden: Brill, 2000), 113–153, has written about the use of the Exodus story in light of eschatological schemes and calculations.

52. Bede the Venerable, *Bede's Ecclesiastical History of the English Nations*, trans. John Stevenson, revised with notes by Dom David Knowles (London: Dent, 1954), chapter 32.

53. Reeves, *Trajectories in Near Eastern Apocalyptic*, 4 (emphasis on "formulaic" has been removed). See the Armenian legend of Ardawazd by Eznik of Kolb, a writer of the mid-fifth century CE. Monica J. Blanchard and Robin

Darling Young, *A Treatise on God Written in Armenian by Eznik of Kolb (Floruit c. 430–c. 450): An English Translation with Notes* (Leuven: Peeters, 1998).

54. S. Wasserstrom, *Between Muslim and Jew*, 48.

55. Reeves, *Trajectories in Near Eastern Apocalyptic*, 76.

56. Translated from Even-Shmuel, in consultation with ibid., 78–80, and Lewis, "Apocalyptic Vision of Islamic History," 313. Many of the words and phrases in brackets are also found in Reeves's translation. On the *Secrets of R. Shim'on ben Yoḥai* and its relationship to the *Prayer of R. Shim'on ben Yoḥai*, see Lewis, "Apocalyptic Vision of Islamic History," and Reeves, *Trajectories in Near Eastern Apocalyptic*. As Reeves notes (77), the *Secrets of R. Shim'on ben Yoḥai* were first published in Salonika in 1743. A version of this text was reprinted in Adolph Jellinek's edited work *Bet ha-Midrasch: Sammlung kleiner Midraschim und vermischter Abhandlungen aus der jüdischen Literatur*, 6 vols. (Leipzig, 1853–1877; repr., Jerusalem: Bamberger & Wahrmann, 1938), 3: 78–82. Yehuda Even-Shmuel subsequently reproduced Jellinek's version in his *Midreshey Ge'ullah*, 2nd ed. (Jerusalem: Mosad Bialik, 1954), 401–403.

57. Usually translated "a pair of horsemen, a chariot [*rekhev*] of asses and a chariot of camels." However, it is read "a pair of horsemen, one riding [*rokhev*] on an ass, one riding on a camel." The Aramaic Bible opts for this reading, as do commentators of the Hebrew text. See Cook and Crone, *Hagarism*.

58. A genizah fragment reads: "*navi shoteh v-ish ha-ruaḥ*," "a demented prophet possessed by a spirit," clearly a revision of the positive estimation of Muhammad found here in the older text.

59. Moshe Gil, *A History of Palestine, 634–1099*, trans. Ethel Broido (Cambridge: Cambridge University Press, 1992), 62.

60. The exact date of the forced conversion is unknown. Whereas S. Baron, *Social and Religious History*, claims that the date is 632, F. E. Peters, *Allah's Commonwealth* (New York: Simon and Schuster, 1973), 38, places it in 634; however, the historicity of the forced conversion is heavily debated. See Joshua Halo, *Byzantine Jewry in the Mediterranean Economy* (Cambridge: Cambridge University Press), 34. See also Walter E. Kaegi, *Heraclius: Emperor of Byzantium* (Cambridge: Cambridge University Press, 2003), who writes: "Heraclius ordered the forcible baptism of Jews in Africa by the prefect of Africa on 31 May 632. The scope and intent of this decree is controversial, though it involved local Jews and Samaritans as well as foreign ones," 216. See also ibid., *Byzantium and the Early Islamic Conquests* (Cambridge: Cambridge University Press, 1992).

61. For a discussion of the debate on dating, see Rachel Adelman, *The Return of the Repressed: Pirqe de-Rabbi Eliezer and the Pseudepigrapha* (Leiden: Brill, 2009), 35–46.

62. This is an embellishment of *Gen. Rab.* 44:15, which does not include the Ishmaelites, but does so here.

63. "The 'kingdom of the Medes and Persians,'" Reeves states, "recognizes the Sasanian domination of the eastern Mediterranean provinces during the decades of the seventh century, and 'Ishmael' is of course a cipher for the Arabs or Islam." Reeves, *Trajectories in Near Eastern Apocalyptic*, 14–15. See also Bakhos, *Ishmael on the Border*, 125–127.

64. See *Shir Hashirim Rabbah* 7:8 for another example of the rabbinic employment of eschatological imagery. *Shir Hashirim Rabbah* draws on many sources such as the *Yerushalmi*, *Genesis Rabbah*, *Leviticus Rabbah*, and *Pesikta de Rav Kahana*, such that it is difficult to date. According to Herman L. Strack and Günter Stemberger, eds., *Introduction to the Talmud and Midrash* (Minneapolis: Fortress, 1992; repr. 1996), 342–343, however, Zunz and Lachs date its final version to the second half of the eighth century.

65. Reeves, *Trajectories in Near Eastern Apocalyptic*, 3.

66. As Gaston demonstrates, Paul's use of the allegory involves "Pythagorean tables of contraries." Two columns are set up in opposition. In one column we have Son (Ishmael), in the other Son (Isaac), for example. See Lloyd Gaston, *Paul and the Torah* (Vancouver: University of British Columbia Press, 1987), 83–91. Each member in the column is analogically related to other members in the same column. See also Daniel Boyarin, *A Radical Jew: Paul and the Politics of Identity* (Berkeley: University of California Press, 1994), and J. Louis Martyn, "The Covenants of Hagar and Sarah," in *Faith and History: Essays in Honor of Paul W. Meyer*, ed. John T. Carroll, Charles H. Cosgrove, and Elizabeth Johnson (Atlanta: Scholars Press, 1990), 160–192.

67. See Acts 15:10, *m.Berakhot* 2:2 and *Sifra* on Lev. 11:43, which mention the yoke of the commandments; but in rabbinic literature this rhetoric serves to affirm the commandments, not as in Acts or Galatians, where they are rejected.

68. For a penetrating discussion of the ramifications of Paul's notion of freedom from Torah in the post-Enlightenment world, see Levenson, *Death and Resurrection of the Beloved Son*, 215–219.

69. A. E. Harvey, "The Opposition to Paul," *Studio Evangelica* 4 (1968): 319–332, for example, refers to them as local synagogue Jews, but this is a misreading of the letter.

70. Ronald E. Heine, *Origen: Homilies on Genesis and Exodus* (Washington, DC: Catholic University of America Press, 1982), 130–131.

71. C. T. R. Hayward, trans., *St. Jerome's Hebrew Questions on Genesis*, (Oxford: Clarendon Press, 1995), 53. For an illuminating discussion of Jerome's Greek exegetical sources, see Adam Kamesar, *Jerome, Greek Scholarship, and the Hebrew Bible: A Study of the "Quaestiones Hebraicae in Genesim"* (Oxford: Clarendon Press, 1993). See, too, Kamesar, "The Evaluation of the Narrative Aggada in Greek and Latin Patristic Literature," *Journal of Theological Studies* 45 (1994): 37–71. See R. Hayward, "Some Observations on St. Jerome's *Hebrew Questions on Genesis* and the Rabbinic Tradition," *Proceedings of the Irish Biblical Association* 13 (1990): 58–76.

72. Eric Plumer, trans. *Augustine's Commentary on Galatians: Introduction, Text, Translations and Notes*, Oxford Early Christian Studies (Oxford: Oxford University Press, 2003), 197–198.

73. See W. H. C. Frend, *The Donatist Church: A Movement of Protest in Roman North Africa* (Oxford: Clarendon Press, 1952), for an extended analysis of the subject matter.

74. My translation is adapted from Edmund Hill, O.P., trans., *Homilies on the Gospel of John 1–40* (Works of St. Augustine: A Translation for the 21st Century) (New York: New City Press, 2009), 222–223.

75. *Treatises on John*, 11, on John 2.23–25; 3.1–5: "The apostle recounts this; and he says that in those two sons of Abraham was a figure of the two Testaments, the Old and the New. To the Old Testament belong the lovers of temporal things, the lovers of the world: to the New Testament belong the lovers of eternal life. Hence, that Jerusalem on earth was the shadow of the heavenly Jerusalem, the mother of us all, which is in heaven."

76. See Pss. 42:10 and 43:2. Note also Song of Songs 1:5. The symbolic nuance of *meshekh* is less clear, but the military context here suggests that the meaning may be the root *mskh*, "to draw," in the sense of "mobilize" or the like (Judith 4:7); or perhaps, to continue the archery image, *meshekh* stands elliptically for *mashakh qeshet*, "draw the bow" (see 1 Kings 22:34). I thank Stephen Geller for furnishing me with excerpts of his forthcoming Psalms commentary.

77. I made minor revisions to this translation taken from Maria Boulding, O.S.B., trans., *Exposition of the Psalms 99–120*, vol. 5 (Works of St. Augustine: A Translation for the 21st Century) (New York: New City Press, 2003), 506–507.

78. See Uri Rubin, "Prophets and Progenitors in the Early Shi'a Tradition," in *Jerusalem Studies in Arabic and Islam*, vol. 1 (1979): 41–65.

79. Wheeler Thackston Jr. trans. *Tales of the Prophets, Muhammad Abd Allah al-Kisa'i*, (Chicago: Great Books of the Islamic World, 1997), 151. Al-Kisa'i also mentions that when Sarah gave birth to Isaac, a light shone from his forehead that lit everything around him. When he first touched the earth he fell down prostrate before God and raised his hands to heaven to proclaim the Divine Unity.

80. In some versions, such as al-Tha'labi's, Abraham travels to Mecca on al-Burāq, the strange creature, a mythical steed, which Muhammad rode when he went on the "Night Journey."

81. Some versions include more details than others. My retelling is adapted from Thackston, trans., *al-Kisa'i's Tales of the Prophets*. See Reuven Firestone, *Journeys in Holy Lands: The Evolution of the Abraham-Ishmael Legends in Islamic Exegesis* (Albany: State University of New York Press, 1990), 76–79, for a discussion of the different versions.

82. For a discussion of the Islamic versions of the story, see Firestone, *Journeys in Holy Lands*, and Bakhos, *Ishmael on the Border*.

83. The story is found in later midrashic compilations, in *Midrash ha-Gadol* and *Yalkut Shim'oni, Wayyera* 95, both dated to the thirteenth century. See critical editions of M. Margoliot, *Midrash ha-Gadol al Hameshah Humshe Torah* (Jerusalem: Mossad Harav Kook, 1947), 1:339–342, and *Yalkut Shim'oni al ha-Torah le Rabbenu Shim'on ha-Darshan*, eds. D. Hyman, D. N. Lerrer, and I. Shiloni (Jerusalem: Mossad Harav Kook, 1973), 1:424–425. The story is also found in *Sefer ha-Yashar*, dated to the beginning of the sixteenth century. See Joseph Dan, *Ha-Sipur ha-'ivri biyeme ha-benayim* (Jerusalem: Keter, 1974), 137–138, who claims that the work is a product of the Jewish Renaissance in Italy.

84. As Hava Lazarus-Yafeh, *Intertwined Worlds* (Princeton: Princeton University Press, 1992), 4, writes: "One should not think in terms of influences or cultural borrowing only, however. It has been said that the Near East

resembles a palimpsest, layer upon layer, tradition upon tradition, intertwined to the extent that one cannot really grasp one without the other, certainly not the later without the earlier, but often also not the earlier without considering the shapes it took later." See also S. Rosenblatt, "Rabbinic Legends in Hadith," *Muslim World* 35 (1947): 237–252, and S. D. Goitein, "The Intermediate Civilization/The Hellenic Heritage in Islam," in Goitein, *Studies in Islamic History and Institutions* (Leiden: Brill, 1966), 54–70. On the role of Christianity and Judaism, in particular, in the origins and development of Islam, see Cook and Crone, *Hagarism*, and M. Cook, *Muhammad* (New York: Oxford University Press, 1983; reissued 1996), 77–89.

85. For an excellent examination of the literary precedent of Q. 2:127, see Joseph Witztum, "The Foundations of the House (Q. 2:127)," *Bulletin of the School of Oriental and African Studies* 72.1 (2009): 25–40.

86. See Firestone, *Journeys in Holy Lands*, 80–93.

87. *'Arā'is al-Majālis fī Qiṣaṣ al-Anbiyā'* or *"Lives of the Prophets": As Recounted by Abū Isḥāq Aḥmad ibn Muḥammad ibn Ibrāhīm al-Thaʿlabī*, trans. and annot. William Brinner (Leiden: Brill, 2002), 149.s

7. The Sacrifice of Isaac and Ishmael

1. See Isabel Speyart van Woerden, "The Iconography of the Sacrifice of Abraham," *Vigiliae Christianae* 15 (1961): 214–255, which contains a list of nearly six hundred items from late antiquity through the twelfth century by Christian artists (the list contains only two Jewish monuments: the famous Dura Europos and Beth Alpha images), and Rachel Hachlili, *Ancient Jewish Art and Archaeology in the Diaspora* (Leiden: Brill, 1998).

2. The following are select works on the subject that range in themes, topics, and perspectives. To date, Lukas Kundert, *Die Opferung/Bindung Isaaks*, 2 vols. (Neukirchen-Vluyn: Neukirchener Verlag, 1998), is the most extensive study of the interpretation of the Aqedah. See Shalom Spiegel, *The Last Trial: On the Legends and Lore of the Command to Abraham to Offer Isaac as a Sacrifice: The Akedah*, trans. Judah Goldin (Woodstock, VT: Jewish Lights, 1993), and Jon D. Levenson, *Death and Resurrection of the Beloved Son* (New Haven: Yale University Press, 1993), 173–219; Geza Vermes, *Scripture and Tradition in Judaism*, 2nd rev. ed., Studia Post-Biblica (Leiden: Brill, 1973), 193–227; Robert J. Daly, "The Soteriological Significance of the Sacrifice of Isaac," *Catholic Biblical Quarterly* 39 (1977): 45–75; James Swetnam, *Jesus and Isaac: A Study of the Epistle to the Hebrews in Light of the Aqedah*, Analecta Biblica 94 (Rome: Biblical Institute, 1981), 4–80; Alan Segal, "'He Who Did Not Spare His Only Son . . .' (Romans 8:32): Jesus, Paul, and the Sacrifice of Isaac," in *From Jesus to Paul*, ed. Peter Richardson and John C. Hurd (Waterloo, Ontario: Wilfred Laurier, 184), 169–184, reprinted as "The Sacrifice of Isaac in Early Judaism and Christianity," in Alan F. Segal, *The Other Judaisms of Late Antiquity*, Brown Judaica Series 127 (Atlanta: Scholars, 1987), 109–130; P. R. Davis and B. D. Chilton, "The Aqedah: A Revised Tradition History," *Catholic Biblical Quarterly* 40 (1978): 514–546, and Philip R. Davies, "Passover and the Dating of the Aqedah," *Journal of Jewish Studies* 30 (1979):

59–67; C. T. R. Hayward, "The Sacrifice of Isaac and Jewish Polemic against Christianity," *Catholic Biblical Quarterly* 52 (1990): 292–306; Hans Joachim Shoeps, "The Sacrifice of Isaac in Paul's Theology," *Journal of Biblical Literature* 65 (1946): 385–392, and Edward Kessler, *Bound by the Bible: Jews, Christians and the Sacrifice of Isaac* (Cambridge: Cambridge University Press, 2004), and Carol Delaney, *Abraham on Trial* (Princeton: Princeton University Press, 1998).

3. Søren Kierkegaard, *Fear and Trembling*, trans. Alastair Hannay (Harmondsworth: Penguin, 1985), 60.

4. Yvonne Sherman, *Biblical Blaspheming: Trials of the Sacred for a Secular Age* (Cambridge: Cambridge University Press, 2013), 333–374, also examines sources that question God's command that Abraham sacrifice his son.

5. Yael Feldman, *Glory and Agony: Isaac's Sacrifice and National Narrative* (Stanford: Stanford University Press, 2010).

6. See for example Deut. 8:2, 13:3–4; Isa. 39; 2 Chron. 32:31. Gen. 18:17–33 might be considered a test to see how Abraham will react to God's intent to destroy Sodom and Gomorrah. See Jacob Licht, *Ha-Nisayon ba-Mikra uva-Yahadut shel tekufat ha-Bayit ha-sheni* [Testing in the Hebrew Bible in the Second Temple Period] (Jerusalem: Magnes Press, 1973), and James Kugel, *Traditions of the Bible: A Guide to the Bible as It Was at the Start of the Common Era* (Cambridge, MA: Harvard University Press, 1998), 296–326.

7. Ten tests are mentioned in *m.Avot* 4:3 and *Avot de Rabbi Natan* 33, in addition to *PRE* 26. See Scott B. Noegel, "Abraham's Ten Trials and a Biblical Numerical Convention," *Jewish Bible Quarterly* 31 (2003): 73–83, and Lewis Barth, "The Lection for the Second Day of Rosh Hashanah: A Homily Containing Ten Trials of Abraham" (Hebrew), *Hebrew Union College Annual* 58 (1987): 1–48. See, too, Jo Milgrom, *The Akedah: A Primary Symbol in Jewish Thought and Art* (Berkeley: Bibal Press, 1988). While Jerome mentions the ten trials in his *Hebrew Questions*, the notion that Abraham endured many trials does not figure prominently in the writings of the church fathers. Hebrews 11:17–22 mentions the test Abraham endured, that of having been commanded to sacrifice Isaac; however, no mention is made of ten trials. The near-sacrifice of Isaac is considered the final test. *Jubilees*, however, ends the litany of Abraham's trials with the purchase of a burial cave for his wife Sarah (Genesis 23). Kugel, *Traditions of the Bible: A Guide to the Bible as It Was at the Start of the Common Era* (Cambridge, MA: Harvard University Press, 1998), 325–326, astutely observes, "If the offering of Isaac was indeed Abraham's last test, then it should have been followed by a period of bliss unalloyed. Instead, it is followed by the mention of Sarah's death (Gen. 23:1–2) and, subsequent to that event, a curious account of how Abraham bought the cave of the Machpelah as a burial plot for her. *That* narrative is then followed by the assertion that God 'blessed Abraham in all things' (Gen. 24:1), which surely would be a fit conclusion to Abraham's final test." According to *Jubilees*, making Abraham negotiate with the Hittites for purchase of the burial plot is the test.

8. James VanderKam, trans., *Book of Jubilees, Corpus Scriptorum Christianorum Orientalium*, vol. 511, Scriptores Aethiopici 88 (Louvain: Peeters, 1989), 105. All translations of *Jubilees* are taken from VanderKam.

9. According to Philo, *On Abraham*, 197, this was an unprecedented test.

10. As Levenson notes, *Death and Resurrection of the Beloved Son*, 139, "the application of Ps 60:6 to the aqedah is generated not only by these near-homophonies, but also by the term 'those who fear God' [*lire'ekha*] in the psalm and the angelic announcement in Gen 22:12 that Abraham is one of them [*yere' 'elohim*]."

11. "And Abraham rose early in the morning," also in Gen. 21:14, is one of the many literary parallels between both sacrificial stories.

12. For a philological discussion of Gen. 21:14, and of the theological and moral issues raised when it is understood in the broader narrative structure, see Larry Lyke, "Where Does the Boy Belong? Compositional Strategy in Genesis 21:14," *Catholic Biblical Quarterly* 56 (1994): 637–648.

13. T. Carmi, *The Penguin Book of Hebrew Verse* (New York: Viking Press, 1981), 201–202.

14. See also 4Q *Pseudo-Jubilees* (4Q225), a nonbiblical Qumran scroll, which shares similarities. For a discussion of the text, see Robert Kugler, "Hearing 4Q225: A Case Study in Reconstructing the Religious Imagination of the Qumran Community," *Dead Sea Discoveries* 10 (2003): 81–103. For an investigation of the weeping angels motif and a detailed examination of the text, see James Kugel, "Exegetical Notes on 4Q225 'Pseudo-Jubilees,'" *Dead Sea Discoveries* 13.1 (2006): 73–98; Menaham Kister, "Observations on Aspects of Exegesis, Tradition and Theology in Midrash, Pseudepigrapha and Other Jewish Writings," in *Tracing the Threads: Studies in the Vitality of Jewish Pseudepigrapha*, Society of Biblical Literature Early Judaism and Its Literature 6, ed. John C. Reeves (Atlanta: Scholars Press, 1994), 1–34; Moshe Bernstein, "Angels at the Akedah," *Dead Sea Discoveries* 7 (2000): 263–291; and F. Garcia Martinez, "The Sacrifice of Isaac in 4Q225," in *The Sacrifice of Isaac: The Aqedah (Genesis 22) and Its Interpretations*, ed. Ed Noort and Eibert Tigchelaar (Leiden: Brill, 2002), 44–57.

15. *Genesis Rabbah* 55:4 also expands the narrative in order to explicate the meaning of "these things" or "these words."

16. *Leviticus Rabbah* 36:5; see also *Lev. Rab.* 36:2; *b.Yoma* 87a, where Israel relies on the merits of the forefathers.

17. *Mekhilta de Rabbi Ishmael, Beshallah* 4.

18. Spiegel, *Last Trial*, 24.

19. Philo of Alexandria, *De Abrahamo*, trans. F. H. Colson, Loeb Classical Library (Cambridge, MA: Harvard University Press, 1959), 97.

20. In her unwavering devotion to God, the mother who martyrs her seven sons possesses a soul like Abraham (4 Macc. 14:20). In *Lamentations Rabbah* 1:50 a comparison is made between Abraham, who built one altar and nearly sacrificed his son, and the mother who built seven altars on which seven sons were sacrificed.

21. The Aqedah is also associated with resurrection. That is, traditions that claim Isaac was slain also assert that he was resurrected. See Spiegel, *Last Trial*, 3–8 and Levenson, *Death and Resurrection of the Beloved Son*.

22. In some sources, Isaac in fact dies but is resurrected. See Spiegel, *Last Trial*. A connection between the idea of resurrection and the Aqedah is found

in Hebrews 11:17–19: "By faith Abraham, when put to the test, offered up Isaac. He who had received the promises was ready to offer up his only son, of whom he had been told, 'It is through Isaac that descendants shall be named for you.' He considered the fact that God is able even to raise someone from the dead— and figuratively speaking, he did receive him back."

23. Samuel Sandmel, *Philo's Place in Judaism: A Study of the Conceptions of Abraham in Jewish Literature* (Cincinnati: Hebrew Union College, 1956); Alan Segal, *The Other Judaisms of Late Antiquity* (Atlanta: Scholars Press, 1987); Philip Davies, "Passover and the Dating of the Aqedah," *Journal of Jewish Studies* 30 (1979): 59–67; and Jon D. Levenson, *The Death and Resurrection of the Beloved Son*.

24. See Yaakov Elbaum, "From Sermon to Story: The Transformation of the Akedah," *Prooftexts* 6 (1986): 97–116.

25. *Reply to Faustus the Manichean* (Contra Faustum), 22.73.

26. *Gen. Rab.* 56:3. Isaac is like one who carries his stake on his shoulder.

27. Melito of Sardis, fragment from Paschal Homily. Robert M. Grant, *Second-Century Christianity: A Collection of Fragments* (Louisville: Westminster John Knox Press, 2003), 32.

28. *City of God*, 16.32. See also Chrysostom, *Homilies on Genesis*, 47:14.

29. Edward G. Mathews, trans., *St. Ephrem the Syrian: Selected Prose Works*, in *The Fathers of the Church*, vol. 91 (Washington, DC: Catholic University of America Press, 1994), 169. Ephrem shows familiarity with the Jewish tradition that the ram was created in the twilight of the eve of Shabbat in the week of Creation.

30. See Edward Kessler's detailed discussion of the church fathers in *Bound by the Bible*.

31. See also Melito of Sardis, who describes Isaac as unafraid "by the sword nor alarmed by the fire nor sorrowful at the offering, he carried with fortitude the model of the Lord" (fragment 9). For a discussion of the fascinating fourth-century Greek poem "Pros Abraham," see Pieter W. van der Horst and Martien F. G. Parmentier, "A New Early Christian Poem on the Sacrifice of Isaac," in *Le Codex Des Visions*, ed. André Hurst and Jean Rudhardt, Recherches et Recontres Publications de la Faculté des lettres de Genevè (Geneva: Librairie Droz S.A., 2002), 155–172.

32. See Kessler, *Bound by the Bible*, 133–135, for a discussion on the controversial nature of the Aqedah between Jews and Christians in late antiquity.

33. Robert C. Hill, trans., *Saint John Chrysostom: Homilies on Genesis 46– 67*, *The Fathers of the Church–A New Translation* 87 (Washington, DC: Catholic University of America Press, 1992), 21–22.

34. Brock, "Two Syriac Verse Homilies," *Le Museon* 99 (1986): 61–129, 108–109.

35. Ibid., 123.

36. Ibid.

37. Ibid., 125.

38. Ibid., 76.

39. William Brinner, trans., *The History of al-Tabari*, vol. 2, *Prophets and Patriarchs* (Albany: SUNY Press, 1987), 96–97. See also ibid., trans. and annot., *'Arā'is*

al-Majālis fī Qiṣaṣ al-Anbiyā' or "Lives of the Prophets": As Recounted by Abū Isḥāq Aḥmad ibn Muḥammad ibn Ibrāhīm al-Thaʿlabi (Leiden: Brill, 2002), 161.

40. Brinner, *The History of al-Tabari*, 97.

41. Ibid., 85.

42. Al-Kisa'i, *Tales of the Prophets*, "On Isaac." Translated in consultation with Wheeler M. Thackston, Jr., trans., Muhammad ibn 'Abd Allah al-Kisā'i, *Tales of the Prophets (Qiṣaṣ al-anbiyā')*, Great Books of the Islamic World (1997), 160–165, and Reuven Firestone, *Journeys in Holy Lands: The Evolution of the Abraham-Ishmael Legends in Islamic Exegesis* (Albany: State University of New York Press, 1990),125–126.

43. See Ignaz Goldziher, *Die Richtungen der islamischen Koranauslegung* (Leiden, 1920), reprinted 1970, 79–81; Reuven Firestone, "Abraham's Son as the Intended Sacrifice *(al-dhabīḥ,* Qur'an 37: 99–113): Issues in Qur'anic Exegesis," *Journal of Semitic Studies* 34 (1989): 95–131, and his *Journeys in Holy Lands*. For a lengthy discussion, see Fred Leemhuis, "Ibrāhīm's Sacrifice of His Son in the Early Post-koranic Tradition," in *The Sacrifice of Isaac: The Aqedah (Genesis 22) and Its Interpretations*, ed. Ed Noort and Eibert Tigehelaar (Leiden: Brill, 2002), 125–139. According to Leemhuis, the Qur'an commentary tradition for many centuries debated the identity of the sacrificial son, whether he is Isaac or Ishmael.

44. Al-Tabari, *History*, 82. According to Firestone, *Journeys in Holy Lands*, 135, there are 130 authoritative statements that consider Isaac to be the intended victim and 133 that consider Ishmael to be the sacrificial son.

45. See Leemhuis, "Ibrāhīm's Sacrifice," who argues that while the traditions may describe opinions as coming from an earlier period, they may well in fact reflect opinions held by later generations.

46. Brinner, *'Arā'is al-Majālis fī Qiṣaṣ al-Anbiyā' or "Lives of the Prophets,"* 138.

47. Ibid., 155.

48. Ibid., 154–155.

49. Ibid., 156.

50. For a more detailed discussion of Ibn Taymiyya's arguments see Younus Y. Mizra, "Ishmael as Abraham's Sacrifice: Ibn Taymiyya and Ibn Kathir on the Intended Victim," *Islam and Christian-Muslim Relations* 24.3 (2013): 277–298. Q. 37:101 refers to the son as *ghulām ḥalīm*, "patient boy." Al-Zamakhshari connects *ḥalīm* to its synonym *ṣabr*. While *ghulām ḥalīm* in Q. 37:101 can refer to either son, by linking it to its synonym, *ṣabr*, an adjective used to describe Ishmael, al-Zamakhshari concludes that Ishmael is the sacrificial son. See Firestone, *Journeys in Holy Lands*, 137.

51. See Mizra, "Ishmael as Abraham's Sacrifice," for an analysis of the differences between the arguments put forth by Ibn Taymiyya and Ibn Kathir.

52. Compare *b.Sanhedrin* 89b. In an early Islamic source Abraham asks God which of the two sons he is to sacrifice, and the Lord says, "The one most beloved to you." Cited in Norman Calder, "From Midrash to Scripture: The Sacrifice of Abraham in Early Islamic Tradition," *Le Museon* 101 (1988): 381.

53. This pilgrimage is noncompulsory and taken anytime, not during Hajj.

54. Firestone, *Journeys in Holy Lands*, 112–113.

55. Brock, "Two Syriac Verse Homilies," 61–129.

56. *Tanhuma* A, translated in consultation with Elbaum, "From Sermon to Story," 106.

57. In *PRE*, chapter 32, it is Samael who informs her of what happened.

58. Sherman, *Biblical Blaspheming*, 365.

59. Firestone, *Journeys in Holy Lands*, 113.

60. *Gen. Rab.* 55:4; and see *b.Sanhedrin* 89b.

61. Brock, "Two Syriac Verse Homilies," 110.

Conclusion

1. *The Church in the Shadow of the Mosque: Christians and Muslims in the World of Islam* (Princeton: Princeton University Press, 2008), 164.

2. Bar Hebraeus, *Chron. Syr.*, 96–97, as cited in Robert Hoyland, *Seeing Islam as Others Saw It: A Survey and Evaluation of Christian, Jewish and Zoroastrian Writings in Early Islam* (Princeton: Darwin Press, 1997), 536–537.

3. Reference to Islam as "the religion of Abraham," which had become widespread, was among the practices denounced. In scholarly circles the meaning of *millat Ibrāhīm* was debated; many reasons for its legitimate use were given, as well as reasons for finding it objectionable. See Madeline C. Zilfi, *The Politics of Piety: The Ottoman Ulema in the Postclassical Age (1600–1800)* (Minneapolis: Bibliotheca Islamica, 1988), 136; and for views on the debate, see Katib Celebi, *Balance of Truth*, trans. G. L. Lewis (London: Allen and Unwin, 1957), 110–123.

Acknowledgments

Over the course of several years of research and writing, I have relied on the generosity and support of many institutions, colleagues, and friends. In 2006 a New Directions Mellon Fellowship afforded me the opportunity to hone my reading of classical Arabic texts and to immerse myself in the field of early Islam. I am grateful to the Mellon Foundation for enabling me to study in Beirut, Damascus, and Princeton, where I benefited immeasurably from interactions with colleagues. I thank the Princeton Department of Near Eastern Studies for hosting me as a visiting fellow during the 2006–7 school year, and owe special gratitude to Michael Cook. He kindly permitted me to sit in on his course, where I was introduced to the skills of the trade and saw up close how one can be both a preeminent scholar and an inspiring teacher. I thank Patricia Crone for inviting me to join her informal Qur'an reading group and guiding me through classical Islamic exegetical material on the story of Noah, but even more for the years of lively conversations and friendship.

In Damascus I had the pleasure and good fortune of working with Isam Eido, whose passion for learning was contagious. Several colleagues, especially in Islamic Studies, have taught me a great deal. I have relied on the wisdom of Walid Saleh, Joseph Witztum, Jon Levenson, Michael Cooperson, Leora Batnitzky, and Andrew Rippin. I am especially indebted to Andrew Rippin for his meticulous reading of the manuscript and for helping me dodge embarrassing pitfalls. The responsibility for any remaining errors is, of course, mine.

My home institution, UCLA, has provided both financial and moral support. I am blessed to have many colleagues in the Department of Near Eastern Languages and Cultures who make UCLA a most congenial place to develop as a scholar. In 2011 and 2012 I spent part of each summer as a visiting scholar at Yarnton Manor, the Oxford Centre for Jewish Studies. I thank the staff of Yarnton who made being there a most enjoyable experience. I must confess that the main attraction of going to Yarnton was to spend time with my dear friend Stephen Geller. Our long walks together were always intellectually invigorating and filled with humor and good cheer.

I owe a belated debt of gratitude to Burton Visotzky, who had confidence in me when I had little in myself. I am deeply grateful to him for warmly welcoming me to the Jewish Theological Seminary, where even many moons later I still consider myself a *bat bayit*.

The idea for this book had a rather extended germination period, but it was Andy Beck who first planted the seed. Many other hands were involved in bringing this manuscript to the light of day. The brilliant Katya Rice made the tedious editing process delightful and fruitful. I thank her for astute comments and suggestions that significantly improved the manuscript. I also enjoyed working with Deborah Grahame-Smith and appreciate the great care and attention she gave the book. I am most fortunate to have worked with Heather Hughes and Sharmila Sen of Harvard University Press, both of whom have been exceedingly supportive. I admire Sharmila's keen mind and value her sage advice and impeccable judgment.

I am grateful to Aaron Hass, my husband, whose patience matches that of Job's. His constant love is a reminder of the good in my life.

Finally, I thank my cousin (mother, friend, sister, confidante) Vivienne Kneider, who encouraged me at the age of fourteen to read Scriptures carefully and to seek out answers. She has been my study partner ever since. During our three decades of wrestling over verses with an intensity born of love, I could always count on her for unconditional acceptance, support, insight, and inspiration. This book is dedicated to her.

Index

Aaron, 20, 36
Abel, 53, 71
Abimelech, 62, 119, 120, 128, 197, 239, 253, 256,
Abraham, 9, 36; birth of, 96–97, 99; chosenness of, 55, 56, 104, 194, 195; covenant of God, 21, 52–53, 55, 58–59, 134, 194; discovery of God, 103, 104–105; faith of, 71, 73, 192; families of, 9, 29, 59–61, 69, 146–153, 215; genealogy of, 52–53, 65, 70–71, 80, 96, 145, 146–153, 152, 161, 240n37, 240n39; in Genesis, 51–65, 80–81; in Gospel of Matthew, 65–66; importance to Christianity, 66–67; interpretation of sources on, 12; and Melchizedek, 58; monotheism of, 1–2, 9, 81, 88, 91, 101, 215; New Testament on, 65–73; Old Testament on, 51–65; as patriarch, 4–6, 64–65, 150–151; in pyre, 92–96; Qur'an on, 65, 73–79, 103–104, 131–132; renunciation of idolatry, 74–78, 81–83, 86–89, 96–101, 103–104; trials of, 191–200
Abraham (Feiler), 5
Abraham Fund (organization), 4
Abrahamic, use of term, 4, 7–8, 217, 218, 222n13, 222n15
Abraham Path Initiative (organization), 4–5
Abraham's Vision (organization), 4

Abram. *See* Abraham
Abu Huraira, 132
Acts of the Apostles, 18, 152
Adam, 21, 25, 34, 51–52, 55, 81, 187
'Adnan, 185–186
Adversus Marcionem (Tertullian), 117
African-American culture, 133–134
Against the Heresies (Irenaeus), 201
Aggadat Bereshit, 114, 254n18
Ajar. *See* Hagar
Alexandrian school of interpretation, 36, 38, 42
Allegory, 35, 36, 37, 40–41, 117, 119, 177–178, 183
Alter, Robert, 53–54
Ambrose of Milan, 119, 129, 200, 255n29
Anderson, Gary, 230n52, 236n6
Angel Gabriel, 19, 92, 99, 124, 184, 207
Anthropomorphism, 44
Antiochene school of interpretation, 36, 37–38, 42
Apocalypse of Abraham, 85–86, 97, 242n56, 244n66, 247n15, 248nn16–18, 250n38
Apocalypses, 18, 169–176
Apocrypha, 16
Aqedah, 19, 193–194, 196, 197, 199, 200–201, 203, 212, 228n39, 246n9, 253n16, 268n2, 270n10, 270n14, 270nn21–22, 271n23, 271n32, 272n43
Aqiba (rabbi), 165, 166–167, 262n39
Arabic language, 16, 21, 186, 225n20

Arabs: Arab Muslims, 125, 155, 156;
   genealogy of, 142–145, 156–157,
   185–186; origin of term, 156
Aram, 139
Aramaic language, 21
Astronomy, 75, 82, 108, 247
Athanasius, 202
Augustine, 41, 66, 115, 117, 129, 179–183,
   200, 201–202, 231n65, 231nn71–72,
   241n41, 266n72, 266n74, 267n77
Avraham. *See* Abraham
Avram. *See* Abraham
Azar, 75–77, 96–98, 101

Babylonia, 16
Babylonian Talmud Gittin, 251n46
Baptism, 90–91, 181
Barnabas, 73, 152, 200
Be'er-lahai-ro'i, 111, 139
Beersheba, 62, 63, 131
Ben Sira, Jesus, 64, 239n34
Ben (Bar) Yohai, Shimon, 89, 110–111,
   164–167, 170, 172–173, 264n49
Berekiah (rabbi), 112–113
Bernstein, Moshe, 227n34, 270n14
Bible: borrowing/intertextuality, 22–23,
   49; canon, 17; covenants of God,
   58–59; exegetical traditions, 23–42;
   literal vs. figurative interpretation,
   32–36, 40–41; relationship with
   Qur'an, 22–25; as revelation, 15;
   scriptural narrative, comparative
   studies, 10–11; translations, 21. *See also*
   New Testament; Old Testament
Biblical Antiquities (Pseudo-Philo), 25, 81,
   91, 93, 100–101, 192, 196, 199
Bidāya wa-l-nihāya, al- (Ibn Kathir),
   46, 123
Binyan av, 30–31
Book of Jubilees, 25, 31, 82–83, 88, 95, 101,
   112, 122, 126, 162–164, 192, 196
Boyarin, Daniel, 226n26, 240n40,
   254n24, 255n36, 266n66
Brinner, William, 225n23, 233n90,
   234n98, 235n106,237n16, 251n42,
   254n22, 256n37,256n39, 256n40,
   256n43, 257n54, 258n11, 268n87,
   271n39, 272n40, 272n46
Brock, Sebastian, 203, 256n48, 256n50,
   271n34, 273n55, 273n61
Buber, Martin, 150

Buddhism, 2
Byzantine Empire, 173

Caesarius of Arles, 90–91
Cain, 36
Calder, Norman, 234n102, 251n40, 272n52
Calvert-Koyzis, Nancy, 9, 222n21, 245n2,
   247n12
Canaan, 57, 60, 64, 80–81
Canon, use of term, 15, 223n3
Catholic, 179, 181
Cave of Treasures, 89, 103, 248n24, 249n29
Chaldeans, 75, 82, 83–84, 95–96, 257n51.
   See also Ur of the Chaldeans
Chosenness: of Abraham, 55, 56, 104,
   194, 195; doctrine of, 3, 53–54; of
   Isaac, 53–54, 139, 142, 145, 155–156,
   169, 177; of Israel, 142, 148; of Jewish
   people, 54–55, 139, 151–152, 155–156,
   170; and relationship to God, 51–52
Christ. *See* Jesus Christ
Christianity: Abraham, importance of,
   66–67, 104; Abraham as patriarch,
   5–6, 64–65; common narratives of,
   6–7; on covenant, 54–55; exegetical
   traditions, 23–24, 32–42; Ishmael,
   references, 177–183; Johannine, 70;
   monotheism of, 1–2, 5; on New
   Testament, 16; on sacrifice of Isaac,
   200–209; on Sarah-Hagar narrative,
   116–121, 125–126. *See also* Bible; New
   Testament; Old Testament
Christiansen, Irmgard, 35
Chronicles of Jerameel, 101
Chrysostom, John, 33, 37–38, 119–120,
   200, 202, 255n32, 271n28, 271n33
Circumcision, 60, 66–67, 161, 178
City of God (Augustine), 117
Clement of Alexandria, 36, 117, 119,
   202
Code of Hammurapi, 160–161, 252n5
Code of Lipit-Ishtar, 161
Commentary on Genesis (Didymus), 38
Commentary on Genesis (Ephrem), 39, 115
Confessions (Augustine), 41
Cook, Michael, 74, 231n75, 243nn58–59,
   243n61, 264n47, 265n57, 268n84
Covenants of God: with Abraham, 52–53,
   55, 58–59, 134, 194, 197; and com-
   mandments, 17; grant, 58–59; with
   Isaac, 53–54, 197

Crone, Patricia, 74, 243nn58–59, 243n61, 264n47, 265n57, 268n84
Cyril of Alexandria, 40–41, 119, 200, 202
Cyrus, 16

Dagorn, René, 250n3, 258n10
David, 36, 65–66, 174
Day of Judgment, 21, 78
Day of Remembrance, 200
Dead Sea Scrolls, 25, 111, 126–127, 227n34, 230n52; 4Q225, 196, 270nn14–15; 4Q252, 227n34
De Doctrina Christiana (Augustine), 41
De Genesi ad Litteram (Augustine), 41
De Principiis (Origen), 37
Deuterocanonical Books, 16
Dhul-Kifl, 183
Dialogue with Trypho, 35
Didymus, 38, 90, 117, 119, 128–129
Diocletian, 179
Diodorus, 36
Donatism, 179–180, 181
Dunn, James D. G., 240n40, 241n5

Ecclesiastica Historia, 157
Ecclesiasticus. See Ben Sira, Jesus
Edom, 139, 158, 172, 174
Eid al-Adha (Feast of the Sacrifice), 206
Eleazar b. Yosi (rabbi), 165
Election. See Chosenness
Eliezer (rabbi), 174
Eliezer (servant), 64, 141–142
Elijah, 17, 170
Enoch, 71, 99, 183
Eph'al, Israel, 156–157, 260n3, 260nn6–7
Ephrem, 38–40, 89, 91, 115, 120, 129, 201
Ephron the Hittite, 64
Epistle of Barnabas, 200
Epistle to the Galatians, 69–70, 151–152, 103, 116–117, 158, 177, 178, 179, 180, 182, 183, 237n20, 241n45, 241n47, 242nn48–49, 251n1, 254n25, 259n19, 266n67, 266n72
Epistle to the Hebrews, 71, 268n2, 237n18
Epistle to the Romans, 66, 71, 151–152, 240n40, 241n41, 242n49, 263n46, 268n2
Esau, 36, 110, 138, 170
Esther, 29
Ethelbert, King of Kent, 171

Ethnocentrism, chosenness as, 54, 155–156
Eve, 25, 51–52
Exodus narrative, 150, 170, 237n17, 238n22
Ezekiel, 183

Faith, 68–69, 71, 73, 192
Fatimah, 168
Feast of the Sacrifice (Eid al-Adha), 206
Feiler, Bruce, 5
Feldman, Louis, 246n9, 247n11, 262n34, 262n36
Festal Letter (Athanasius), 202
Firestone, Reuven, 226n27, 236n9, 244n64, 267nn81–82, 268n86, 272nn42–44, 272n50, 272n54, 273n59
Fishbane, Michael, 227n30, 237n17
Fraade, Steven D., 228n34
Fredrickson, Paula, 241n40, 259n18

Gager, John, 240n40, 241n46, 242nn47–48
Garden of Eden, 52
Gaston, Lloyd, 240n40, 241n45, 242nn47–48
Geller, Stephen, 237n10, 248n23, 267n76
Genealogy: of Abraham, 52–53, 65, 70–71, 80, 96, 145, 146–153, 152, 161, 240n37, 240n39; of Arabs, 142–145, 156–157, 185–186; emphasis on, 142–144; Islamic tradition, 143–146; of Jesus, 65–66; of Muhammad, 121; theological vs. biological, 150–151, 216
Genesis, Book of: on Abraham, 51–65, 80–81; on Hagar, 59, 60, 62–63; on Isaac, 52, 53, 54, 57, 60–64, 68; on Ishmael, 157; on Keturah, 53, 54, 64; on Sarah, 53, 54, 56, 57, 59, 60–64, 127
Genesis Apocryphon, 25, 111, 126–127, 227n32
Genesis Rabbah, 28–30, 88–89, 93, 95, 110–111, 113–114, 127–129, 131, 140, 142, 146–151, 167, 175, 193, 197–199, 228n37, 248n20, 259n15, 266n64, 270n15
Gentiles, 60–70, 151–152
Gezera shavah, 30
Gilliot, Claude, 43–44, 231n73, 232nn75–76, 233nn83–84, 233n86
Gnosticism, 34, 42, 117

God: on covenanted people, 52–53, 197; covenants of, 17, 52–55, 58–59, 134, 194, 197; love of, 3; obedience to, 17; revelation of, 15, 19–20; word of, 16, 19, 24, 37, 49–50, 71, 215

Goitein, S. D., 263n45, 268n84

Goldziher, Ignaz, 258n6, 272n43

Gomorrah, 61–62, 130

Goodman, Martin, 243n60, 251n47, 252n6, 253n10, 254n25, 255n28, 256n45

Gospel of John, 70–71, 152, 216, 266n74

Gospel of Matthew, 34, 65–66

Great Flood, 28–29, 51, 102, 232n76

Gregory bar Hebraeus, 217–218

Gregory I (Pope), 171

Gregory of Nyssa, 35, 200

Griffith, Sidney, 217, 221n4, 222n10, 224n14, 225n15, 225nn19–20, 230nn60–61, 230n63

Hackett, JoAnn, 159

Ḥadīth traditions, 43–45, 131, 143

Hagar, 6, 10, 78; in African-American culture, 133–134; children of, 29, 150; Christian interpretations of, 116–121; expulsion of, 62–63, 78, 120, 122, 123–124; idolatry of, 111, 113, 114–115, 125, 126, 169; Islamic interpretations of, 121–126, 144–145; Jewish interpretations of, 106–109; marginality of, 109–110, 115, 136; Philo on, 107–108; present-day interpretations of, 132–136; rabbinic literature on, 109–115; Sarah-Hagar allegory, 38, 116–119, 135, 216–217; Sarah on, 59, 62, 106–107, 122–123, 137–139

Hajar. *See* Hagar

Hajj, 187–188

Hajun, 116

Ham, 91

Hammurapi. *See* Code of Hammurapi

Ḥanīf, 9, 73–75, 243n58, 244nn60–62

Haran, 80, 83, 93–95, 237n12, 246n8, 247n10, 249n29, 250n36, 250n38

Hawting, Gerald, 74, 75, 222n10, 234n102, 243nn60–61, 244n63, 245n69, 251n40

Hebrew language, 16, 21, 38

Hebrew Questions on Genesis (Jerome), 40

Hebron, 58, 64

Heinemann, Joseph, 146

Hekkesh, 31

Heraclius, Emperor of Byzantium, 173

Herberg, Will, 54

Hexapla (Origen), 37

Hillel, seven rules of, 49

Hinduism, 2

History of the Prophets and Patriarchs, The (al-Tabari), 45, 48, 99, 122, 233n90, 256n37, 256n40, 271n39

Hiyya (rabbi), 93–94

Hodge Johnson, Caroline, 241n40, 254n25

Homilies on Genesis (Origen), 118, 119, 178, 201

Hoyland, Robert, 264n47, 273n2

Hud, 20

Hughes, Aaron, 7, 221n4

Ibn Abbas, 187

Ibn al-Kalbi, 185–186

Ibn al-Mu'tazz, 145

Ibn Ezra, 131

Ibn Kathir, 43, 46–47, 99, 123, 208–209

Ibn Nuwas, 144

Ibn Taymiyya, 43, 208

Ibn Yasar, 122

Ibrahim. *See* Abraham

Idolatry/idols, 5, 56, 111; Azar worship of, 75–77; dwelling among, 90, 93; Hagar worship of, 111, 113, 114–115, 125, 126, 169; Ishmael worship of, 111, 164–167, 178; Ka'bah as house of, 176–187; renunciation of, 74, 75–78, 81–83, 86–89, 96–101, 103–104; selling, 93–94, 97; Terah worship of, 81, 82–83, 86–87, 93–94, 99, 216

Idris. *See* Enoch

Ignatius, 73

Isaac, 9, 10, 64, 76, 154–155; Abrahamic lineage by, 54, 117; birth, 121, 163–164; blessing of, 110, 148; chosenness of, 53–54, 139, 141–142, 145, 155–156, 169, 177; covenant of God, 53–54, 60–61, 150, 177; inheritance rights, 120, 140, 149, 160–162; Paul on, 177–178; as prophet, 78; rivalry with Ishmael, 137–142, 160, 216; sacrifice (binding) of, 63, 71, 104, 122, 141, 190–213; as typos for Jesus, 200

Iscah, 80

Isfara'ini, Abu Hamid al-, 44
Ishaq, 8. *See also* Isaac
Ishbak, 54
Ishmael, 8–9, 10, 20, 21, 64, 121, 131; in
  apocalyptic imagination, 169–176;
  Arabic, 144, 156; birth, 59, 114, 123;
  blessed by God, 53; Christian references, 177–183, 188; exclusion of, 61,
  109–110; expulsion of, 63, 78, 120, 122,
  123–124, 155, 195, 200; as great nation,
  60, 62; idolatry of, 111, 164–167, 178;
  inheritance rights, 120, 140, 160–162,
  252n5; in Islamic tradition, 183–189;
  Jewish, 156–164, 188; marriage, 168,
  186; and *metsaheq*, 62–63, 158–159, 162,
  164–169; Muhammad genealogy by,
  121, 125, 186; portrayals of, 154–156,
  168, 216; as prophet, 78; Qur'an on,
  155–156, 183; rivalry with Isaac,
  137–142, 160, 216; role in Islam, 6, 156,
  168–169; sacrifice of, 78, 194, 206–207,
  209–210; Sarah on, 106, 107, 159–164
Ishmael (rabbi), 165, 175; thirteen rules
  of, 49
Ishmaelites, 139, 149, 156–158, 169–176
Islam/Muslims: Abraham as prototype,
  73, 104, 215–216; Abrahamic motifs,
  96–101; apocalyptic impulse in,
  176; Arab Muslims, 125, 142–145,
  155, 156; common narratives of, 6–8;
  exegetical traditions, 23–24; genealogical tradition, 143–146; interchange
  with Jews, 185; on Ishmael, 6, 156,
  168–169, 183–189; monotheism of,
  1–2, 5; Persian Muslims, 125, 142,
  144–146, 155; on sacrifice of Isaac,
  204–209; on Sarah-Hagar narrative,
  121–126, 135–136. *See also* Qur'an
Isma'il, 8. *See also* Ishmael
Isnād, 42–44, 233n85
Israel, 142, 148, 174, 197–198; Israelites,
  16, 150
Isrā'īliyyāt, 44, 46–47, 234n99, 234n100,
  234nn102–104, 235n105

Jacob, 9, 21, 76; Abrahamic lineage by,
  54, 78, 142–143; as Jewish forefather,
  150; rivalry with Esau, 138, 170
Jacobs, Andrew S., 241n40
Jacobson, Howard, 93, 227n32, 245n2,
  249n31

Jaffee, Martin, 2, 3
Jāmi' al-bayān 'an ta'wīl ay al Qur'ān
  (al-Tabari), 44
Jay, Pierre, 231n66, 248n25
Jellinek, Adolph, 265n56
Jerome, 38–40, 95–96, 101–102, 103, 112,
  157, 178
Jesus Christ, 9, 20, 21, 202; Adam as
  typos of, 34; as fulfillment of scripture,
  17–18; genealogy of, 65–66, 70, 71;
  Isaac as typos of, 200; priesthood of,
  72; resurrection of, 41
Jewish Antiquities (Josephus), 26, 84,
  108–109, 163–164, 247n9–10, 253n9
Jewish people. *See* Judaism/Jewish people
Job, 36
Jokshan, 54
Joktan, 92
Josephus, 26, 84, 85, 88, 101, 107–109,
  157, 163–164, 196, 199, 214, 244n66,
  246n9, 247n10–11, 250n38, 253n10,
  260n8, 262n32, 262n34, 262n36
Jubilees. *See Book of Jubilees*
Judahites, 156
Judaism/Jewish people, 23; Abraham as
  patriarch, 5–6, 52–53, 84, 104, 215–216;
  apocalyptic visions, 170–171; chosenness
  of, 54–55, 139, 151–152, 155–156, 170;
  common narratives of, 6–7; exegetical
  traditions, 23–24; interchange with
  Muslims, 185; monotheism of, 1–2, 5;
  on Old Testament, 16; on Sarah-Hagar
  narrative, 106–109, 125–126, 135. *See also*
  Old Testament; Torah
Judea, 18, 241–242n48
Judgment Day, 21, 78
Judith, Book of, 83, 84, 101, 199, 250n38,
  267n76
Jurhum tribe, 124, 184–186, 188
Justin Martyr, 104, 117

Ka'bah, 9, 123, 155, 183, 186–187, 188, 204
Kabbalah, 31
Kadizadeli movement, 218
Kaminsky, Joel, 236n6, 238n27, 261n21,
  264n51
Kannengiesser, Charles, 33, 229nn42–43,
  229nn48–50, 230n55, 230nn59–60
Kant, Immanuel, 190
Kashf wa'l-bayān 'an tafsīr al-Qur'ān,
  al- (al-Thal'abi), 46

Kelal uperat, 31, 233n92
Keturah, 29, 54, 64, 78, 106, 109–116,
    147, 150, 156
Kierkegaard, Søren, 190–191
Kingdom of Edom, 173–174
Kingdom of Ishmael, 173
Kisa'i, Muhammad ibn 'Abd Allah al-,
    99–100, 183, 206, 207, 210–211
Kister, Menachem, 229n52, 235n104,
    244n67, 270n14
Kugel, James, 82, 95, 227n31, 235n109,
    244nn65–66, 245nn3–4, 246n8,
    250n38, 269nn6–7, 270n14

Lazarus-Yafeh, Hava, 224n11, 225n20,
    226n24, 227n28, 267n84
Letter of Barnabas, 152
Levenson, Jon, 7, 221n4, 222n11, 222n16,
    236n4, 237n17, 238n22, 238n24,
    238n27, 239n31, 240n40, 251n47,
    256n47, 261n22, 261n28, 264n51,
    266n68, 268n2, 271n23, 275
Levi (rabbi), 28, 89, 210
Leviticus Rabbah, 198, 212
Lewis, Bernard, 263n47
Liber Antiquitatum Biblicarum. See *Biblical
    Antiquities*
Lipit-Ishtar. *See* Code of Lipit-Ishtar
Lot, 20, 56–58, 72, 80, 91, 129–130,
    158
Lowin, Shari, 88–89, 226n27, 244n64,
    244nn67–68, 248n22, 250n36, 251n41,
    251n46, 263n45

Madrashe (*madrasha*, singular), 38–39
Making of a Forefather, The (Lowin), 88,
    226n27, 244n64, 244nn67–68, 250n36,
    251n41
Malachi, 17
Mamre, 58
Maqām Ibrāhīm, 187
Marcion, 34, 73, 117
Marumath, 85–86
Marwah, al-, 125
Mashal (*meshalim*, plural), 30, 148, 150
Massignon, Louis, 4, 221n4
Mastema, 196
Masudi, al-, 144, 145
McAuliffe, Jane Dammen, 42, 44,
    231nn73–74, 232n75, 232nn77–78,
    233n87, 234n100, 236n9, 243n61

Mecca, 9, 44, 76, 78,123–124, 184, 186,
    187, 237n14, 267n80
Medan, 54
Mekhilta de Rabbi Ishmael, 199, 270n17
Melchizedek, 58, 72–73
Melito of Sardis, 200–202
Mesopotamia, 64, 83
Metatron, 172–173
Metsaheq, 62–63, 158–159, 162, 164–169,
    262n39
Midianites, 158
Midrash: exegetical traditions, 25–32;
    halakhic, 30–31, 49; motifs, 19;
    understanding of, 11–12. *See also specific
    works*
Midrash ha-Gadol, 31, 101, 168
Milcah, 80
Millat Ibrāhīm, 5
Mishnah Avot, 192
Monotheism: of Abraham, 1, 5, 9, 81, 88,
    99, 101, 215; elective, 2–3; forms of,
    1–3, 12, 189, 245n69; Josephus on, 84;
    prophets on, 21
Moriah, 63
Mosaic law, 69, 177
Moses, 9, 16, 20, 21, 35, 73, 76, 197, 207
Moses ben Nachman. *See* Nachmanides
Mount Sinai, 69, 116–117, 177
Muhammad, 9, 103–104; Abraham as
    precursor of, 76, 218; birth of, 99;
    Isaac genealogy of, 145–146; Ishmael
    genealogy of, 121, 125, 186; on Ka'bah,
    187; prophetic message of, 143;
    revelation of God, 19; stories of, 46–48
Münz-Manor, Ophir, 230n62
Muqatil ibn Sulayman al-Balkhi, 43–44,
    99, 125, 207, 232n81
Muslims. *See* Islam/Muslims
Muwaffaq, al-, 144

Nabī, defined, 20, 183
Nachmanides, 128
Nahon, 85
Nahor, 64, 80, 81, 83, 91
Nebuchadnezzar, 236n10, 250n36, 251n46
Nehemiah, 16, 18, 64, 115, 156
Nehemiah (rabbi), 28, 29, 112, 147
Nestorianism, 37
Neuwirth, Angelica, 23, 227n29
New Testament, 16–18; Abraham's family
    in, 151; common narratives of, 6–8;

exegetical traditions, 33–42; literal vs. figurative interpretation, 32–35; unity with Old Testament, 33–34

Niehoff, Maren, 228n34, 252n2, 252n5, 261n29

Nimrod, 81, 91–101, 111, 125, 130, 204, 249nn29–30, 250n35, 251n46

Nissah, use of term, 193

Nistarot (Shimon ben Yohai), 172–173

Noah, 20, 71, 99, 102

Nuwas, Abu, 114

Old Testament, 16, 64; on Abraham, 51–65; common narratives of, 6–8; exegetical traditions, 32–42; vs. Jewish Bible, 18; literal vs. figurative interpretation, 32–36, 40–41; summation of, 51–52, 56; unity with New Testament, 33–34; Vulgate translation, 40

On Abraham (Ambrose), 129

On Abraham (Philo), 107

On Christian Teaching (*De Doctrina Christiana*, Augustine), 41

On Genesis (Didymus), 129

On the Preliminary Studies (Philo), 108

Oral traditions, 23, 26–27, 133, 185

Origen, 36–37, 38, 40, 115, 117, 118–119, 121, 178–179, 200, 201, 229n44, 229n52, 230n56, 242n51, 254n19, 255n28, 255n30, 256n70

Oshaya (rabbi), 29

Otherness, 110, 115

Palestine, 27, 38–39

Paradise, 184

Paschal Homilies, 201

Patristics, study of, 36

Paul, 18, 33, 34; on Abraham, 68–70, 104, 151–152; centrality of, 66; on Isaac, 177–178; on Ishmael, 158–159, 177–178; on salvation/faith, 68–69; on Sarah-Hagar narrative, 116–118, 120–121

Pentateuch, 16, 17. *See also* Torah

People of the Book, 5

Persian Muslims, 125, 142, 144–146, 155–156

Pharaoh, 110–111, 127, 129–130

Philology, 31, 33, 37

Philo of Alexandria, 33, 84–90; as interpreter of scriptures, 35; on

Ishmael, 162; on sacrifice of Isaac, 198–199; on Sarah/Hagar, 38, 106–108, 116, 117–118; on trials of Abraham, 196; use of allegory, 35

Pinchas (rabbi), 28

Pirke de Rabbi Eliezer (PRE), 31, 113–114, 141, 169, 173–176, 212

Pirqe Avot, 50

Piyyutim, 38

PRE. See *Pirke de Rabbi Eliezer*

Promised Land, 16, 59, 128, 155

Pseudo-Barnabas, 35

Pseudo-Jonathan, 199

Pseudo-Philo, 25, 81, 91, 100–101, 192, 199

Qathan, 185

Qiṣaṣ al-anbiyā, 46–47, 75, 234n99

Qiṣaṣ al-anbiyā (al-Tha'labi), 46–47, 96, 116, 234n98, 235n106, 237n16, 251n42, 254n22, 256n39, 256n43, 257n54, 258n11, 268n87, 271n39, 272n46

Qummi, al-, 211

Qumran, 26

Qur'an, 19–21; on Abraham, 65, 73–79, 103–104, 131–132; borrowing/intertextuality, 22–23, 49; common narratives of, 6–8; covenant of God, 55–56; exegetical interpretation, 42–50; on Hagar, 121; on Ishmael, 155–156, 183; relationship with Bible, 22–25; revelation in, 20; on trials of Abraham, 192

Quraysh, 186

Rachel, 147

Rashi, 31–32

Rasūl, defined, 20, 183

Rebekah, 64, 138

Red Sea parting, 35, 198

Reeves, John, 171, 172, 229n41, 244n67, 264n49, 264n53, 265nn55–56, 265n63, 266n65, 270n14

Revelation of God, 15, 19–20

Reynolds, Gabriel, 225n23, 236n9, 244n62

Righteousness, 66–68, 102

Rippin, Andrew, 231n75, 232n81, 233n96, 234n99, 101, 236n9, 243n58, 243n61

Rosh Hashanah, 199, 200, 212

Rubin, Uri, 243n58, 243n61, 264n47, 267n78

Ryan, Patrick, 10

Safa, al-, 125
Saḥīḥ al-Bukhārī, 124–125, 131–132
Saleh, Walid, 20, 224n14, 225n20,
  232nn79–80, 233n96
Salih, 20
Salvation, 65, 67–68, 170–171, 202, 240n37
Samael, 139–140
Saracens, 157
Sarah, 6, 10, 56–57, 62, 78, 184, 203, 211;
  Abrahamic lineage from, 54, 60, 80;
  Christian interpretations of, 116–121;
  death, 64; on Hagar, 59, 62, 106–107,
  122–123, 137–139; on Ishmael, 106,
  107, 159–164; Islamic interpretations
  of, 121–126; Jewish interpretations of,
  106–109; present-day interpretations
  of, 132–136; sacrifice of, 126–132;
  Sarah-Hagar allegory, 38, 116–119,
  135, 216–217
Sarai. *See* Sarah
Sarna, N., 139, 258n1, 260n12, 261nn26–27
Satan, 76, 122, 196–197, 205, 211–212
Savant, Sarah, 144, 145, 258nn7–8, 259n13
Schwartz, Joshua, 260n16, 261n18, 261n21
Schwartz, Seth, 255n36
Schwartzbaum, Haim, 234n98
Seal of Prophecy, 6, 19, 121
Seal of the Messengers, 145
Second Temple period, 25
Sefer ha-Yashar, 101, 250n37, 267n83
Seforno, Ovadiah, 159–160
Segal, Alan, 268n2, 271n23
Segal, Michael, 227n31, 245n4
Semitism, use of term, 3
Shari'ah, 143
Shekhinah, 141–142
Sherman, Yvonne, 212, 269n4, 273n58
Shi'ite sources, 183, 211
Shimon ben (bar) Yohai (rabbi), 89,
  110–111, 164–167, 170, 172–173, 264n49
Shintoism, 2
Shuah, 54
Shu'ayb, 20
Shu'ūbīs, 144
Shu'ūbiyya literature, 144, 153
Sifre Deuteronomy, 103–104
Siker, Jeffrey, 68–69, 72–73, 239n35,
  240n39, 241n44, 242n47, 242n50,
  242n53
Simonetti, Manlio, 229nn47–48, 230n54
Sirach. *See* Ben Sira, Jesus

Smith, Jonathan Z., 223n3
Sodom, 61–62, 130
Sozomenus, 157
Stendahl, Krister, 240n36, 242n48
Stern, David, 228n38
Stromateis (Clement), 118, 255nn27–28
Suddi, al-, 122
Sunni narratives, 44, 88
Swetnam, James, 71–72, 242n52, 268n2
Syren, Roger, 238n28, 262n32
Syriac traditions, 38, 129, 202–203

Tabari, Abū Ja'far Muhammad ibn Jarir
  al-, 44–45, 48, 49, 122, 124, 125, 145,
  204–205, 207. *See also specific works*
Tabarsi, al-, 211, 212
Tafsīr, 42–45, 75, 102
Tafsīr al-Qur'ān al-'aẓīm (Ibn Kathir), 46
Tafsīr al-Tabari, 44
Taḥrīf, 19, 208, 224nn11–13, 242n52, 268n2
Tales of the Prophets (al-Kisa'i), 99
Tales of the Prophets (al-Tha'labi), 46–48,
  96, 116
Talmud, 11, 32, 157, 196, 248, 249;
  b.'Eruvin, 249n30; *b.Hullin*, 249n30;
  b.Pesaḥim, 249n15; *b.Sanhedrin*, 196,
  248n19, 258n2, 272n52, 273n60; *b.Yoma*,
  270n16
TaNaKh, 8, 16–19, 29, 51. *See also* Old
  Testament; Torah
Tanḥuma, 150, 246n7, 249n34, 256n38,
  256n51, 258n2, 273n56
Taoism, 2
Targum Neofiti (also *Neophyti*), 199, 250n36
Targum Onkelos, 157
Targum Pseudo-Jonathan, 111, 125
Ta'rīkh al-rusul wa'l-mulūk (al-Tabari),
  45, 48, 99, 122, 233n82
Taymiyya, Ibn, 43, 208, 272nn50–51
Terah, 87–88, 216, 237n10, 237n12,
  246nn7–8, 247n10, 250n36; idol
  worship by, 81, 82–83, 85–87, 93–94,
  99, 216; lineage, 80; and Nimrod, 96;
  repentance of, 101
Tertullian, 117, 254n26
Tha'labi, Ahmad b. Muhammad al-, 43,
  46, 47–48, 96–99, 122–124, 125, 132,
  187, 204, 207, 233n82, 234n98,
  235n106, 237n16, 251n42, 254n22,
  258n11, 268n87, 272n39. *See also specific*
  works